THE CAMBRIDGE COMPANION TO SUFISM

Often described as the 'mystical' dimension of Islam, Sufism embraces specific aesthetic, literary, ritual, and devotional manifestations of the Islamic tradition. The origins of Sufism stretch back to the early formative period of Islam, but it was in the ninth to tenth centuries CE that celebrated individuals appeared from the mists of historical myth. By the medieval period the Sufi orders (or brotherhoods) emerged in Islamic lands, many of which still exist in the contemporary age. *The Cambridge Companion to Sufism* traces the evolution from the formative period to the present, addressing specific themes along the way within the context of the times. The first section of this book analyses the early period with a focus on ascetic devotions, gender, and ethics. The section of the medieval period examines antinomian forms of Sufism, the ways that Sufis understood 'mystical experience', and Sufi poetry. The final section assesses the forms of Sufism that can be found in the modern age, explaining the controversies that took place in the colonial period and how as a transnational movement Sufism has responded to the challenges of modernity and has developed and grown in the West. This inimitable volume sheds light on a multifaceted and alternative aspect of Islamic history and religion; it covers a wide range of manifestations of the Sufi way of life during more than one thousand years of history, encompassing Sufism in the traditional Middle Eastern and North African heartlands, sub-Saharan Africa, and newly emerging forms in the West.

Lloyd Ridgeon is Reader in Islamic Studies at the University of Glasgow, Scotland. His previous publications include *Javanmardi: A Sufi Code of Honour* (2011) and *Morals and Mysticism in Persian Sufism* (2010).

CAMBRIDGE COMPANIONS TO RELIGION

A series of companions to major topics and key figures in theology and religious studies. Each volume contains specially commissioned chapters by international scholars which provide an accessible and stimulating introduction to the subject for new readers and non-specialists.

OTHER TITLES IN THE SERIES

The Cambridge Companion to Christian Doctrine
edited by Colin Gunton (1997)
9780521471183 hardback; 9780521476959 paperback

The Cambridge Companion to Biblical Interpretation
edited by John Barton (1998)
9780521481441 hardback; 9780521485937 paperback

The Cambridge Companion to Dietrich Bonhoeffer
edited by John de Gruchy (1999)
9780521582582 hardback; 9780521587815 paperback

The Cambridge Companion to Karl Barth
edited by John Webster (2000)
9780521584760 hardback; 9780521585606 paperback

The Cambridge Companion to Jesus
edited by Markus Bockmuehl (2001)
9780521792615 hardback; 9780521796781 paperback

The Cambridge Companion to Feminist Theology
edited by Susan Frank Parsons (2002)
9780521663274 hardback; 9780521663809 paperback

The Cambridge Companion to Martin Luther
edited by Donald K. McKim (2003)
9780521816489 hardback; 9780521016735 paperback

The Cambridge Companion to St Paul
edited by James D.G. Dunn (2003)
9780521781558 hardback; 9780521786942 paperback

The Cambridge Companion to Postmodern Theology
edited by Kevin J. Vanhoozer (2003)
9780521790628 hardback; 9780521793957 paperback

The Cambridge Companion to John Calvin
edited by Donald K. McKim (2004)
9780521816472 hardback; 9780521016728 paperback

The Cambridge Companion to Hans Urs Von Balthasar
edited by Edward T. Oakes, SJ, and David Moss (2004)
9780521814676 hardback; 9780521891479 paperback

(*continued after the Index*)

The Cambridge Companion to Sufism

Edited by

LLOYD RIDGEON
University of Glasgow

CAMBRIDGE
UNIVERSITY PRESS

CAMBRIDGE
UNIVERSITY PRESS

32 Avenue of the Americas, New York, NY 10013-2473, USA

Cambridge University Press is part of the University of Cambridge.

It furthers the University's mission by disseminating knowledge in the pursuit of education, learning, and research at the highest international levels of excellence.

www.cambridge.org
Information on this title: www.cambridge.org/9781107679504

First published 2015

A catalog record for this publication is available from the British Library.

Library of Congress Cataloging in Publication Data
The Cambridge companion to Sufism / Lloyd Ridgeon.
pages cm. – (Cambridge companions to religion)
I. Ridgeon, Lloyd V. J.
BP189.C36 2015
297.4–dc23 2014034130

ISBN 978-1-107-01830-3 Hardback
ISBN 978-1-107-67950-4 Paperback

Contents

Figures

Contributors

RON GEAVES is currently Visiting Professor of Muslim Culture and Enterprise at University College Suffolk. He has written and edited nineteen books and contributed to around twenty-five edited collections and numerous journal articles. His works include *Sectarian Influences in Islam in Britain* (1994), *Sufis in Britain* (2000), *Islam and the West Post 9/11* (2004), *Aspects of Islam* (2005), *Islam Today* (2010), *Islam in Victorian Britain: The Life and Times of Abdullah Quilliam* (2010), and *Sufis of Britain* (2014). He is currently working on the history of Islam in Britain in the Edwardian era.

AHMET T. KARAMUSTAFA is Professor of History at the University of Maryland, College Park, USA. His expertise is in the social and intellectual history of Sufism in particular and Islamic piety in general in the medieval and early modern periods. He has also conducted research on Islamic cartography as well as on Muslim religious literature. His publications include *God's Unruly Friends* (1994) and *Sufism: The Formative Period* (2007). He is currently working on two book projects: *The Flowering of Sufism* and *Vernacular Islam: Everyday Muslim Religious Life in Medieval Turkey*.

LEONARD LEWISOHN is Senior Lecturer in Persian and Iran Heritage Foundation Fellow in Classical Persian and Sufi Literature at the Institute of Arab and Islamic Studies at the University of Exeter. He is the author of *Beyond Faith and Infidelity: The Sufi Poetry and Teachings of Mahmud Shabistari* (1995) and the editor of three volumes on *The Heritage of Sufism* – vol. 1: *The Legacy of Mediaeval Persian Sufism*; vol. 2: *Classical Persian Sufism from Its Origins to Rumi*; and vol. 3 (with David Morgan): *Late Classical Persianate Sufism: The Safavid and Mughal Period* (1999). He is editor of the *Mawlana Rumi Review*, an annual journal devoted to Jalal al-Din Rumi. He is also editor (with Christopher Shackle) of *The Art of Spiritual Flight: Farid al-Din 'Attar and the Persian Sufi Tradition* (2006), co-translator (with Robert Bly) of *The Angels Knocking on the Tavern*

Door: Thirty Poems of Hafiz (2008), and editor of *Hafiz and the Religion of Love in Classical Persian Poetry* (2010).

BEVERLY MACK is a Professor of African Studies in the Department of African and African American Studies at the University of Kansas. Prior to joining KU, she taught at Georgetown University and Yale University. Since 1995 she has taught courses on Women and Islam, Islamic Literature, and Introduction to Arabic and Islamic Studies at KU. Her books include *Hausa Women in the Twentieth Century* (with Catherine Coles) (1990), *Muslim Women Sing: Hausa Popular Song* (2004), and several works on the nineteenth-century Sufi scholar Nana Asma'u with her colleague Jean Boyd, including: *The Collected Works of Nana Asma'u, Daughter of Shehu Usman dan Fodiyo, 1793–1864* (1997); *One Woman's Jihad: Nana Asma'u, Scholar and Scribe* (2001); and *Educating Muslim Women: The West African Legacy of Nana Asma'u* (2013).

CHRISTOPHER MELCHERT got his doctorate in History at the University of Pennsylvania in 1992. Since 2000, he has taught at the University of Oxford. He has published two books, *The Formation of the Sunni Schools of Law, 9th–10th Centuries C.E.* (1997) and *Ahmad ibn Hanbal* (2006), as well as more than forty journal articles. His next book will be a projected history of Islamic piety before Sufism.

ERIK S. OHLANDER is Associate Professor of Religious Studies at Indiana University–Purdue University, Fort Wayne. He obtained his PhD from Michigan University in 2004. He has published *Sufism in an Age of Transition: 'Umar al-Suhrawardi and the Rise of Islamic Mystical Brotherhoods* (2008) and is joint editor (with John Curry) of *Sufism in Society: Arrangements of the Mystical in the Muslim World 1200–1800* (2011). He is the editor of the *Journal of Sufi Studies.*

LLOYD RIDGEON is Reader in Islamic Studies at Glasgow University. His recent publications include *Javanmardi: A Sufi Code of Honour* (2011), *Morals and Mysticism in Persian Sufism: A History of Sufi-futuwwat in Iran* (2010), and *Sufi Castigator: Ahmad Kasravi and the Iranian Mystical Tradition* (2006). He is the editor of the *British Journal of Middle Eastern Studies.*

LAURY SILVERS works on Sufism in the formative period, in particular women, gender, Sufi metaphysics, and North American Muslim women's religious authority. She is the author, co-editor, and co-author of books and articles on these subjects, including *A Soaring Minaret: Abu Bakr al-Wasiti and the Rise of Baghdadi Sufism* (2011) and *A Jihad for Justice: Honoring the Life and Work of Amina Wadud* (co-editor with Kecia Ali and Julianne Hammer; 2012). She is co-author (with Ahmed Elewa and Yasmin Amin) of a translation and introduction to the women's accounts in Ibn al-Jawzi's *Sifat al-safwa* (in progress); *'God Loves Me': Early Pious and Sufi Women and the Theological Debate over God's Love*; and *'I am One of the People': A Survey and Analysis of Legal Arguments on Woman-Led Prayer in Islam* (with Ahmed Elewa). She teaches at the University of Toronto.

KNUT S. VIKØR is Professor of Middle Eastern History at the University of Bergen, Norway. Among his books are *The Oasis of Salt: A History of Kawar, a Saharan Centre of Salt Production* (1999); *Sufi and Scholar on the Desert Edge: Muhammad b. Ali al-Sanusi and His Brotherhood* (1995); *Between God and Sultan: A History of Islamic Law* (2005); and *The Maghreb Since 1800: A Short History* (2012).

ITZCHAK WEISMANN is Professor of Islamic Studies and Director of the Jewish-Arab Center at the University of Haifa. His research interests focus on modern Islam, particularly fundamentalist and radical Islamic movements and Sufism. He completed his PhD dissertation at Haifa University and gained a Post-Doctorate at Princeton University (Rothschild Foundation) and Oxford University (the British Council). He is the author of *Taste of Modernity: Sufism, Salafiyya, and Arabism in Late Ottoman Damascus* (2001); *The Naqshbandiyya: Orthodoxy and Activism in a Worldwide Sufi Tradition* (2007); *Ottoman Reform and Islamic Regeneration* (forthcoming, co-editor); and *Islamic Myths and Memories: Mediators of Globalization* (forthcoming, co-editor).

PNINA WERBNER is Professor Emerita of Social Anthropology at Keele University and author of *"The Manchester Migration Trilogy": The Migration Process* (1990/2002), *Imagined Diasporas among Manchester Muslims* (2002), and *Pilgrims of Love: The Anthropology of a Global Sufi Cult* (2003). She recently published *The Making of an African Working Class: Politics, Law, and Cultural Protest in the Manual Workers Union of Botswana* (2014), and she is the editor of several theoretical collections on hybridity, cosmopolitanism, multiculturalism, migration, and citizenship, including *Anthropology and the New Cosmopolitanism: Rooted, Feminist and Vernacular Perspectives* (2008) and the *Political Aesthetics of Global Revolt: Beyond the Arab Spring* (2014).

SAEKO YAZAKI gained her PhD at Edinburgh University and is currently Lord Kelvin Adam Smith Fellow in Theology and Religious Studies at the University of Glasgow. Her areas of research include early Sufism, the Judaeo-Islamic tradition in al-Andalus, and their continuing relevance to the present. She is also pursuing comparative study of monotheistic and non-monotheistic faiths, focusing on Sufism and Zen. She is the author of *Islamic Mysticism and Abu Talib al-Makki: The Role of the Heart* (2013).

Preface

The so-called mystical tradition of Islam has been the focus of a number of admirable surveys and studies, each with its own specific focus. Worthy of mention are works by Annemarie Schimmel (*The Mystical Dimensions of Islam*), Alexander Knysh (*Islamic Mysticism: A Short Introduction*), and Julian Baldick (*Mystical Islam*). These works provide an excellent background to many elements of the Sufi tradition, but they lack any significant discussion of Islam and Sufism in the modern period; rather, they focus primarily upon the formative and medieval period. Other introductions have concentrated on aspects of the tradition that reflect its "high" and intellectual approach, with examples taken largely from the medieval period. Typical of this is William Chittick's attention to Sufi ritual and theology in his *Sufism: A Short Introduction*. Carl Ernst's *The Shambhala Guide to Sufism* covers more territory in terms of chronology, but its scope is far from comprehensive, and it serves instead as a first-rate introduction to the topic. In assembling the present volume, a conscious effort has been made to move away from the phenomenological presentation of Sufism in its various geographical guises, which is a feature of Seyyid Hossein Nasr's *Islamic Spirituality*. Moreover, the issue- or theme-based nature of this collection of articles dispenses with the need to capture absolutely everything, and thus avoids the danger of presenting a very thin coverage of the phenomenon of Sufism in its entirety.

The present work attempts to build on the achievements of the aforementioned works by addressing a range of questions that are of concern to academics and students across a broad range of disciplines. Aside from the more "traditional" chapters that focus on the early formation of Sufism, Sufi rituals and belief, and love within the Sufi tradition – all of which are indispensible topics for such a volume – this work includes thematic chapters on issues relating to gender, identity formation, mysticism, marginalisation, ethics, and the impact of modernity, colonialism, and globalisation. In this respect it offers a very different history of Sufism, one that takes readers on an intellectually challenging journey. It is designed to help readers through and beyond the "introductory" level.

Of necessity this introduction is very brief because of space constraints as well as the difficulties of defining what Sufism is. With more than one thousand years to its history, there have been diverse interpretations of what Sufism has been and is, and it would be futile to attempt to offer a definition within a few sentences or paragraphs. My own chapter on "Sufism and Mysticism" should indicate the kinds of problems that appear when attempting to define the tradition. Suffice it to say that Sufism is a form of Islamic spirituality that by the early medieval period had developed specific rituals that were meant to focus the believer's attention upon God – in some cases leading to claims of direct experience with God. The implications of this belief are all too readily apparent in political, social, and literary realms – which the following twelve chapters address.

I have no wish to summarise the articles in this volume – it would be an injustice to the scholarship that has gone into these twelve chapters. By studying the whole of this book the reader will emerge with a very sound basis for comprehending Sufi history and for engaging in further and more detailed study. Should this be the case, then I will have achieved my aim. Gratitude is due to a number of individuals in the production of this book, including Marigold Acland, Sarika Narula, and William Hammell, and I also wish to thank the authors for their patience and goodwill over the past couple of years as this book was being prepared.

PART I

THE EARLY PERIOD

1

Origins and Early Sufism

Christopher Melchert

Sufism is widely defined as Islamic mysticism, particularly the form that took shape around the Baghdadi master al-Junayd (d. 298/911?). In the early eleventh century CE, biographers worked out a spiritual lineage for Sufism going back to the Companions of the Prophet. The immediate forbears of the Sufis they identified as eighth- and ninth-century renunciants known as *zuhhād, nussāk*, or *ʿubbād* (the most important extant biographical dictionaries are those of al-Sulamī and Abū Nuʿaym).[1] They underwent austerities, devoted extraordinary amounts of time to Qur'ānic recitation and prayer, and generally cultivated a solemn attitude towards life. Some spoke of thinking often and steadily of God, but the ideas of mutual love and mystical union were yet to come. A few wore wool, but express references to *ṣūfiyah* before the later ninth century usually have to do with marginal, disreputable figures not identified as forbears by the later Sufi biographers. Modern research has largely confirmed that Sufism grew out of this earlier, ascetic tradition.[2]

By a process not yet convincingly mapped in detail, there arose in the mid-ninth century a mystical trend, identified in Iraq with persons called Sufis. They talked of reciprocal love between themselves and God, and found that God addressed them through things of the world. This aroused opposition from pious Sunni circles determined to protect divine transcendence, and in 264/877–8, a Sufi inquisition was instituted in Baghdad. Some Sufis were arrested, although released without punishment, while others went into exile. By the end of the century, something like classical Sufism had developed in Baghdad, from where it would spread and absorb other pious movements over the next two

1 Al-Sulamī, *Kitāb Ṭabaqāt al-ṣūfiyya*. Edited by Johannes Pedersen (Leiden: E. J. Brill, 1960); Abū Nuʿaym al-Iṣbahānī, *Ḥilyat al-awliyā'*, 10 vols (Cairo: Maṭbaʿat al-Saʿādah and Maktabat al-Khānjī, 1352–7/1932–8).

2 Louis Massignon, *Essay on the Origins of the Technical Language of Islamic Mysticism*. Translated by Benjamin Clark (Notre Dame, Ind.: University of Notre Dame Press, 1997).

centuries. This chapter traces its emergence, as understood by twentieth-century scholarship, out of the earlier ascetical or renunciant tradition.

RENUNCIATION

The predominance of different themes in the Qur'ān and in surviving, dateable inscriptions suggests that piety was the main character of Islam in the seventh century. On the basis of inscriptions firmly dated in the seventh century, Fred Donner finds that pleas for divine forgiveness and express hopes for entry into paradise are so predominant that virtually no other features of the new religion can be made out.[3] The argument here is that such a piety, however prevalent among the earliest Muslims, could not outlast mass conversion to Islam. Ascetical, renunciant piety came under suspicion of demanding too much by the later eighth century; by the late ninth century, it had given way to the admittedly élitist, mystical piety of Sufism.

As for austerity, many early exemplars of piety were notable for their poverty. When the anti-caliph Ibn al-Zubayr (d. Mecca, 73/693) came home, he saw three bed rolls (*muthul*). One sufficed for himself, he said, and one for his wife, but the third was for Satan so they threw it away.[4] The Basran Mālik ibn Dīnār (d. 130/747–8?) gave away a pot because he feared its being stolen.[5] He was found in a house without any light or anything but the ground to lay his bread on.[6] The Kufan Dāwūd al-Ṭāʾī (d. 165/781–2?) moved from one room to another as his house gradually fell into ruin.[7]

There are many stories of renunciants who ate little. The Basran al-ʿAlāʾ ibn Ziyād (d. 94/712–13) ate one loaf a day, fasted till he turned green, and prayed till he dropped.[8] Al-Ḥasan al-Baṣrī (d. 110/728) said that the believer was properly sad morning and evening, satisfied with what satisfies a kid, mainly a handful of *tamarrud* (probably a dish of dates softened in milk) and a drink of water.[9] The Medinese Saʿīd ibn Muḥammad (d. 160s/777–87) made

[3] F. Donner, *Narratives of Islamic origins* (Princeton: Darwin Press, 1998), chap. 2; Solange Ory, "Aspects religieux des textes épigraphiques du début de l'Islam", 30–9 in *Les premières écritures islamiques*, Alfred-Louis de Prémare (ed.) (Aix-en-Provence: Édisud, 1990).

[4] Ibn al-Mubārak, *al-Zuhd wa-al-raqāʾiq*. Edited by Ḥabīb al-Raḥmān al-Aʿẓamī (Malegaon: Majlis Iḥyāʾ al-Maʿārif, 1386). Reprinted with different pagination, same numbers (Beirut: Dār al-Kutub al-ʿIlmīyah, 1419/1998). no 761.

[5] Abū Nuʿaym, *Ḥilyat al-awliyāʾ* 2:364.

[6] Abū Nuʿaym, *Ḥilyah* 2:365–6, 6:189.

[7] Abū Nuʿaym, *Ḥilyah* 7:347.

[8] Ibn al-Mubārak, *al-Zuhd*, no 965.

[9] Aḥmad ibn Ḥanbal (attrib.), *al-Zuhd*, edited by ʿAbd al-Raḥmān ibn Qāsim (Mecca: Maṭbaʿat Umm al-Qurá, 1357). Reprinted (Beirut: Dār al-Kutub al-ʿIlmīyah, 1403/1983). References to the latter in *italic*.

his living from a small tract of salty land that yielded two dinars per year. He would go to banquets when invited but eat nothing, saying, "I dislike to accustom my belly to good food, which would make it dissatisfied with what I normally feed it."[10] Aḥmad ibn Ḥanbal (d. 241/855) doubted whether a satiated man would find softening (*riqqah*) in his heart.[11]

Given the widespread preference for night-time devotions, it is unsurprisingly common to read of sleep deprivation. The Kufan Masrūq (d. 63/682–3?) did not sleep on pilgrimage save in prostration (i.e. overcome as he performed supererogatory ritual prayers).[12] The wife of the Medinese *qāḍī* Abū Bakr ibn Muḥammad ibn ʿAmr ibn Ḥazm (d. 110/728–9?) testified that he did not lie on his bed at night for 40 years.[13] The Basran Muʿādha al-ʿAdawīya (*fl.* early 8th cent.) would not sleep by day, fearing it would be her last, or by night, likewise fearing it would be her last, and wore thin clothes so that the cold would keep her awake.[14]

Some preferred at least short-term withdrawal from society. The Muʿtazilah (literally, "withdrawers") were probably distinguished at first by their renunciant piety rather than a peculiar theology,[15] and they were by no means the only ones who practiced withdrawal from sinful society. The Kufan al-Rabīʿ ibn Khuthaym (d. 63/682–3?) and the Basran Muṭarrif ibn Shikhkhīr (d. 95/713–14) are quoted as calling for one to learn jurisprudence, then withdraw.[16] A Shiʿi source quotes Jaʿfar al-Ṣādiq (d. 148/765): "Bowing in the mosque is the monasticism (*rahbānīyah*) of the Arabs. The believer's session is his mosque and his cell is his house."[17] Others restricted their conversation, at the very least. The Companion Ibn Masʿūd (d. Medina, 33/653–4?) said, "By God, if a man speaks a frivolous word (*kalimah fī al-rafāhiyah*) for his companions to laugh at, his downfall will be greater than between heaven and earth."[18] There are many injunctions to restrict

10 Ibn Saʿd, *K. al-Ṭabaqāt al-kabīr*, edited by Eduard Sachau et al., 9 vols in 15 (Leiden: E. J. Brill, 1904–40). Reprinted as *al-Ṭabaqāt al-kubrá*, 9 vols (Beirut: Dār Ṣādir, 1957–68). References to the latter in *italic*: 5:305, *5:411*.

11 Aḥmad ibn Ḥanbal (attrib.), *Kitāb al-Waraʿ*, edited by Zaynab Ibrāhīm al-Qārūṭ (Beirut: Dār al-Kutub al-ʿIlmīyah, 1403/1983). Also edited by Muḥammad Sayyid Basyūnī Zaghlūl (Beirut: Dār al-Kitāb al-ʿArabī, 1409/1988). References to latter in *italic*: 100 *82*.

12 Ibn al-Mubārak, *Zuhd*, no. 975; Aḥmad, *Zuhd*, 349, *418*.

13 Ibn Ḥajar, *Kitāb Tahdhīb* al-Tahdhīb, 12 vols (Hyderabad: Majlis Dā'irat al-Maʿārif al-Niẓāmīyah, 1325–7) (repr. Beirut: Dār Ṣādir, n.d.), 12:39.

14 Aḥmad, *Zuhd*, 208, *257*.

15 Sarah Stroumsa, "The beginnings of the Muʿtazilah, reconsidered", *Jerusalem Studies in Arabic and Islam*, no 13 (1990), 265–93.

16 Aḥmad, *Zuhd*, 240, 333, *294*, *401–2*.

17 Al-Kulaynī, *al-Kāfī, k. al-ʿishrah, bāb al-ittikā' wa-al-iḥtibā'*; edited by ʿAlī Akbar al-Ghaffārī, corrected by Muḥammad al-Ākhundī, 8 vols (Tehran: Dār al-Kutub al-Islāmīyah, 1389, 1391/2010–12), 2:662.

18 Ibn al-Mubārak, *Zuhd*, no 993.

speech, especially in the mosque; for example, from the Medinese Saʿīd ibn al-Musayyab (d. after 90/708–9): "Whoever sits in the mosque sits with God, so how much he should not say anything but good."[19] But whereas reports of conversations between Muslim ascetics and Christian hermits are numerous, reports of long-term withdrawal by Muslims seem rare; for example, al-ʿAbbās al-Majnūn (*fl.* early 3rd/9th cent.?), who lived in Mount Lebanon, wore wool, ate only twice a month, and gave himself over to ritual worship for 60 years.[20] The famous Companion Ibn Masʿūd is supposed to have actively discouraged some Kufans who had established themselves out of town to worship: "What induced you to do what you have done?" They said, "We wished to go away from the crowd." Ibn Masʿūd said, "If the people did what you have done, who would fight the enemy? I will not go away till you return."[21]

As noted, some early renunciants wore wool (Arabic: *ṣūf*), which was scratchy, smelly when wet, and liable to become ragged. Mālik ibn Dīnār wore a woollen garment.[22] The Kufan ʿAwn ibn ʿAbd Allāh (d. before 120/738) wore wool so that people would not be afraid to sit with him (i.e. so as to appear properly humble).[23] It was often related that the pious forbears had worn wool; for example, the Kufan Khaythamah ibn ʿAbd al-Raḥ mān (d. after 80/699) related that ʿĪsá and Yaḥyá (Jesus and John) had been cousins, the first wearing wool, the second skins.[24] However, the term "Sufi" did not appear until the later eighth century, and few of the renunciants whom later Sufi writers regarded as their forbears were expressly called 'Sufis' in their lifetimes.

More than particular austerities, early Muslim renunciants had in common their devotion of extraordinary amounts of time to Qur'ānic recitation and ritual prayer. The Meccan ʿAmr ibn Dīnār (d. 126/743–4) divided his nights into a third each for sleep, *ḥadīth* (i.e. reviewing his own notebooks), and ritual prayer.[25] The Basran Sulaymān al-Taymī (d. 143/761) would spend all night in prayer, praying the dawn prayer on the previous evening's ablution. He would circulate among mosques with his son all night, praying here and there until dawn.[26]

[19] Ibn al-Mubārak, *Zuhd*, no. 416.
[20] Abū Nuʿaym, *Ḥilyah* 10:145.
[21] Ibn al-Mubārak, *Zuhd*, no. 1104.
[22] Abū Nuʿaym, *Ḥilyah* 2:368.
[23] Ibid., 4:246.
[24] Ibid., 4:117.
[25] Ibid., 3:348.
[26] Ibn Saʿd, *Ṭabaqāt* 7/2:18, *7:253*.

Early renunciants were so devoted to reciting the Qur'an that *qāri'* ("reciter") became another term for "renunciant". The Companion Ibn Mas'ūd is said to have recited the Qur'an every three days, seldom making use of daylight,[27] although he is also quoted as saying, "Recite the Qur'ān in seven; do not recite it in three."[28] The Basran Abū 'Amr ibn al-'Alā' (d. 154/770–1?), one of the famous seven readers of the Qur'ān, burnt his books when he devoted himself entirely to Qur'ānic recitation, according to one source,[29] or when he devoted himself more generally to worship according to another,[30] indicating the equivalence of recitation with the life of devotion. Rather than reciting the whole Qur'ān, some ascetics meditated on small parts of it; for example, al-Rabī' ibn Khuthaym would recite one verse all night, bending and prostrating himself.[31] Night-time devotions had the advantage of taking place outside of most people's observation, and hence were less likely to be performed merely to impress them. A *ḥadīth* report from the Prophet states that "There are three eyes that will never be burnt by the fire: an eye that has wept from fear of God, an eye that has stayed awake at night with the Book of God, and an eye that has kept watch on the path of God."[32]

Celibacy was not unknown among early ascetics. 'Āmir ibn 'Abd Qays (d. ca. 55/674–5), usually associated with Basra, is a prominent early example.[33] More common are those who married but did not maintain normal conjugal relations. For example, the Kufan 'Amr ibn 'Utba (d. early 30s/650s) married at the insistence of his parents, reinforced by pressure from the caliph 'Uthmān. But he divorced two wives in succession after they said they would not give birth to children (from lack of sex), after which his parents left him alone.[34] The Kufan traditionist Sufyān al-Thawrī (d. 161/777?) said, "Do not be

[27] Ibn Abī Shaybah, *al-Muṣannaf, k. al-ṣalāh 826, fī al-Qur'ān fī kam yukhtam.* Edited by Muḥ ammad 'Abd Allāh al-Jum'ah and Muḥammad Ibrāhīm al-Luḥaydān, 16 vols (Riyadh: Maktabat al-Rushd, 1425/2004), 3:575.

[28] Ibn Abī Shaybah, *Muṣannaf, k. al-ṣalāh* 826, *fī al-Qur'ān fī kam yukhtam* = ed. Jum'ah & Luḥ aydān, 3:578.

[29] Al-Jāḥiẓ, *al-Bayān wa-al-tabyīn.* Edited by 'Abd al-Salām Muḥammad Hārūn. Maktabat al-Jāḥiẓ 2, 4 vols in 2 (Cairo: Maṭba'at Lajnat al-Ta'līf wa-al-Tarjamah wa-al-Nashr, 1367–9/1948–50), 1:321.

[30] Ibn al-Jazarī, *Ghāyat al-nihāyah fī ṭabaqāt al-qurrā'.* Edited by Gotthelf Bergsträßer, 3 vols (Cairo: Maktabat al-Khānjī, 1351–2/1932–3); (repr. Baghdad: Maktabat al-Muthanná, n.d.; repr. Beirut: Dār al-Kutub al-'Ilmīyah, 1400/1980), 1:290.

[31] Aḥmad, *Zuhd*, 336, *405*.

[32] Ibn al-Mubārak, *Kitāb al-Jihād.* Edited by Nazīh Ḥammād (Beirut: Dār al-Nūr, 1971/1391). Reprinted with different pagination, same nos, (Beirut: al-Maktabah al-'Aṣrīyah, 1409/1988), no 188; Ibn Abī Shaybah, *Muṣannaf, k. al-jihād* 1, *mā dhukira fī faḍl al-jihād* = Jum'ah & Luḥ aydān, 7:21; sim., Abū Nu'aym, *Ḥilyah* 5:209.

[33] Ibn Sa'd, *Ṭabaqāt* 7/1:74–7, *7:104–8*.

[34] Aḥmad, *Zuhd*, 354–5, *424–5*.

fooled by someone with dependents", since the need to support them would tempt him to attract presents by dictating invented *ḥadīth*.[35]

Licit gain (*kasb*) was a major concern of early Muslim ascetics. The most prominent sources of gain that they tried to avoid were payments from rulers and the yield of land improperly appropriated. For example, the Basran Muḥammad ibn Wāsiʿ (d. 123/740–1) reproached Mālik ibn Dīnār for accepting something from a ruler, even though he had spent it on buying a slave to set free.[36] "He ate only by the gain of his hand" is a common characterization, showing that someone ensured that his provision involved no fraud. Some statements indicate distrust of all trading. Mālik ibn Dīnār said, "The market increases wealth but takes away religion."[37] A Shiʿi source quotes Jaʿfar al-Ṣādiq as saying, "A believer's profit off a believer is usury [*ribḥ al-mu'min 'alá mu'min ribā*]."[38] Some stories commend economic recklessness. For example, ʿAmr ibn 'Utba is said to have bought a mare for 4,000 dirhams. When it was objected that he had paid too much, he said he would not like to have a dirham for each time it raised and put down its hoof.[39] But trade also had its defenders: the Basran Ḥassān ibn Abī Sinān (*fl.* first half 2nd/8th cent.) traded for the sake of giving alms to the poor.[40]

Morally, the early ascetics cultivated sadness and fear – especially sadness over past sins and fear of judgement to come. Al-Ḥasan al-Baṣrī said, "The believer is sad in the morning and sad in the evening." Asked to describe al-Ḥasan himself, someone said, "When you saw him, it was as if he had just buried his mother. When he sat, it was as a prisoner sits who is about to have his head struck off. When he talked, he talked the talk of a man who has been condemned to the Fire."[41] Extreme fear of the Last Judgement is attributed to a number of early figures; for example, the Kufan Abū Maysara (d. 63/682–3) took to his bed and said, "Would that my mother had never borne me." His wife said, "Abū Maysarah: God has done well by you, having guided you to Islam." He said, "Yes, but God has made it clear to us that we are bound for the Fire, without making clear to us that we are going out of it."[42] Early

35 Abū Nuʿaym, *Ḥilyah* 6:381–2.
36 Ibid., 2:353–4.
37 Ibid., 2:385.
38 Al-Barqī, *Kitāb al-Maḥāsin* (Najaf: al-Maṭbaʿah al-Ḥaydarīyah, 1384/1964), 77.
39 Aḥmad, *Zuhd*, 352 422.
40 Abū Nuʿaym, *Ḥilyah* 3:115–16.
41 Aḥmad ibn Ḥanbal, *K. al-Jāmiʿ fī al-ʿilal wa-maʿrifat al-rijāl.* Edited by Muḥammad Ḥusām Bayḍūn, 2 vols (Beirut: Mu'assasat al-Kutub al-Thaqāfīyah, 1410/1990), 1:65–6; sim., Jāḥiẓ, *Bayān* 3:171.
42 Ibn al-Mubārak, *Zuhd*, no. 312, alluding to Q. 19:71.

ascetics interpreted the Qur'ān as enjoining such sadness and fear. Many examples are quoted of weeping at hearing the Qur'ān recited. Al-Rabīʿ ibn Khuthaym wept all night over Q. 45:21: "Or do those who commit evil deeds reckon that We shall make them as those who believe and do righteous deeds . . . ?"[43]

The chief point of austerity was, of course, moral, so as to keep one's attention on the important things, mainly God and the judgement to come. Ṭalḥa ibn ʿUbayd Allāh (d. 36/656) sold an estate for 700,000 dirhams but stayed awake all night fearing for the money and so gave it away in the morning.[44] Al-Ḥasan al-Baṣrī said, "Beware of the distractions of the world. The world has many distractions. A man can scarcely open one door of distraction to himself without that door's leading on to ten more doors."[45] Because the point of austerity was mainly moral, early ascetics are often associated with measures to conceal their austerities from public view. Ibn Masʿūd said, "Ritual prayer at night is worth more than by daytime as secret almsgiving is worth more than public."[46] Many wore wool underneath more respectable fabrics, so that people could not see that they were suffering from scratchiness; for example, the Basran Hārūn ibn Rabāb (*fl.* early 2nd/8th cent.).[47] Several persons are said to have covered up the Qur'ān from which they were reading if someone approached, such as Ibrāhīm al-Nakhaʿī.[48]

Concomitant with concern for attention to God was a certain indifference to good works in the world. We certainly have stories of almsgiving. For example, ʿAlī Zayn al-ʿĀbidīn (d. Medina, 93/711–12?) gave alms in secret. His back was found to have been blackened from carrying sacks of food at night for the poor of Medina.[49] But many are also quoted as preferring ritual devotions. For example, Kaʿb al-Aḥbār (d. late 30s/650s) said, "By him in whose hand is my soul, I should prefer to weep from fear of God until my tears flow down my cheeks to giving in alms a mountain of gold."[50] Many ascetics spent time in warfare on the frontier. The Kufan Abū Wā'il (d. *ca.* 99/717–18) had a reed house for himself and his horse, which he would dismantle and give away as alms on going to war, then rebuild if he safely returned;[51] the emphasis here is on his willingness to die. But the statement of the Meccan

43 Jones's translation; Aḥmad, *Zuhd*, 329, *397*.
44 Aḥmad, *Zuhd*, 145, *181*.
45 Ibn al-Mubārak, *Zuhd*, no. 535.
46 Ibn Abī Shaybah, *Muṣannaf*, *zuhd* 12, *kalām Ibn Mas'ūd*, = ed. J&L, 12:213.
47 Abū Nuʿaym, *Ḥilyah* 3:55.
48 Ibn al-Mubârak, *Zuhd*, nos 1100–1; Aḥmad, *Zuhd*, 365, *437*.
49 Abū Nuʿaym, *Ḥilyah* 3:136.
50 Ibid., 5:366.
51 Ibn Saʿd, *Ṭabaqāt* 6:68, *6:101*; Aḥmad, *Zuhd* 357, *427–8*.

ʿAbd Allāh ibn ʿAmr (d. 63/683?) – "The recollection of God morning and evening is better than breaking swords in the path of God and pouring out wealth" – apparently indicates that private spiritual struggle might take priority over the physical.[52] Sufyān ibn ʿUyayna calculated that spiritual *jihād* was worth ten times as much as war on the infidels.[53]

Miracle stories seem less prominent in the literature of early Islamic asceticism than in, say, biographies of contemporary Christian saints. Still, they can be found. Answered prayer (*al-daʿwah al-mustajābah*) is mentioned fairly often (there are many examples in Ibn Abī al-Dunyā, *Mujābū al-daʿwah*).[54] One of the most common forms of miracle has to do with performing the ritual prayer; for example, ʿAmr ibn ʿUtba was protected by a lion as he prayed.[55] Another is the appearance of food, as when the Basran Ḥabīb al-Fārisī (*fl.* late 1st/early 2nd cent.) bought grain to relieve famine, then paid it back miraculously from sacks he had put under his bed empty before praying.[56]

THE EVOLUTION OF RENUNCIATION

The historical study of renunciation remains undeveloped. Modern scholarship follows the medieval Islamic consensus in considering the renunciants of the eighth century the forbears to the Sufis of the later ninth century and after. Scholars have long been exercised by the problem of whether Islamic renunciant piety and later Sufism were originally Islamic or were borrowed from other religious traditions. The thesis of Buddhist origins would seem to require that the earliest signs of Islamic mysticism were manifest early on, when Buddhism was strongest, and in the easternmost parts of the Islamic world, whereas mysticism seems to show up first in the ninth century, not the late seventh, and in Egypt and Iraq, not Khurasan. The same goes for alleged Indian origins more generally. Louis Massignon argued strongly for the endogenous development of Islamic renunciation and subsequent mysticism, although allowing for some influence from Christian monasticism.[57] He adduced the Qur'ānic origin of the Sufis' technical vocabulary.

[52] Ibn al-Mubārak, *Zuhd*, no. 1116.

[53] Abū Nuʿaym, *Ḥilyah* 7:284.

[54] Ibn Abī al-Dunyā, *Mujābū al-daʿwah*. Edited by Muḥammad ʿAbd al-Qādir ʿAṭā (Beirut: Dār al-Kutub al-ʿIlmīyah, 1406/1986).

[55] Aḥmad, *Zuhd*, 353, 423.

[56] Abū Nuʿaym, *Ḥilyah* 6:150.

[57] Massignon, *Essay*.

Christian parallels are not trivial. At the level of vocabulary, "asceticism" is a conventional translation of Arabic *zuhd*, which means more precisely *renunciation* or at least *unconcern*, mainly with the world. (The active participle occurs once in the Qur'ān, at 12:20, where the merchants who sell Yūsuf are described as *zāhidīn fīh* – "indifferent about him".) It corresponds to the Greek term *apatheia*. A close Arabic analogue to *askētikos* – literally, "given to exercise" – is *mujtahid*, used in the renunciant tradition especially of persons who spent extraordinary amounts of time in supererogatory ritual prayer. There are also close parallels at the level of practice.[58] Massignon stressed Qur'ānic origins partly as a riposte to Muslim modernists who were happy to dismiss Sufism as an alien superfluity. The works of Donner and other researchers suggest that the question of external influence should be reconceived as one of differentiation[59] – that is, somewhat as Christianity had taken some time to become differentiated from Judaism, it probably took some time for Islam to become differentiated from other Middle Eastern monotheisms. To say that Islamic renunciation was to some extent a variant development of earlier Middle Eastern traditions is not to discredit it, for the same should now be said equally of Islamic law and theology. It might be added that the early renunciants certainly saw themselves as living in continuity with a longer tradition. The Yemeni Wahb ibn Munabbih (d. 114/732?) is particularly associated with stories of pre-Muḥammadan prophets (he would not have thought of them as pre-Islamic), while a source as late as Aḥmad's *Zuhd* (compiled in the late ninth century) includes as many stories and sayings of pre-Muḥammadan prophets as of Muḥammad himself.

As for identifying stages in the history of renunciation, piety in this style seems to have prevailed for most of the seventh and eighth centuries. The Qur'ān has no theme so pervasive as the call to be mindful of God and not heedless. Surviving inscriptions confirm that early believers responded to the promise of salvation and the threat of perdition. In the extant literature, obsessive fear and sadness, to the extent of wishing one could avoid the Resurrection, is attributed only to fairly early figures, mainly Companions and Followers. We may doubt the precise accuracy of many quotations, partly because the same statements are sometimes found ascribed to multiple early

[58] Andrae Tor, "Zuhd und Mönchtum", *Le monde oriental* (Uppsala) 25 (1931): 296–327; Ofer Livne-Kafri, "Early Muslim ascetics and the world of Christian monasticism", *Jerusalem Studies in Arabic and Islam*, no 20 (1996), 105–29; Göran Ogén, "Did the term "*ṣūfī*" exist before the Sufis?", *Acta Orientalia* 43 (1983): 33–48.

[59] Fred M. Donner, *Muhammad and the Believers: at the origins of Islam* (Cambridge, Mass.: Belknap Press of Harvard University Press, 2010) and Julian Baldick, *Mystical Islam: an introduction to Sufism* (London: I.B. Tauris, 1989), chap. 1.

personalities and partly because we often find different sources offering variant wordings. However, on the general principle that later writers will not bother to project backwards what is strange to themselves, it seems likely that such a mood really did characterize the early period.

Poetry is less vulnerable than prose to alteration in the course of transmission, so disparagement of austerity for outward show is securely attested by the second half of the eighth century.[60] This is an old theme one might expect to be almost as old as renunciation itself.[61] Therefore, although again the precise attribution and wording are not secure, there is probably nothing anachronistic in, for example, al-Ḥasan al-Baṣrī's warning to wearers of wool: "Piety is not in one's clothing. It settles in the heart and is confirmed by one's work and deed."[62] The tendency of such warnings is that inward dispositions should match outward. There is no need to interpret such warnings as disparagement of austerity itself.

Actual disparagement of outward austerity seems most likely to have arisen in about the last third of the eighth century. Sufyān al-Thawrī is quoted as saying, "Renunciation means shortness of hope (*qiṣar al-amal*), not eating or dressing poorly."[63] Similarly, Sufyān ibn ʿUyayna is quoted as saying, "Renunciation concerns what God has forbidden. As for what God has made licit, God has made it allowable. The prophets married, rode, dressed, and ate, but (when) God forbade them something, they avoided it, and were renunciant concerning it."[64] This is not to call for inward dispositions to match outward, nor even for practising one's austerities out of public view, but rather to call for inward renunciation alone. It seems likely that mass conversion to Islam was a major reason for growing distrust of outward renunciation. It was practical for Muslims to spend most of the night in Qur'ānic recitation and supererogatory ritual prayer when they were a tiny minority at the top of society, living off tribute. When most people were Muslims, normal devotional life could no longer be allowed to hinder making a living.

[60] Geert Jan Van Gelder, "Musāwir al-Warrāq and the beginnings of Arabic gastronomic poetry", *Journal of Semitic Studies* 36 (1991): 309–27, esp. 311–13.

[61] cf. Zech. 13:4, disparaging those who wear wool in order to deceive.

[62] Aḥmad, *Zuhd*, 267 *327*; cf. Jāḥiẓ, *Bayān* 3:134, 144.

[63] Ibn Qutaybah, *ʿUyūn al-akhbār*, 4 vols (Cairo: Dār al-Kutub al-Miṣrīyah, 1343–9/1925–30). 2:356; sim. Abū Nuʿaym, *Ḥilyah* 6:386.

[64] Al-Dhahabī, *Siyar aʿlām al-nubalāʾ*. Edited by Shuʿayb al-Arnaʾūṭ. et al., 25 vols (Beirut: Muʾassasat al-Risālah, 1401–9/1981–8), 8:413.

THE EMERGENCE OF SUFISM

There are two solutions to the problem of maintaining a rigorous piety and allowing believers to make a living. One is to turn piety inward, reducing demands for outward observances such as time-consuming rituals to what is practical for most persons. This is the Protestant solution in the Christian tradition and that of the "Ḥadīth Folk" in the Islamic.[65] The other is to create a specialist caste of full-time religious specialists, supported by alms from ordinary believers. This is the monastic solution in the Christian and Buddhist traditions, among others, and to a great extent the Sufi solution in the Islamic. In the early ninth century, even as proto-Sunni disparagement of outward austerity gained ground, there apparently arose more extreme forms of austerity. Shaqīq al-Balkhī (d. 194/809–10) rejected all deliberate pursuit of gain, teaching that the pious should live on alms alone. *Tawakkul* ("dependence") came to be practised with such recklessness as for renunciants to set off on journeys across the desert without carrying food or water, expecting to be sustained accidentally – that is, by divine provision alone. As it crystallized around al-Junayd, Sufism repudiated the most extreme forms of austerity in favour of inward dependence on God.[66] As mystics, the Sufis found it easy to be generous towards nonspecialist Muslims and hopeful of their prospects for salvation, taking some of the offence out of their hierarchicalism. This seems to be the characteristic Sunni position.

Several problems need to be disengaged in order to make out the emergence of classical Sufism. One is the term "Sufism" itself. The earliest person to be called a "Sufi" was famously a Kūfan named Abū Hāshim (d. 150/767–8?), although the wearing of wool for pious reasons is well attested before him.[67] But for the next century, persons called "Sufis" by their contemporaries seem to have been disreputable, marginal figures, often involved with political opposition and certainly not demonstrably mystics. Only in the second half of the ninth century does it appear that there were persons called Sufis who were also acceptable to the Sunni mainstream, notably the circle of Abū Ḥātim al-ʿAṭṭār in Basra.[68] There are some intersections between it and the circle of al-Junayd in Baghdad in the late ninth century. By one report, Abū Ḥātim al-ʿAttār was even one of al-Junayd's teachers. Abū al-Ḥasan

[65] C. Melchert, "The piety of the hadith folk", *International Journal of Middle East Studies* 34 (2002): 425–39.

[66] On which see Benedikt Reinert, *Die Lehre vom* Tawakkul *in der klassischen Sufik*. Studien zur Sprache, Geschichte u. Kultur des islamischen Orients, n.s. 3 (Berlin: W. de Gruyter, 1968).

[67] R. A. Nicholson, "An historical enquiry concerning the origin and development of Sufism", *Journal of the Royal Asiatic Society* 38 (1906), 303–48, esp. 305; also Massignon, *Essay*, 104–7.

[68] Melchert, "Baṣran origins of Classical Sufism", *Der Islam* 82 (2005): 221–40.

al-Būshanjī (d. 348/959–60) famously said of Sufism, "It is a name without a reality. It used to be a reality without a name."[69] The historian's problem of having only names to deal with means that a reality without a name may be difficult to pin down; it also indicates the problem of transition periods, when names will be applied inconsistently to different things. But careful scholarship will avoid applying the term "Sufi" to such persons as the Baghdadi al-Muḥāsibī (d. 243/857–8) and the Egyptian Dhū al-Nūn (d. 245/860?), who were not known as Sufis in their own lifetimes, however much their teaching and examples were valued by the later Sufi tradition.

A separate problem is the emergence of mysticism. Effectively beginning with Max Weber, sociologists of religion have used "asceticism" to refer to the piety that stresses obedience to a transcendent deity. They contrast it with "mysticism" – the piety that stresses communion with an immanent deity.[70] Its closest Arabic analogue is *maʿrifah* ("knowing", contrasted with *ʿilm*, knowledge passed on orally by human teachers, whereas the Arabic *taṣawwuf* refers to the wearing of wool, not religious experience. Nevertheless, it is entirely just to describe Sufism as "Islamic mysticism". Islamic law is a major expression of Islamic asceticism in this sense, while Sufism is a major expression of Islamic mysticism. A predominantly mystical piety seems to emerge in the literary record in the mid-ninth century, in the generation before al-Junayd. "Mysticism" is a term with a fairly clear history in Christian usage, meaning knowledge of God by direct apprehension. Some Christian writers have tried to keep it Christian, distinguishing between true forms that approach God through Jesus Christ and inferior, delusory forms that do not. Resistance to the term "mysticism" from Muslims largely has to do with traditional reluctance to liken anything Islamic to anything non-Islamic. Exclusive definitions such as these are completely unhelpful to comparative religious scholarship and will not be heeded here.

It is a puzzle that early Islamic renunciation looked so similar to contemporary Christian asceticism, whereas it took centuries for Islamic mysticism to appear, even though there was already a well-developed Christian mystical tradition (going back to Evagrius and Origen, for example) for it to have taken up as well. Part of the solution is that although mysticism was one strand of the Christian ascetical tradition, another strand (represented, for example, by

[69] Ahmet T. Karamustafa, *Sufism: the formative period* (Edinburgh: University Press, 2007), 100, 111n

[70] Gert H. Mueller, "Asceticism and mysticism: a contribution towards the sociology of faith", pp. 68–132 in *International yearbook for the sociology of religion* 8: *sociological theories of religion/religion and language*. Edited by Günter Dux, Thomas Luckmann and Joachim Matthes (Opladen: Westdeutscher Verlag, 1973).

Athanasius' biography of St. Antony) was sternly anti-mystical.[71] But it remains to be explained why only the anti-mystical strand seems to have impressed the early Muslims. It shows, anyway, that whatever borrowing went on from one community to another, the Muslims as borrowers took over what made sense to them, not everything they encountered.

Along with the indiscriminate application of the term "Sufi", careful scholarship will resist the characteristic inclination of mystics to find significance in virtually everything, so that it becomes impossible to find a time when mysticism did not prevail. Talk of disinterested love from the Basran Rābiʿah al-ʿAdawīya (d. 185/801–2?), for example, has been interpreted as mysticism, overlooking that it crucially avoids any suggestion of mutuality (at least as her doctrine is reported in the early literature). It does point to the most probable path, at the experiential level, from renunciation to mysticism, mainly single-minded concentration on God. For example, the Syrian Abū Sulaymān al-Dārānī (d. 215/830–1) is quoted as reviewing different definitions of renunciation (*zuhd*) current in Iraq: "Some say it is leaving off meeting people, some say it is leaving off desires, and some say it is leaving off satiety. Their definitions are similar to one another. I think that renunciation is leaving off whatever distracts you from God."[72] When Dhū al-Nūn refers to God's select servants whose bodies are in the world but whose spirits are hung up in the kingdom,[73] we seem to be in unmistakably mystical territory – all the more when a disciple to Abū Yazīd al-Basṭāmī (d. 261/875?) asks him about a sob that he had seen tear the veil between him and God, to which Abū Yazīd responds by lauding the sob that means there is no veil to tear.[74]

It has often been alleged, but never convincingly demonstrated, that Shiʿism was decisively important to the emergence of Sufism. Sometimes it is alleged that the esoteric element of Sufism depended on Shiʿi precedents, such as finding allusions to ʿAlī and his house in the Qur'ān. Sometimes it is alleged that whenever Sufi sources quote a Shiʿi imam, especially Jaʿfar al-Ṣādiq, it betrays a Shiʿi background, no matter how Sunni the quotation sounds. Sometimes it is alleged that Sufi ideas of charismatic individuals must have been modelled on early Shiʿi ideas. The weakness of the case is ever and again the lack of Shiʿi literature securely dated before the emergence of Sufi mysticism in the mid-ninth century, so that alleged Shiʿi precedents can only be assumed, not demonstrated. Extant Shiʿi literature from the late ninth and

[71] Andrew Louth, *The origins of the Christian mystical tradition from Plato to Denys* (Oxford: Clarendon Press, 1981), 100.
[72] Abū Nuʿaym, *Ḥilyah* 9:258.
[73] Ibid., 9:349.
[74] Ibid., 10:38.

early tenth centuries (al-Barqī, al-Ahwāzī, Ibn Hammām al-Iskāfī and al-Kulaynī) present Shiʿi versions of Sunni renunciant sayings. For example, Jaʿfar al-Ṣādiq is quoted as saying, "If you are not weeping, pretend to weep."[75] In the Sunni tradition, the same is attributed to the Prophet,[76] Abū Bakr the first caliph,[77] and Abū Mūsá al-Ashʿarī, another prominent Companion.[78] Early Shiʿi books do not present Shiʿi versions of later Sufi sayings, unless extravagant Shiʿi claims for imams are (unnecessarily) taken as the basis of extravagant later claims for Sufi saints.[79]

Mystical claims provoked new hostility from ascetics. The most spectacular manifestation of hostility was the Inquisition of 264/877–8, in which Ghulām Khalīl (d. 275/888), a popular preacher from Basra, procured the indictment of seventy-odd Sufis for allegedly saying they no longer feared God but, rather, loved him. Ruwaym (d. 303/915–16) and al-Nūrī (d. 295/907–8) were among those who fled Baghdad. Al-Junayd himself escaped arrest by asserting that he was not a Sufi at all but a student of jurisprudence.[80] In the event, no one was put to death, but al-Junayd went on to develop a language to deal with mystical experience that would not offend more old-fashioned ascetics. Notably, triads such as separation-union-separation (*farq-jamʿ-farq*) and subsistence-annihilation-subsistence (*baqāʾ-fanāʾ-baqāʾ*) replaced the old dichotomies (e.g. *farq-jamʿ*). One spoke of the first sobriety, seeing the world in common daylight, followed by the drunkenness of ecstatic absorption by God, followed by the second sobriety, in which one was conscious of the world again but in a way that was transformed by the experience of drunkenness. Thus, a mystic could speak of his union with God in a way that recognized the validity of his experience but also reassured the ascetically

[75] Kulaynī, *Kāfī, k. al-duʿāʾ, bāb al-raghbah wa-al-rahbah*, 2:483.

[76] Ibn Mājah, *al-Sunan, k. al-zuhd* 19, *bāb al-ḥuzn wa-al-bukāʾ*, no 4196; Abū ʿUbayd. *Faḍāʾil al-Qurʾān*. Edited by Marwān al-ʿAṭīyah, Muḥsin Kharābah, and Wafāʾ Taqī al-Dīn (Damascus: Dār Ibn Kathīr, 1415/1995), 135; Hannād ibn al-Sarī. *Kitāb al-Zuhd*. Edited by ʿAbd al-Raḥmān ibn ʿAbd al-Jabbār al-Faryawāʾī, 2 vols (Kuwayt: Dār al-Khulafāʾ lil-Kitāb al-Islāmī, 1406/1985), 1:270; Aḥmad, *Zuhd*, 27, *36*.

[77] Ibn al-Mubārak, *Zuhd*, no 131; Wakīʿ, *al-Zuhd*. Edited by ʿAbd al-Raḥmān ʿAbd al-Jabbār al-Faryawāʾī, 3 vols (Medina: Maktabat al-Dār, 1404/1984). Reprinted Riyadh: Dār al-Ṣumayʿī, 1415/1994, 1:254; Aḥmad, *Zuhd*, 108, *135*; Ibn Abī Shaybah, *Muṣannaf, k. al-zuhd* 92, *mā qālū fī al-bukāʾ*, 12:424.

[78] Aḥmad, *Zuhd*, 199 *247*; Abū Nuʿaym, *Ḥilyah* 1:261.

[79] James W. Morris, "Revisiting religious Shiʿism and early Sufism: the fourth/tenth-century dialogue of the sage and the young disciple", pp. 102–16 in *Reason and Inspiration in Islam*. Edited by Todd Lawson (London: I.B. Tauris, 2005).

[80] Richard Gramlich, *Alte Vorbilder des Sufitums* 1: *Scheiche des Westens* and 2: *Scheiche des Ostens*. *Alte Vorbilder* 1:384–5, Akademie der Wissenschaften und der Literatur, Mainz, Veröffentlichungen der orientalischen Kommission 42/1–2 (Wiesbaden: Harrassowitz, 1996), 1: 384–5.

minded that he recognized divine transcendence. Al-Junayd also pushed mysticism in an inward direction, offering a style of mystical piety that would not interfere so clearly with the collection of *ḥadīth*, the study of jurisprudence, making a living, and so on. Tension between mystics and ascetics did not go away, and the prominent Sufis al-Ḥallāj and Ibn ʿAṭāʾ were put to death in 309/922. However, whereas al-Junayd was molested in the Inquisition of Ghulām Khalīl, he was left alone when al-Ḥallāj was tried.[81]

The transition from early renunciation to Sufism of course involved continuity and discontinuity. A notable point of continuity was austere living: Sufis were known for "eating little, speaking little, sleeping little, and withdrawal from people" – all typical activities of the early renunciants as well. When Ruwaym asked for some water on a hot day, a slave girl exclaimed, "A Sufi who drinks during the day!" and threw down the jug of water she was carrying. Ever after, Ruwaym fasted by day, evidently living up to the normal expectation.[82] Until modern times, moderate austerity remained an important part of ideal deportment among all Muslims.

As for discontinuity, mysticism meant more tolerance of hierarchy: masters and disciples, full- and part-time devotees, initiates and non-initiates. A related phenomenon was the rise of the Sufi shaykh as an intermediary between the servant and God (on which more below). Discontinuity here is probably related to the spread of Islam from city to country. However, charismatic leadership had precedents in the early period, when important renunciants and jurisprudents were commonly the same men (e.g. al-Ḥasan, al-Baṣrī and Ibrāhīm al-Nakhaʿī), interpreting God's will to laymen, and when notable *ḥadīth* transmitters were sometimes identified as *abdāl* ("substitutes") by whose intercession fell rain.[83]

The expectation of communion with God was a greater point of discontinuity, which explains why it was precisely this issue over which Sufis were attacked at the Inquisition of Ghulām Khalīl. So were some Sufi practices, notably "audition" (*samāʿ*), the cultivation of rapture by listening to music,

[81] Much has been much written about Al-Ḥallāj: Massignon, *The Passion of al-Hallāj, mystic and martyr of Islam*, translated by Herbert Mason (Princeton: University Press, 1982), looks at his life from a religious point of view; Carl W. Ernst, *Words of Ecstasy in Sufism* (Albany: State University of New York Press, 1985), proposes a political interpretation of his prosecution; while S. A. Arjomand, "The crisis of the imamate and the institution of occultation in Twelver Shiʿism" (*International Journal of Middle East Studies* 28 (1996): 491–515, stresses Shiʿism.

[82] Al-Sarrāj, *The Kitáb al-Lumaʿ fi ʾl-taṣawwuf.* Edited by Reynold Alleyne Nicholson (Leiden: E. J. Brill and London: Luzacs, 1914), 163; Alexander D. Knysh, (translator), *Al-Qushayri's epistle on Sufism* (Reading: Garnet, 2007), 48.

[83] See list in G. H. A. Juynboll, *Encyclopedia of canonical ḥadīth* (Leiden: Brill, 2007), 731–2; cf. Karamustafa, *Sufism*, 106, 139–40nn.

which seems to have burgeoned from about the middle of the ninth century.[84] More significant is the theoretical elaboration of the mystical path. The renunciants of old had collected stories and sayings, but it was especially the Sufis who seem to have sat about trading definitions of technical terms and only Sufis (except for al-Muḥāsibī, it appears) who wrote treatises.

Although they reportedly had masters and disciples in common and are quoted complementarily, al-Junayd is sometimes opposed in the tradition to Abū al-Ḥusayn al-Nūrī. For example, al-Nuri is quoted as saying,

> I wished to see one of these miracles. I took a cane from some boys and stood between two boats. Then I said, "By your mightiness, if a three-pound fish does not come out to me, let me drown myself." Then there came out to me a fish weighing three pounds. When al-Junayd heard of this, he said, "It should have been a snake come out to him in order to bite him".[85]

Al-Junayd is wary, here, that miracle-working may encourage self-importance.

> One day Nūrī said to Junayd, who had decided reluctantly to speak in public and was lecturing in a theoretical mystical vocabulary, while he, Nūrī, was preaching out of fraternal devotion: "You defraud them, and they have let you sit in their pulpits, but as for me, who wanted to warn their souls, they have thrown me into the rubbish heap".[86]

There are a number of stories of al-Nūrī getting into trouble. He was once brought before the caliph for insulting the muezzin at the call to prayer by saying *labbayk* at the barking of a dog ("at your service", normally addressed to God at the circumambulation of the Kaʿba). Al-Nūrī explained that the muezzin had been calling inattentively, while the dogs had been praising as best they could without knowing how and without hope of reward.[87] A Ḥanbali source apparently says that he executed the Muslim's duty to command the right and forbid the wrong (*al-amr bi-al-maʿrūf wa-al-nahy ʿan al-munkar*) by smashing jugs of wine bound for the caliphal palace.[88] Probably, al-Nūrī represents a more populist, demonstrative line of Sufi teaching and practice, perhaps continuing the line of al-Kharrāz (d. 277/890–1?) a little before him and anticipating ʿAbd Allāh Anṣārī (d. 481/1089) and others after him.

84 Jean During. "Musique et rites: le *samāʿ*", 157–72 in *Les voies d'Allah: les ordres mystiques dans l'islam des origines à aujoud'hui*. Directed by Alexandre Popovic and Gilles Veinstein (Paris: Fayard, 1996); Arthur Gribetz, "The *samāʿ* controversy: Sufi vs. Legalist", *Studia Islamica*, no 74 (1991), 43–62; for Qushayrī's apology, see Knysh, *Al-Qushayri's epistle*, 342–57.

85 Sarrāj, *Lumaʿ*, 327; Knysh, *Al-Qushayri's epistle*, 369.

86 Massignon, *Passion*, 1:79.

87 Sarrāj, 5; cf. Knysh, *Al-Qushayri's epistle*, 268.

88 Richard Gramlich, 1:75.

SUFISM TRIUMPHANT

The tenth century was one of consolidation and spread. As for consolidation, the earliest biographical dictionaries of Sufism were evidently written by Abū Saʿīd ibn al-Aʿrābī (d. 340/952?), a Basran who joined the circle of al-Junayd in Baghdad for a time before settling in Mecca, and Jaʿfar al-Khuldī (d. 348/959), a Baghdadi associated with al-Junayd. These survive only in quotation, likewise the great *Tārīkh al-ṣūfiyya* of the Nishapuran al-Sulamī (d. 412/1021); however, a shorter version of al-Sulamī's work covering a little over a hundred personalities is extant.[89] Comprehensive treatments of Sufi doctrine also appeared, defining terms and quoting the greatest figures of the (not-distant) past. Foremost among them is al-Sarrāj (d. 378/988), *Kitāb al-Lumaʿ*. In the eleventh century, there appeared, besides the biographies and other works of al-Sulamī, al-Khargūshī (d. 407/1016?), *Tahdhīb al-asrār*, similar to *al-Lumaʿ*, *Ḥilyat al-awliyā'* of the *ḥadīth* collector Abū Nuʿaym al-Iṣbahānī (d. 430/1038), which combines sayings of renunciants and Sufis along with *ḥadīth* they related, and the influential *Risāla* of al-Qushayrī (d. 465/1072),[90] also important as a theologian and Qur'ān commentator. (Al-Khaṭīb al-Baghdādī's biography of al-Qushayrī portrays him as an Ashʿarī without mentioning Sufism.) Also in the later eleventh century there began to appear Persian Sufi literature, notably the *Kashf al-maḥjūb* of Hujwīrī (d. 465/1072–3?),[91] from Lahore, and a collection of aphorisms, a biographical dictionary, and other works by ʿAbd Allāh Anṣārī, from Herat.

As for the spread of Sufism, two parties of the pious seem to have contested supremacy in Nishapur (northeastern Iran) in the later ninth century: the undemonstrative Malāmatīyya and the more populist Karāmīyya (also spelt Karrāmīyah). Sufism, so-called, was evidently introduced from Baghdad by Abū Bakr al-Wāsiṭī (d. after 320/932), although his teaching was soon reinforced by Nishapurans who had travelled to Baghdad and back. By the early eleventh century, it had absorbed the Malāmati tendency,[92] and perhaps the Karāmi as well, inasmuch as the *khānaqāh* began as a Karāmi institution but continued as a central Sufi one from the eleventh century.[93] The first

[89] Rkia E. Cornell, translator. *Early Sufi Women* by al-Sulamī (Louisville, Ky.: Fons Vitae, 1999).

[90] Knysh, *Al-Qushayri's Epistle.*

[91] R. A. Nicholson, translator. *Kashf al-maḥjúb* by ʿAlī ibn ʿUthmān al-Hujwīrī (Leiden: E. J. Brill and London: Luzac & Co., 1911).

[92] Jacqueline Chabbi, "Remarques sur le développement historique des mouvements ascétiques et mystiques au Khurasan," *Studia Islamica*, no 46 (1977), 5–72; Jean-Jacques Thibon, *L'œuvre d'Abū 'Abd al-Rahmān al-Sulamī (325/937–412/1021) et la formation du soufisme* (Damascus: Institut Français du Proche-Orient, 2009).

[93] Jacqueline Chabbi. "Khānḳāh," *Encyclopaedia of Islam*, new edition, s.v.

Andalusian to be called a Sufi was one ʿAbd Allāh ibn Naṣr (d. 315/927–8).[94] In Basra, Sahl al-Tustarī (d. 283/896?) seems to have stood apart from Abū Ḥātim al-ʿAṭṭār and his circle. The Baghdadi Ḥanbali leader al-Barbahārī (d. 329/941) is said to have been his disciple, and traces of his doctrine have been detected in a creed attributed to al-Barbahārī (see below, p. 22). Locally, Sahl's doctrine was maintained and extended for a time by Ibn Sālim (d. 350s/961–70) and the Sālimi school. Abū Ṭālib al-Makkī (d. 386/996), *Qūt al-qulūb*, probably represents the culmination of Sālimi doctrine. The school seems to have been absorbed by Baghdadi Sufism after him. The magnificent synthesis of al-Ghazālī (d. 505/1111), *Iḥyāʾ ʿulūm al-dīn*, is heavily reliant on the *Qūt* in many places (without acknowledgement).

Sahl al-Tustarī and the Basran tradition after him make a good example of the distorting effect of Sufi spread and consolidation, for Sufi writers like al-Sarrāj quote Sahl as though he had been at the centre of the Sufi movement of his time, not its periphery. (Massignon inferred rather that al-Sarrāj was himself a leading Sālimi, implying that he was an outsider who saw something attractive in Sufism).[95] The effect of such quotation is to disguise disagreement. Overlooking disagreement came easily to Sufi historians, who as mystics were used to discovering meaning in almost everything and so could easily see the affinity of Sahl's teaching with their own ideas. However, it forces responsible modern scholars to read Sufi histories against the grain. The exact relations between Baghdadi Sufism and local traditions outside Baghdad is a promising topic for further research.

The period from al-Sarrāj to al-Qushayrī has been identified especially with the production of handbooks, interpreted as seeking to reassure ascetical, law-oriented outsiders. To the contrary, some scholars have recently protested that the handbooks were principally intended as summaries of Sufi doctrine for insiders. Remonstrations against persons who starve themselves to the point of being too weak to perform the ritual prayer at the appointed time[96] or who cite the Qur'ānic story of al-Khaḍir and Moses (Q. 18:60–82) to justify preferring saints to prophets[97] are presumably sincere. Still, when al-Sarrāj explains near the beginning (for example) that knowledge is completed when the servant experiences only the present time and exists always by means of and for God, permanently diverted from everything except God, later quotes Ibn ʿAṭāʾ as

[94] Manuela Marín, "The early development of *zuhd* in al-Andalus," pp. 83–96 in Frederick de Jong (ed.), *Shiʿa Islam, Sects and Sufism* (Utrecht: M. Th. Houtsma Stichting, 1992), p. 85.

[95] Massignon, *Passion* 2:130.

[96] Sarrāj, *Lumaʿ*, 417.

[97] Sarrāj, *Lumaʿ*, 422–3.

saying that the recollection of God will do away with human nature, then near the end declares it a gross error to speak of the falling away of human nature when one leaves changeability behind, it does sound as though he believes in the experience but wants mystics not to describe it in language obnoxious to the ascetical-minded orthodox, jealous of divine transcendence.[98]

Starting somewhat before the stage of writing handbooks and culminating somewhat afterwards appears to be the rise of the Sufi shaykh. Fritz Meier outstandingly drew attention to a series of shaykhs in Khurasan whose reported doctrine increasingly stressed the essential importance of a teacher who not only lectured to his disciples in the manner of al-Junayd, among others, but closely followed their spiritual progress to the point of assigning particular exercises according to their particular needs at the time.[99] For example, al-Qushayrī concludes his *Risāla* with a full account of the new training programme (*bāb al-waṣīyah lil-murīdīn*), with rules for such steps as the master's assignment of divine names for different novices to recite at the appropriate points in their development. By contrast, al-Sarrāj, *al-Luma'*, al-Khargūshī, *Tahdhīb al-asrār*, and even al-Sulamī, *Ādāb al-ṣuḥba*, know little of the new formality.[100] Al-Qushayrī says of himself:

> As a beginner I would never enter into the presence of my master Abu 'Ali unless I was fasting. I would also perform a full ablution. ... When I overcame my timidity and entered the school, I would be overcome by a sense of numbness in the middle of it to such an extent that one could stick a needle into me without my taking notice of it.[101]

Earlier teachers certainly gave directions for the best way to live, but earlier writers do not describe such extravagant devotion to them. In the course of the tenth century, special buildings for Sufis begin to appear in the sources, variously called by the names *khānaqāh*, *zāwiya*, *duwayra*, and others. They appear to have begun as meeting places, but become in the eleventh century regular halls of residence for the disciples of a particular master.[102]

[98] Sarrāj, *Luma'*, 40, 219, 427.

[99] Fritz Meier, "Khurāsān and the end of Classical Sufism," 189–219 in *Essays on Islamic Piety and Mysticism*. Translated by John O'Kane with Bernd Radtke (Leiden: Brill, 1999); Laury Silvers-Alario, "The teaching relationship in early Sufism: a reassessment of Fritz Meier's definition of the *shaykh al-tarbiya* and the *shaykh al-ta'līm*," *Muslim World* 93 (2003): 69–97.

[100] Al-Sulamī. *Kitāb Ādāb al-ṣuḥbah*. Edited by M. J. Kister (Jerusalem: Israel Oriental Society, 1954).

[101] Knysh, *Al-Qushayri's Epistle*, 305–6.

[102] Karamustafa, *Sufism*, 121, 125–7.

Al-Junayd and the early Sufis tended to be identified with the Shāfiʿi school in law and Ashʿarism in theology, or more broadly with the compromise tendency to base law and belief on Qur'ān and *ḥadīth* while allowing reason considerable scope to combine texts and extrapolate implicit rules and doctrines. This set them apart from the extreme Sunni traditionalists on the one side, who preferred to do without theological speculation and argument, and such rationalists on the other side as the Muʿtazila. The Muʿtazila were also opposed to Sufism by their disbelief in miracles by other than prophets. The Ashʿarīyah accommodated miracles by means of occasionalism, explaining that God recreated everything from one moment to the next so that miracles are simply departures from his habit (*kharq al-ʿādah*), disrupting the accustomed chain of cause and effect. Only prophets were associated with *muʿjizāt*, miracles that "rendered incapable" others of doing the same, but the *awliyā'* ("friends", mainly of God) might be honoured with *karāmāt*, "charismata".[103] Lines were still fairly blurred in the tenth century, however. The Ḥanbali creed of al-Barbahārī (but also attributed to the earlier anti-Sufi Ghulām Khalīl) warns against direct contemplation of God (*al-fikra fī Allāh*), in agreement with Sahl al-Tustarī, also against those who call to longing for and love of God rather than fear of him.[104] The Egyptian Ḥ anafi al-Ṭaḥāwī (d. 321/933) includes in his creed the superiority of prophets to *awliyā'*, against anyone who ranked the *awliyā'* higher, notably the Transoxanian al-Ḥakīm al-Tirmidhī (d. *ca.* 295/907–8?). However, he also affirms belief in their *karāmāt*. The North African Ibn Abī Zayd al-Qayrawānī (d. 386/996–7?), Māliki in law and Ashʿari in theology, allows contemplation of (*al-tafakkur fī*) God's signs but not his essence. He includes all the saved among the *awliyā'*, although his main concern was probably to disallow Shiʿi ideas, not Sufi (*al-Risālah, bāb mā tanṭiqu bihī al-alsinah*). Among Sufi writers, al-Qushayrī and Hujwīrī were particularly notable for integrating *kalām* theological views with Sufism. By contrast, ʿAbd Allāh Anṣārī was identified with Ḥanbalism and probably preserved a more populist, demonstrative line of Sufi teaching that was disdainful of theology and other rational sciences.[105]

To summarize, widespread acceptance of renunciant piety in most of the seventh and eighth centuries CE seems to have been succeeded by growing distrust from the later eighth century. Sufism went from designating disreputable, marginal figures to accepted Sunnis at about the middle of the ninth

[102] Karamustafa, *Sufism*, 121, 125–7.

[103] Annemarie Schimmel, *Mystical Dimensions of Islam* (Chapel Hill: University of North Carolina Press, 1975), 206.

[104] Melchert, 'The Ḥanābila and the early Sufis, *Arabica* 48 (2001), 361–2.

[105] Karamustafa, *Sufism*, 93–6, 101–6.

century. At the same time, it also became identified with an emerging mystical piety. It survived a notable attack, the Inquisition of Ghulām Khalīl, by the development of a less offensive style of discourse in the circle of al-Junayd. The new Sufism spread from Baghdad in the tenth century and had effectively absorbed most rival pious movements by the middle of the eleventh century.

FURTHER READING

Andrae, Tor. *In the Garden of Myrtles*. Translated by Birgitta Sharpe. Muslim spirituality in South Asia. New York: State University of New York Press, 1987.

Al-Ḥakīm al-Tirmidhī. *The Concept of Sainthood in early Islamic Mysticism: Two Works by Al-Ḥakīm al-Tirmidhī*. Translated with an introduction by Bernd Radtke and John O'Kane. Curzon Sufi series. Richmond: Curzon Press, 1996.

Ibn al-Jawzī. *Talbīs Iblīs*. Abridged and translated by D. S. Margoliouth as '"The Devil's Delusion" by Ibn al-Jauzi', *Islamic Culture* 9 (1935): 1–21, 187–208, 377–99, 533–57; 10 (1936): 20–39, 169–92, 339–68, 633–47; 11 (1937): 267–73, 393–403, 529–33; 12 (1938): 108–18, 235–40, 352–64, 447–58; 19 (1945): 69–81, 171–88, 272–89, 376–83; 20 (1946): 58–71, 181–90, 297–310, 408–22; 21 (1947): 73–9, 172–83, 394–402; 22 (1948): 75–86. The section on Sufis and the like begins at 10 (1936): 339. Collected as *Talbis Iblis* ("Delusion of the Devil"). Translated by D. S. Margoliouth. Edited by N. K. Singh. New Delhi: Kitab Bhavan, 2003.

Al-Kalābādhī. *The Doctrine of the Sufis*. Translated by Arthur John Arberry. Cambridge: Cambridge University Press, 1935.

Karamustafa, Ahmet T. *Sufism. The Formative Period. The New Edinburgh Islamic surveys*. Edinburgh: Edinburgh University Press, 2007.

Knysh, Alexander. *Islamic Mysticism: A Short History. Themes in Islamic studies 1*. Leiden: Brill, 2000.

Massignon, Louis. *Essay on the Origins of the Technical Language of Islamic Mysticism*. Translated by Benjamin Clark. Notre Dame, Ind.: University of Notre Dame Press, 1997.

Al-Qushayrī. *Al-Qushayri's Epistle on Sufism*. Translated by Alexander D. Knysh, reviewed by Muhammad Eissa. *Great Books of Islamic Civilization*. Reading: Garnet Publishing, 2007.

Sells, Michael A., editor and translator. *Early Islamic mysticism: Sufi, Qur'an, Mi'raj, Poetic and Theological Writings*. Classics of Western spirituality. New York: Paulist Press, 1996.

Al-Sulamī. *Early Sufi Women*. Edited and translated by Rkia Elaroui Cornell. Louisville, Ky.: Fons Vitae, 1999.

2

Early Pious, Mystic Sufi Women

Laury Silvers[1]

There is a significant obstacle to writing a history of early Sufi women: women are substantially missing from the major sources. The texts that have come to define the history, practice, and thought of Sufism from the early period onward contain few female figures.[2] Some reports of pious and Sufi women survived orally and in written form over the intervening centuries in collections of biographical notices of noted individuals, such as Abū ʿAbd

[1] Thanks to Kecia Ali, Yasmin Amin, Aisha Geissinger, Alan Godlas, Nate Hofer, Christopher Melchert, Kristian Petersen, Lloyd Ridgeon, Karen Ruffle, and others for answering any number of questions, sharing sources, helping to identify figures, and reading drafts (especially Geissinger); and thanks to Basit Iqbal for his meticulous editing work. All errors are mine. Death dates and locations are only given, when known, to help situate the women in their place and time. Due to the word limit, primary source citations are not exhaustive and I have cited only secondary sources specific to the issue at hand and which provide relevant bibliographies. References to Ibn al-Jawzī's *Ṣifāt al-ṣafwa* are cited by entry number as "IJ, #000"; except where noted, these translations are by Silvers and Ahmed Elewa or Silvers and Yasmin Amin. References to Abū ʿAbd al-Raḥmān al-Sulamī's *Dhikr al-niswa* are cited by the pagination of R. Cornell's translation (*Early Sufi Women:* Dhikr an-niswa al-mutaʿabbidāt aṣ ṣūfiyyāt *by Abū ʿAbd ar-Raḥmān ās-Sulamī* [Louisville, KY: Fons Vitae, 1999]) as "AARS, 000–000."

[2] Abū Nuʿaym al-Iṣfahānī's (d. 430/1038) *Ḥilyat al-awliyā*ʾ [28 women/649 men]; Nūr al-Din ʿAbd al-Raḥmān Jāmī's (d. 897/1492) *Nafahāt al-uns* [35w/564m]; ʿAbd al-Wahhāb b. Aḥmad al-Shaʿrānī's (d. 973/1565) *Ṭabaqāt al-kubrā* [16w/412m]. But the majority of the women named in these works, and those mentioned below, are members of the Prophet's family, companions, or Qur' ānic figures. Likewise, see the women named in al-Qushayrī's *al-Risāla fī ʿilm al-taṣawwuf* [biographical section: 0w/83m], Abū al-Ḥassan ʿAlī b. ʿUsman al-Jullabī al-Hujwīrī's *Kashf al-maḥjub* [12w/109m], Farīd al-Dīn al-ʿAṭṭar's (d. 628/1230) *Tadhikirat al-awliyā*ʾ [1w/72m], Khargūshī's *Tahdhīb al-asrār* [7 women] (see C. Melchert, "Khargūshī, *Tahdhīb al-asrār*", *Bulletin of the SOAS*, 73/1 [2010], 32 [corrected from 7% to 7 women]), Abū l-Ḥasan al-Sīrjānī's (d. *ca.* 470/1077) *Kitāb al-bayāḍ wa-l-sawād* [8w/478m] (see B. Orfali and N. Saab [eds], *Sufism, Black and White: A Critical Edition of* Kitāb al-Bayāḍ wa-l-Sawād *by Abū l-Ḥasan al-Sīrjānī* [d. *ca.* 470/1077] [Leiden: Brill, 2012]) [thanks to the editors for sharing this volume with me]; finally, see R. Roded, *Women in Islamic Biographical Collections: From Ibn Saʿd to Who's Who* (Boulder, CO: Lynne Rienner, 1994).

al-Raḥmān al-Sulamī's (d. 402/1012) *Dhikr al-niswa al-mutaʿabbidāt as-ṣūfiyyāt*, and Abū al-Faraj Ibn al-Jawzī's (d. 597/1200) *Ṣifāt al-ṣafwa*, as well as Muḥammad Ibn Saʿd's (d. 230/845) *Ṭabaqāt al-kubrā*.[3] Despite likely access to such resources, however, major Sufi manuals and treatises such as Abū Ṭālib al-Makkī's (d. 386/996) *Qūṭ al-qulūb*, Abū Bakr al-Kalabādhi's (d. *ca.* 380/990) *Taʿarruf*, Abū Nasr al-Sarrāj's (d. 378/988) *Kitāb al-lumaʿ*, Abū al-Qāsim al-Qushayrī's (d. 465/1072) *al-Risāla*, and Abū al-Ḥassan al-Ḥujwīrī's (d. 470/1077) *Kashf al-maḥjūb* only mention by name the near-legendary Rabīʿa al-ʿAdawiyya (Basra, d. 185/801) and a few other pious and Sufi women. While a number of women do appear in these texts, they are most often anonymous, and moreover are depicted as supporting players in accounts of more famous men.[4] In al-Sulamī and Ibn al-Jawzī's works, a few of these men are depicted making an effort to transmit women's knowledge with women at the centre of the accounts.[5] Individual women are mentioned in some early Sufi texts, such as al-Ḥakīm al-Tirmidhī's (d. 320/910) account of his wife's extraordinary spiritual station.[6] Certainly, men's names have been dropped from the sources. But the sheer number of extant reports of men compared to women in the formative literature means that women are read as marginal to the development, transmission, and preservation of Sufi practices, knowledge, and teaching.

3 Abū al-Faraj ibn al-Jawzī, *Ṣifāt al-ṣafwa* (Beirut: Dār al-Kutub al-ʿIlmiyya, 1999); Cornell, *Early Sufi Women*; Muḥammad b. Saʿd, *al-Ṭabaqāt al-kubrā* (Lebanon: Dar Iḥyāʾ al-Turāth al-ʿArabiyya, 1996). See Nana Asmaʾu's "Sufi Women" for the rare, possibly unique, biographical collection (in the form of a poem) by a woman about women (in Beverly Mack and Jean Boyd (eds), *Collected works of Nana Asmaʾu* (East Lansing, MI, 2012); also see Mack's chapter on Asmaʾu in this volume (Chapter 8).

4 Cornell, *Early Sufi Women*, 15–20; also see A. Afsaruddin, "Gender and the poetics of narrative", *The Muslim World* 92 (2002), 461–480; V. Hoffman, "Oral Traditions as a Source for the study of Muslim women: Women in the Sufi orders", in A. El-Azhary Sonbol (ed.), *Beyond the Exotic: Women's Histories in Islamic Societies* (Cairo: American University of Cairo Press, 2006), 365–380. On "restraint" in naming women other than family members (and then as supporting players) in one source, see Marín, "Saints, women, and family relationships", and using family genealogies as sources, see F. Chiabotti, "ʿAbd al-Karīm al-Qushayrī: Family ties and transmission in Nishapur's Sufi milieu", both in C. Mayeur-Jaoun and A. Papas (eds), *Family Portraits with Saints: Hagiography, Sanctity, and Family in the Muslim World* (Berlin: Klaus Schwarz Verlag, 2013) [thanks to the editors for sharing this volume with me pre-publication]. On the sources available to authors, see A. K. Alikberov, "Genre tabakāt in early Sufi tradition", ACTAS XVI Congreso UEAI (1995), 23–30.

5 Notably reports attributed to Dhū al-Nūn (d. 244/859) and Aḥmad b. Abū al-Ḥawārī (d. 230/845 or 246/860). For Dhū al-Nūn's transmissions, see IJ, #620, #881, #908, #909, #974, #975, #991, #992, #993, #994, and #995; and AARS, 142–145. For Hawārī's transmissions, see IJ, #601, #731, #822, #823, #824, #825, #827, and #830; AARS, 82–83, 84–85, 86–87, 120–121, 124–125, and 126–127.

6 D. Reynolds, trans., "The Autobiography of al-Hakim al-Tirmidhi (with substantial contributions from his wife's dreams)", in D. F. Reynolds (ed.), *Interpreting the Self: Autobiography in the Arabic Literary Tradition* (Berkeley: University of California Press, 2001), 120–131.

Most surviving accounts of women in the formative period (namely, between the 1st/7th and 4th/10th centuries) concern those in the early piety movement – that is, prior to the rise of Sufism in the late 3rd/9th century.[7] These "vigorous worshippers" (*mutaʿabbidāt*) were known for their intense ritual practice, scrupulous ethics, and ability to inspire a sense of intimacy with God, but cannot be called Sufis in the historical sense of the term.[8] Rather, pious women such as the famous Rabīʿa al-ʿAdawiyya were cast as "Sufis" when Sufism was said to be "a reality without a name".[9] Likewise, Sufi literature tended to co-opt individuals identified with other mystical movements, such as the Malāmatiyya, as their own.[10] The Ḥanbalī scholar Ibn al-Jawzī did the same, sharing the contributions of these women in keeping with his own perspective on worthy piety.[11] Despite the authors' agendas, these sources offer valuable insights into the diverse pious and mystical movements of the early period. This chapter offers a summary of the reported thought and practices of early pious, mystical, and Sufi women in the contexts of the theological movements of their day, their social lives, and their teacher–student relationships.

These reports raise numerous methodological concerns. Some scholars are extremely sceptical of their historical reliability, but others, such as Shahzad Bashir, Nadia Maria El-Cheikh, and Aisha Geissinger, have written convincingly that such biographical reports retain some historical value.[12] These reports can offer important clues about the existence of individuals,

[7] "Piety" is used here in a general sense to refer to devotional thought and practices prior to the rise of Sufism and sometimes concurrent with it, including those called *nussāk* (the devout), *abrār* (the righteous), *zuhhād* (renunciants), and *ʿubbād* (worshippers). On these terms, see Knysh, *Islamic Mysticism: A Short History* (Leiden: Brill, 2000), 5–7.

[8] S. Sviri, "Sufism: Reconsidering Terms, Definitions, and Processes in the Formative Period of Islamic Mysticism", in G. Gobillot and J-J. Thibon (eds), *Les Maîtres Soufis et Leurs Disciples IIIe-Ve Siècles de l'hégire (IXe-XIe s.) Enseignement, Formation et Transmission* (Beirut: Institute Français du Proche-Orient, 2012).

[9] A. Karamustafa, *Sufism: The Formative Period* (Edinburgh: University Press, 2007), 100.

[10] M. Ngyuen, *Sufi Master and Qur'an Scholar: Abū'l-Qāsim al-Qushayrī and the* Laṭā'if al-ishārāt (New York: Oxford University Press, 2012), 68–69; J. A. Mojaddedi, *The Biographical Tradition in Sufism: The Tabaqāt Genre from al-Sulamī to Jāmī* (Richmond, Surry, UK: Curzon Press, 2001), ch. 1; on mystical traditions in the formative period see Karamustafa, *Sufism*; Knysh, *Islamic Mysticism*; and S. Sviri, *Perspectives on Early Islamic Mysticism: The World of al-Hakīm al-Tirmidhī and his Contemporaries* (New York: Routledge, 2010).

[11] On Ibn al-Jawzī, see "Ibn D̲jawzī", *EI2*.

[12] For examples of extreme scepticism, see S. A. Mourad, *Early Islam between Myth and History: Al-Ḥasan al-Baṣrī (d. 110H/728 CE) and the Formation of his Legacy in Classical Islamic Scholarship* (Leiden: Brill, 2005) and D. A. Spellberg, *Politics, Gender, and the Islamic Past: The Legacy of ʿA'isha Bint Abi Bakr* (New York: Columbia University Press, 1994).

movements, and doctrines, as well as social realities.[13] A single report will typically reflect several competing and complementary purposes. For example, it is reported that the mother of Misʿir b. Kidam (Kufa, d. 155/772) prayed at the mosque five times a day and that Misʿir walked her there and back.[14] This seems straightforward enough; walking one's mother to the mosque is common practice even now, where women are permitted to attend. But consider too that while the notice is ostensibly about his mother, it also highlights Misʿir b. Kidām's good character, demonstrating his reliability as a Hadith transmitter. The report may also indicate that at least older women in the city of Kufa around the mid-2nd century were permitted to pray regularly in the mosque. It may even have been intended to take a stand on a matter of dispute at the time by claiming that a respected Hadith transmitter approved of older women's mosque attendance.[15]

As I will show, the textual marginalization of these women does not seem to reflect their actual participation in pious or mystical circles. Sufi authors excised or downplayed women's roles for any number of interrelated social, economic, and political reasons, such as shifting modes of authority in the Seljuk period and the rise of the Sufi orders; personal reasons, such as Abū Ṭālib al-Makkī's distaste for women; and to control controversy, whether due to criticism of women's relatively open participation or other concerns.[16] Over time, transmitters and authors transformed some women's socially engaged lives, even in worship, into near total seclusion and silence, presenting the woman untouched by the world as the ideal.[17] For instance, ʿAmma, the sister of Abū Saʿīd b. Abū al-Khayr (d. 441/1049), told her brother that his words were like an ingot of gold. He replied, " . . . but your silence is an

[13] See S. Bashir, *Sufi Bodies: Religion and Society in Medieval Islam* (New York: Columbia University Press, 2011); N. M. El-Cheikh, "Women's history: A study of al-Tanūkhī", in M. Marín and R. Deguilhem (eds), *Writing the Feminine: Women in Arab Sources* (London: IB Taurus, 2002); and A. Geissinger, *Gender and the Construction of Exegetical Authority: A Rereading of the Classical Genre of Qur'an Commentary* (Leiden: Brill, 2014).

[14] IJ, #467.

[15] IJ, #474; B. Sadeghi, *The Logic of Lawmaking in Islam: Women and Prayer in the Legal Tradition* (Cambridge: Cambridge University Press, 2013), ch. 5.

[16] Ngyuen, *Sufi Master and Qur'an Scholar*, 36–45; Karamustafa, *Sufism*, ch. 5; Beatrix Immenkamp, *Marriage and Celibacy in Medieval Islam: A study of Ghazali's* Kitāb ādāb al-nikāḥ (Dissertation for the Faculty of Oriental Studies, Kings College, Cambridge, 1994), 116–118; F. Sobieroj, "The Muʿtazila and Sufism", F. de Jong and B. Radtke (eds), *Islamic Mysticism Contested: Thirteen Centuries of Controversies and Polemics* (Leiden: Brill, 1999); and L. Ridgeon, "The controversy of Awḥad ad-dīn Kirmānī and handsome, moon-faced youths: A case study of *Shāhid Bāzī* in medieval Sufism", *Journal of Sufi Studies* 1 (2012), 1–28.

[17] See Silvers, "Disappearing women: The case of Hafsa bt. Sirin", in progress.

unpierced pearl".[18] The Hadith, legal, and biographical literature of the first few centuries of Islam demonstrates that there was an overall trend to restrict the manner in which women engaged in public life.[19] Although much of this literature presents free women's seclusion as normative and religiously mandated, non-elite free women and enslaved women's public activities (manual labour, buying and selling, teaching, socializing, etc.) could not be controlled.[20] Nor could religious behaviour outside the direct control of authorities. As I will argue, other reports seem to vouch for women's socially unconventional behaviour such as privately and publicly visiting with men, attending mixed-gender gatherings, and, in some cases, setting up camp at the Kaaba or even preaching in the streets.

Writing a history of women's religious life raises the question of whether there is a distinct "women's spirituality". Gendered social expectations and obligations not only shaped how women were depicted in these sources, but also how women lived, worshipped, gave guidance, or received it. Maria Dakake has identified a common "language of domesticity" in early women's sayings. These sayings imagine God as the masculine object of feminine longing, while sayings attributed to men imagine God as the veiled beloved with whom they seek an elusive rendezvous.[21] Dakake writes that, for women, God is the idealized male guardian who protects, comforts, consoles, and shares in intimacy with his obedient and loving servant.[22] That said, while some reports recreate the trope of divine guardianship with gratitude and love, other reports depict women wracked with fear of displeasing him and thus suffering his abandonment in this world, or, worse, punishment in the

[18] Moḥammad Ebn-e Monavvar, *The Secrets of God's Mystical Oneness* (Asrār al-towḥīd) (New York, Mazda Publishers, 1992), 412.

[19] For example, see M. H. Katz, *Prayer in Islamic Thought and Practice* (Cambridge: Cambridge University Press, 2013), 177–214; L. Halevi, *Muhammad's Grave: Death Rites and the Making of Islamic Society* (New York: Columbia University Press, 2007); and M. Tillier, "Women before the *Qāḍī* under the Abbasids", *Islamic Law and Society* 16 (2009), 280–301; on women's marginalization in Hadith scholarship during the 2nd–3rd/8th–9th centuries, see A. Sayeed, *Women and the Transmission of Religious Knowledge in Islam* (Cambridge: Cambridge University Press, 2013), 76–107.

[20] For example, see M. Yazigi, 'Some accounts of women delegates to Caliph Muʿāwiya: Political significance", *Arabica* 52/3 (2005), 437–449; Y. Rapoport, *Marriage, Money, and Divorce in Medieval Islamic Society* (Cambridge: Cambridge University Press, 2005); M. Shatzmiller, "Aspects of women's participation in the economic life of later medieval Islam: Occupations and mentalities", *Arabica* 35/1 (1988), 36–58; A. Ghabin, *Hisba: Arts and Crafts in Islam* (Weisbaden: Harrassowitz Verlag, 2009).

[21] M. Dakake, "Guest of the inmost heart: Conceptions of the divine beloved among early Sufi women", *Comparative Islamic Studies* 3/1 (2007), 72.

[22] Dakake, "Guest of the inmost heart", 75–79.

next.[23] Rkia Cornell has identified a thread in women's sayings, which she calls a "theology of servitude", marking their extreme sense of submission to God alone.[24] The degree to which such depictions were the imaginings of male transmitters is open to debate, but it is demonstrably the case that women's domestic obligations and other gendered social norms would have an effect on their theological perspectives and ritual lives.[25] Gender norms are also complicated by social class, political associations, environmental issues, and other factors. There is nothing inherent to women about any of these socio-historical contexts. Thus, there is little historical value in identifying a "spirituality" particular to women, unless it refers to the dynamic and intersecting socio-historical narratives that name certain types of bodies, experiences, and articulations "female".

WOMEN AND THEOLOGY IN CONTEXT

Scholastic theologians argued their positions in technical language drawn from traditional sources as well as the Greek philosophical tradition.[26] Their views mainly reached the populace from mosque pulpits and circles of learning, and were sometimes enforced by Caliphal authorities.[27] Nevertheless, theology was not a top-down affair. Accounts demonstrate that male and female scholars and preachers who were familiar with the language of scholastic theology (*kalām*) but were not theologians themselves, as well as untrained popular preachers, revered pious folk, and perhaps even one's grandmother, had a stake in defining the proper boundaries of the divine–human relationship and took stands on controversial issues (such as whether one could comprehend God or see him in this world or the next).[28]

[23] L. Silvers, "God loves me": The theological content and context of early pious and Sufi women's sayings on love", *Journal for Islamic Studies* 30 (2010), 33–59.

[24] Cornell, *Early Sufi Women*, 54–60.

[25] Cornell, *Early Sufi Women*, 54–60; Dakake, "Guest of the inmost heart", 73–97; and see examples below.

[26] "Kalām", *EI*².

[27] A. El Shamsy, "The social construction of orthodoxy", in T. Winter (ed.), *The Cambridge Companion to Classical Islamic Theology* (Cambridge: Cambridge University Press, 2008).

[28] On high/low distinctions, see A. Karamustafa, *God's Unruly Friends: Dervish Groups in the Islamic Later Middle Period, 1200–1550* (Salt Lake City: University of Utah Press, 1994), ch. 1; on the relationship between popular and elite theologies, see El Shamsy, "The social construction of orthodoxy"; D. Ephrat, *Spiritual Wayfarers, Leaders in Piety: Sufism and the Dissemination of Islam in Medieval Palestine* (Cambridge, MA: Harvard University Press, 2008); D. Talmon-Heller, *Islamic Piety in Medieval Syria: Mosques, Cemeteries and Sermons under the Zangids and Ayyūbids (1146–1260)* (Leiden: Brill, 2007); J. Berkey, *Popular Preaching and Religious Authority in the Medieval Islamic Near East* (Seattle: University of Washington Press, 2001).

And why not? People's understanding of the divine–human relationship generally arises from an effort to negotiate their lives in a meaningful way.[29] Whatever the historical reliability of the reports, they demonstrate that it was not unheard of for women to adopt such positions and that the popular voice mattered. One report has an unnamed woman clinging to the Kaaba, calling out,

> O You whom eyes do not see, with whom imaginings (*al-awhām*) and conjecture (*al-ẓunūn*) cannot intermix, whom the things of this world (*al-ḥawādith*) cannot change, whom the describers cannot describe, O You who knows the weight of the mountains, the measure of the seas, the number of the raindrops and the leaves of the trees, and the number of everything upon which night falls and the day breaks. Heaven cannot hide itself from Him, nor the earth, nor the mountain its impassable terrain, nor the sea its depths.[30]

Elite theologians had no choice but to respond to popular theological positions, whether by adopting, reshaping, or opposing them. Thus the two developed in conversation with one another, making it difficult to draw a clean line between them.

The first "properly theological dispute" in Islamic history developed out of early political divisions.[31] Sayings from regions dominated by dissenters who held the political leadership responsible for the murder of the Prophet's family typically reflect a desire for people to be held accountable for their actions, meaning that God is bound to punish wrongdoing and reward good deeds.[32] For instance, Umm Ibrāhīm al-ʿĀbida (Basra, d. *ca.* late 3rd/9th century) was furious when she saw pilgrims on Hajj engaging in trade. She declared that on the Last Day, their actions would be exposed and they would be unable to escape punishment. She called out to God loudly enough for the pilgrims to hear, "My Love, they are engaged with this world and have left You!" Then she screamed and collapsed on the ground. When she came to her senses, her companion remonstrated with her for such extraordinary behaviour. She scolded him in turn, saying, "You layabout! When He is decreeing [either paradise or hell], for whom would God fake his pleasure?"[33]

[29] J. Z. Smith, "Map is not territory", in J. Z. Smith, *Map is not Territory: Studies in the History of Religions* (Chicago: University of Chicago Press, 1993), 289–310.

[30] IJ, #973.

[31] K. Blankinship, "The early creed", in T. Winter (ed.), *The Cambridge Companion to Classical Islamic Theology* (Cambridge: Cambridge University Press, 2008), 38.

[32] S. A. Jackson, *Islam and the Problem of Black Suffering* (New York: Oxford University Press, 2009), 29–30.

[33] IJ, #600.

Those regions dominated by the Ahl al-Ḥadīth, who promoted quietism in the face of these injustices, argued, by contrast, that the political situation was the will of God and judgment belonged to God alone.[34] Reports associated with these regions typically reflect a tendency towards notions of predestination in which God alone decides one's fate in the afterlife. Naqīsh bt. Sālim of Mecca was overheard calling out in grief, "O Master of Humankind, misdeeds weigh heavily on me. Sadness has darkened my eyelids like kohl. I swear by Your majesty I shall never enjoy laughter until I know my destination in the final abode. Oh, what will be my home?"[35]

Gender intersects with other socio-historical factors in shaping one's understanding of the divine–human relationship. Some men and women depicted God in anthropomorphic terms, with women reportedly imagining God as the idealized male lover and guardian. In the following account, a woman claims that her love for God outstrips even her good works in ensuring his good treatment of her in the afterlife:

> "By God, I am so tired of life that if I were to find death for sale, I would buy it out of longing for Him and my love of meeting Him." So I said to her, "Are you so certain of your works?" "No, by God, rather out my love for Him and beautiful opinion of Him. Would He torment me when I love Him so?'[36]

Taking the opposite position on human responsibility, Mu'mina bt. Bahlūl (Baghdad, lived late 3rd/10th century) is reported to have loved her guardian so abjectly that he had complete power over her. She feared that he would withdraw his intimacy from her and punish her in the afterlife. The gendered social dynamic of male guardianship established in the Qur'an is at play here. Men are made guardians over women and directed to correct them through progressively stringent means, involving abandonment of the marital bed, then physical punishment (Q. 4:34).[37] Mu'mina said, "The world and the Hereafter are not pleasurable except through You. So do not overwhelm me with the loss of You and the punishment that results from it!"[38]

[34] See T. Nagel, *The History of Islamic Theology from Muhammad to the Present*, trans. T. Thornton (Princeton: Princeton University Press, 2000), ch. 2.

[35] IJ, #230.

[36] IJ, #1015; see also IJ, #596; and Dakake, "Guest of the inmost heart", 92, n. 17.

[37] Silvers, "God loves me", 44–46. On conceptions of the divine–human relationship in terms of idealized heterosexual and patriarchal gender roles, see S. Murata, *The Tao of Islam: A Sourcebook on Gender Relationships in Islamic Thought* (Albany: SUNY Press, 1992); and M. Malamud, "Gender and spiritual self-fashioning: The master-disciple relationship in classical Sufism", *Journal of the American Academy of Religion* 64/1 (1996), 89–117.

[38] AARS, 86–87; IJ, #365.

As the reader may have noticed, reports from the early period – irrespective of theological position on free will or predestination – typically emphasize fear and sadness when contemplating judgment in the next world. Although there were periods and places of relative calm and wealth, the people of the formative period lived through civil wars that tore Muhammad's community apart, local (sometimes violent) challenges to political authority, cycles of plague, and periods of famine. Coupled with the Qur'an's emphasis on the threat of punishment and the promise of reward, it is not surprising that popular theological positions were deeply coloured by the fear of divine judgment even as they expressed hope – and certainty – of salvation.[39] Reports characterize some people as particularly fearful (*al-khāʾifūn*).[40] It was reported that Umayyah bt. Abū al-Muwarriʿ (Mawsul, lived *ca.* early 2nd/8th century) was among them:

> When mentioning the Fire, she would say, "They have been doomed to the Fire, eaten from the Fire, drunk from the Fire, yet they live on [in the Fire]." Then she would weep at length and shudder as if she were a seed on a hot frying pan. At times when the Fire was mentioned she would even weep blood.[41]

CONTEMPLATING THE NEXT WORLD AND THE PRACTICE OF SORROW

Among men and women alike, fear and love were associated with moderate to extreme renunciation (*zuhd*) in the form of scrupulous behaviour, lengthy prayers, supererogatory fasting, and, as already seen, weeping.[42] In most regions, but especially in Basra, there were men and women who wept in contemplation of the transience of this life and the return to God. These weepers are remembered in the literature with great flourish; one man is said to have wept so much in prayer that the pebbles beneath him would become soaked.[43] Lay people were encouraged to weep, too. Prophetic reports condemned wailing for the dead, but encouraged pious weeping as a ritually expiatory practice.[44] Women and men alike visited weepers who were able to

[39] C. Melchert, "Exaggerated fear in the early renunciant tradition", *Journal of the Royal Asiatic Society* 21/3 (2011), 283–300.

[40] IJ, #630, #729, and #824; Melchert, "Exaggerated fear", 288.

[41] IJ, #729.

[42] On *zuhd*, see C. Melchert, "Origins and early Sufism", in this volume (Chapter 1).

[43] Melchert, "Exaggerated Fear", 288.

[44] L. G. Jones, "He cried and made others cry", in E. Gertsman (ed.), *Crying in the Middle Ages: Tears of History* (New York: Routledge, 2011), 103; for regional context, see Ephrat, *Spiritual Wayfarers*, 24.

inspire others to weep. For women, pious weeping offered them a certain amount of religious and social authority that challenged scholarly efforts to direct orthodoxy, orthopraxy, and women's role in public religious practice, and also challenged social expectations such as marriage.

Weeping is portrayed in the reports as a highly personal response to one's relationship with God, but personal experience manifests in and responds to historical contexts. Weeping is part of a constellation of phenomena that includes political protest, social approbation, and personal experiences of transformation.[45] In some respects, women's practice of weeping is portrayed as an acceptable redirection of the practice of wailing for the dead. Prior to the coming of Islam, and for a short time afterwards, women acted as public and private mourners. Professionals, as well as friends and family, wailed and wept to help people grieve in public and private social rites. Wailing and elaborate funeral rituals were criticized by early authorities as out of step with a prophetic attitude of restraint and also as belying God's promise that true life would be found after death.[46] But in dominantly pro-ʿAlid garrison cities such as Kufa and Basra, women's wailing also played a role in fomenting rebellion against Caliphal powers and anticipated Shiʿa rituals of mourning and protest for the injustices perpetrated against the Prophet's family.[47] Prohibitions against women's wailing for the dead was most stringent in Kufa.[48] Nevertheless, it seems to have been a difficult practice to restrain.[49]

Reports seem to advise that if women are to weep and wail, then they should direct their grief more properly towards contemplation of the next world. One report makes a connection between the wailing of a mother who has lost her child and wailing for God's sake. Ḥakīma al-Makkiyya (Mecca, lived early 2nd/8th century) lived with other women gathered around the Kaaba who engaged in constant worship. She waited day and night for the Kaaba to open. It is said that "[w]hen she saw its door open, she screamed like a mother whose child has died. She wept until she fell down faint".[50] Another report from the same period indicates that it may have been difficult to restrain women from visiting gravesites to wail for the dead, and advises that such practices be redirected towards the remembrance of death in the

[45] See Jones, "He cried and made others cry", 102–135; and S. Mahmood, "Rehearsed spontaneity and the conventionality of ritual: Disciplines of 'Ṣalāt", *American Ethnologist* 28/4 (2001), 827–853.

[46] Ibid., 119–127.

[47] Ibid., 132–134.

[48] Ibid., 127–135.

[49] Ibid., 135–138.

[50] IJ, #229.

service of worshipping God. The unnamed woman in the report seems to belong to a group of women who visit graveyards as mourners. While visiting a graveyard, she suddenly comes across a skull that sends her into an agitated state of repentance. When they want to know what happened, she replies, "My heart cried out from remembering death when I saw skulls inside the tomb! Leave me! Not one of you is serious about worshipping God and has come here longing to serve Him."[51]

Pious weeping and its associated practices of fasting and praying at length seemed to excuse women from certain gender expectations and offer them religious authority. Some reports may address concerns that weeping and fasting were ruining women's chances at marriage, and thus motherhood, by destroying their looks.[52] Accounts seem to vouch for these women by presenting their ruined bodies as a great loss to men and thus presented as a sacrifice for God's sake,[53] nowhere so explicitly as in the case of Khansāʾ bt. Khidām. She reportedly "had a resounding voice and was a great beauty like a fattened camel adorned for sacrifice", but she fasted until she was skin and bones, and wept until she lost her eyesight.[54]

The marks of renunciation on women's bodies testified to their sincerity and the soundness of their views and practices.[55] Shaʿwāna (al-Uballa, lived mid-2nd/8th century) received elite validation by Abū Mālik b. Ḍaygham b. Mālik (d. 180/796), a respected Hadith scholar and renunciant, after he determined the exact place in the eye from which her tears fell. The evidence of her body would not only have demonstrated that she was no charlatan, but would also have served to vouch for her authority as a teacher and the propriety of her gatherings, in which she led men and women into ecstatic states through music and perhaps dance (*samāʿ*).[56]

51 IJ, #204.

52 IJ, #234, #603, and #615; Cornell, *Early Sufi Women*, 56–60.

53 On the construction of maternity and male control of women's reproductive bodies, see K. Kueny, *Conceiving Identities: Maternity in Medieval Muslim Discourse and Practice* (Albany, NY: SUNY Press, 2013).

54 IJ, #251 (she may be the young companion [Ibn Māja, Book of Marriage, 1/602]).

55 Transmitters exaggerated or imagined lives of sorrow and renunciation to bolster the authority of early and late scholars (see S. A. Mourad, *Early Islam between Myth and History*; M. H. Reid, *Law and Piety in Medieval Islam* [Cambridge: Cambridge University Press, 2013]; and on feigned weeping, see Jones, "He cried and made others cry", 104). Nevertheless public weeping was a common practice before and after the coming of Islam (see Jones, "He cried and made others cry"; and M. H. Katz, *The Birth of the Prophet Muhammad: Devotional Piety in Sunni Islam* [New York: Routledge, 2007], 142).

56 On *samāʿ*, see K. Avery, *A Psychology of Early Sufi* Samāʿ*: Listening and Altered States* (New York: Routledge, 2004).

My father said to him one day, "Describe her weeping for me."

I said, "O Abū Mālik, I will describe it for you. By God she weeps day and night almost without stopping!"

My father said, "This is not what I asked you to describe. How does she begin her weeping?"

I replied, "Yes O Abū Mālik, whenever she begins a session of invocation (*samā*ʿ) you will see tears pouring from her eyelids like rain."

My father asked, "Which were more abundant – the tears coming from the inner corner of the eye beside the nose, or the tears coming from the outer corner beside the temple."

I replied, "O Abū Mālik, her tears were too numerous to distinguish one from another. From the moment she begins her invocation, they flow, all at once, from the four corners of her eyes."

My father wept and said, "It seems to me that fear has burnt up her entire heart." Then he said, "It has been said that an increase or decrease of tears is proportional to the extent of the burning of the heart. When the heart has been fully consumed, the person who maintains the station of sorrow (*al-ḥazīn*) can weep whenever he wants. Thus, the smallest amount of invocation will cause him to weep."[57]

WOMEN'S WORSHIP IN CONTEXT: FAMILY, SLAVES, AND MARGINAL WOMEN

Widowed and Married Women

Domestic duties and other labour restricted most women's time for worship, but older free women had the greatest flexibility to pursue lengthy prayers. Women who were widowed, with grown children or without children, and who had help caring for their needs could pray throughout the night and day, sleeping for just a few hours in the morning or the afternoon without concern for domestic obligations. They worshipped in mosques, or even in graveyards, but mainly at home or the homes of friends. Munayfa bt. Abū Ṭāriq of Bahrain only began praying at length in the last forty years of her life, after she had been widowed and her children were grown. While visiting overnight, her friend Amma observed her standing in prayer for hours, weeping as she repeated one verse of the Qur'an over and over: "And how could you disbelieve while the verses of God are recited to you and among you is His Messenger? And whoever holds firmly to God has been guided to a straight path" (Q. 3:101). She is reported to have prayed throughout the day (when

[57] AARS, 98–99; IJ, #630.

domestic duties would be performed) until the afternoon, when she would sleep until sunset (perhaps to avoid visitors).[58]

Older women without anyone to care for them would have to be up in the morning to perform domestic chores or other labour, thus limiting the time they spent awake in prayers at night. In some cases, these women prayed a portion of the night and considered their daytime work as part of their renunciant path.[59] Māwardiyya (Basra, d. 466/1073) only took up regular fasting, nightly prayers, and practicing *niswān* (female chivalry) after the age of thirty (when, if she had children, they would no longer require her constant attention).[60] She probably continued her labour of making and selling rosewater. She lived until the age of eighty and ground her own flour and baked her own bread every day. In renunciant style, she ground her flour out of legumes rather than grain (a luxury food), and ate little meat, oil, or grapes.[61]

Married women are depicted admiringly as they encourage their immediate family to be more scrupulous, take up more ritual worship, or enter into extremes of renunciation.[62] Some women cajoled while others scolded their husbands. One unnamed woman, who was known for her assiduous worship and sharp tongue, performed one hundred cycles of mid-morning prayer every day (taking at least two hours to complete, they could be performed after her morning chores and before the midday meal), recited either chapter 112 from the Qurʾan or its opening verse ("Say He is God, One") 10,000 times a day while going about her business, and stood in prayer through the night:

> She would say to her husband, "Get up! Take care! How long are you going to sleep? Get up, you heedless man! Get up, you idle oaf! How long are you going to be heedless? I swear that you will only provide for us by permissible means. I swear to you that you will not enter the Fire on account of me. On the piety of your mother, pray that God has mercy on you! Do not slack, for God will decide your case!"[63]

In many accounts, married women are portrayed as having the admiration of their husbands and grown children. Jawhara's husband, Abū ʿAbd Allāh

[58] IJ, #654; on avoiding visitors, see IJ, #623, #853, #931, and #934.

[59] IJ, #614.

[60] IJ, #619; on female chivalry, see below, p. 49.

[61] See Waines, "Luxury foods of medieval Islamic societies", *World Archaeology* 34/3 (2003), 571–580.

[62] On the problem of using the English word "family" in this and later periods, see "Introduction", Mayeur-Jaoun and Papas (eds), *Family Portraits with Saints*.

[63] IJ, #1011; see also IJ, #595.

b. Abū Jaʿfar al-Barāthī (Baghdad, d. 300/912), a well-known renunciant (possibly Sufi), found her to be a worthy partner who prodded him to even greater feats of renunciation. The two only had mats woven from reeds to sit on, which she talked him into giving up by saying, "Isn't it said in the Hadith, 'The earth says to the child of Adam, "You put a barrier between you and I, and tomorrow you will be inside me"?' "[64] In some cases, a husband or grown children express concern for his wife or their mother's health due to the intensity of her worship. Umm al-Aswad's (Kufa, d. *ca.* 100/718) legs were disabled and her daughter worried about her standing in prayer at such length.[65] ʿŪwayd b. Abū ʿImrān al-Jūnī (Basra, d. *ca.* 123/740) tried to curtail his wife's worship after she injured her legs standing in prayer such that she had to wrap them tightly in cloth.[66]

Marriage, Sex, and Worship

The biographical material on Rābiʿa bt. Ismāʿīl (lived *ca.* 200/800) offers insight into the way that marriage and sex intersected with worship for these devout women. Although socially disapproved of, it seems to have been possible for non-elite women to choose to live alone, with other women, or avoid marriage entirely. For instance, the famed Rābiʿa al-ʿAdawiyya, who was reportedly a freed slave or an impoverished orphan, lived alone at times, but also shared her home with her companions and servants, Maryam, until Maryam's death, then ʿAbda bt. Abū Shawwāl, who was with Rābiʿa when she died.[67] And Ḥasna al-ʿĀbida, reportedly a great beauty, was in a position to declare, "Farewell to men!"[68] But Rābiʿa bt. Ismāʿīl was a wealthy widow, and thus if she desired to undertake a life of worship outside the protection of her family or a husband it would have been socially ruinous for her.[69] Women's convents (sing. *ribāṭ*) had not yet developed, so a woman of Rābiʿa bt. Ismāʿīl's social status had little choice but to marry a man who would permit her a life of worship.[70]

[64] IJ, #360; see also IJ, #614.
[65] IJ, #466.
[66] IJ, #613.
[67] Cornell, *Early Sufi Women*, 63; AARS, 84–85.
[68] IJ, #603.
[69] B. Shoshan, "High culture and popular culture in medieval Islam", *Studia Islamica* 73 (1991), 67–107; S. M. Ali, "The rise of the Abbasid public sphere: The case of al-Mutanabbi and three middle ranking patrons", *al-Qantara* 29/2 (2008), 467–494.
[70] On women's use of *ribāṭs*, see Rapoport, *Marriage, Money and Divorce*, 38–44; on convents as an escape from marriage, see C. W. Bynum, *Holy Feast, Holy Fast: The Religious Significance of Food to Medieval Women* (Berkeley: University of California Press, 1988), 222.

Rābiʿa reportedly offered the well-known shaykh Aḥmad b. Abū al-Ḥawārī (d. 230/845 or 246/860) and his companions some seven thousand to thirty thousand dirhams, requested that their marriage be celibate, and encouraged him to take other wives.[71] Aḥmad is the narrator of her life of piety: "She told me, 'I do not love you in the way that married couples do, instead I love you as do the brothers [on the path]. I want to be with you only to serve you.' "[72] Aḥmad is portrayed here as a great lover of women, soul and body. In soul, he admired Rābiʿa, acknowledged her as his spiritual equal, and took the trouble to transmit anecdotes about her and other accomplished women.[73] In body, he enjoyed the physically intimate company of his other wives, and possibly Rābiʿa.[74] The reports' depiction of Aḥmad's admiration of Rābiʿa and his virility are not unconnected. The narrative construction of Rābiʿa and Aḥmad's piety is framed in terms of their faithfulness to the marital norms of their day; a clear link is made between submitting to one's husband and submitting to God.[75]

Rābiʿa would enter the relationship as his spiritual equal, but her social standing as a wife would require her obedience, including constant sexual availability.[76] She would be socially and legally obligated to check with him first before fasting through the day or praying throughout the night, in case he might want to have sex with her.[77] He is depicted expressing his pride in his wife's resolve to worship God in these moments by demonstrating how she both resisted his overtures and acknowledged his right to sex with her. In the following narration, he amplifies her piety by phrasing her resistance as almost desperate:

> If I wanted to have sex with her during the day she would say, "I implore you in the name of God, do not make me break my fast today." And if I wanted her during the night, she would say, "I implore you in the name of God to grant me this night for God's sake."[78]

[71] IJ, #823; S. Bashir, "Islamic tradition and celibacy", in C. Olson (ed.), *Celibacy and Religious Traditions* (New York: Oxford University Press, 2007), 140–141.

[72] AARS, 316–317; IJ, #823.

[73] See footnote 5, this chapter.

[74] Knysh, *Islamic Mysticism*, 37–38.

[75] A. Chaudhry, *Domestic Violence and the Islamic Tradition* (Oxford: Oxford University Press, 2013), 41–44. On obedience in marriage and discipleship, see Malamud, "Gender and Spiritual Self-Fashioning"; and M. Dakake, "'Walking upon the path of god like men?' Women and the feminine in the Islamic mystical tradition", in J-L. Michon and R. Gaetani (eds), *Sufism: Love and Wisdom* (Bloomington: World Wisdom, 2006), 133.

[76] See K. Ali, *Marriage and Slavery in Early Islam* (Cambridge, MA: Harvard University Press, 2010), 66–96.

[77] IJ, #823.

[78] AARS, 316–317; IJ, #823.

Having sex would be no small interruption to such a woman's worship. During the day, she would not be able to return to fasting. At night, she would have to perform the major ablution to return to her prayers. Public baths would not be available to her so late, so during much of the year she would have to wash herself in the cold.[79]

The following report demonstrates his pride in having a wife who understands her place in the marital hierarchy but who loves God above all else. By marrying him, she gives her body to the man whom she admires and who admires her, but her love belongs to God alone:

> I also heard her say while in a state of intimacy [with God]:
> I have made You the One who speaks to me in the depths of my soul,
> While I made my body lawful for the one who desires to sit with me.
> My body is my intimate gift to my worldly companion
> While my heart's Beloved is my true Intimate in the depths of my soul.[80]

Whatever their life together may have been like, the narrative portrays the idealized link between women's piety and submission to their husbands, the need for a man to vouch for a woman's unusual behaviour, and real world compromises that women like Rābiʿa might have had to negotiate.

Brothers and Sisters

There are a number of stories of brothers and sisters who shared homes or who worshipped together. Abū Sulaymān al-Dārānī (d. 205/830) seems to have been close to his sisters, ʿAbda and Āmina, and describes their intellect and dedication to worship as exalted.[81] Bishr al-Ḥāfī (d. *ca.* 235/850) and his sisters, Muḍgha, Zubda, and Mukhkha, lived and worshipped together in Baghdad, where they visited Aḥmad b. Ḥanbal (d. 855/241) and received visits from scholars and other pietists such as Āmina al-Ramliyya.[82] They tended the home and wove textiles for income, which was a common trade for women and considered a legitimate source of income for the scrupulously pious.[83] Sisters Ghaḍba and ʿĀliyya worshipped late through the night, and

[79] The warmest nights, given the average weather temperatures in Damascus in her era, would have been 60F/15C, but would often fall below freezing in winter. With or without a nearby fire, this would have been at least uncomfortable and perhaps even physically dangerous.
[80] AARS, 316–317.
[81] IJ, #822.
[82] IJ, #828.
[83] IJ, #382; M. Shatzmiller, "Women and wage labour in the medieval Islamic West", *Journal of the Economic and Social History of the Orient* 40 (1997), 174–206; Rapoport, *Marriage, Money and Divorce*, 31–38.

had much (if not all) of the Qur'an memorized. One of them was heard reciting six of the lengthiest chapters of the Qur'an in just one cycle of prayer.[84] Ḥafṣa bt. Sīrīn's (d. *ca.* 100/718) father built her and her brothers private prayer spaces out of roofing planks to give them space for reflection in their bustling childhood home.[85]

Mothers

There are few accounts of women with their dependent children. As mentioned above, the literature sometimes places the stress on women's solitary worship, and so downplays the women's identities as mothers or grandmothers and thus erases their social bonds.[86] Historically, however, women raised their children as part of a community of other women in which the shared experience of the cycles of life created strong social bonds. Ḥafṣa bt. Sīrīn's story is unusual in detailing a loving relationship between her and her son, whom she reportedly doted on and who cared for her in her old age. Hudhayl is even said to have stayed up with her during her long nightly prayers, feeding a quick-burning fire to make sure she was warm. His early death affected her deeply.[87] From the few sayings we have, it is easy to imagine that mothers took an active role in guiding their children. Umm Ṭalq warned her son of vanity: "How beautiful is your voice when you recite the Qur'an. I only hope that your voice will not lead to evil consequences for you on the Day of Judgment."[88] The advice reportedly struck him so deeply that he wept until he fainted. An unnamed woman was overheard advising her son, whom she brought to al-Barathī's gatherings, that nothing in this world could compensate for Paradise or be worth the suffering of Hell.[89] Other women worshipped alongside their children, some of whom excelled them in faith and practice.[90]

84 IJ, #605 and #606; also see IJ, #475.

85 Ibn Saʿd, *Ṭabaqāt al-kubrā*, #3065.

86 See A. Papas, "The son of his mother: Qalandarī celibacy and the 'destruction' of family", in Mayeur-Jaoun and Papas (eds), *Family portraits with saints*, 420–444; A. Schimmel, *My Soul is a Woman: The Feminine in Islam* (London: Continuum, 1997), 89–97; and Bashir, *Sufi Bodies*, 152–153.

87 IJ, #585. On attitudes towards children, see A. Giladi, "Herlihy's thesis revisited: Some notes on investment in children in medieval Muslim societies", *Journal of Family History* 36/3 (2011), 235–247.

88 AARS, 294–295; IJ, #597.

89 IJ, #368; see also IJ, #938.

90 IJ, #587.

There are a few examples of women lamenting the birth of a child or mistreating their children in pursuit of their worship. Notably, these stories are not treated negatively in the literature. Not unlike those pious men who rejected their children, the strangeness of a woman's rejection of her own child seems to function as a testament to a life of worship in total commitment to God. In a woman's case it also serves to neuter her, thus transforming her into an exceptional "woman". Nusiyya bt. Salmān (Basra, lived mid-2nd/late-8th century) reportedly said, "O Lord, you do not see me as someone worthy of your worship, otherwise you not have preoccupied me with a child."[91] Other women are distracted by their love of their children or grieve over their children's waywardness.[92] ʿAthāma (Syria, lived early 2nd/8th century) was so distracted by having to remind her son to perform his prayers that she lamented to herself:

> O ʿAthāma, why are you so distracted?
> Your house must have been invaded by a trickster.
> Weep so that you may complete your prayers on time,
> If you were to weep at all today!
> And weep while the *Qur'ān* is being recited.
> For once you, too, used to recite it,
> You used to recite it with reflection,
> While tears streamed down from your eyes.
> But today, you do not recite it
> Without having a reciter with you.
> I shall lament for you with fervent love,
> For as long as I live![93]

Slaves

Enslaved women who were married to other slaves, mothers, unmarried housekeepers, or used for sex by their owners had similar limits placed on their time for worship. But unlike a free woman, an enslaved woman would not gain significant time when her children were grown or hope that her domestic duties would be lightened until her old age. One woman, Hinayda, was married to another slave with whom she had a child. As a domestic or agricultural slave, she would have to fulfil her duties for her owner as well as her own domestic chores. Hinayda found solitude by waking to pray through

[91] AARS, 92–93.
[92] IJ, #937.
[93] AARS, 310–311; IJ, #820.

part of the night. Her husband and child admired her hard work and devotion, gladly accepting her encouragement in their own practice.[94] Enslaved women could fit worship into their full days by fasting, but for some women fasting most likely proved debilitating. Ibrāhīm al-Nukhʿay (Kufa, d. 96/715) expressed concern for one of his slaves who fasted despite the extraordinary heat.[95] Khālid al-Warrāq (Basra, lived *ca.* 275/888) believed his slave was worshipping too much, given her circumstances, and advised her to slow down. She replied that there can be no slowing down in the race to achieve Paradise. Weeping, she said, "Khālid, don't let anyone slow you down, for there is no second place for those who lost the opportunity to serve."[96] Sometimes slaves had the chance to worship when they travelled with their owners on Hajj, or were able to visit the House if they lived in Mecca.[97] When not in service to their owners' needs while on pilgrimage, social barriers would have been broken down, allowing slaves the freedom to worship that they might not have had otherwise.[98]

Slaves are occasionally portrayed in informal teaching roles, such as Khalid al-Warraq's slave (mentioned above). When ʿAwn b. Abū ʿAmāra (Basra, d. 210/825) complained to a slave owned by his family that profits were tightening, she advised him to be content with God alone.[99] The well-known Hadith transmitters Āṭā (d. 114/732) and Mujāhid (d. 104/722) discretely visited a black slave in Mecca whose words would move them to tears.[100] A common narrative trope depicts slaves used for sex teaching their more sophisticated, and sometimes scholarly, owner a truth about God's love through their simple purity of faith. These well-known men are so humbled by the women's understanding that they release them.[101] In this vein, slaves sometimes play a romantic role in the literature because their abject submission to their owners is analogous to abject submission to God. In a case of abject devotion, a young female slave is depicted hanging onto the curtains of the Kaaba, weeping and imploring God until, it is said, she died.[102] The manumitted slave of the caliph

[94] IJ, #935; see also #475.

[95] IJ, #616 (she is called both *mamlūka* and *mawla* [K. Ali has remarked, in some cases, *mawla* denotes a slave not a client]); and IJ, #908.

[96] IJ, #618.

[97] IJ, #785.

[98] A. Geissinger, "Portrayal of the Ḥajj as a context for women's exegesis: Textual evidence in al-Bukhārī's (d. 870) 'al-Saḥīḥ'", in S. Günther (ed.), *Insights into Classical Arabic Literature and Islam* (Leiden: Brill, 2005), 267.

[99] IJ, #621.

[100] IJ, #233.

[101] Silvers, "God loves me", 53–58.

[102] IJ, #620; also see #785.

Muʿawiyya, Zajlah al-ʿĀbida (lived *ca.* late 1st/7th century) instructs that the free should obey God just as completely as they expect their slaves to obey them.[103] In some of these stories, black skin seems to articulate the ideal of spiritual poverty by connecting the lowest social status, an enslaved black woman, with the highest spiritual status. For instance, Shaʿwāna's spiritual stature is affirmed by her protest, "[I am] nothing but a sinful black slave!"[104]

Although domestic slaves might be treated as trusted members of the family, and were protected as such if released, they were still slaves and so were subject to their owners' decency or lack thereof. The average slave-owner must not have been particularly decent to their property, since the good treatment of slaves is so worthy of remark in the literature. The entirety of an entry describing the piety of one Kufan woman depicts how she restrained herself out of fear of God from whipping her slave.[105] Narratives about men releasing their slaves used for sex who teach them about divine love serve to illustrate the scholars' great humility, but also suggest that sex-slavery is not for "exceptional" women.[106] In a similar vein, the story of a slave who had gone mad from her total submission to God romanticizes slavery as abject submission, but also seems to acknowledge some discomfort with the practice. It is said that she wore a wool shirt with the words "Not for Buying or Selling" embroidered on it, suggesting that someone who literally has been bought and sold transcends her body while in the presence of God and, as she is said to have put it, is satisfied with her state.[107] The transmitters' assurance that she has transcended her body seems to try to compensate for the implications of the trade in human bodies. It suggests that for some transmitters, at least, transcending the body through suffering does not erase the injustice that may have caused the suffering in the first place.

Marginal Women

A number of women lived on the margins of society. They were impoverished, homeless, wanderers, or considered mad. Women on the margins faced

103 IJ, #604; also see #597.

104 IJ, #630. Likewise, skin blackened by fasting is a mark of exceptional piety (IJ, #478, #604). al-Sīrjānī transmits a story in which a black man transcends the lowness of his skin color. As he draws near to God, his skin turns white. For that story and others marking the color black as low and even sinful, see B. Orfali and N. Saab, *Sufism, Black and White*, 12–16.

105 IJ, #477.

106 On male piety, virility, treatment of slaves used for sex, and related issues, see A. Geissinger, " 'Are men the majority in paradise, or women?' Constructing gender and communal boundaries in Muslim's (d. 261 A.H./875 CE) *Kitāb al-Janna*", in S. Günther and T. Lawson (eds), *Roads to Paradise: Eschatology and Concepts of the Hereafter in Islam* (Leiden: Brill, 2015). K. Ali, *Marriage and Slavery in Early Islam.*

107 IJ, #628; see also IJ, #479.

serious hardships, but these reportedly did not diminish their commitment to a renunciant life. As a result of her scrupulous behaviour, the daughter of Abū al-Ḥasan al-Makkī (d. 224/838) gave up her allowance from her father for one year and was forced to pick through the garbage heaps for her food.[108] While the poor received some charity in food from the government and individuals, the report demonstrates that it was not unheard of for the impoverished to resort to scavenging.[109] One report may be either an attack on the Quraysh for not caring for their own or praise for Qurayshi piety; whichever the case, it makes the point that some women must have been homeless. ʿAbd al-Raḥmān b. al-Ḥakam said, "There was an old woman of the Quraysh in Mecca who had sought refuge in a burrow since she did not have any other home. Someone asked her if she was satisfied with her situation. She replied, 'Isn't this plenty for someone who is dying [to this world]?'"[110] Whether by choice or in a state of homelessness, Muṭayyaʿa al-ʿĀbida (Basra, possibly lived late 2nd/8th century) lived in a graveyard without any family for fifty-four years.[111]

Madness (*jadhba* or *junūn*) is regarded positively in Sufi literature; so much so, it becomes a well-worn romantic trope. Some Sufis are even said to have toured mental hospitals or private homes to catch some insight in the unreserved speech of "the mad".[112] Their imagined or real social isolation and suffering may have been understood in terms of the emotional and physical suffering displayed by renunciants demonstrating their intimacy with God and perceived as redemptive. To her brother's distress, Bukhkha (Kufa, lived *ca.* late second century) had lost her mind and had to be kept confined in a room on the roof of his house for some ten years. He brought doctors in to care for her, but she rejected them in favour of seclusion with the divine physician. Despite her torment, he reports she was able to keep herself ritually clean and perform her daily prayers. She was miraculously cured when she was offered a choice in a dream between being cured now or being patient with her condition and so gain Paradise in the next. She chose patience, but

[108] IJ, #232.

[109] See M. Bonner, "Poverty and charity in the rise of Islam" and I. Mattson, "Status-based definitions of need in early Islam and maintenance laws", in M. Bonner, M. Ener, and A. Singer (eds), *Poverty and Charity in Middle Eastern Contexts* (Albany: SUNY Press, 2003).

[110] IJ, #240.

[111] IJ, #607.

[112] M. W. Dols, *Majnūn: The Madman in Medieval Islamic Society* (Oxford: Clarendon Press, 1992), 391–392, 388–422. On the difficulty of translating these terms, Dols' sometimes romantic treatment of the subject, the ill-treatment of those considered mad, and the role of state and religious power in determining madness, see B. Shoshan, "The state and madness in medieval Islam", *International Journal of Middle East Studies* 35/2 (2003), 329–340.

politely bargained, "...but God is unstinting to His creation. Nothing is beyond Him. If He willed it, He could unite the two for me." And so she was granted both a cure and salvation.[113]

Mad or sane women who travelled or wandered on their own were open to harassment, such as children throwing rocks at them in the street, but also robbery and sexual assault.[114] Dhū al-Nūn reportedly encountered a number of these women, one of whom was dressed as a man, suggesting the dangers of being a woman alone on the road.[115] Transmitters seem to have protected the women whose stories they relayed from accusations of illicit sex, even if she were a victim of sexual assault. One report seems to be assuring us that Maymūna al-Sawdā' of Kufa, a black shepherd lost in ecstasy, was protected by God from such assaults. She is depicted carrying a cane and a wool cloak embroidered with the words, "Not for sale. If the sheep are with wolves, the wolves don't eat the sheep and the sheep don't fear the wolves." ʿAbd al-Wāḥid b. Zayd (Basra, d. 176/793) remarks to her, "I see the wolves are with the sheep! The sheep do not fear the wolves nor do the wolves eat the sheep. How could that be?" She replied, "Leave me alone! I fixed what is between me and my Master, and so He has taken care of the wolves and the sheep."[116]

GATHERINGS OF LIKE-MINDED WOMEN AND MEN

News of pious folk, mystics, and Sufis travelled far and wide. Stories about them were sought out; people would visit them for inspiration, to collect their insights, or simply to criticize or marvel at them. Reports indicate that when the pious or Sufis gathered, they might ask about and share stories of the remarkable people they met, including women. Sufyān al-Thawrī (Basra, d. 161/777) was at a gathering when he mentioned a woman from Kufa, and his friends inquired if he memorized any of her sayings.[117] The reports attest that women welcomed women and men in their homes and visited others.

[113] IJ, #480; Ibn Ḥabīb al-Naysabūrī, *ʿUqala al-majānīn*, ed. ʿUmar al-Asʿad (Beirut Dar al-Nafā'is, 1987), 294–295.

[114] Dols, *Majnūn*, 396; see M. Tolmacheva, "Female piety and patronage in the medieval Hajj", in G. R. G. Hambly (ed.), *Women in the Medieval Islamic World* (New York: St. Martin's Press, 1999), 167; and H. Azam, *Sexual Violence in Maliki Ideology: From Discursive Foundations to Classical Articulation* (PhD diss., Duke University, 2007).

[115] IJ, #974.

[116] IJ, #479. ʿAbd al-Wāḥid b. Zayd reportedly visited an institution to hear the insights of the mad where he heard a patient claim that Maymūna would be his wife in Paradise, after which ʿAbd al-Wāḥid sought her out (Dols, *Majnūn*, 391); also see IJ, #472.

[117] IJ, #476, #630.

For instance, it is reported that ʿAthāma travelled a great deal in search of knowledge.[118] They taught women and men and learned from them. They chatted with women and men in public, and met at private and public gatherings. They travelled for Hajj, where mixed-gender encounters were common on the road and during the pilgrimage.[119]

Mixed-gender gatherings may have been comfortable for many of those involved, but stories indicate that there were concerns about the propriety of these meetings, in particular the character of the women. Complaints are not uncommon in the literature, and there was even an accusation of sexual assault involving men from Junayd's circle.[120] Some narratives seem to address these concerns by vouching for the character of the women and men alike. In these narratives, a well-known man encounters a woman in her home or in public. The man says something the woman disapproves of, she upbraids him, and he is humbled. In the most familiar set pieces, a man makes an unwelcome comment about the physical beauty of the woman he is visiting. The most well-known story may be that of Abū Yazīd al-Bisṭāmī's visit with Umm ʿAlī (Balkh, d. 240/854), the wife of Abū Ḥamid Aḥmad b. Khiḍrawayh, during which he notices henna on her hands. Umm ʿAlī dismissively insults him, marking her as an exceptional woman and beyond moral reproach.[121] Typically, the man is not shamed by telling the story; on the contrary, it demonstrates his humility, itself a cornerstone of religious authority. In some cases, the man desires to marry the woman because of her commitment to worship or out of a sense of guardianship. Malīka bt. Muḥammad al-Munkadar of Medina dismisses two men from Basra, one of whom offered to marry her, by saying she would only consider marrying the famed Mālik b. Dīnār (d. 130/748) or Ayyūb al-Sakhtiyānī (d. 131/748). After the two men reveal themselves to be Mālik and Ayyūb, she responds, "Uff! I would have thought remembering God would have kept you too preoccupied to speak to women!"[122]

Other accounts, for instance some of those depicting women as having bodies ruined from fasting or weeping, as being childless or distracted by children, or as being called "men" on the path, seem to vouch for the

118 IJ, #820.

119 Cornell, *Early Sufi Women*, 60–70.

120 Karamustafa, *Sufism*, 23; Outside this period, see A. Dahlén, "Female Sufi saints and disciples: Women in the life of Jalal al-din Rumi", *Orientalia Suecana* 57 (2008); and K. Pemberton, "Women *pirs*, saintly succession, and spiritual guidance in South Asian Sufism", *The Muslim World* 96/1 (2006), 61–87.

121 A. Azad, "Female mystics in Islam: A quiet legacy", *Journal of the Economic and Social History of the Orient* 56 (2013), 76.

122 IJ, #200; see also #615.

propriety of women visited by men by denying their sexual availability, rendering them, in effect, sexually neuter.[123] Other stories even suggest that the onus was on men to control themselves in women's presence.[124] Although these stories demonstrate the respect these men had for the women, they do not challenge gender norms by recognizing the women's exceptional status; rather, they serve to reinforce the social status quo. When men vouch for women's exceptional status by rendering them sexually neuter, depicting them as having transcended their bodies, or by calling them "men", their praise only confirms that men hold the power to authorize women's value and women were typically perceived as spiritually and morally weak.[125] Analogously, given the slave narratives discussed above, extraordinary slaves used for sex must be "free", just as extraordinary women must be sexless or "men". As Carolyn Heilbrun remarks, "exceptional women are the chief imprisoners of nonexceptional women, simultaneously proving any woman could do it and assuring, in their uniqueness among men, that no other woman will".[126]

Informal Gatherings

Women and men regularly gathered on an informal basis.[127] It seems that ʿAmada al-ʿUfiyya of Syria had a great love of books and had gatherings in which to discuss them.[128] Aḥmad al-Ḥawārī passed along reports heard at social gatherings attended by Rābiʿa bt. Ismāʿīl, such as Ḥukayma's gloss on the verse of the Qur'an, "Except for who comes to God with a peaceful heart" (Q. 26:89). She said, "The 'peaceful heart' is the one that meets God without anything other than God in it."[129] One man's father sent him to sit and learn from Ṭalḥa al-ʿAdawiyya, who would sit with baskets of raisins, buckthorn, and fresh beans before her, counting praises to God with them and snacking on them in turn.[130] Ghufayra (Basra, d. *ca.* 100/718), Jawhara (Baghdad, lived early 3rd/9th century), and Ubayda bt. Abū Kilāb (Basra, lived 2nd/8th

[123] For instance, IJ, #251, #259, #470, #478, #589, #604, #616; Cornell, *Early Sufi women*, 59–60; Schimmel, *My Soul is a Woman*, 69–88.
[124] IJ, #253, #944, and #945; A. Knysh, trans., *al-Qushayri's Epistle on Sufism* (Berkshire: Garnet Publishing, 2007), 97.
[125] For example, see IJ, #946; see also Cornell, *Early Sufi Women*, 18; and Spellberg, *Politics, Gender, and the Islamic Past*, 58–60.
[126] C. Heilbrun, *Writing a Woman's Life* (New York: W. W. Norton 1988), 81.
[127] IJ, #238.
[128] IJ, #826.
[129] AARS, 126–27; see also IJ, #731.
[130] IJ, #930.

century) received groups of regular visitors in their homes or other sites, such as a graveyard, for discussion.[131] And, of course, Rābiʿa al-ʿAdawiyya welcomed well-known scholars and renunciants to her home for discussion and guidance.[132] In some cases, there are reports of women with great spiritual mastery, such as Fāṭima, the wife of Abū ʿAlī al-Rūdhbārī (Cairo, d. 322/934), whom we might expect to have held gatherings, but there seem to be no reports of it.[133] Some women, though, did not welcome being visited at home by men. Several women prayed at length while uninvited men waited, thus shaming them into leaving.[134] Lubaba seems to have been sought out to answer questions about ritual law, but tired easily of human interaction and at those times would retreat into seclusion for her devotions.[135] According to reports, men and women also met in public and stopped to chat, whether this be in their hometown, travelling, or on Hajj.[136]

Other reports allude to informal networks in which women supported each other in their practices. Such women might be depicted in the literature as solitary worshippers, but these accounts suggest that women's devotions were taken up through networks of shared experience. A number of women found in Basra, Baghdad, and Mecca are reported to have used a variation of an old and well-known supplication: "The stars have sunk, the eyes are asleep, the kingdom has shut its gates, and your door is open. Every lover is alone with his lover, and so I stand before you."[137] If not a transmitter's interpolation, the supplication may have been shared by some women. In any case, pious, mystic, and Sufi women were engaged socially with one another. They visited each other at home, met at gatherings, travelled to spend time with each other, passed along accounts of each other's knowledge or practices, worshipped with one another, and caught up with each other's news.[138] The narrative frames of some transmissions show that they shared their knowledge in casual social interactions as one might expect. Ḥukayma's gloss on the Qurʾan may have a formal feel to it, but it arose during a chat with Rābiʿa bt. Ismāʿil in

[131] IJ, #368, #593, #594, #598, #601, #604, #607, #609, and #632.

[132] On depictions of Rābiʿa al-ʿAdawiyya as a guide in some Sufi sources, see Cornell, *Early Sufi Women*, 59–63; and H. A. Ford, *Constructing Sanctity: Miracles, Saints, and Gender in Yūsuf ibn Ismāʿīl al-Nabhānī's* Jāmiʿ karāmāt al-awliyāʾ (Dissertation for the Department of Near Eastern and Languages and Cultures, Indiana University, 2000), 221–224.

[133] IJ, #851; AARS, 186–187.

[134] IJ, #623, #853, #931, and #934.

[135] AARS, 82; IJ, #783.

[136] See IJ, #787, #830, #880, #933, and #939; sections on women met at the Kaaba, IJ, #968–978; sections on women met on the road, IJ, #991–995.

[137] IJ, #201, #590, #596, and #615; and see Dakake, "Guest of the inmost heart", 85; noted in Malik, *Muwatta*, Kitab al-salat/al-ʿamal fi duaʿ, #505 (pointed out to me by A. Geissinger).

[138] IJ, #589, #590, #591, #592, #608, #654, #824, and #827.

response to her news that Aḥmad had taken another wife. It was Ḥukayma's way of saying that she was not impressed with his lack of judgment.[139]

Some women also belonged to a female counterpart to *futuwwa* (male chivalry) called *niswān*, dating back at least to the early 3rd/9th century in Khurasan.[140] Sufi treatises present *futuwwa* "as a collection of virtues necessary for a pious believer, such as generosity, munificence, modesty, chastity, trustworthiness, loyalty, mercifulness, knowledge, humility and piety, and it was considered one of the stations that a 'traveller' passes on his way to God".[141] For women in the early period, such as Umm ʿAlī, the wife of Aḥmad b. Khaḍrawayh (Balkh, d. 240/854), *niswān* most likely referred to an informal association of women who undertook a commitment to developing and upholding shared character traits.[142] Other women, such as Fāṭima al-Khānaqahiyya, made formal vows of service to *futuwwa* organizations themselves.[143]

Women also entered into female-only groups in the performance of Hajj.[144] But some women stayed there for years, a few seemingly attaching themselves to the walls of the Great Mosque. A number of women wearing shifts made of wool and donkey hair were observed secluding themselves in the mosque area and refusing to speak during the day.[145] One woman, who had devoted herself to the Kaaba since childhood, reportedly wore an iron ring around her wrist to which she would chain herself (presumably) to a mosque wall.[146] It is not clear if chaining herself demonstrated her attachment, kept her from giving up her commitment, or kept others from removing her. Although contested then and now, the ritually liminal space of Kaaba seemed to allow for a degree of social and ritual egalitarianism.[147]

Formal Gatherings

Other reports indicate more formal teaching environments in which people visited women and men as subordinates.[148] Shaʿwāna and Baḥriyya held

139 AARS, 126–127.
140 Cornell, *Early Sufi Women*, 67.
141 K. Gevorgyan, "*Futuwwa* varieties and the *futuwwat-nāma* literature: An attempt to classify *futuwwa* and Persian *futuwwat-nāmas*", *British Journal of Middle Eastern Studies* 40/1 (2013), 4.
142 L. Ridgeon, *Morals and Mysticism in Persian Sufism: A History of sufi-futuwwat in Iran* (New York: Routledge, 2010), 10, 35; Cornell, *Early Sufi Women*, 65–69.
143 Cornell, *Early Sufi Women*, 68.
144 Geissinger, "Portrayal of the Ḥajj", 170.
145 IJ, #784.
146 IJ, #786; also see IJ, #784.
147 Geissinger, "Portrayal of the Hajj", 165.
148 On Sulamī's use of scholarly titles and Cornell's account of women's institutions in Sufism, see Cornell, *Early Sufi Women*, 58–73.

formal mixed-gender gatherings at which they led regular visitors and followers in *samāʿ* (ecstatic concert).[149] Shaʿwāna's followers included Kurdiyya bt. ʿAmr and visitors such as Fuḍayl b. ʿIyāḍ (d. 187/803).[150] Fāṭima bt. ʿImrān of Damaghān is said to have taught the *fuqarāʾ*, "the poor ones" who had devoted their lives to God.[151] Scholarly pious women, such as Ḥafṣa bt. Sīrīn, also held teaching circles.[152] Women who preached in the streets or in graveyards seem to have had regular gatherings and followers.[153] In a report that reads as an upbraiding tale vouching for her authority to act in the capacity of preacher, a man saw a black woman preaching in the street to a crowd that then followed her into a nearby house and sat around her in a circle. He was outraged by her behaviour and approached her disrespectfully, demanding she account for herself. Standing over her while she was seated with her followers, he asked in an incredulous tone, "Have you no fear of pride?" She raised her head to look at him and said, "How could one who has not been informed about his return to God be proud of his works?"[154]

Women were also regulars at gatherings of pious and Sufi leaders such as Sarī al-Saqatī, Ibrāhīm Khawwās, and al-Junayd of Baghdad; Abū ʿUthmān al-Hīrī of Nishapur; and Aḥmad ibn Abū al-Ḥawārī and Sulaymān al-Dārānī of Syria.[155] Miskīna al-Ṭafāwayya and Shaʿwāna both visited the gatherings of ʿĪsā b. Zādān in Ubulla, near Basra. The renowned Umm al-Ḥusayn al-Qurayshiyya of Nasa visited the circles of Abū al-Ḥusayn al-Khiḍrī in Baghdad and Abū al-Qāsim al-Naṣrābādhī in Naysabur.[156] She reportedly berated al-Naṣrābādhī with criticism until he snapped at her to be quiet, to which she replied, "I will be quiet when you are quiet!"[157] In some cases, the teacher–student relationship was grounded in a household bond. Abū Sulaymān al-Dārānī's sisters, ʿAbda and Āmina, were his students. Ibrāhīm al-Khawwās (d. 291/904) taught his sister Maymūna.[158] Abū ʿUthmān al-Hīrī

[149] IJ, #601 and #630.

[150] IJ, #608; AARS, 116–117.

[151] IJ, #678.

[152] IJ, #585; and, for instance, IJ #366, #367, #783, #819, #821, #829; Cornell, *Early Sufi Women*, 63–64; also see A. Geissinger, *Gender and the Construction of Exegetical Authority*; and Sayeed, *Women and the Transmission of Religious Knowledge in Islam.*

[153] IJ, #607 and #932.

[154] IJ, #625; also see IJ, #239.

[155] IJ, #369, #370, #371, and #689, Cornell, *Early Sufi Women*, 32 nt. 52, 154, 172.

[156] AARS, 250–251.

[157] AARS, 224–225.

[158] IJ, #822.

taught his daughter, ʿĀʾisha.[159] And Zaytūna was a servant and student of three Baghdadī Sufis, Nūrī, Junayd, and Abū Hamza.[160]

A number of women seem to have had only female students. It is not clear if they led small circles of committed students or if, like other pious and Sufi teachers, there was a lay following as well. Muʿādha al-ʿAdawiyya (d. *ca.* 1st/7th century) taught women such as Ghufayra who, in turn, taught others in Basra renunciant practices including prayer, fasting, and night vigils.[161] Rābiʿa bt. Ismāʿīl studied under Ḥukayma.[162] Umm al-Bunayn bt. ʿAbd al-ʿAzīz b. Marwān, the sister of ʿUmar, is reported to have had female students to whom she transmitted Hadith and instructed in pious worship and gaining intimacy with God.[163] Shabaka of Basra seems to have had a circle of very serious female students who undertook rigorous spiritual seclusion in underground cells dug into the floor of her home, where they likely fasted, prayed, and recited litanies.[164] An unnamed Syrian woman is reported to have taught other women at the mosque in Hims. The report suggests that women were not only welcome to pray in this mosque, but that women were permitted to teach and study there at that time. It is said that she instructed them in Qurʾan, Hadith, and the religious obligations, as well as offering them inward guidance.[165]

Conclusion

That women were widely integrated into these circles or paths as leaders and followers should not be taken as proof that the pious and mystical paths were free of patriarchal assumptions or restrictions such as sexual availability in marriage and social hierarchies such as slavery, nor should they support an essentialized notion of "women's spirituality". On the contrary, I have argued that such women lived in complex social networks and that their experience and articulation of their relationship with God, and their transmitters' reworking of it, was profoundly shaped by their socio-historical circumstances. Women's lives were impacted by egalitarian impulses, but those impulses were formed within a patriarchal system of values, gender norms,

[159] IJ, #689.
[160] AARS, 158–161.
[161] Cornell, *Early Sufi Women*, 61; AARS, 88–89; IJ, #593.
[162] AARS, 126–127.
[163] IJ, #821.
[164] AARS, 90–91.
[165] IJ, #829.

social hierarchies, and structures of authority. That said, so much more textual and historical analysis is still needed to clarify, correct, and add to our understanding of the historical situation of early women as well as the diverse agendas at work in the narrative constructions about women's lives.

FURTHER READING

Abū ʿAbd ar-Raḥmān ās-Sulamī, Early Sufi Women: Dhikr an-niswa al-mutaʿ abbidā t aṣ ṣū fiyyā t by Abū ʿAbd ar-Raḥmān ās-Sulamī, trans. and ed. Rkia Cornell (Louisville, KY: Fons Vitae, 1999).

ʿĀʾishah al-Bāʿūniyyah, *The Principles of Sufism*, trans. and ed. Emil Homerin (New York: New York University Press, 2014).

Afshan Bokhari, "Between patron and piety: Jahān Ārā Begam's Sufi affiliations and articulations in seventeenth century Mughal India" in *Sufism and Society: Arrangements of the Mystical in the Muslim World, 1200–1800*, eds John J. Curry and Erik S. Ohlander (London, UK: Routledge, 2012), 120–142.

Beverly Mack, *One Woman's Jihad: Nana Asma'u, Scholar and Scribe* (Bloomington, IN: Indiana University Press, 2000), 198.

Razia Sultanova, *From Shamanism to Sufism: Women, Islam, and Culture in Central Asia* (London, UK: IB Tauris, 2011).

Kelly Pemberton, *Women Mystics and Sufi Shrines in India* (Columbia, SC: University of South Carolina Press, 2010).

Cemalnur Sargut, *Beauty of Light: Sufi Teachings of a Living Female Saint*, eds Tehseen Thaver and Omid Safi (Louisville, KY: Fonsvitae, 2015).

3

Early Sufi Rituals, Beliefs, and Hermeneutics

Erik S. Ohlander

Historically speaking, Sufism has comprehended an astounding diversity of conceptual, practical and institutional forms. These forms, perhaps most usefully classed under the taxon of "mystico-ascetic religiosity",[1] have served an equally astounding variety of interests and needs, both individual and communal, in different times and in different places.[2] As such, it is difficult to speak of things truly "essential" in relation to Sufi ritual, belief, and

[1] The individual terms of the compound, "asceticism" and "mysticism", both of which depend upon modern significations often foreign to their assumed pre-modern nominal signifiers, are understood here simply in relation to the weaving together of a religious theory and praxis which hopes for the attainment of a state of righteousness (asceticism), and a religious theory and praxis which hopes for the attainment of a state of experiential communion with the divine (mysticism). In their respective Islamic contexts, asceticism (*zuhd*) looks to achieve its goal through the free and deliberate renunciation of the things of the world, typically through embracing various austerities or mortifications, although it is the renunciatory aspect which is most prominent. While often embracing an ethos of renunciation and the practice of certain austerities or mortifications, mysticism (for which there was no meaningful word in the pre-modern Islamic tradition) typically looks to achieve its goal thorough a form of mild asceticism coupled with the deliberate practice of various contemplative or meditative disciplines. Both are present, and often interwoven, within the pre-modern mystico-ascetic tradition referred to as *taṣawwuf* ("Sufism").

[2] An informative example of the wide ranging concerns of contemporary scholarship on diverse areas and aspects of Sufism within and across multiple geo-historical contexts may be found in Dina Le Gall, "Recent Thinking on Sufis and Saints in the Lives of Muslim Societies, Past and Present", *International Journal of Middle East Studies*, 42, no. 4 (2010), 673–687, to which the individual contributions in a number of recent collective volumes treating the subject clearly speak, viz. John J. Curry and Erik S. Ohlander, eds., *Sufism and Society: Arrangements of the Mystical in the Muslim World, 1200–1800* (Abingdon, Oxon and New York: Routledge, 2012); Rachida Chih, Catherine Mayeur-Jaouen, et al., eds., *Le soufisme à l'époque ottoman, XVIe–XVIIIe siècle* (Cairo: Institut français d'archéologie orientale, 2010); and Ron Geaves, Markus Dressler, and Gritt Klinkhammer, eds., *Sufis in Western Society: Global Networking and Locality* (Abingdon, Oxon and New York: Routledge, 2009).

hermeneutics in the sense of a body of discretely definable elements which might be understood to stand for all Sufis or all of Sufism at all times and at all places.[3] Much the same, of course, can be said about many of the other Islamic religious sciences, amongst which Sufism (*taṣawwuf*) was, it should be noted, an admitted latecomer.[4]

Securing its place, though never squarely, within the Islamic tradition in the period following that which witnessed the crystallization of legal, institutional, exegetical, theological and other basic structuring elements of Muslim religious life, Sufism nevertheless came, by the seventh/thirteenth century certainly, to assert a particularly visible presence within and across Muslim societies.[5] This is a position which, the profoundly sweeping transformations which the early modern and modern periods wrought across Muslim societies aside, it still maintains to the present day. Partially as a result of the successful efforts of a series of prolific and influential Sufi scholar-apologists of the fifth/eleventh century and partially as a result of shifting social and political realities rooted in the breakdown of centralized authority and the migrations of Inner Asian pastoralists into the citied world of the eastern and central Islamic lands between that time and the mid-seventh/thirteenth century, over the course of the middle and later periods of Islamic history Sufism asserted a

[3] Which is not to say that such has not been attempted, especially in the guise of scholarship informed by the modern religio-philosophical movement known as Perennialism and the associated movement of Traditionalism (on which, in relation to Islamic studies generally, see Carl Ernst, "Traditionalism, the Perennial Philosophy and Islamic Studies", *MESA Bulletin*, 28, no. 2 [1994], 176–180; and, more broadly, Mark Sedgwick, *Against the Modern World: Traditionalism and the Secret Intellectual History of the Twentieth Century* [Oxford and New York: Oxford University Press, 2004]). In relation to this, it is important to note that several different, often mutually exclusive, conceptual and interpretive schema have been applied to the subject generally within modern and contemporary academic literature, on which see Nile Green, *Sufism: A Global History* (Malden, Mass.: Wiley-Blackwell, 2012), 1–5; Erik S. Ohlander, "Sufism in Medieval Muslim Societies", *History Compass*, 8, no. 6 (2010), 518; Alexander Knysh, "Historiography of Sufi Studies in the West", in *A Companion to the History of the Middle East*, ed. Youssef M. Choueiri (Malden, Mass.: Blackwell Publishing, 2005), 106–131; Carl Ernst, *The Shambhala Guide to Sufism* (Boston: Shambhala Publications, 1997), 1–18; and R. Caspar, "Muslim Mysticism: Tendencies in Modern Research", in *Studies in Islam*, ed. and trans. M. Swartz (New York: Oxford University Press, 1988), 164–184.

[4] Short approachable synthetic overviews of the historical development of Sufism and its periodization may be found in Alexander Knysh, "Sufism", in *The New Cambridge History of Islam*, vol. 4, ed. Robert Irwin (Cambridge: Cambridge University Press, 2010), 60–104; Ohlander, "Sufism in Medieval Muslim Societies", 518–523; and Fritz Meier, "The Mystic Path", in *Islam and the Arab World: Faith, People, Culture*, ed. Bernard Lewis (London: Thames and Hudson Ltd., 1976), 117–128.

[5] A sketch of the main outlines of which may be found in Ohlander, "Sufism in Medieval Muslim Societies", 521–523.

marked and extraordinarily vibrant presence within the social, cultural, and religious life of Muslim societies.[6]

Over the course of this period, Sufi communities flourished as far afield as the Atlantic shores of North Africa in the west to the reaches of Chinese Turkestan in the east, and from central Anatolia in the north to the Malay Archipelago in the south.[7] Wherever Islam went, so too did Sufis, taking with them certain elements associated, to one degree or another, with ideas, traditions, and ways of viewing Islam, the world, the self, and others which were self-referentially conceptualized and referred to as having to do with *taṣawwuf*.[8] Of course, as with other forms of Muslim religious expression, the nature, role, and general tenor of the expression of Sufi religiosity varied dramatically across the wide geographical landscapes embraced by the Abode of Islam over the broad temporal and geographical sweep of its pre-modern history. At the same time, however, just as with jurisprudence, mosque architecture, religio-scholarly pedagogy, or the performance of basic ritual duties such as the five-times-a-day canonical prayer or daytime fasting during the month of Ramadan, there were elements similar enough within and across Sufi communities which made them recognizable *qua* Sufi communities to, say, a transregional traveller such as the famed Ibn Baṭṭūṭa (d. ca. 770/1368–1369).[9] It is these elements to which this exposition

[6] On this latter point see Jonathan P. Berkey, *The Formation of Islam: Religion and Society in the Near East, 600–1800* (Cambridge: University Press, 2003), 231–247; Ira M. Lapidus, *A History of Islamic Societies*, 2nd edn. (Cambridge: University Press, 2002), 137–141, 158–166, 172–182; and, the inspiration for the foregoing, Marshall G.S. Hodgson, *The Venture of Islam: Conscience and History in a World Civilization; vol. 2: The Expansion of Islam in the Middle Periods* (Chicago and London: The University of Chicago Press, 1974), 201–254, and index (s.v. Ṣûfism, Ṣûfis).

[7] Informative sketches covering major areas of the pre- and early modern Muslim world may be found in Green, *Sufism: Global History*, 125–176, and Knysh, "Sufism", 90–104, with detailed representative overviews divided by geographical region being found in Alexandre Popovic and Gilles Veinstein, eds., *Les Voies d'Allah: Les Orders Mystiques dans le Monde Musulman des Origines à Aujourd'hui* (Paris: Fayard, 1996), 261–447, to which the brief survey in Julian Baldick, *Mystical Islam: An Introduction to Sufism* (New York and London: New York University Press, 1989), 86–131, is usefully added.

[8] It should be noted that the idea, still widely cited, that Sufis self-consciously served as missionaries for Islam, and were singularly responsible in numerous instances for the conversion of peoples living in peripheral regions of the Muslim heartlands has proven to be largely false. On this, see Ernst, *The Shambhala Guide to Sufism*, 138–141; and, for the related issue of the "vernacularization" of Sufism in the medieval period, Green, *Sufism: A Global History*, 103–112.

[9] On whom see Marina A. Tolmacheva, "Ibn Baṭṭūṭah", in *Essays in Arabic Literary Biography*, ed. Joseph E. Lowry and Devin J. Stewart (Wiesbaden: Harrassowitz Verlag, 2009), 126–137; and for his encounters with Sufi communities in different parts of the late medieval Muslim world, *Travels of Ibn Battuta A.D. 1325–1354*, 5 vols., trans. H.A.R. Gibb (vol. 4 with C.F.

attends, particularly in relation to key ideas and forms of expression necessary to a general understanding of matters which were of significance within and across the inextricably intertwined conceptual and ritual landscapes of pre-modern Sufi communities.

THE CONCEPTUAL LANDSCAPE

An important and relatively early theme in Sufi literature is that of impatience, the insatiable and all-consuming desire to know or to experience God in the here and now rather than in the hereafter.[10] As it has often been understood in the tradition, the impetus of such impatience does not, however, lie in a wholly conscious or freely willed aspiration, but rather in a deeply set existential yearning rooted in the inborn longing of the human spirit (*rūḥ*) to return to its source. This source, of course, is God, the divine reality from which all things originate and to which all things ultimately return. From a fairly early period onward this notion has often been evoked in Sufi literature in relation to a short Qur'ānic vignette (Q. 7:172) recounting the events of what later interpreters would come to call the "Day of the Primordial Covenant" (*yawm al-mīthāq*) or the "Day of 'Am I Not [Your Lord]'" (*yawm alastu [bi-rabbikum]*), in which God addresses the pre-created souls of the progeny of Adam with a critical question, to which they respond in the affirmative:

Beckingham; vol. 5 compiled by A.D.H. Bivar) (Cambridge: Hakluyt Society, 1958–2000), vol. 5, index.

10 An impulse which reflects a shift from the concerns of asceticism to mysticism, on which see Green, *Sufism: A Global History*, 16–29; Éric Geoffroy, *Introduction to Sufism: The Inner Path of Islam*, trans. Roger Gaetani (Bloomington, Ind.: World Wisdom Inc., 2010), 65–67, 68–69; Knysh, "Sufism", 61–68; Ahmet T. Karamustafa, *Sufism: The Formative Period* (Berkeley and Los Angeles: University of California Press, 2007), 1–7; Christopher Melchert, "Asceticism", in *The Encyclopaedia of Islam Three* (Leiden: Brill, 2007; hereafter *EI3*), fasc. 2007-1, 163–169; idem, "Baṣran Origins of Classical Sufism", *Der Islam*, 82, no. 2 (2005), 221–240 (which revises his "The Transition from Asceticism to Mysticism in the Middle of the Ninth Century C.E.", *Studia Islamica* 83, no. 1 [1996], 51–70; to which may be added the vigorous critique and presentation of other data by Bernd Radtke in his "Von den hinderlichen Wirkungen der Extase und dem Wesen der Ignoranz", in Bernd Radtke, *Neue kritische Gänge: Zu Stand und Aufgaben der Sufikforschung / New Critical Essays: On the Present State and Future Tasks of the Study of Sufism* [Utrecht: M.Th. Houtsma Stichting], 251–291); Alexander Knysh, *Islamic Mysticism: A Short History* (Leiden: Brill, 2000), 5–42; Christopher Melchert, "The Ḥanābila and the Early Sufis", *Arabica*, 48, no. 3 (2001), 352–367; G.-C. Anawati and Louis Gardet, *Mystique Musulmane: Aspects et Tendences, Expériences et Techniques*, 4th rev. edn. (Paris: J. Vrin, 1986), 23–31; and Annemarie Schimmel, *Mystical Dimensions of Islam* (Chapel Hill, NC: The University of North Carolina Press, 1975), 23–47.

And when thy Lord took from the Children of Adam,
from their loins, their seed, and made them testify
touching themselves, "Am I not your Lord?"
They said, "Yes, we testify" . . .[11]

It is in realizing, recapturing, or otherwise actualizing, in the here and now, the existential implications of this Qur'ānic *in illo tempore*[12] to which the aspiring Sufi ultimately endeavours, a striving which, in its impatience, projects a wider, yet ultimately intimately individualized, mythic drama firmly unto the plane of lived human experience. It is within the profound and momentous structuring frames of such all-encompassing mythic narratives that Sufi thinkers, practitioners, affiliates, and others understood and positioned themselves, their doctrines, their ritual praxes. This ever in relation to the broader personal and communal drama of working out the entailments, in time and in space, of membership in a historically constituted elective monotheistic community which envisioned itself as the product of the final and summative divine dispensation prior to the inevitable resolution of the cosmic process so vividly detailed in Qur'ānic eschatological narratives.[13]

Evinced in literature belonging to a fairly early period in the history of Sufism, the overarching metaphysical orientation of this mythopoesis was one which differentiated between two complementary layers of phenomenal existence, namely that which is apparent, plain, outer, and exoteric (*ẓāhir*) and that which is hidden, obscure, inner, and esoteric (*bāṭin*).[14] It is this basic metaphysical binary which has served, more so than any other, as a master structuring or framing device within and across diverse levels of act and discourse amongst Sufi communities from the formative period forward. Within the structuring logic of an ethical monotheism such as Islam, to understand reality as something which is embedded within layers of deeper meaning not readily apparent is to simultaneously aver that such layers are nevertheless conceptually, discursively, and even physically accessible.

[11] A.J. Arberry, trans., *The Koran Interpreted*, 2 vols. (London: George Allen & Unwin Ltd, 1955), vol. 1, 192.

[12] That is, the primordial "in-that-time" of myths of origin. The expression, often used in his comparative writings on the subject, is borrowed from Mircea Eliade. On the *yawm al-mīthāq* see Louis Massignon, "Le "jour du covenant" (*yawm al-mīthāq*)", *Oriens*, 15 (1962), 86–92.

[13] An illuminating discussion of the broader narrative architecture of Islamic configurations of salvation history, but one example of the totalizing discourse of elective monotheisms in general, may be found in Martin S. Jaffee, "One God, One Revelation, One People: On the Symbolic Structure of Elective Monotheism", *Journal of the American Academy of Religion*, 69, no. 4 (2001), 753–775.

[14] On this concept in general, see I. Poonawala, "al-Ẓāhir wa'l-Bāṭin", in *The Encyclopaedia of Islam, New Edition*, 12 vols. (Leiden: E.J. Brill, 1954–2004; hereafter *EI2*).

This is, however, something which is only possible – as much socially as conceptually – in relation to its being grounded within a common mythos in which narrative touchstones, such as the "Day of the Primordial Covenant", serve both as a kind of communicative mechanism or media within and between groups of like-minded individuals while simultaneously linking such groups, although not always with comfort and ease, to a broader corporate confessional order. Thus, all of those things known through or by revelation – whether they be ubiquitous ritual praxes such as the five-times-a-day canonical prayer or formulaic creedal assertions such as the Muslim profession of faith – are construed as part of a wider reality shared between Sufis and their non-Sufi coreligionists, a reality which while shared between all, is one in which only the former are aware of its actual fullness, that is both its exoteric and esoteric dimensions. The idea, essentially a kind of exemplarism, was that while all good Muslims could, to one extent or another, be assured of being able to reclaim the *in illo tempore* of the Qurʾānic primordial covenant in the world to come through adhering to the clear and unambitious externals of the Qurʾānic "straight path", in having access to its deeper, hidden meanings only the Sufis could taste it in advance.

By at least the time of the profoundly influential Sufi teacher al-Junayd al-Baghdādī (d. 298/910),[15] such conceptualizations were both understood and expressed in relation to an epistemology which posited a qualitative distinction between rational, discursive knowledge (*ʿilm*) and its soteriological implications and entailments, and non-rational, experiential knowledge (*maʿrifa*) and its mystical implications and entailments.[16] Whereas both were understood as necessary and cohesively integral parts of the perpetuation of the Islamic revelation in time and space, being as they were made possible in the first place through the authoritative transmission of the totalizing religio-ethical order vouchsafed by the Prophet to his community until the end of days, it was only through *maʿrifa* that the fullness of that order – that is, its *bāṭin* as well as its *ẓāhir* – could be wholly known. Whereas, for example, the conditions structuring the performance of obligatory ritual praxes or the validity of theological truth claims communicated in scripture were known by jurists and theologians through the application of deductive or inductive reasoning, knowledge of their deeper, esoteric significances were

[15] On whom see Green, *Sufism: A Global History*, 36–39; Karamustafa, *Sufism: The Formative Period*, 15–18; Knysh, *Islamic Mysticism*, 52–56; Baldick, *Mystical Islam*, 44–46; and Schimmel, *Mystical Dimensions of Islam*, 57–59.

[16] On these epistemological constructs and their ramifications for metaphysical speculation, see Knysh, *Islamic Mysticism*, 311–314; Baldick, *Mystical Islam*, 44–46; and Anawati and Gardet, *Mystique Musulmane*, 129–145.

obtainable to Sufis through immediate, experiential, and non-discursive forms of cognition. In contradistinction to deductive and other rational speculative methods rooted in the employment of the rational mind (*ʿaql*) in which knowledge of revelation was gained through the mechanisms of reasoned personal opinion (*raʾy*), analogy (*qiyās*), or simply the reception of authoritative pronouncement (*naql*), the Sufis claimed the same through appeals to direct and non-mediated mechanisms of knowing such as *kashf* ("unveiling"), *ilhām* ("inspiration"), *mushāhada* ("direct witnessing"), *dhawq* ("tasting"), and such like. While not wholly tied to it, discussions of the nature of such mystical epiphanies, discussions of which become increasingly ubiquitous in Sufi literature from the late fourth/tenth century forward, were very much rooted in the assumption that such suprasensible forms of cognition are not only directly related to the psycho-spiritual transmutations which the individual Sufi undergoes as he journeys along the mystical path or way (*ṭarīq* / *ṭarīqa*), but also serve as an essential undergirding for a hermeneutical model which came to be applied to the interpretation of the Qurʾān.

On this latter point, it should be noted that while a diversity of exegetical styles have always operated, antagonistically or otherwise, alongside one another in the collective exegetical endeavours of the Muslim religio-scholarly elite (a fact as true today as it was in the early and middle periods of Islamic history),[17] pre-modern Sufi authors have often found themselves drawn to a style of scriptural exegesis which relied, more so than anything else, on the discursively elusive dynamics of experiential knowing. Typically referred to as "exegesis by allusion" (*tafsīr bi-l-ishāra*), this hermeneutical model is one which not only recognizes the presence of multifold layers of meaning embedded in the Qurʾānic text – that is, its *ẓāhir* and *bāṭin* – but also assumes that such meaning is accessible through a reflective and contemplative process rooted in the cultivation of a deep, inward "listening" (*ḥusn al-istimāʿ*), a type of eisegesis in which the hidden verities or significances enunciated in the Qurʾānic text are "extracted" (*istinbāṭ*) though the identification of symbolical, metaphorical, or allegorical allusions (*ishārāt*) to verities or significances confirmed by the listener's own mystical experiences.[18] Evinced already in

[17] Approachable overviews of which may be found in Andrew Rippen, "Tafsir", in *The Encyclopedia of Religion, Second Edition*, 15 vols., ed. Lindsay Jones (Detroit: Macmillan Reference USA, 2005), vol. 13, 8949–8955; Claude Gilliot, "Exegesis of the Qurʾān: Classical and Medieval", in *Encyclopaedia of the Qurʾān*, 6 vols., ed. Jane Dammen McAuliffe (Leiden: Brill, 2001–2006; hereafter *EQ*), vol. 2, 99–124; and, Rotraud Wielandt, "Exegesis of the Qurʾān: Early Modern and Contemporary", in *EQ*, vol. 2, 124–142.

[18] On this see Alexander D. Knysh, "Ṣūfism and the Qurʾān", in *EQ*, 137–159; Alan Godlas, "Sufism", in *The Blackwell Companion to the Qur'an*, ed. Andrew Rippin (Oxford: Blackwell,

exegetical glosses attributed to the late second/ninth-century associate of the aforementioned al-Junayd al-Baghdādī, Ibn ʿAṭāʾ al-Adamī (d. 309/922),[19] this hermeneutical model is well represented in exegetical compilations edited by the well-known Sufi scholar Abū ʿAbd al-Raḥmān al-Sulamī (d. 412/1021),[20] such as a series of interpretive glosses attributed, pseudonymously, to Jaʿfar al-Ṣādiq (d. 148/765)[21] in the former's *Verities of Qurʾānic Exegesis* (*Ḥaqāʾiq al-tafsīr*), of which the following gloss on a Qurʾanic verse (Q. 55:11) otherwise interpreted, exoterically, as a description of paradise furnishes a representative example:

> "*In it are fruit and date palms with unfolding calyxes.*" Jaʿfar said: The real made the hearts of his friends into gardens of his intimacy. He planted in them the trees of knowing, roots firm in the secrets of their hearts, branches standing in the presence of witness. In every time they father the fruits of intimacy. That is what is meant by his saying "*In it are fruit and date palms with unfolding calyxes*," that is, of all kinds. Each one fathers from it a kind according to the capacity of his labor and what is unveiled for him of the manifestations of knowing and the traces of friendship with the divine.[22]

As typically understood within the Sufi tradition, attaining the type of elevated spiritual state necessary to effectively detect and extract such subtle allusions from revelation requires a long and difficult process of psycho-spiritual transmutation. This process is often likened to the journey of an intrepid traveller making his way along a difficult and winding path, a journey in which the aspirant reaches various "halts" or "way stations" (sing., *maqām*;

2006), 350–361; Kristin Sands, *Ṣūfī Commentaries on the Qurʾān in Classical Islam* (London: Routledge, 2006); Gerhard Böwering, "The Scriptural "Senses" in Medieval Ṣūfī Qurʾān Exegesis", in *With Reverence for the Word: Medieval Scriptural Exegesis in Judaism, Christianity, and Islam*, ed. Jane Dammen McAuliffe, Barry D. Walfish, and Joseph W. Goering (Oxford and New York: Oxford University Press, 2003), 346–365; Gerhard Böwering, "Ṣūfī Hermeneutics in Medieval Islam", *Revue des Études Islamiques*, 55–57, no. 1 (1987–1989), 255–270; and Paul Nwyia, *Exégèse Coranique et Langage Mystique* (Beirut: Dar al-Machreq Editeurs, 1970).

19 On whom see Richard Gramlich, *Abu l-ʿAbbās b. ʿAṭāʾ. Sufi und Koranausleger* (Stuttgart: Franz Steiner, 1995).

20 On whose exegetical compilations see, with further references, Jean-Jacques Thibon, *L'œuvre d'Abū ʿAbd al-Rahmān al-Sulamī (325/937–412/1021) et la Formation du Soufisme* (Damascus: Institut Français du Proche-orient, 2009, 396–406; Gerhard Böwering, "al-Sulamī", In *EI2*, vol. 9, 811–812; idem, "The Major Sources of Sulamī's Minor Qurʾān Commentary", *Oriens* 35 (1996), 35–56; and idem, "The Qurʾān Commentary of Al-Sulamī", in *Islamic Studies Presented to Charles J. Adams*, ed. Wael B. Hallaq and Donald P. Little (Leiden: E.J. Brill, 1991), 41–56.

21 On him see, the sixth Imām of the Shiʿites and a figure associated, often pseudonymously, with contributions to a variety of fields of knowledge in early Islam, see M.G.S. Hodgson, "Dj̲aʿfar al-Ṣādiḳ", in *EI2*, vol. 2, 374–375.

22 Michael A. Sells, ed. and trans., *Early Islamic Mysticism: Sufi, Qur'an, Mi'raj, Poetic and Theological Writings* (New York and Mahwah, NJ: Paulist Press, 1996), 87 [italics in original].

pl. *maqāmāt*) and experiences various "states" (sing. *ḥāl*; pl. *aḥwāl*) as he progressively overcomes the machinations of his carnal soul or ego-self (*nafs*), until his person is divested of all of those base qualities which estrange his spirit from its source.[23] The first of these halts or way stations, whose exact order and enumeration have often been interpreted differently by different Sufis, is typically identified as the station of "repentance" (*tawba*), with the last being the stations of "annihilation [in God]" (*fanāʾ* [*bi-llāh*]) and "abiding [in God]" (*baqāʾ* [*bi-llāh*]). Whereas a *maqām* is typically understood to be earned or attained as a result of effort, the *ḥāl*, of which many more are typically enumerated in the classical Sufi handbooks, are typically understood as being freely given and ephemeral "graces" which come and go without effort on the part of the mystic. These altered states of consciousness are often enumerated in dichotomous pairs such as "contraction" and "expansion" (*basṭ* and *qabḍ*), "absence" and "presence" (*ghayba* and *ḥuḍūr*), and "awe" and "intimacy" (*hayba* and *uns*). An important, if not essential, element of wayfaring through these states and stations is the mystic's experience of hardship and trial (*balāʾ*), an element which lends an air of extreme gravity to the endeavour, one quite fitting to the momentousness of recapturing the existential implications of the Qurʾānic *in illo tempore* evoked by the events of the Day of the Primordial Covenant.

In a simile oft referenced in Sufi literature, the structural form of the totality of wayfaring towards a reunion with the divine reality is likened to an almond. In this simile, the tough, outer protective husk of the fruit is representative of the *sharīʿa*, the revealed law of Islam, its inner shell is representative of the *ṭarīqa*, the Sufi path or way, and the kernel found at its centre is representative of the *ḥaqīqa*, the divine reality itself. Embedded within this simile is the idea of progressive and methodical transmutation of the mystic's entire person, his outer self being purified through the actualization (*taḥqīq*) of the verities of the *sharīʿa* and his inner self being illuminated through the actualization of the verities of the *ṭarīqa*; this so that he is adequately prepared to re-encounter his lord in the original, essential, and primordial state in which he, as spirit, existed prior to the calling into being of the phenomenal creation in which he, as corporealised being, has now found himself in relation to the *ḥaqīqa*. Often evoked in a *ḥadīth* in which the Prophet is reported to have said that "the *sharīʿa* are my words (*aqwālī*), the *ṭarīqa* are my actions (*aʿmālī*),

[23] On this conceptualization, and its various formulations, see Knysh, *Islamic Mysticism*, 301–311; Ernst, *The Shambhala Guide to Sufism*, 98–108; Schimmel, *Mystical Dimensions of Islam*, 99–148; Hodgson, *The Venture of Islam*, vol. 2, 232–227; and A.J. Arberry, *Sufism: An Account of the Mystics of Islam* (London: George Allen & Unwin Ltd, 1950), 74–83.

and the *ḥaqīqa* is my interior states (*aḥwālī*)",[24] from a fairly early point onwards the idea amongst Sufi communities was that this totality of wayfaring was a communal patrimony passed on by the Prophet himself to certain elect amongst his companions through the mechanism of initiatic transmission, thus coming to form *silsila*s or "chains" of transmission through which Sufi masters, generation after generation, perpetuate the inner, esoteric dimensions of the Islamic revelation to their own companions,[25] dimensions which when attuned to properly allow for the kind of fulfilment in the here and now of what other members of the wider confessional community, who as members of that community otherwise simply maintain adherence to the *sharīʿa* alone, anticipate achieving in the world to come at an undetermined point in the future. Not content to wait, however, the Sufis necessarily move beyond the *sharīʿa* – this simply so as to be able to realize in the present what is otherwise promised in the future.

As in the confessional community at large, the numerically smaller community created by its more impatient members who, due to their impatience, have taken on the task of perpetuating the inner, esoteric dimensions of the Islamic revelation handed down by the Prophet to the elect amongst his companions, and they to the next generation and so forth and so on, are themselves internally differentiated by levels of spiritual achievement and realization. At the top – or at the centre, depending on the conceptualization – stand those who have through their wayfaring become "friends" or "intimates" of God (sing., *walī*; pl. *awliyāʾ*), individuals who possess a kind of saintly authority (*walāya*) and from that a resulting spiritual-temporal jurisdiction (*wilāya*).[26] This latter quality has, at least in the more complex schematizations of the corporate body of the *awliyāʾ* evinced first in the late third/ninth century in the writings of the enigmatic al-Ḥakīm al-Tirmidhī and brought to a certain conclusion in the detailed presentations of Ibn

[24] Schimmel, *Mystical Dimensions of Islam*, 99; on which see further Geoffroy, *Introduction to Sufism*, 59–64.

[25] On this idea and its historical ramifications, see Green, *Sufism: A Global History*, 81–91; Geoffroy, *Introduction to Sufism*, 99–116; Knysh, *Islamic Mysticism*, 169–244; Ernst, *The Shambhala Guide to Sufism*, 120–137; Baldick, *Mystical Islam*, 69–77; Schimmel, *Mystical Dimensions of Islam*, 228–258; and Hodgson, *The Venture of Islam*, vol. 2, 214–217.

[26] Examinations of specific manifestations of which in various pre-modern Muslim societies may be found in Green, *Sufism: A Global History*, 92–103; John Renard, *Friends of God: Islamic Images of Piety, Commitment, and Servanthood* (Berkeley, Los Angeles, and London: University of California Press, 2008); B. Radtke et al., "Walī", in *EI2*, vol. 12, 109–124; Vincent J. Cornell, *Realm of the Saint: Power and Authority in Moroccan Sufism* (Austin, Texas: University of Texas Press, 1998); and Ernst, *The Shambhala Guide to Sufism*, 58–80.

al-ʿArabī[27] in the early seventh/thirteenth century, often been understood in relation to a kind of saintly hierarchy at whose head stands a supreme saint, the *quṭb* ("pole") or "succor" (*ghawth*) who has been charged by God with maintaining an kind of equilibrium in the world and under whom stand lesser saints such as the *awtād* ("pillars"), *abdāl* ("substitutes"), *abrār* ("godly"), and the *akhyār* ("selected").[28] In addition to such cosmically important figures, other more prosaic designations emerged fairly early on within Sufi communities so as to more effectively map and position individuals within both expanding conceptual and social ambits, the latter especially in relation to the institutional forms of Sufi organization and practice which began to solidify in the late sixth/twelfth into the seventh/thirteenth century, in which differentiations were drawn between those who have obtained the goal, those who are *ṣūfī*s properly speaking, and the *mutaṣawwif* ("aspiring Sufi") who is still striving to obtain that goal.[29]

THE RITUAL LANDSCAPE

The oft-quoted third/ninth-century Sufi Bāyazīd Bisṭāmī[30] is said to have remarked that "he who has no master takes Satan for his master." This

[27] On these two figures respectively, see Knysh, *Islamic Mysticism*, 105–113, 163–168; Baldick, *Mystical Islam*, 42–44, 82–85; and Schimmel, *Mystical Dimensions of Islam*, 56–57, 263–274. An approachable biography and study of Ibn al-ʿArabī is to be had in Stephen Hirtenstein, *The Unlimited Mercifier: The Spiritual Life and Thought of Ibn ʿArabī* (Oxford and Ashland, OR: Anqa Publishing and White Cloud Press, 1999).

[28] On the hierarchy of saints in general see Geoffroy, *Introduction to Sufism*, 125–126; Knysh, "Sufism", 86–90; Karamustafa, *Sufism: The Formative Period*, 127–134; Jacqueline Chabbi, "Abdāl", in *Encyclopaedia Iranica*, ed. Ehsan Yarshater (London [et cetera]: Routledge and Kegan Paul [et cetera], 1982–; hereafter *EIr*), vol. 1, 173–174; Schimmel, *Mystical Dimensions of Islam*, 199–204; Hodgson, *The Venture of Islam*, vol. 2, 227–230; and I. Goldziher, "Abdāl", in *EI2*, vol. 1, 94. On the ideas of al-Ḥakīm al-Tirmidhī and Ibn al-ʿArabī see, respectively, Bernd Radtke and John O'Kane, trans., *The Concept of Sainthood in Early Islamic Mysticism: Two works by Al-Ḥakīm Al-Tirmidhī* (Richmond, Surrey: Curzon Press, 1996), and Michel Chodkiewicz, *Seal of the Saints: Prophethood and Sainthood in the Doctrine of Ibn ʿArabī*, trans. Liadain Sherrard (Cambridge: The Islamic Texts Society, 1993).

[29] Both the conceptual and practical dimensions of this differentiation are well evinced in the particularly well-documented example of the influential *ribāṭ*-directing Sufi master of late Abbasid Baghdad, Abū Ḥafṣ ʿUmar al-Suhrawardī (d. 632/1234), on which see idem, "Institutionalized Mashyakha in the Twelfth Century Ṣūfism of ʿUmar al-Suhrawardī", *Jerusalem Studies in Arabic and Islam*, 36 (2009), 381–424; Arin Salamah-Qudsi, "The Idea of *Tashabbuh* in Sufi Communities and Literature of the Late 6th/12th and Early 7th/13th Century in Baghdad", *Al-Qanṭara*, 32 (2011), 175–197; and Erik S. Ohlander, *Sufism in an Age of Transition: ʿUmar al-Suhrawardī and the Rise of the Islamic Mystical Brotherhoods* (Leiden: Brill, 2008), 148–154, 187–247 (passim).

[30] On Bisṭāmī (d. 234/848 or 261/875), see Gerhard Böwering, "Besṭāmī (Basṭāmī)", in *EIr*, 2:183–186.

apophthegm encapsulates a great deal concerning pre-modern Sufi conceptualizations of the centrality of the master-disciple relationship in relation to the successful reclamation of the primordial Qurʾānic *in illo tempore*. Rooted simultaneously in wider Islamic conceptualizations regarding the communal duty of ensuring the perpetuation of the final divine dispensation on the plane of history up to the very moment of the eschaton, the notion of the original prophetic bequest of the discipline of Sufism as a communal patrimony thenceforth preserved in *silsila*s, and the ubiquitous social formulation of patron-protégé relationships within all manners of vocational endeavour in pre-modern Muslim societies generally, the master-disciple relationship stood as a central organizing principle within and across pre-modern Sufi communities. The nature of this relationship is well captured in the denominations used to describe its participants: *shaykh* or *pīr* ("elder") and *murshid* ("guide") for the master, and *ṭālib* or *shāgird* ("student") and *murīd* ("aspirant") for the disciple. As a realized *ṣūfī* authorized by a previous master to take on disciples of his own, the *murshid* stands in as a representative (*nāʾib*) of the Prophet, serving to guide the impatient aspirants of his own day just as the Prophet guided the elect amongst his companions. As such, when auspicated into the Sufi path by a master, the disciple takes an oath of allegiance (*bayʿa*), pledging thereby to place full faith and trust in the direction of the master, yielding to him, as the saying often goes, like "a corpse in the hands of an undertaker",[31] and following his direction as a son would his father, without question or complaint, knowing that in his wisdom the master, as his spiritual father, always has his best interests in mind.[32]

From at least the later third/ninth century such masters, whose earlier roles as simple "teaching-masters" (*shaykh al-taʿlīm*) began to give way to that of "directing-masters" (*shaykh al-tarbīya*) by the fifth/eleventh century, increasingly started gather around themselves ever larger groups of followers.[33] Such groups, consisting of more than associates who in an earlier period may have

[31] Schimmel, *Mystical Dimensions of Islam*, 103.

[32] On the master-disciple relationship in general, and on rituals of initiation in particular, see Geoffroy, *Introduction to Sufism*, 142–158; Knysh, "Sufism", 84–86; Ohlander, *Sufism in an Age of Transition*, 214–216; Knysh, *Islamic Mysticism*, 172–179; J. Spencer Trimingham, *The Sufi Orders in Islam*, with a new foreword by J. Voll (New York and Oxford: Oxford University Press, 1998), 181–193; Ernst, *The Shambhala Guide to Sufism*, 141–145; Hodgson, *The Venture of Islam*, vol. 2, 206–210, 214–217; and Arberry, *Sufism*, 84–92.

[33] On this process see Karamustafa, *Sufism: The Formative Period*, 114–127; Fritz Meier, "Khurāsān and the End of Classical Sufism", in *Essays on Islamic Piety and Mysticism*, trans. John O'Kane and ed. Bernd Radtke (Leiden: Brill, 1999), 189–219 (to which is usefully added Laury Silvers-Alario, "The Teaching Relationship in Early Sufism: A Reassessment of Fritz Meier's Definition of the *shaykh al-tarbiya* and the *shaykh al-taʿlīm*", *The Muslim World*, 95 [2003], 69–97).

been more apt to engage in occasional companionship (*ṣuḥba*) with them so as to benefit from their guidance rather than placing themselves under their long-term care, increasingly came to be associated with intentionally constructed residential centres. Appearing already in the later fourth/tenth century, by the fifth/eleventh and then into the sixth/twelfth century residential hospices or cloisters, known in Arabic as *ribāṭ* or in Persian as *khānaqāh*, began to appear with increasing ubiquity across the Abode of Islam.[34] Serving as both the primary residence of a Sufi master and as a meeting place for his disciples, such institutions, which were supported by everything from modest charitable donations gathered by the brethren to large income-generating endowments effected through the legal institution of *waqf*, became the primary stage of Sufi ritual praxis. It was within *ribāṭ*s and *khānaqāh*s, rather than within mosques or madrasas (although the former could, and often did, incorporate smaller versions of the latter, especially in dense urban landscapes) that Sufi aspirants would be initiated into the path, would be taught its arcana, and would engage, under the watchful eye and careful direction of the master of the *ribāṭ* or *khānaqāh*, in those ritual praxes which, more so than anything else, visibly marked out Sufi communities as a distinctive sodality within the Muslim corporate order.

As far as scholars are able to reconstruct it, life within a medieval Sufi *ribāṭ* or *khānaqāh* was tightly structured and highly regulated.[35] Every member of the community, from the master down to the lowliest disciple and domestic servant, had a carefully defined place within the sodality, with each affiliate being expected to adhere with utmost attention to a formally defined set of courtesies (sing. *adab*; pl. *ādāb*). These courtesies structured everything from verbal intercourse to bodily comportment, from the performance of supererogatory ritual duties to table manners, and from manners of dress to modes of social interaction.[36] In short, the comprehensive, synthetic view of a divinely-ordained way to properly navigate the world so vividly expressed in the minutia of Islamic orthopraxy, in which acts of servanthood (*ʿibādāt*)

34 On the development of such institutions in general see Gerhard Böwering and Matthew Melvin-Koushki, "K̲ānaqāh", in *EIr*, vol. 15, 456–466; Ohlander, *Sufism in an Age of Transition*, 27–34; Trimingham, *The Sufi Orders in Islam*, 166–173; Jacqueline Chabbi, "Ribāṭ", in *EI2*, 8:493–506; and idem, "K̲h̲ānḳāh, in *EI2*, vol. 4, 1025–1026.

35 See, for example, the discussion of the rules and regulations for life in such institutions promulgated by the aforementioned ʿUmar al-Suhrawardī in Ohlander, *Sufism in an Age of Transition*, 187–247 passim.

36 On which in general see Geoffroy, *Introduction to Sufism*, 158–162; Erik S. Ohlander, "Adab, in Ṣūfism", in *EI3*, fasc. 2009–1, 40–43; Ernst, *The Shambhala Guide to Sufism*, 145–146; and, in the case of the wide-ranging prescriptive treatises of the aforementioned ʿUmar al-Suhrawardī, Ohlander, *Sufism in an Age of Transition*, 203–206.

enmesh with social acts (*muʿāmalāt*) into a seamless and synthetic whole which sacralized the community's entire lifeworld, became for medieval Sufi communities a signally actable, and eminently replicable, life-orientational frame within which the entailments of a spiritual impatience rooted in the drama of estrangement from the state of pre-creation could be worked out at both a communal and individual level. As such, the meticulous focus on matters of *adab* noted in Sufi literature, especially that produced during the later medieval period, serves not only as evidence of the increasing acculturation of modes of Sufi religiosity within and across Muslim societies in the post-formative period, but perhaps more immediately it evinces the Islamically-oriented expression of such modes in the first place. That is, as modes of mystico-ascetic religiosity associated with self-reflexively defined Sufi communities in different parts of the pre-modern Muslim world continued to ensconce themselves into the social and communal fabric of the societies which both bore and housed them, so too did such communities need to find ways, organically speaking, to integrate these into the wider realities of those societies.[37] In the case of codes of *adab*, the paradigmatic sympathy between both their underlying ethos and its formal expression served, visibly, to credential those adhering to them as legitimate defenders of an intracommunal patrimony in which, at least practically speaking, Sufi *adab* was presented as so deftly alloyed to wider forms of Islamic socio-religious expression as to be inseparable from them.

At the same time, it should be noted that whereas adherence to formal codes of behaviour and comportment within Sufi *ribāṭ*s or *khānaqāh*s, as embedded within the wider lifeworld of living Muslim societies, gelled well with wider Islamic conceptualizations of how one should be in the world, the matter of specifically intracommunal ritual praxes, especially those of an extra-canonical or supererogatory nature, were typically less well accommodated. Here, it is important to note that within the wider Sufi landscape of pre-modern Islamic societies two major streams of mystico-ascetic religiosity can be discerned. The first, the praxis of the minority often not associated with established *ribāṭ* or *khānaqāh* communities, embraced overtly antinomian figurations of wayfaring on the Sufi path. The second, the praxis of the majority which was often closely associated with *ribāṭ* or *khānaqāh* communities, embraced adherence *to sharīʾa* norms as a sine qua non of the same.

[37] Of which the various Sufi-tinged *futuwwa* associations that emerged with vigour beginning in the later sixth/twelfth century are excellent examples. On this in general see Lloyd Ridgeon, *Morals and Mysticism in Persian Sufism: A History of Sufi-futuwwat in Iran* (London and New York: Routledge, 2010).

The former, rooted in the renunciative logic of *malāma*, or "drawing blame" to oneself through the intentional flouting of social and religious norms, looked to tame the *nafs* through a wilful disinterest in the judgmental gaze of society.[38] In contradistinction, the latter envisioned the wilful perfection of such norms as an essential aide in effectively traversing the Sufi path. It is in relation to these two opposing streams that the variety of extra-canonical and supererogatory praxes associated with pre-modern Sufi religiosity generally should be viewed. Both embraced the concept of voluntary physical and spiritual poverty (*faqr*) as a basic orienting principle framing wayfaring on the Sufi path, but whereas the discourse of the former is clearly rooted in the assumption that it is through the actualization of the verities of the *sharī'a* that the aspirant's outer self is best purified and, as such, that fastidious adherence to *sharī'a* norms is both individually and communally desirable, the discourse of the latter envisioned slavish conformity to social custom and religious pedantry as roadblocks to such inner transformation. As such, alternative praxes needed to be found. Both perspectives are well evinced in the sources, the former being well displayed in popular prescriptive texts authored by seminal *sharī'a*-minded Sufi teachers such as Abū Ṭālib al-Makkī (d. 386/996), Abū Ḥāmid al-Ghazālī (d. 505/1111), ʿAbd al-Qādir al-Jīlānī (d. 561/1166), and Abū Ḥafṣ ʿUmar al-Suhrawardī (d. 632/1234),[39] whereas the latter is equally well displayed in both the activities of intentional mystico-ascetic sodalities such as the various Qalandar movements of the later medieval and early modern periods and in a series of instances of the more

38 On this strand of mystico-ascetic religiosity in northeastern Iran, and the development of the later Malāmatiyya movement in Ottoman Turkey, see Green, *Sufism: A Global History*, 46; Geoffroy, *Introduction to Sufism*, 67–68; Karamustafa, *Sufism: The Formative Period*, 48–51, 60–65; Knysh, *Islamic Mysticism*, 94–99, 274–277; Sara Sviri, "Ḥakīm Tirmidhī and the *Malāmatī* Movement in Early Sufism", in *The Heritage of Sufism*, vol. 1, Classical Persian Sufism from its Origins to Rumi (700–1300), ed. Leonard Lewisohn (Oxford: Oneworld, 1999), 583–613; Popovic and Veinstein, *Les Voies d'Allah*, index (s.v. Malamati, Malamatis; Malâmatiyya; Malâmi, Malāmis, Melâmi); F. de Jong et al., "Malāmatiyya", in *EI2*, vol. 6, 223–228; and Jacqueline Chabbi, "Remarques sur le développement historique des mouvements ascétiques et mystique au Khurasan, IIIe/IXe siècle – IVe/Xe siècle", *Studia Islamica*, 46 (1977), 32–34, 53–57.

39 On Abū Ṭālib al-Makkī, see Saeko Yazaki, *Islamic Mysticism and Abū Ṭālib al-Makkī: The Role of the Heart* (Abingdon, Oxon: Routledge, 2013); Erik S. Ohlander, "Abū Ṭālib al-Makkī", in *EI3*, fasc. 2010–1, 27–30; and Knysh, *Islamic Mysticism*, 121–122. On Abū Ḥāmid al-Ghazālī, see Eric L. Ormsby, *Ghazali: The Revival of Islam* (Oxford: Oneworld, 2008); Knysh, *Islamic Mysticism*, 140–149; and Schimmel, *Mystical Dimensions of Islam*, 91–97. On ʿAbd al-Qādir al-Jīlānī, see Knysh, *Islamic Mysticism*, 179–191; André Demeerseman, *Nouveau Regard sur la Voie Spirituelle d'ʿAbd al-Qadir al-Jilani et sa Tradition* (Paris: J. Vrin, 1988); and Schimmel, *Mystical Dimensions of Islam*, 246–248. On Abū Ḥafṣ ʿUmar al-Suhrawardī see Ohlander, *Sufism in an Age of Transition*, esp. 57–136; Knysh, *Islamic Mysticism*, 195–207; and Angelika Hartmann, "al-Suhrawardī, Shihāb al-Dīn Abū Ḥafṣ ʿUmar", in *EI2*, vol. 9, 778–782.

individualized expressions of isolated Sufi wayfarers who embraced the generalized ethos of *malāma* and "drunken" (*sukr*) forms of Sufi religiosity.[40]

At the same time, both steams shared a ritual universe which, perhaps more so than anything else, served to distinguish expressions of Sufi religiosity as something visibly different or distinctive framing the day-to-day activities of either within the purview of the wider Islamic ritual landscape. While *sharīʿa*-minded Sufi masters often enjoined upon their disciples the fastidious discharge of their basic Islamic ritual duties – typically supplemented with the performance of canonical supererogatory devotions such as added liturgical prayers, Qurʾānic recitation, voluntary fasting, and such like – this was inevitably done in concert with the programmatic performance of other ritual praxes. Typically, such praxes, which were generally of a contemplative or ascetical nature, were understood to serve as integral components of the Sufi path, discrete ritual mechanisms handed down through the initiatic lineages deriving ultimately from the Prophet himself, which served to secure advancement towards the final realization in the here and now of the *in illo tempore* of the Qurʾānic primordial covenant. Among these practices it is the practice of *dhikr* ("anamnesis"), which takes pride of place.[41] Possessing explicit Qurʾānic associations, as a contemplative praxis *dhikr* refers to the methodical and ritualized repetition of particular religious formulae, normally coupled with specific breathing patterns, visualizations, or bodily

[40] On which see, with further references, Geoffroy, *Introduction to Sufism*, 69–71; Karamustafa, *Sufism: The Formative Period*, 155–166; Knysh, *Islamic Mysticism*, 68–82, 272–274; Ernst, *The Shambhala Guide to Sufism*, 114–119; Ahmet T. Karamustafa, *God's Unruly Friends: Dervish Groups in the Islamic Later Middle Period*, 1200–1550 (Salt Lake City: The University of Utah Press, 1994); Tahsin Yazıcı, "Ḳalandar", and "Ḳalandariyya", in *EI2*, vol. 4, 472–473, 473–474; and Schimmel, *Mystical Dimensions of Islam*, 46–51, 62–77.

[41] On the subject of *dhikr* within Sufism generally, along with pertinent examples of its diverse forms of expression in relation to various confraternities, see Geoffroy, *Introduction to Sufism*, 162–170; Ohlander, *Sufism in an Age of Transition*, 222–225; Knysh, *Islamic Mysticism*, 317–322; M.I. Waley, "Contemplative Disciples in Early Persian Sufism", in *The Heritage of Sufism*, vol. 1, 502–511; Trimingham, *The Sufi Orders in Islam*, 200–207, and glossary of Arabic terms (s.v. *dhikr* (√remember, recollect)); Ernst, *The Shambhala Guide to Sufism*, 92–98, 108–111; Éric Geoffroy, *Le Soufisme en Egypte et Syrie sous les Derniers Mamlouks et les Premiers Ottomans* (Damascus: Institut Français de Damas, 1995), 408–411; Jamal Elias, *The Throne Carrier of God: The Life and Thought of ʿAlāʾ ad-Dawla as-Simnānī* (Albany: State University of New York Press, 1995), 124–134; Anawati and Gardet, *Mystique Musulmane*, 187–234; Richard Gramlich, *Die Schiitischen Derwischorden Persiens*, 3 vols. (Wiesbaden: Franz Steiner Verlag, 1965–1981), vol. 2, 370–430; Schimmel, *Mystical Dimensions of Islam*, 167–178; Hodgson, *The Venture of Islam*, vol. 2, 210–214; Ernst Bannerth, "Dhikr et khalwa d'après Ibn ʿAṭāʾ Allāh", *Mélanges de l'Institut Dominicain d'études Orientales du Caire*, 12 (1974), 65–90 passim; L. Gardet, "Dhikr", *EI2*, 2:223; and Fritz Meier, *Die Fawāʾiḥ al-Ǧalāl des Naǧm al-Dīn al-Kubrā* (Wiesbaden: Franz Steiner Verlag, 1957), 200–214.

movements. While *dhikr* could be performed aloud or silently, alone or in congregation, in quantifiably set cycles or in endless repetition, and while marked differences exist between various Sufi confraternities as to its form, commonly cited *dhikr* formulae include the first-half of the Muslim profession of faith (*lā ilāha illā 'llāh*, "there is no god but God"), the recitation of any or all of the ninety-names of God, and the progressively apocopated utterance of the Arabic third-person masculine singular pronoun *huwa* ("he") as in the phrase *allāh hu* ("God, him"), which after many repetitions is progressively shortened to *hu* and, finally, to just a breathy, plosive utterance which evokes, both phonologically and conceptually, the essence of the original formula. In the context of pre-modern Sufi confraternities, the initiatic ritual in which a new aspirant was auspicated by a Sufi master often included, in addition to the taking of a formal oath of allegiance and investiture with the Sufi habit (*khirqa*), the "inculcation of the mystical formula" (*talqīn al-dhikr*), passed on by the *shaykh* or *pīr* in the context of a meaning-event which was understood to replicate the original giving of *dhikr* formulae by the Prophet to the elect amongst his companions, especially to the person of his cousin and son-in-law ʿAlī b. Abī Ṭālib (d. 40/661), the fourth of the rightly-guided caliphs of the Sunnis and the first Imām of the Shiites.

Within the ritual praxis of many, but certainly not all, Sufi confraternities in pre-modern Muslim societies the communal performance of the *dhikr* was connected with the much more controversial practice of *samāʿ* – literally "hearing" or "audition". Perhaps best described as a type of "mystical concert" in which a groups of aspirants and affiliated parties gather, under the direction of a Sufi master, to listen to the stylized recitation of religious litanies or mystically-themed poetry by a professional or semi-professional reciter (*qawwāl*) supported by melodic or percussive accompaniment, as a form of group ritual the *samāʿ* was understood as a contemplative exercise whose proper execution, and the individual and group experience thereof, had a potentially efficacious bearing on the participants' spiritual development.[42] Participating in the *samāʿ*, for example, was understood to elicit the

[42] On the practice of *samāʿ* within Sufism generally see, with further references, Geoffroy, *Introduction to Sufism*, 170–174; Kenneth S. Avery, *A Psychology of Early Sufi samāʿ: Listening and Altered States* (Abingdon, Oxon: RoutledgeCurzon, 2004); Knysh, *Islamic Mysticism*, 322–325; Fritz Meier, "The Dervish Dance: An Attempt at an Overview", in *Essays on Islamic Piety and Mysticism*, 23–48; Ernst, *The Shambhala Guide to Sufism*, 179–198; Jean During, "Samāʿ", in *EI2*, vol. 8, 1018–1019; idem, "Musique et rites: *le samâʿ*", in *Les Voies d'Allah*, 157–172; idem, *Musique et Extase: l'audition Spirituelle dans la Tradition Soufie* (Paris: Albin Michel, 1988); Schimmel, *Mystical Dimensions of Islam*, 178–186; and Marjian Molé, "La danse extatique en Islam", in *Les Danses Sacrées* (Paris: Éditions du Seuil, 1963), 145–280.

manifestation of mystical states, especially that of "ecstasy" (*wajd*), in the attendees, who in contemplating the varied levels of the multisensory performance taking place in front of them could be led to various inner breakthroughs not otherwise available through other mystico-ascetic or contemplative praxes. Closely associated with the *samāʿ*, and certainly one of its more controversial aspects, was the ritualized practice of "gazing upon (beardless) young men" (*naẓar ilā l-murd*; *shāhid-bāzī*), a practice in which the physical beauties of the object of visual contemplation were understood, ideally, as being symbolical representations of inner spiritual truths.[43] Due to the innate liability of *samāʿ*, and especially practices such as *naẓar ilā l-murd* / *shāhid-bāzī*, to be either misunderstood or to be perceived as merely "secular", if not religiously suspect, entertainment, many medieval Sufi prescriptive manuals and handbooks make it a point to deal explicitly with the rules and regulations structuring the performance of the *samāʿ*. In such texts, it is not uncommon to come across detailed prescriptions concerning the *adab* to which participants in and attendees at the *samāʿ* are to adhere, such as how and where to sit, when and when not to move, how to comport oneself when overcome with ecstasy, how a *khirqa* or other item of clothing rent and tossed off by one experiencing the latter is to be divided amongst those in attendance, how young men are, or are not to be, included in the ritual, and such like.[44]

While others could be cited, in addition to the practices of *dhikr* and *samāʿ*, there was perhaps no more ubiquitous a form of mystico-ascetic praxis within and across various figurations of Sufi religiosity in pre-modern Muslim societies than that of solitary spiritual retreat, or *khalwa* ("solitude"/"seclusion").[45] Evoking the Judeo–Christian–Islamic religious valuation given to the number forty (e.g. Moses' forty-day stay on Mt. Sinai; Jesus' forty day vigil in the wilderness; the enunciation of Muḥammad's prophethood in his fortieth year; et cetera), *khalwa* was typically done for forty days at a time, thus its alternate denominative as "a period of forty [days]" (Arabic:

[43] On which, in relation to seventh/thirteen-century controversies over the appropriateness of the practice within Sufi communal ritual praxis, see Lloyd Ridgeon, "The Controversy of Shaykh Awḥad al-Dīn Kirmānī and Handsome, Moon-Faced Youths: A Case Study of Shāhid-Bāzī in Medieval Sufism", *Journal of Sufi Studies*, 1, no. 1 (2012), 3–30.

[44] See, for example, the rules and regulations, and various objections to them, detailed in Ohlander, *Sufism in an Age of Transition*, 239–242.

[45] On which see, with further references, Geoffroy, *Introduction to Sufism*, 176–181; Ohlander, *Sufism in an Age of Transition*, 220–222; Knysh, *Islamic Mysticism*, 314–317, Trimingham, *The Sufi Orders in Islam*, glossary of Arabic terms (s.v. *khalwa* (√*khalā*, to be alone)); Ernst, *The Shambhala Guide to Sufism*, 111–114; Herman Landolt, "Khalwa", in *EI2*, vol. 4, 990; and Bannerth, "Dhikr et khalwa", 65–90 passim.

arbaʿīniyya; Persian: *chilla*). Conceived of as a wilful detachment from all of those things in which the *nafs* delights, as a response to the tension obtaining between the negative valuation given to permanent monasticism (whether anchoritic or cenobitic) in the Islamic tradition on the basis of prophetic tradition and the necessary practical entailments of a worldview in which the recapturing in the here and now of a primordial state of being is understood to be dependent upon overcoming the corporeally, sensually, and materially-socially driven egoism of the lower self, like *dhikr* and *samāʿ* the practice of *khalwa* amongst medieval Sufis was a carefully delineated mystico-ascetic endeavour. In the context of intentional Sufi communities in which a *ribāṭ* or *khānaqāh* served to provide a ritual-physical space within which keys elements of wayfaring on the Sufi path were pursued, the ritual of *khalwa* was often associated with specially built one-man cells or nooks (*zāwiya*) within a *ribāṭ* or *khānaqāh* in which the retreatant would isolate himself, neither leaving it nor having contact with others save during those times when he must quit the cell in order to pray the mandatory congregational prayers or attend to other absolutely necessary duties (although even when away from his cell, the retreatant was neither to speak with nor to acknowledge the presence of others). Under the instruction of his Sufi master, while in *khalwa* the retreatant was enjoined to perform various and discrete exercises, mystico-ascetic and contemplative praxes which may elicit the manifestation of certain psychic and visionary phenomena (*waqāʾiʿ*) which he is to later report back to the *shaykh* or *pīr* for interpretation.

CONCLUSION

As a diverse and multifaceted form of Muslim religiosity which joins a system of mystically-minded metaphysics, doctrines, and hermeneutics to various mystico-ascetic and contemplative practices aimed at the cultivation of an intimate, unmediated, or unitive encounter with God, the Sufis hope to experience in this life what other Muslims hope to experience in the life to come. While a diversity of doctrines and practices, along with a diversity of attitudes and forms of social and institutional organization, developed in relation to both individual and communal efforts to realize this hope within and across premodern Muslim societies, certain key ideas and forms of expression bound them together. As we have seen, these key ideas included the idea that the human spirit is possessed of a deeply set existential yearning to return to its source, the concept of the existence of esoteric dimensions of revelation, and indeed of reality itself, and the primacy of non-rational, unmediated, experiential knowing in coming to knowledge of these hidden dimensions, whether in relation to a hermeneutical model of Qur'ānic interpretation which looks to detect and validate meaning through reference to inner, spiritual experience, or in relation to an envisioning of a path of spiritual advancement and inner transmutation rooted in the actualization of the hidden verities contained therein. In addition, we have noted the importance of the communal and social resonances of these concepts, both in the idea that the Sufi path as mediated by *shaykhs* and *pīrs* represents a communal patrimony of the Muslim community passed on by the Prophet himself to certain of its elect members, and in the idea that those inheriting this patrimony create a community of "friends" or "intimates" of God who serve to maintain a kind of equilibrium in the world until the final resolution of the grand Qur'ānic drama at the end of time.

Within the ritual landscape of pre-modern Sufi communities, the centrality of the master-disciple relationship, the institutional and organizational forms housing such relationships, and the significance of *adab* as a structuring framework through which both are brought into meaningful, replicable connection has also been noted. So too have important structuring ideas pertaining to the relationship – multifaceted and not without tensions – between the outer, revealed law of Islam and wayfaring on the Sufi path and, following therefrom, the ubiquity of mystico-ascetic and contemplative ritual praxes such as *dhikr*, *samā*ʿ, and *khalwa*. As with the ultimately instrumental if not pedagogical nature of key elements of the conceptual landscape of pre-modern Sufi communities outlined above, however, it is important in the end to understand that it has been the actual results of mystico-ascetic and contemplative praxes, rather than the praxes themselves, that have commanded the most attention amongst Sufis, generally speaking. That is to say, that for all intents and purposes those observable dimensions of Sufi ritual represent but an outward veneer of a much deeper set of life-orientational attitudes in which the content, rather than the form, takes pride of place.[46]

FURTHER READING

Anawati, G.C. and Louis Gardet. *Mystique Musulmane: Aspects et Tendences, Expériences et Techniques*. 4th rev. edn. Paris: J. Vrin, 1986.

Arberry, A.J. *Sufism: An Account of the Mystics of Islam*. London: George Allen & Unwin, Ltd., 1950.

Baldick, Julian. *Mystical Islam: An Introduction to Sufism*. London: I.B. Tauris, 1989.

Chittick, William. *Sufism: A Short Introduction*. Oxford: Oneworld, 2000.

Ernst, Carl. *The Shambhala Guide to Sufism*. Boston: Shambhala Publications, 1997.

[46] On the Sufi conceptualization of the contextual relationship between knowledge and action in general see Erik S. Ohlander, "Action (ʿAmal), in Ṣūfism", in *EI3*, fasc. 2009–2, 44–46.

Geoffroy, Éric. *Introduction to Sufism: The Inner Path of Islam.* Translated by Roger Gaetani. Bloomington, Ind.: World Wisdom Inc., 2010.
Green, Nile. *Sufism: A Global History.* Malden, Mass.: Wiley-Blackwell, 2012.
Karamustafa, Ahmet T. *Sufism: The Formative Period.* Edinburgh: Edinburgh University Press, 2007.
Knysh, Alexander. *Islamic Mysticism: A Short History.* Leiden: Brill, 2000.
Lewisohn, Leonard, ed. *The Heritage of Sufism*, 3 vols. Oxford: Oneworld Publications, 1999.
Popovic, Alexandre and Gilles Veinstein, eds., *Les Voies d'Allah: Les Orders Mystiques dans le Monde Musulman des Origines à Aujourd'hui.* Paris: Fayard, 1996.
Schimmel, Annemarie. *Mystical Dimensions of Islam.* Chapel Hill: University of North Carolina Press, 1975.
Trimingham, J. Spencer. *The Sufi Orders in Islam.* With a new foreword by J. Voll. New York and Oxford: Oxford University Press, 1998.

4

Morality in Early Sufi Literature

Saeko Yazaki

INTRODUCTION

Ethics is by nature practical, since the knowledge of what the individual ought to do or refrain from doing needs to be applied. Thus, as religion often determines codes of behaviour, Islam also concerns morality. Ethical literature on *ādāb* (sing. *adab*, originally meaning a praiseworthy, effective norm of conduct), for example, starts to flourish during the second/eighth century, and by the fifth/eleventh century Islamic moral thought (*akhlāq*, sing. *khulq* or *khuluq*) has gradually taken form. This period sees the production of numerous works on cultured behaviour and ethical themes in various fields (Ḥadīth, literature, philosophy, etc.), from authors such as Yaḥyā b. Ādām (d. 203/818), Muḥammad al-Bukhārī (d. 256/870), Ibn Qutayba (d. 276/889), Ibn Abi'l-Dunyā (d. 281/894), Abū Naṣr al-Fārābī (d. 338–9/950), Abū Ḥayyān al-Tawḥīdī (d. 414/1023), and so on.[1] As part of this wider trend, early Sufism (*taṣawwuf*) also produced a rich literature on proper living, in line with the significance it assigned to ethical conduct – as a famous quotation has it, "The whole of *taṣawwuf* is etiquette."[2]

[1] For a wide variety of meanings of *adab* and a survey of *adab* literature, see, e.g., S. M. Toorawa, "Defining *Adab* by (Re)defining the *Adīb*: Ibn Abī Ṭāhir Ṭayfūr and Storytelling", in ed. P.F. Kennedy, *On Fiction and Adab in Medieval Arabic Literature* (Wiesbaden: Harrassowitz, 2005), 287–308; S.A. Bonebakker, "*Adab* and the Concept of *Belles-lettres*", in J. Ashtiany et al. (eds), *ʿAbbasid Belles-Lettres* (Cambridge: Cambridge University Press, 1990), 16–30; *Encyclopedia of Arabic Literature*, s.v. "*Adab*" (H. Kilpatrick). Cf. *Encyclopaedia of Islam [EI2]*, s.v. "*Adab*" (F. Gabrieli) and "*Akhlāḳ*" (R. Walzer); *EI3*, s.v. "*Adab* b) and Islamic scholarship in the ʿAbbāsid period" (S. Enderwitz), "*Adab* c) and Islamic scholarship after the 'Sunnī revival'" (T. Bauer), and "*Adab* e) modern usage" (B. Hallaq). I express sincere thanks to Stephen R. Burge and Ben Young for their helpful comments on earlier drafts of this article; all the deficiencies that remain are, needless to say, mine alone.

[2] Attributed to Abū Ḥafṣ al-Nīsābūrī al-Ḥaddād (d. c. 265/878–9); Abū ʿAbd al-Raḥmān al-Sulamī, *Kitāb ṭabaqāt al-ṣūfiyya: Texte Arabe avec une introduction et un index*, ed. J. Pedersen (Leiden: E.J. Brill, 1960), 110.

Sufi morality has both an external and an internal dimension. Internal morality is thought of as the basis for bodily action, since refined manners are strongly connected with spiritual realisation. Sufis often convey the impression of focusing solely on esoteric and other-worldly dimensions of faith; however, humans are physical beings: believers are enjoined to address the difference between their physicality and their spirituality, and must attempt to achieve an equilibrium between them. In Sufism, this balance is often considered as being closely linked to the connection between two fundamentally different and yet related categories, such as this world and the hereafter, or the human and the Divine. A.J. Arberry once described Sufism as a response to an "uncompromising Monotheism", representing the human yearning for personal experience of God.[3] From such a perspective, the Sufis' main concern becomes the metaphysical separation between God and His created beings, where one way to respond to this state of separation is to live in complete accordance with God's will, awaiting the Divine mercy which allows the believer to experience intimate knowledge of Reality. A number of early believers identified elements of Islamic piety which they saw as crucial to living according to Divine guidance and seeking purity both within and without; these principles they set down in treatises which came to be used as manuals by later Sufis.

This chapter explores these classical guidebooks on devotion in order to examine the way in which they conceive Sufi morality in their understanding of the essential components of faith.[4] Those writings are *Kitāb lumaʿ fi'l-taṣawwuf* ("The Book of Sparkling Lights in Sufism") by Abū Naṣr al-Sarrāj (d. 378/988), *Kitāb al-taʿarruf li-madhhab ahl al-taṣawwuf* ("The Book of Acquaintance with the Path of Sufis") by Abū Bakr al-Kalābādhī (d. 380s/990s), *Qūt al-qulūb* ("The Nourishment of Hearts") by Abū Ṭālib al-Makkī (d. 386/996), *Jawāmiʿ ādāb al-ṣūfiyya* ("A Collection of Sufi Rules of

3 A.J. Arberry, *Sufism: An Account of the Mystics of Islam* (Mineola, NY: Dover Publications, 2002), 12.

4 Although little research has focused specifically on morality in the formative period of Sufism, useful recent works on Sufism and ethics include: P.J. Awn, "The Ethical Concerns of Classical Sufism", *The Journal of Religious Ethics* 11, no. 2 (Fall, 1983), 240–63; P.L. Heck, "Mysticism as Morality: The Case of Sufism", *Journal of Religious Ethics* 34, no. 2 (2006), 253–86; F. Meier, "A Book of Etiquette for Sufis", in idem, *Essays on Islamic Piety and Mysticism*, trans. J. O'Kane (Leiden: Brill, 1999), 49–92; L. Ridgeon, "Reading Sufi History through *Ādāb*: The Manners of Sufis, Jawānmardān and Qalandars", a draft article for the Proceedings for *Ethique et Spiritualité en Islam: l'adab Soufi*, forthcoming (I would like to express my thanks to Lloyd Ridgeon, who kindly shared his draft with me). For an account of the ethical concept of *Futuwwa* in Persian Sufism (chivalry, generosity; *javānmardī* in Persian), see L. Ridgeon, *Morals and Mysticism in Persian Sufism: A History of Sufi*-futuwwat *in Iran* (Abingdon, Oxon: Routledge, 2010).

Conduct") and *Kitāb ādāb al-ṣuḥba wa-ḥusn al-ʿishra* ("The Book of Rules of Companionship and Excellent Social Relations") by Abū ʿAbd al-Raḥmān al-Sulamī (d. 412/1021), and *al-Risāla al-Qushayriyya* ("The Treatise of al-Qushayrī") by Abu'l-Qāsim al-Qushayrī (d. 465/1072). The writings of al-Sarrāj and al-Kalābādhī are the earliest extant Sufi survey guides; the works of al-Makkī and al-Sulamī represent early devotional discussions on ethics and manners; and the treatise by al-Qushayrī has been one of the most popular Sufi manuals, combining hagiography and an overview of Sufi concepts and notions.[5]

The chapter commences with a brief overview of the Sufi understanding of ethics in the period prior to the main timeframe under investigation. It then introduces the lives and works of the five authors, before analysing their discussion of morality as regards their understanding of 1) the core components of Islamic tenets and the position of Sufism, 2) the importance of the Qur'ān and Ḥadīth in Sufi ethics, and 3) the harmonious relations between inner and outer moral obligations. As we will see, ethical conduct is conceived of as an acquired habit, requiring knowledge (of good and bad deeds), choice (of the former) and action (based on knowledge and choice). After examining the key themes in the writings of these five scholars, the concluding remarks address whether they represent an advance on the discussions in existing moral teachings as regards elucidating the extent of human free will in choosing good over bad, and whether they provide a deeper understanding of what makes good actions good, so that one can differentiate between good and bad conduct. In addition to these theological issues, reflection on the social contextualisation of ethical systems might suggest that the rules of conduct mirror the socio-political conditions extant at the time. The six works in question were written in different periods and locations: the conclusion will consider whether any change in the discourse on morality can be perceived between the earlier and the later works.

THE EARLY PERIOD

The period between the late fourth/tenth century and the early sixth/twelfth century, during which these treatises were compiled, is of significance for the history of Sufism in a number of ways. This century is often called the

[5] Although the focus of this article is on these five scholars, other renowned authors in this period include Abū Saʿd al-Khargūshī (d. 406/1015 or 407/1016), Abū Nuʿaym al-Iṣfahānī (d. 430/1038), ʿAlī b. ʿUthmān Hujwīrī (d. bet. 465/1073 and 469/1077), ʿAbd Allāḥ Anṣārī (d. 481/1089), Abū Ḥāmid al-Ghazālī (d. 505/1111), and the anonymous author of *Adab al-mulūk*.

"systematisation" period of Sufism, when Sufi teachings were given a theoretical basis and set down in documents. It is also a transitional period regarding the way in which the Sufi path was learned and taught. Sufism began to be institutionalised in the fifth-sixth/eleventh-twelfth centuries; before this period, the master–follower relationship was not as rigid or formalised as it would become after the establishment of Sufi orders (*ṭuruq*, sing. *ṭarīqa*).[6] The change in the nature of the learning style changed the focus of Sufi literature as regards morals and ethics. Unlike later Sufi *adab* literature, which often contained etiquette guides for novices, in the early Sufi survey works written during the pre-institutionalised period *adab* and moral vision (*khulq*) were directed towards God and His created beings in general.[7] We will see this in more detail below. The authors of these writings attempted to consolidate existing Sufi teachings as an intellectual discipline, promoting Sufism as the ideal way of living for believers. The Sufi moral disposition is therefore not a new product of the fourth/tenth century, and it is clear that the fundamental ethical concerns had currency before those early manuals were compiled.

A renunciatory form of piety (*zuhd*) emerged in the second/eighth century, with a focus on cultivation of the internal life. A letter from the renowned preacher al-Ḥasan al-Baṣrī (d. 110/728) to the Umayyad Caliph describes the lowly status of earthly beings: "This world has neither worth nor weight with God" because He "has created nothing more hateful to Him than this world".[8] Rejection of this world is also manifest in a saying by the famous Persian Sufi Abū Yazīd al-Bisṭāmī (d. c. 261/875): "This world is nothing; how can one renounce it?"[9] *Zuhd* in this period often takes the form of poverty, withdrawing from earthly affairs and yearning for the life beyond this world. However, as long as humans will be judged on the Last Day according to their conduct in this world, believers are not in a position to ignore physical and material reality. *Zuhd* can be regarded as an ethical way of life,[10] and the separation of the external and internal dimensions and the emphasis on knowledge of hidden matters (*ʿilm al-bāṭin*) seems to be proposed as a

6 Although there is disagreement over the nature of the early Shaykhs, both Meier and Silvers-Alario agree that the institutionalisation of Sufism begins around the fifth/eleventh century; Meier, *Essays*, 189–219; L. Silvers-Alario, "The Teaching Relationship in Early Sufism: A Reassessment of Fritz Meier's Definition of the *Shaykh al-tarbiya* and the *Shaykh al-taʿlīm*", *The Muslim World* 93 (January 2003), 69–97. Cf. C.E. Farah, "Rules Governing the Šayḫ-Muršid's Conduct", *Numen* 21, fasc. 2 (August 1974), 81–96.

7 Cf. *EI3*, "Adab, in Ṣūfism" (E.S. Ohlander); Heck, "Mysticism as Morality", 254 no. 1.

8 Arberry, *Sufism*, 34.

9 *Encyclopaedia Iranica*, s.v. "Besṭāmī (Basṭāmī), Bāyazīd" (G. Böwering).

10 Cf. L. Kinberg, "What is meant by *Zuhd*", *Studia Islamica* 61 (1985), 27–44.

means of finding a balance between the physicality and spirituality of human beings. As the renowned Sufi Abū Ḥafṣ al-Ḥaddād (d. c. 265/878–9) from Nīshāpūr states: "mannered behaviour of the exterior is the sign of mannered behaviour of the interior, because the Prophet – may God bless him and grant him salvation – said that if one's heart is humble, his limbs are humble". Proper social conduct is thus considered to be a measure of faith and hence a religious duty.[11]

The control of the lower self (*nafs*) was a crucial theme in ethical training. The importance of examining the self (*muḥāsabat al-nafs*) appears even in the name of the renowned Sufi ethicist from Baghdad, al-Ḥārith al-Muḥāsibī (d. 243/857). Al-Muḥāsibī preached that the core function of the heart is to fulfil God's will, a function that is easily hindered by various forms of egoism derived from the lower self, including "egoistic self-display (*riyāʾ*)", "pride (*kibr*)", "vanity (*ʿujb*)", and "self-delusion (*ghirra*)".[12] This dichotomous view of the lower self, and the heart (*qalb*) which was oriented towards God, can also be found outside the Baghdadi tradition, such as in the teachings of Sahl al-Tustarī (d. 283/896, Basra), and of al-Ḥakīm al-Tirmidhī (d. bet. 295/905 and 300/910, present-day Uzbekistan). For Sahl al-Tustarī, life in this world was a struggle between the heart and the *nafs*, while al-Tirmidhī similarly laid emphasis on the importance of conquering the lower self by following Divine law.[13] How to control the selfish ego, *nafs*, was thus one of the central issues in Sufi teachings, albeit issuing in a variety of different methods and approaches. Amid the varying opinions, however, there is a shared assumption regarding the importance of morality and the interconnectedness between external deeds and internal behaviour.

It should be recognised here that not all Sufi behaviour was considered socially acceptable; indeed, much of it was regarded as highly controversial. Unlike the "sober" type of Baghdad Sufi represented by al-Muḥāsibī and Abu'l-Qāsim al-Junayd (d. 298/910), their "intoxicated" counterparts were known for their seemingly intemperate utterances. The most frequently cited examples of such utterances include "Glory be to me (*subḥānī*)" from al-Bisṭāmī, and "I am the Truth (*ana al-ḥaqq*)" from al-Ḥusayn b. Manṣūr

[11] Al-Sulamī, *Ṭabaqāt*, 110. The first part also appears in: Abu'l-Qāsim al-Qushayrī, *al-Risāla al-Qushayriyya* (Beirut: Dār al-Kutub al-ʿIlmiyya, 2009), 45.

[12] M. A. Sells, *Early Islamic Mysticism: Sufi, Qur'an, Miʿraj, Poetic and Theological Writings* (Mahwah, NJ: 1996), 172.

[13] G. Böwering, *The Mystical Vision of Existence in Classical Islam: The Qurʾanic Hermeneutics of the Sufi Sahl at-Tustarī (d. 283/896)* (Berlin: Walter de Gruyter, 1980), 241; A.T. Karamustafa, *Sufism: The Formative Period* (Edinburgh: Edinburgh University Press, 2007), 45.

al-Ḥallāj (d. 309/922); the latter is one of the most famous figures of the "drunken" type, and his execution is sometimes considered to be a turning point in the history of Sufism. The reaction to such ecstatic sayings (*shaṭaḥāt*, sing. *shaṭḥ*), as uttered from a "higher" level of consciousness, led to a number of Sufis stressing the importance of appropriate interpretation of their "true" meaning and an appreciation of their proper context.[14] Although moral precepts had already existed in Sufism, as discussed above, the advocacy of *adab* in early Sufi literature was a means by which authors attempted to emphasise the legitimacy of the Sufi tradition in Islamic belief and practice.

LIVES AND WORKS

The first author to be discussed here, Abū Naṣr al-Sarrāj (d. 378/988), was originally from Ṭūs in Khurāsān. Travelling widely in Persia, Iraq, Syria, and Egypt, al-Sarrāj associated with prominent Sufi figures, including leading representatives of the Baghdadi tradition of al-Junayd, Ibn Khafīf al-Shīrāzī (d. 371/982) in Persia, Jaʿfar al-Khuldī (d. 348/960) in Baghdad, and Abu'l-Ḥasan Aḥmad Ibn Sālim (d. c. 356/967) in Basra – the latter being a disciple of Sahl al-Tustarī and the head of the Sālimiyya school.[15] Al-Sarrāj collected the sayings of around 200 Sufi authorities from written and oral sources, including thirty-nine Sufis whose teachings he noted in person; arranging these according to themes, he thus composed one of the earliest Sufi survey works, *Kitāb lumaʿ fi'l-taṣawwuf* ("The Book of Sparkling Lights in Sufism"), which also provides explanations of key Sufi concepts and terms.[16] By discussing the doctrines and practices of past Sufi masters based on the spirit of the Qur'ān and Ḥadīth, al-Sarrāj attempted to clarify the nature of Sufism, urging the reader to distinguish genuine from the pseudo-Sufis, whose number had

[14] Many Sufi classics contain chapters on *shaṭḥ* and *wajd* (the ecstatic state attained through the encounter with the Divine); e.g. Abū Naṣr al-Sarrāj, *The Kitāb al-lumaʿ fi'l-taṣawwuf of Abū Naṣr al-Sarrāj*, ed. R.A. Nicholson (Leiden: E.J. Brill, 1914), 302–4 on those who have reached the state of *wajd* (including al-Ḥallāj), 346–7 on *shaṭḥ*, 380–95 on al-Bisṭāmī (page numbers are from the Arabic part of the book [henceforth (Ar)]); Abū Bakr al-Kalābādhī, *al-Taʿarruf li-madhhab ahl al-taṣawwuf*, ed. ʿAbd al-Ḥalīm Maḥmūd and Ṭāhā ʿAbd al-Bāqī Surūr (Cairo: Dār Iḥyāʾ al-Kutub al-ʿArabiyya, 1380/1960–1), 112–13 on *wajd*, cf. 113–17.

[15] *EI2*, s.v. "al-Sarrādj" (P. Lory); A. Knysh, *Islamic Mysticism: A Short History* (Leiden: Brill, 2000), 118; Karamustafa, *Sufism*, 67.

[16] For Arabic editions, see *Lumaʿ*; missing chapters are in *Pages from the Kitāb al-lumaʿ of Abū Naṣr al-Sarrāj*, ed. A.J. Arberry (London: Luzac, 1947). The complete German translation is available as *Schlagrichter über das Sufitum*, trans. R. Gramlich (Stuttgart: Freiburger Islamistudien, 1990); and partial English translations appear in J. Renard, *Knowledge of God in Classical Sufism: Foundations of Islamic Mystical Theology* (New York; Mahwah, NJ: Paulist Press, 2004) 65–99, and Sells, *Mysticism*, 196–231.

become so large by his time that the true meaning of Sufism was thought to be misunderstood.[17] The many later authors who refer to al-Sarrāj's careful research include al-Kalābādhī, al-Sulamī, al-Qushayrī, and the famous Islamic thinker Abū Ḥāmid al-Ghazālī (d. 505/1111).

Another early Sufi survey work, *Kitāb al-taʿarruf li-madhhab ahl al-taṣawwuf* ("The Book of Acquaintance with the Path of Sufis"), was authored by Abū Bakr al-Kalābādhī (d. c. 385/995).[18] Although little is known about his life, it appears that he was from Bukhārā, studied the Ḥanafī school of law, and left a Ḥadīth commentary in addition to the *Taʿarruf*. Unlike al-Sarrāj, who is the only contemporary authority to appear in this treatise, al-Kalābādhī did not associate with any Sufi teachers, and (except for one figure) all the sayings of past masters he collected were drawn from written sources.[19] In the introduction al-Kalābādhī states that he has set out to clarify Sufi doctrines for the benefit of those who had misunderstood the true meanings of the allusions and expressions that Sufis often use, so that his book may refute "the false accusations by slanderers" and "the evil interpretation of the ignorant". At the same time, he hoped that his work would serve as a guide to those who yearned to embark on God's path, singling out his own local community in Transoxania as the main prospective readership.[20] Al-Kalābādhī's concise treatise on Sufi teachings was soon translated into Persian, and it attracted a number of commentaries, including one by the famous Ḥanbalī Sufi, ʿAbd Allāh Anṣārī (d. 481/1089).[21]

The fame of the third author, Abū Ṭālib al-Makkī (d. 386/996), lies in his work on ethics, *Qūt al-qulūb* ("The Nourishment of Hearts").[22] After being

[17] Al-Sarrāj, *Lumaʿ*(Ar), 2–3.

[18] Arabic edition: *Taʿarruf*; complete English translation: *The Doctrine of the Ṣūfīs: Kitāb al-taʿarruf li-madhhab ahl al-taṣawwuf*, trans. A. J. Arberry (Cambridge: Cambridge University Press, 1935); partial English translation: Renard, *Knowledge*, 100–11.

[19] Karamustafa, *Sufism*, 69; al-Kalābādhī, *Doctrine*, x–xi.

[20] Al-Kalābādhī, *Taʿarruf*, 20; cf. Karamustafa, *Sufism*, 70–1.

[21] Al-Kalābādhī, *Doctrine*, xii; Karamustafa, *Sufism*, 71; cf. C. Brockelmann, *Geschichte der Arabischen Litteratur* (Leiden: Brill, 1943), vol. 1, 217 and SI, 360.

[22] Among a number of Arabic editions, I use *Qūt al-qulūb fī muʿāmalat al-maḥbūb wa waṣf ṭarīq al-murīd ilā maqām al-tawḥīd*, 3 vols, ed. Maḥmūd b. Ibrāhīm b. Muḥammad al-Raḍwānī (Cairo: Dār al-Turāth, 2001), as it seems to be the only edition which has a description of the edited manuscripts. The complete German translation is available with a useful index: *Die Nahrung der Herzen: Abū Ṭālib al-Makkīs Qūt al-qulūb*, trans. R. Gramlich, 4 vols (Stuttgart: Franz Steiner Verlag, 1992–5); partial English translations: Renard, *Knowledge*, 112–263; W. Mohd Azam b. Mohd Amin, "An Evaluation of the *Qūt al-qulūb* of al-Makkī with an Annotated Translation of his *Kitāb al-tawba*" (unpublished PhD thesis, University of Edinburgh, 1991), 53–154; S. Yazaki, *Islamic Mysticism and Abū Ṭālib al-Makkī: The Role of the Heart* (Abingdon, Oxon: Routledge, 2013), 46–84; E.H. Douglas, "The Beard", *The Muslim World* 68, issue 2 (April 1978), 100–10.

educated in Mecca, al-Makkī went to Basra, where he became associated with the Sālimiyya school, and his final years he lived in Baghdad. He probably learned the Sufi way while in Mecca and Basra, either directly or indirectly from Ibn al-Aʿrābī (d. 341/952), a prominent Sufi teacher and Ḥadīth scholar who was affiliated with al-Junayd, as well as from Ibn Sālim, the head of the Sālimiyya school.[23] Al-Makkī also received a solid education in Ḥadīth, as evidenced by the thorough Ḥadīth orientation manifest in his *Qūt*. That work, possibly the only extant work of al-Makkī,[24] is often considered to be one of the earliest Sufi manuals, together with the *Lumaʿ* of al-Sarrāj and the *Taʿarruf* of al-Kalābādhī – although the latter two treatises differ from the *Qūt* in a number of ways (see below for further discussion: p. 84). Al-Makkī's influence can be seen in many later writings within and beyond Sufism, especially in the works of the Ḥanbalī scholar Ibn al-Farrāʾ (d. 458/1066), the famous thinker al-Ghazālī, Ibn ʿAbbād al-Rundī (d. 792/1390) from al-Andalus, and the Salafī reformer Jamāl al-Dīn al-Qāsimī (d. 1914); a possible link with a Jewish judge in al-Andalus has also been discussed.[25]

The next two treatises to be examined, *Jawāmiʿ ādāb al-ṣūfiyya* ("A Collection of Sufi Rules of Conduct") and *Kitāb ādāb al-ṣuḥba wa-ḥusn al-ʿishra* ("The Book of Rules of Companionship and Excellent Social Relations"), were authored by the well-known Sufi hagiographer and Qurʾān commentator Abū ʿAbd al-Raḥmān al-Sulamī (d. 412/1021).[26] Born in Nīshāpūr and educated by his grandfather Abū ʿAmr Ismāʿīl b. Nujayd (d. 366/976–7), a famous Ḥadīth scholar and a leader of the Malāmatiyya, al-Sulamī received a thorough education in the study of Ḥadīth and the Sufi tradition, as well as in Kalām (especially Ashʿarī) and jurisprudence (especially Shāfiʿī). His Sufi teachers include Abu'l-Qāsim al-Naṣrābādhī (d. 367/977–8), a Shāfiʿī Ḥadīth scholar and follower of Abū Bakr al-Shiblī

[23] The same Ibn Sālim whose gatherings al-Sarrāj often attended. There is no evidence for al-Makkī and al-Sarrāj having known each other; see Yazaki, *al-Makkī*, 96.

[24] For the works of al-Makkī, see Yazaki, *al-Makkī*, 22–8; for the authenticity of his alleged work, *ʿIlm al-qulūb*; see idem, "A Pseudo-Abū Ṭālib al-Makkī?: The Authenticity of *ʿIlm al-qulūb*", *Arabica* 59 (2012), 650–84.

[25] For the life of al-Makkī, a comparison of the three treatises, an account of his influence, and a possible link between al-Makkī and an Andalusian Jewish judge, see Yazaki, *al-Makkī*, 12–21, 85–94, 95–144, 145–73.

[26] Arabic editions: *Jawāmiʿ ādāb al-ṣūfiyya and ʿUyūb al-nafs wa-mudāwātuhā*, ed. E. Kohlberg (Jerusalem: Jerusalem Academic Press, 1976); *Kitāb ādāb aṣ-ṣuḥba*, ed. M. J. Kister (Jerusalem: Israel Oriental Society, 1954). There is a complete English translation of the *Jawāmiʿ* with a useful survey at the beginning: *A Collection of Sufi Rules of Conduct*, trans. E. Biagi (Cambridge: Islamic Texts Society, 2010). The two works contain a great deal of repetition and their structure is somewhat random. Helpful summaries for the *Jawāmiʿ* include: *Collection*, xxxiv–xxxvii; *Jawāmiʿ*, 11–13; for *al-Ṣuḥba*: *Collection*, xix–xxi; *Ṣuḥba*, 5–6.

(d. 334/946) in Baghdad. Al-Sulamī travelled widely in Khurāsān and Iraq, returned to his town after the pilgrimage, and established a small Sufi convent. A prolific author, he wrote a number of books on topics including Sufi hagiography, Qur'ān commentary, and Sufi ideas. But many of his works are lost: probably the best-known work by al-Sulamī, *Ṭabaqāt al-ṣūfiyya* ("Sufi Biographical Dictionary"), is a summary of his massive *Ta'rīkh al-ṣūfiyya* ("Sufi History"), which is no longer extant. He composed many books on Sufi *ādāb*, but again the major opus, *Sunan al-ṣūfiyya* ("Sufi Practices and Customs"), is lost. Its contents, however, are reflected in his extant short writings on Sufi manners, including the *Jawāmiʿ* and *al-Ṣuḥba*.[27] Al-Sulamī was an outstanding scholar among his contemporaries, with a large number of followers, including another renowned Sufi author, al-Qushayrī, who refers to al-Sulamī on almost every page of his *Risāla*.[28]

Abu'l-Qāsim al-Qushayrī (d. 465/1072), the final author to be discussed here, is known for his famous compendium of Sufism, *al Risāla al-Qushayriyya* ("The Treatise of al-Qushayrī").[29] Al-Qushayrī was born in northern Khurāsān and received the education typical of a "country squire" of his time: *adab*, Arabic language and literature, chivalry, and weaponry.[30] While in Nīshāpūr, he frequently attended lectures by the well-known Sufi master Abū ʿAlī al-Daqqāq (d. 405/1015), who was a disciple of al-Naṣrābādhī and belonged to the Baghdadi Sufi tradition. Al-Qushayrī was later introduced to al-Sulamī, another notable Sufi and follower of al-Naṣrābādhī, and his respect for both al-Daqqāq and al-Sulamī can be seen in their recurrent appearances in the *Risāla*. As with al-Sulamī, the themes which al-Qushayrī studied included Ḥadīth, Ashʿarī Kalām, and Shāfiʿī jurisprudence. His writings, while focusing on Sufi ideas, indicate his deep knowledge of Islamic sciences: for example, his important interpretation of the Qur'ān introduces subtle meanings (*laṭā'if*) of the verses based on the principles of revealed law and Kalām.[31]

[27] Abū Bakr Aḥmad al-Bayhaqī (d. 458/1066) incorporates extracts from the *Sunan* in his works; cf. al-Sulamī, *Collection*, xxxiii.

[28] For the life of al-Sulamī, see, e.g. al-Sulamī, *Ṭabaqāt*, 19–32; *EI2*, s.v. "al-Sulamī" (G. Böwering); al-Sulamī, *Collection*, xv–xvi.

[29] Arabic edition: *Risāla*; apart from a complete English translation: *Al-Qushayri's Epistle on Sufism*, trans. A.D. Knysh (Reading: Garnet, 2007), there are partial English translations (for details, see K. Honerkamp, review of the *Epistle*, *Journal of Islamic Studies* 23, issue 3 (2012), 376–7). A German translation is also available: *Das Sendschreiben al-Qušayrīs über das Sufitum*, trans. R. Gramlich (Wiesbaden: F. Steiner, 1989).

[30] *EI2*, s.v. "al-Ḳushayrī" (H. Halm).

[31] Abu'l-Qāsim al-Qushayrī, *Tafsīr al-Qushayrī laṭā'if al-ishārāt*, ed. ʿAbd al-Ḥalīm Maḥmūd, 6 vols in 3 (Cairo: al-Maktaba al-Tawfīqiyya, n.d.). See also a careful survey of the *Laṭā'if* by M. Nguyen, in *Sufi Master and Qur'an Scholar: Abū'l-Qāsim al-Qushayrī and the Laṭā'if al-ishārāt* (Oxford: Oxford University Press, 2012). For the life of al-Qushayrī, see Nguyen,

ISLAM AND SUFISM

At the outset of the *Luma*ʿ, al-Sarrāj emphasises that God has clearly set the foundations of religion in the Qurʾān by placing "the most excellent" of the believers in faith just after the angels: "God bears witness that there is no god but He – and the angels, and men possessed of knowledge – upholding justice" (3:18/16).[32] This is reiterated by a saying of the Prophet: "Those possessing knowledge are the heirs of the prophets" (*al-ʿulamāʾ warathat al-anbiyāʾ*).[33] Al-Sarrāj argues that the elevated believers with proper knowledge are "those who adhere (*muʿtaṣimūn*) to the Book of God Most High, those who strive (*mujtahidūn*) to follow God's Messenger – may God bless him and grant him salvation –, those who are guided (*muqtidūn*) by the Companions and Successors, and those who follow (*sālikūn*) the path of His God-fearing friends and His virtuous servants".[34]

Among the heirs of the prophets, al-Sarrāj identifies three types of scholars: followers of Ḥadīth, students of jurisprudence, and Sufis. All draw upon the same three religious sciences – the knowledge of the Qurʾān, the Sunna, and the realities of belief – but they differ as regards knowledge (*ʿilm*) and action (*ʿamal*). This is a key matter in faith, because, according to al-Sarrāj, "knowledge is connected to action, and action is connected to sincere devotion (*ikhlāṣ*)", since the believer is supposed to serve God both in his knowledge and in action.[35] After describing the characteristics of the scholars of Ḥadīth and jurisprudence, al-Sarrāj states that the Sufis' knowledge and methods are not in disagreement with those scholars. However, based on those "exoteric sciences" (*al-ʿulūm al-ẓāhir*), Sufis ascend to higher stages of "various devotional services, the true nature of pious deeds, and graceful moral characteristics (*akhlāq*)", because the Sufi path is the most solid in respect of religious matters.[36]

A similar argument appears in the *Taʿarruf*. At the outset of the seventy-five chapters, al-Kalābādhī extols Sufis for being "excellent, noble and pious"

Sufi Master, 23–54; *EI2*, s.v. "al-Ḳushayrī" (H. Halm); al-Qushayrī, *Epistle*, xxi–xxiii; Karamustafa, *Sufism*, 97–8 (see also 111 nos 35, 39).

32 The translation of the Qurʾān is from *The Koran Interpreted*, trans. A.J. Arberry (Oxford: Oxford University Press, 1998). However, since the numbering Arberry uses is different from the standard system, I include both verse numbers when they are different: standard number / verse number in Arberry's *Koran*, for the sake of convenience.

33 Al-Sarrāj, *Lumaʿ*(Ar), 5.

34 Ibid.

35 Ibid.(Ar), 5–6. *Ikhlāṣ* also designates "purification of faith", which is an important Qurʾanic concept. See, e.g., T. Izutsu, *Ethico-Religious Concepts in the Qurʾān* (Montréal: McGill University Press, 1966) 192–3; idem, *God and Man in the Koran: Semantics of the Koranic Weltanschauung* (Tokyo: Keio Institute of Cultural and Linguistic Studies, 1964), 102–3.

36 Al-Sarrāj, *Lumaʿ*(Ar), 10–11.

among God's created beings, because "He confined them to the God-fearing word and turned their souls away from this world". Sufis are those who "understand God, journey towards God, and avert themselves from what is other than God", as their "ears are attentive and their innermost parts are pure". Sufis possess "virtues" (*faḍāʾil*), they are "luminous" and "chosen", since, according to al-Kalābādhī, Sufis are those who follow the true path of Islam.[37] All the religious obligations are clearly set out in the Qurʾān and Ḥadīth, and Sufis agree, al-Kalābādhī emphasises, that those obligations are not to be neglected "in any way by anyone", even by "a righteous one, a friend of God (*walī*), a gnostic", or one who has "reached the highest degrees and the noblest religious stations".[38]

Al-Makkī does not discuss the position of Sufism within Islam in his *Qūt*, although his understanding of the core components of faith based on the Islamic texts is the same. The *Qūt* begins with thirteen Qurʾanic verses emphasising the importance of proper conduct in this world.[39] These verses stress that true faith in God and right deeds are the key to being close to Him and for entry to Paradise – the first verse, for example, reads: "And whosoever desires the world to come and strives after it as he should, being a believer – those, their striving shall be thanked" (17:19/20). Over the following sections, al-Makkī describes the merits of worship and prayer in detail.[40] The *Lumaʿ*, *al-Taʿarruf*, and the *Qūt* are sometimes considered to be the earliest extant Sufi manuals, but the character of the *Qūt* differs markedly from that of the other two works. Unlike al-Sarrāj and al-Kalābādhī, who seek to clarify Sufi teachings by beginning their books with an overview of Sufism and the position of Sufism in Islam, al-Makkī makes no such effort in the *Qūt*. Nor does combating the misrepresentation of Sufi doctrines – clearly a prime motivation for al-Sarrāj and al-Kalābādhī in compiling their works – seem to be his main motivation. The *Qūt* is full of warnings and teachings, and seems to present itself as an encyclopaedic moral guide for Islam in general, rather than a specifically Sufi survey work like the *Lumaʿ* and the *Taʿarruf*.[41]

Unlike al-Makkī, and similar to al-Sarrāj and al-Kalābādhī, the status of Sufism within Islam is a great concern for al-Sulamī. In the introduction to the *Jawāmiʿ*, al-Sulamī states that this is a book on *ādāb* of "those who have

[37] All of the citations so far are from al-Kalābādhī, *Taʿarruf*, 19–20.

[38] Ibid., 58–9.

[39] Q. 17:19, 42:20, 53:39–41, 69:24, 6:132, 34:37, 7:43, 32:17, 29:58–9, 6:127.

[40] Al-Makkī, *Qūt*, vol. 1, 10–156; the Qurʾanic verse is from p. 10.

[41] Despite the different motivations, a wide range of topics related to Islamic piety in the *Qūt* cover items discussed among Sufis, and this is part of the reason why the *Qūt* is usually considered a Sufi work; cf. Yazaki, *al-Makkī*, 92–4, 140–4.

reached spiritual states" and "those who are well-advanced among friends of God (*awliyāʾ Allāh*)"; those people are called Sufis who follow the path of the venerable ancestors, and who shape their nature with morals. However, according to al-Sulamī, some people disapprove of the Sufis without knowing the true meaning of their knowledge, despite the deep understanding of Islamic tenets manifest in Sufism. He hopes that, through his treatise, the ignorant will learn about "their way of life and their rules of conduct (*ādāb*)", and regard them as "they deserve".[42]

In the *Risāla*, a well-arranged Sufi survey work, al-Qushayrī expresses grave concerns about both the misunderstanding of Sufi theories and practices, and that the true Sufis are now very few in number. He begins by stating that this is a book for the "Sufi community" (*jamāʿat al-ṣūfiyya*), understood as the community of the chosen friends of God to whom He has expressed preference "over all of His servants, and after His messengers and prophets". God has granted Sufis "success in performing *ādāb* of servitude", so that they are capable of fulfilling all their obligations. The *Risāla* is hence intended to elucidate the proper manners (*ādāb*) of past masters, their "morals (*akhlāq*), their relations among themselves (*muʿāmalāt*), and their belief (*ʿaqāʾid*) in their hearts".[43]

Al-Qushayrī classifies the best Muslims after the Prophet Muḥammad into chronological groups. The first three are: the Companions (*ṣaḥāba*), the Followers (*tābiʿūn*) who are the adherents of the Companions, and the Followers of the Followers (*atbāʿ al-tābiʿīn*). After this, people become increasingly diverse; among the excellent are those who have renounced the world (*zuhhād*) and those who serve God alone (*ʿubbād*). According to al-Qushayrī, the term *taṣawwuf* began to be used for the greatest believers before the second/ninth century.[44] The fundamental principles of faith lie in the complete recognition of Divine oneness (*tawḥīd*), upon which the true Sufi path is based. Among the many sayings cited in the book concerning this topic, al-Qushayrī emphasises that the first obligation imposed on God's created beings is to obtain experiential knowledge (*maʿrifa*) of Him, since belief is acceptance of "what the Truth lets [the heart] know among the Hidden".[45] Al-Qushayrī laments, however, that the true Sufis have disappeared, leaving only their traces in the present age, because "piety has

[42] All of the citations so far are from al-Sulamī, *Jawāmiʿ*(Ar), 1–2.
[43] All of the citations in this paragraph are from al-Qushayrī, *Risāla*, 8–9.
[44] Ibid., 21.
[45] Ibid., 11–12, 14.

vanished" and "greed has become stronger".[46] In his *Risāla*, al-Qushayrī attempts to elucidate the real – yet jeopardised – Sufi doctrines and practices as based on proper understanding of the Islamic texts.

THE QURʾĀN AND ḤADĪTH IN SUFI ETHICS

Based on what he asserts as the correct interpretations of the Qur'ān and Ḥadīth, al-Sarrāj attaches great importance to proper manners in religion. The *Lumaʿ* includes an extended section on *ādāb*, wherein he quotes a saying of the Prophet – "God educated me and made my manners exquisite" – as well as one by Ibn al-Mubārak (d. 181/797), who wrote a famous book on *zuhd* – "We are in greater need of a little manners than of abundant knowledge." A number of quotes from the Prophet and past masters, cited at the beginning of that section, affirm the significance of *ādāb* in seeking to be close to God. According to al-Sarrāj, people are divided into three classes in terms of ethical conduct: "the people of this world, the people of religion, and the distinguished people among the people of religion". The *ādāb* of the worldly people mostly concern eloquence of language, rhetoric, and poetry, while religious people mainly engage with discipline of the body and mind, abandonment of lusts, and pious deeds.[47]

The Sufis, the third group, devote themselves to purification of the heart and mindfulness of what is innermost, and their *ādāb* is outstanding among all others, touching upon every avenue of life. Al-Sarrāj then enumerates rules of conduct for Sufis in a wide range of situations from religious obligations (ablution, prayer, almsgiving, fasting, pilgrimage) and everyday life activities (when at home, dressing, companionship, for those who are married and have children, for those sitting alone, and those sitting in a group), to specific occasions (for mealtimes, gatherings, receptions, travel, hunger, sickness, death) and Sufi-related affairs (at the time of *samāʿ* practice, ecstasy (*wujūd*); for Shaykhs, aspirants; when given a worldly thing).[48] Apart from the last group, the topics covered here are not related specifically to Sufis, and appear in many Ḥadīth collections, notably in the book on *adab* in the *Ṣaḥīḥ al-Bukhārī*. In delineating the wide coverage of Sufi ethics, al-Sarrāj demonstrates not only the importance of the Qur'ān and Ḥadīth in the Sufi tradition,

[46] Ibid., 8. (After complaining about the decline of Sufism, al-Qushayrī gives a justification for his action, since speaking ill of others is not commendable. According to al-Qushayrī, he is simply worried about the Sufi path, he has been moderate in laying blame, and so on; ibid., 9.)
[47] All the quotes so far are from al-Sarrāj, *Lumaʿ*(Ar), 142–3.
[48] Ibid.(Ar), 143–211.

but also the excellence of Sufi understanding and application of key Islamic teachings.

The prominence of the Qurʾān and Ḥadīth in Sufi morality also appears in the *Taʿarruf*, where al-Kalābādhī stresses that the salient duty of believers is to follow the rules of conduct (*ādāb*) in the revealed law. No one can abolish the religious obligations prescribed in the Qurʾān and Ḥadīth, and variation upon them can be based only on what the "Muslims have agreed upon" and as set out by the "principles of the Sharīʿa".[49] According to al-Kalābādhī, this is agreed by all Sufis. It is important to note that although he places Sufis highest among believers, this implies no concessions for them as regards moral obligations. The only possible exceptions are those that can be legitimised through agreement of all believers (not only Sufis) and according to the revealed law.[50] What is special about Sufis is, as stated in the introduction to the *Taʿarruf*, their understanding and their diligence in following the path towards God.

Al-Makkī also bases his argument upon the Islamic texts. The *Qūt* is full of citations from the Qurʾān, Ḥadīth, and the sayings of pious ancestors, being distinguished from the other works discussed in this chapter primarily by its tendency to rely on Tradition-oriented accounts, drawing quotations from Ḥadīth scholars and past masters rather than other Sufi scholars.[51] Following the revealed law has paramount importance for al-Makkī. Concerning the meaning of the word "knowledge" in a well-known Ḥadīth – "the quest for knowledge is a religious duty upon every Muslim" – al-Makkī states that this knowledge refers to the Five Pillars upon which Islam is based. Al-Makkī underlines the close link between action and knowledge, saying that "conduct is never right without knowledge of it, since the beginning of conduct is knowledge of it"; accordingly, knowledge of action is just as much a moral obligation as is action itself.[52] Later in the *Qūt*, al-Makkī includes a section on the Five Pillars, providing a detailed clarification of the duties upon believers.[53] Through his deep reading of the Qurʾān and Ḥadīth, ethics for al-Makkī becomes a private and public demonstration of the harmonious relationship between knowledge and action.

49 Al-Kalābādhī, *Taʿarruf*, 59.

50 Here al-Kalābādhī seems to differ from Sahl al-Tustarī, who states that the prophets and God's close friends are destined to enter Heaven without going through the final judgement (but not other mortals); Karamustafa, *Sufism*, 42.

51 See the discussion on the religious authorities cited in the *Qūt*, in Yazaki, *al-Makkī*, 43–5.

52 Al-Makkī, *Qūt*, vol. 1, 363, 367.

53 Ibid., vol. 3, 1171–268.

The significance of reconciling one's behaviour on both the internal and the external dimensions, based on proper understanding of the Islamic tenets, also appears in the *Jawāmiʿ*. According to al-Sulamī, Sufis must follow the *ādāb* of the revealed law, must place their trust in God completely, and "ought not to do secretly anything that he is ashamed to [do] publicly".[54] As it is declared in the Qur'ān, "Ah lo! thou art a tremendous nature (*khuluq ʿaẓīm*)" (68:4/3),[55] God bestowed the "most sublime adornment in the *adab*" upon the Prophet Muḥammad.[56] This is confirmed by a saying of the Prophet already cited above: "Verily, God educated me and made my manners exquisite. He then ordered me to be noble-hearted with moral traits."[57] Al-Sulamī then quotes numerous sayings which reiterate the importance of ethical conduct for believers: "Every matter has something which renders a service to it. What serves faith is *adab*"; *adab* is "excellent companionship (*ḥusn al-ṣuḥba*) with the elderly", respecting them and observing the example of their rules of conduct and morals, as well as with one's comrades and friends.[58] In his treatise, al-Sulamī discusses certain themes which are specific to Sufis (e.g. *samāʿ* and *khalwa*); however, the majority of the topics he addresses have wider relevance to ethical values in Islam, or even for human concerns in general – for example, kindness, generosity, and consideration for others before oneself.[59]

The universal validity of Islam's ethical rules is expressed more explicitly in al-Sulamī's other treatise, *al-Ṣuḥba*, the contents of which are very similar to those of the *Jawāmiʿ*, but with more focus on social behaviour. Introducing the text with the same Qur'anic verse as he uses for the *Jawāmiʿ* (68:4/3), al-Sulamī praises the Prophet Muḥammad for his "excellent social relationships" and "noble companionship", since, with mercy from God, the Prophet was never "harsh and hard of heart" to others, as shown at 3:159/153.[60] The Prophet is naturally the exemplar of right behaviour for all believers, and *al-Ṣuḥba* thus contains approximately eighty Ḥadīth reporting on his morality and detailing his manners in dealing with others. The ethical injunctions that al-Sulamī enumerates in this short treatise again reflect moral values that are common across cultures: for example, forgiveness (*ṣafḥ*), toleration

54 Al-Sulamī, *Jawāmiʿ*(Ar), 22, 25.

55 The translation here is from *The Meaning of the Glorious Qur'an*, trans. M.M. Pickthall (New Delhi: Adam Publishers & Distributors, 2002).

56 Al-Sulamī, *Jawāmiʿ*(Ar), 1–2.

57 This is a well-known Ḥadīth among Sufis. The first part of the report is also quoted by al-Sarrāj (*Lumaʿ*(Ar), 142); see above, p. 86.

58 Al-Sulamī, *Jawāmiʿ*(Ar), 3–5.

59 Ibid.(Ar), 35, 62, 50, 10; 11, 8, 14–15, 41–2.

60 Al-Sulamī, *Ṣuḥba*(Ar), 22.

(*iḥtimāl*), maintaining a sound heart (*salāmat al-ṣadr*) towards others, keeping their secrets, and honouring them more than oneself.[61]

Relying heavily on the teachings of al-Sulamī, al-Qushayrī organises Sufi doctrines according to themes, each of which is supported by numerous Qur'anic verses and Ḥadīth. In the section on morality (*khuluq*), which begins with the same Qur'anic verse as the treatises by al-Sulamī (68:4/3), al-Qushayrī confirms the close link between being the best believer and having the noblest character. Citing numerous sayings, al-Qushayrī emphasises that "Sufism is morality", and that morality should also apply to non-humans – he includes a story against the mistreatment of a chicken. The Prophet says: "indeed you will not satisfy people with your money, but satisfy them [with] your delightful facial expression and excellent ethical nature"; thus, this-worldly desire is not commended, but believers are not to focus solely on their own spiritual growth either.[62] Interaction with others reveals one's true character, since *khuluq* is about forgiveness, as in Sura 7:199, even if a slave girl accidently killed one's infant son, or thieves took all of one's belongings.[63]

Khuluq also encompasses acceptance of harsh treatment from other created beings without any vexation or anger appearing in one's heart in return – as the Prophet says, "Indeed I have been sent [to induce] mercy, not punishment."[64] Al-Qushayrī includes a story designed to show that it is not right to benefit from others' bad behaviour, nor to deprive those others of benefits for the same reason. Constant self-examination is therefore essential for believers, since those with bad character tend to focus on the character of others.[65] In the section on *adab*, al-Qushayrī further confirms that the moral precepts of Sufism are based on the fundamental principles of Islam, since the true recognition of Divine oneness (*tawḥīd*) is an obligation which requires faith (*īmān*); faith is an obligation which necessitates the revealed law (*sharīʿa*); and the observation of the law is an obligation which must be fulfilled with good manners (*adab*). The one who has no *adab* has therefore "neither the revealed law, nor faith, nor [declaration of] *tawḥīd*".[66]

[61] Ibid.(Ar), 29, 49, 33, 45, 44.
[62] Al-Qushayrī, *Risāla*, 275–6.
[63] Ibid., 278, 276–7.
[64] Ibid., 278, 280.
[65] Ibid., 279.
[66] Ibid., 316–7.

INNER AND OUTER MORALITY

Faith exists not only in the mind of believers, but also in their communal life. Religious knowledge, al-Sarrāj emphasises, is therefore both outward (*ẓāhir*) and inward (*bāṭin*). As stated in the Qur'ān, both aspects are indispensable for belief: "He has lavished on you His blessings, outward and inward" (31:20/19). External deeds reflect the conduct of the body, including acts of devotion (*ʿibādāt*) and obeying legal precepts (*aḥkām*), while internal deeds reflect the condition of the heart, being religious stations (*maqāmāt*) and states (*aḥwāl*).[67] Although knowledge of both the exterior and interior is important, al-Sarrāj emphasises that believers are in need of the science of the interior, that is the religious stations and states, and self-exertion (*mujāhada*), through which Sufis devote themselves to attain experiential knowledge (*maʿrifa*).[68] A distinctive characteristic of Sufism is not only its understanding of "rules of conduct (*ādāb*), spiritual states and various types of knowledge", but also the practical way in which it applies its theoretical understanding.[69]

In a chapter on belief (*īmān*), al-Kalābādhī also reiterates the importance of external conduct among Sufis. According to the Prophet, belief consists of "a confirmation with the tongue, a certification with the heart, and an act with the limbs". Faith is both internal and external; neither can be overlooked. Performing moral duties with the body is therefore a crucial component of belief.[70] Al-Kalābādhī stresses that "internal faith without external [faith] is a weak faith", such that even if believers succeed in improving their inward qualities through "strength and religious certainty (*yaqīn*)", they will be diminished if the Divine obligations are not performed.[71]

As indicated by the title of his work, *The Nourishment of Hearts*, for al-Makkī the proper behaviour of the heart is crucial for faith. The role of the heart is to understand the quality of the Divine, and this is the place where God resides in this world.[72] Cardio-gnosis closely relates to bodily conduct in ethics, since the internal activity of the heart is the source of the external behaviour of the limbs; and, conversely, the outward mannered conduct of believers is a measure of the inner activity of their hearts. According to al-Makkī, believers should first strive to control their external actions against their lower selves and this-worldly desires;[73] then, upon attaining full

[67] Al-Sarrāj, *Lumaʿ*(Ar), 23–4.
[68] Ibid.(Ar), 18.
[69] Ibid.(Ar), 11.
[70] Al-Kalābādhī, *Taʿarruf*, 79–80.
[71] Ibid., 81–2.
[72] Al-Makkī, *Qūt*, vol. 1, 343, 333.
[73] Ibid., vol. 1, 339.

understanding of the meaning of the revealed law, the conduct of believers among people will be praiseworthy rather than ostentatious. Although the title of his work appears to stress the spiritual aspects of faith, in his *Qūt* al-Makkī never fails to emphasise the paramount importance of practical activity in the believer's life.

According to al-Makkī, the Qur'ān identifies five characteristics of those who possess knowledge of God and the hereafter: fear of God, submission, modesty, moral character (*ḥusn al-khulq*), and renunciation.[74] A believer must pursue the training of both mind and body, seeking improvement both in individual virtue as well as life in community. Al-Makkī clearly separates knowledge of the interior from that of the exterior; however, "neither of them can manage without the other" – they are as inseparable as "Islam and faith" and "the body and the heart".[75] Not all types of knowledge meet with his approval, however: the quest for "superfluous knowledge" (*fuḍūl al-ʿilm*) is of no value for the hereafter, and does not bring one closer to God. "Excellent knowledge" (*al-ʿilm al-mifḍal*) is also insufficient, since it is abstracted from action.[76] Al-Makkī quotes al-Ḥasan al-Baṣrī to this end: "know what you wish to know, but, by God, God Most High will not reward you for it until you act [upon it]".[77] Those who have real knowledge, al-Makkī implies, do not simply transmit Traditions, but also observe them; a true person of action also behaves nobly towards others, for religious knowledge does not only concern full awareness of the Oneness of God, but also a complete understanding of ethical injunctions and the difference between the permissible (*ḥalāl*) and the forbidden (*ḥarām*).[78]

Al-Sulamī also emphasises the importance of both external and internal codes of behaviour (*ādāb al-ẓawāhir* and *ādāb al-bawāṭin*), based on the same Qur'anic verse as cited in the *Lumaʿ* (31:20/19), and he includes a wide range of topics in the *Jawāmiʿ*.[79] Sufis ought to apply their knowledge both outwardly and inwardly, al-Sulamī claims, citing a saying of al-Muḥāsibī: "If one strives internally, God will bequeath him excellent behaviour externally, and if one improves his behaviour externally and internally, God will bequeath him the right guidance to Him."[80]

[74] Ibid., vol. 1, 407; the Qur'anic verses cited here are: 35:28, 3:199, 15:88–9, 3:159, 28:80.
[75] Ibid., vol. 1, 366.
[76] Ibid., vol. 1, 369.
[77] Ibid., vol. 1, 373.
[78] Ibid., vol. 1, 375, 365. In the last section of the *Qūt*, al-Makkī clarifies the lawful and unlawful, and discusses the dubious matters that lie between them (ibid., vol. 3, 1711–38).
[79] Al-Sulamī, *Jawāmiʿ*(Ar), 1.
[80] Ibid.(Ar), 59–60 (almost the same quote appears on p. 25 of that publication).

Harmonious coordination of both types of *ādāb* is essential, since innermost manners (*adab al-sirr*) are required to purify the heart from weakness, while the code of conduct for the bodily members is designed to keep them from sin and wicked acts.[81] The thoughts of a believer must be constantly directed towards God alone, and Sufis should keep their lower self (*nafs*) under constant scrutiny, never feeling satisfied with its condition.[82] Arrogance clouds judgement and humility must be observed, as one of the sayings in the *Jawāmiʿ* reiterates: "The one who examines the defects of others is blind to defects of his self."[83]

Al-Sulamī also addresses the rules of conduct for the exterior: for example, Sufis ought to eat little, drink little, sleep little, speak little, share food, wear rags, and behave properly.[84] The *adab* of poverty (*faqr*) and of isolation (*tajrīd*) from this world is commended throughout the book.[85] However, earning one's own living also has its place in a Sufi's life, as long as s/he avoids indulgence in desire, since begging should also be avoided.[86] The essential point is to embrace *ādāb* both in the heart and in the body. Al-Sulamī cites the saying, "if you see the sign of a poor man in his appearance, do not anticipate anything admirable from him",[87] implying that vanity and ostentation are strictly forbidden. The discussion in the *Ṣuḥba* bears a great deal of similarity to that in the *Jawāmiʿ*, emphasising the importance of a harmonious relationship between the internal and external faiths.[88]

Drawing on his previous teachings, al-Qushayrī highlights three important qualities of a believer: excellent *adab*, high morality, and the ability to avoid suspicious matters.[89] Action is absolutely necessary, as stressed in the quote from Ibn al-Mubārak regarding the priority of manners over knowledge (cited above), which is also cited in the *Lumaʿ*.[90] In addition to the two sections specific to *khuluq* and *adab*, al-Qushayrī includes sections on humility, modesty, patience, chivalry, generosity, rules of travel, companionship, and advice for aspirants. *Adab* is the "combination of all excellent characteristics", both inward and outward. Al-Qushayrī also stresses the

81 Ibid.(Ar), 14.
82 Ibid.(Ar), 58, 6, 8.
83 Ibid.(Ar), 37.
84 Ibid.(Ar), 12, 40–4.
85 E.g. ibid.(Ar), 8, 29, 40; 16, 47.
86 Ibid.(Ar), 18, 20, 56.
87 Ibid.(Ar), 29–30 (lit. "the light (*ḍawʾ*) of a poor man").
88 Al-Sulamī, *Ṣuḥba*(Ar), 29.
89 Al-Qushayrī, *Risāla*, 318.
90 Ibid., 317; cf. al-Sarrāj, *Lumaʿ*(Ar), 142.

importance of proper education from childhood, since good manners are an acquired habit.[91]

CONCLUDING REMARKS

This chapter has examined the essential principles of Islam, the importance of morality in the Qurʾān and Ḥadīth, and the significance of a harmonious balance between internal and external ethical behaviour, as they appear in the writings of five prominent authors in the early history of Sufism: al-Sarrāj, al-Kalābādhī, al-Makkī, al-Sulamī, and al-Qushayrī. As can be seen in his extensive list of *ādāb*, for al-Sarrāj ethical conduct essentially concerns every matter humans might encounter in this world, regardless of the division between internal and external, because God's presence should be felt in each moment of life. At the beginning of the *Lumaʿ*, al-Sarrāj refers to a famous Ḥadīth in which the Prophet questions Gabriel regarding submission (*islām*), belief (*īmān*), and *iḥsān* (lit. doing well). *Islām* concerns the external dimension, *īmān* both the external and internal, and *iḥsān* refers to the ultimate reality of the external and internal dimensions. According to the Prophet, *iḥsān* means: "You serve God as if you saw Him, for even though you do not see Him, He sees you."[92] The constant feeling of Divine presence should lead believers to pursue proper behaviour, both inside and outside, in all aspects of life. In his *Lumaʿ*, al-Sarrāj confirms that Sufis are those who follow this important Islamic principle.

The high status of Sufism in Islam is also praised in the *Taʿarruf*. Al-Kalābādhī begins his text by citing two lists of works on Sufism: one on the sciences of allusions (*ʿulūm al-ishāra*), and the other on conduct (*muʿāmalāt*). In the latter, he enumerates ten earlier Sufi authors, claiming that those authors combined the science of Ḥadīth with "jurisprudence, Kalām, linguistics and the science of the Qurʾān".[93] Throughout his treatise, al-Kalābādhī lays strong emphasis on the importance of appropriate behaviour, both inward and outward, based upon correct understanding of Islamic tenets. The excellence of the Sufis lies in their devotional performance in fulfilling this principal obligation.

91 Al-Qushayrī, *Risāla*, 316.

92 Al-Sarrāj, *Lumaʿ*(Ar), 6; cf. Q. 7:56.

93 Al-Kalābādhī, *Taʿarruf*, 32–3. The *Taʿarruf* is sometimes called "apologetic" (e.g. Knysh, *Mysticism*, 123). However, al-Kalābādhī does not appear to be defensive about Sufism, and, rather than an apologia, his work can be regarded as a scholarly survey on Sufi doctrines, as Karamustafa also remarks (*Sufism*, 69).

The *Qūt* has a more explicitly preaching style than the previous two works. Al-Makkī warns several times that this world is a test from God and that believers must live well both inwardly and outwardly, since every heart contains a devil which can only be controlled on the basis of sound action. It is therefore paramount that believers be mindful, possess proper knowledge of their duties, and act upon that knowledge both in their hearts and with their limbs.[94] The Qurʾān is the source of knowledge, al-Makkī claims: "the people of faith are the people of the Qurʾān, and the people of the Qurʾān are the people of God and those He has chosen".[95] As Renard notes, al-Makkī's approach is characterised by the fact that he "so prominently canonizes the way of . . . the ancestors in faith as the standard of belief and action".[96] In the *Qūt*, al-Makkī draws on that canon to formulate a code of behaviour for believers, emphasising that their relations with God and fellow humans must be based on sound knowledge, and that they must act upon that knowledge both internally and externally.

Al-Sulamī's two treatises, the *Jawāmiʿ* and *al-Ṣuḥba*, are also clearly intended to be edifying. Given al-Sulamī's introductory comments in the *Jawāmiʿ* – to the effect that he hopes that those who criticise Sufism will gain a better understanding of Sufi norms from his writing – it seems that the intended readership is both Sufis and those who "misunderstood" them. As for *al-Ṣuḥba*, apart from the Sufi sayings (among others) quoted in the work, neither the title nor the contents clearly indicate that this treatise is specifically aimed at Sufis. The language employed in both works is rather plain, and frequent references to the Qurʾān and Ḥadīth appear throughout them. Like the other authors in this chapter, al-Sulamī thus appears to be clearly making the point that Sufi customs and practices derive directly from a correct understanding of the fundamental Islamic texts. The *Jawāmiʿ* and *al-Ṣuḥba* can be regarded as examples of early Sufi *adab* literature. However, just as Biagi, the English translator of the *Jawāmiʿ*, tries to place that work within the *adab* tradition in Arabic literature, it is important to contextualise so-called Sufi writings within the wider literary movement on Islamic piety.[97] Both the *Jawāmiʿ* and *al-Ṣuḥba* can be used as general pedagogical guidebooks for those who seek to live in complete accordance with Divine will both individually and communally.

94 Al-Makkī, *Qūt*, vol. 1, 344–5, 347.
95 Ibid., vol. 1, 384.
96 Renard, *Knowledge*, 112.
97 Al-Sulamī, *Collection*, xii–xiii, xxiv–xxxiii.

Throughout his treatise, al-Qushayrī strikes a rather defensive posture in his attempt to prove that the Sufi path can be perfectly well supported on the basis of fundamental Islamic tenets. Even though he is able to deploy such sound scholarly knowledge that his defence may well be considered successful, it remains that his *Risāla* is often regarded as conveying a "clear apologetic message".[98] Knysh observes that al-Qushayrī had only a small number of disciples, commenting that his persona was "academic and methodical rather than charismatic and inspirational".[99] According to Karamustafa, a popular jurisprudential approach in Nīshāpūr at the time when the *Risāla* was composed involved using a combination of Shāfiʿī and Ashʿarī principles.[100] Al-Qushayrī seems to have made the maximum use of his scholarly knowledge to legitimise Sufism within the Islamic tradition, covering a wide variety of subjects with a specific intent to demonstrate the excellent quality of true Sufi manners, morality, relationships, and belief, such that this can be readily accepted by Sufis and non-Sufis alike.

The five scholars discussed in this chapter provide eloquent accounts of what constitutes *akhlāq* and *ādāb* in Islam. Many of their arguments overlap, as do the documents to which they appeal in their support, and their moral concerns are not specifically mystical or other-worldly, nor exclusively Sufi or Islamic. As noted at the beginning of this chapter, our concluding aim is to examine whether these texts elucidate the extent of human free will – and whether they provide an explanation of what makes good actions good, and how to differentiate between good and bad acts.

It is notable, however, that none of these six works provides a full discussion of the relevant theological issues in relation to moral traits and habits. Concerning human free will and predestination, the five authors do not deny God's omnipotence, yet they still proceed on the assumption that humans have free will, since ethics – what one ought and ought not to do – must by definition be based on personal choice. As al-Makkī keeps emphasising, this world is a test from God. The Final Judgement will be made on the basis of the choices humans have made during their lives. Although God is the Creator of the universe and everything within it, human intentions and actions must yet be accounted for on the Last Day. Believers must strive to be as good as possible on earth – and, emphatically, must not do nothing and simply hope that Divine mercy will annul all their bad behaviour. The antinomy of free

[98] Al-Qushayrī, *Epistle*, xxiv.
[99] Ibid., xxiii.
[100] Karamustafa, *Sufism*, 97.

will and predestination is often discussed, especially within Kalām.[101] However, even al-Sulamī and al-Qushayrī do not touch upon this issue in their discussion on ethics, despite their thorough education in the Ashʿarī teachings. All five authors discussed in this chapter seem to assume that humans do have the power of choice, and that proper internal and external moral conduct is an obligation upon believers for the hereafter.

The other main question which is not touched upon is what makes good actions good. Are things good because they are endorsed by Islamic teachings, or do Islamic teachings endorse them because they are right? This question leads to another: What is it that makes the recommended ethical conduct distinctively *Sufi* – or even Islamic? And if the answer is given that it is because the documents cited in its favour are the fundamental Islamic texts, is there then any essential difference in the level of virtue achieved through revelation and that achieved through reason? If an excellent action counts towards personal salvation, could it then properly be called selfless? Would it even be an ethical act at all? Furthermore, although ethics requires that the individual exercise his or her own judgement, as is hinted in the Qurʾān, the authors discussed in this chapter seem to assume that humans already know what is good and what is bad, even though they often fail to follow the good.[102] The role of these six works, therefore, is fundamentally as a much-needed reminder or warning, rather than an elucidation of the underlying theological concerns.

While living in geographically different areas and in different periods, all five authors discussed in this chapter agree that Islam concerns ethics, and that Sufism essentially comprises teachings about the moral path. The fundamental argument advanced in each of the six works is similar in terms of contents and assumptions, although one slight difference should be noted as regards their perceptions of contemporary Sufis. The three earlier scholars – al-Sarrāj, al-Kalābādhī, and al-Sulamī – believe that Sufism has been misunderstood, and they express their concerns that the fake Sufis outnumber the genuine in their period; but according to the latest author, al-Qushayrī, true Sufism has actually died out.[103] This change may be expressive of a widely shared sentiment

[101] See, e.g. Awn, "Ethical Concerns", 249.

[102] E.g. al-Makkī emphasises the importance of listening to the heart, since it knows what is right and wrong (*Qūt*, vol. 1, 326–7). Cf. *Encyclopaedia of the Qurʾān*, s.v. "Ethics and the Qurʾān" (A.K. Reinhart).

[103] Al-Makkī does not explicitly mention his opinion on this in the *Qūt* (the nature of his work is different from the other Sufi survey works as discussed above). Al-Qushayrī is not the only figure who expresses this view; see, e.g. ʿAlī b. ʿUthmān Hujwīrī, *Kashf al-maḥjūb of al-Hujwīrī 'The Revelation of the Veiled': An Early Persian Treatise on Sufism*, trans. R.A. Nicholson, E.J.W. Gibb Memorial Trust (Wiltshire: Aris & Phillips, 2000), 7; ʿAbd al-Raḥmān Ibn al-Jawzī, *Talbīs Iblīs*, ed. Muḥammad Munīr al-Dimashqī (Cairo: Idārat al-Ṭibāʿa

of his time, reflecting the wider political state of society. Yet the discourse on morality expressed in his work remains almost the same as in the earlier authors', despite their changing attitudes towards Sufism and its adherents.

Ethical conduct and good manners are acquired on an individual basis. However, the strong social implications of these virtues require each individual to bridge the division between personal and communal living. Religion, too, concerns both the private and public aspects of life, and Sufism in particular emphasises sustaining a good balance between one's internal and external deeds. It is no surprise therefore that Sufis should be concerned with ethical conduct and anxious that people be properly instructed with regards to it. Al-Sarrāj, al-Kalābādhī, al-Makkī, al-Sulamī, and al-Qushayrī all identify ethical conduct with living in perfect conformity with Divine will. This requires establishing harmonious relationships with God, the self, and all others. The ethical approach presented in this chapter seems to have currency beyond the specific periods and locations in which these authors formulated it, and indeed much of it seems to transcend the specific moral frameworks represented by Sufism and Islam. Although the Sufi way is sometimes considered to be distinctive of the Islamic tradition,[104] the path of Sufism is better regarded as expressing the path to being a good believer. As demonstrated in the ethical precepts running throughout those early and influential Sufi works, a good believer is someone who leads a moral life.

FURTHER READING

Awn, P.J. "The Ethical Concerns of Classical Sufism", *The Journal of Religious Ethics* 11, no. 2 (Fall, 1983), 240–63.

Bonebakker, S.A. "*Adab* and the Concept of *Belles-lettres*", in J. Ashtiany et al. (eds), *'Abbasid Belles-Lettres* (Cambridge: Cambridge University Press, 1990), 16–30.

Heck, P.L. "Mysticism as Morality: The Case of Sufism", *Journal of Religious Ethics* 34, no. 2 (2006), 253–86.

Meier, F. "A Book of Etiquette for Sufis", in idem, *Essays on Islamic Piety and Mysticism*, trans. J. O'Kane (Leiden: Brill, 1999), 49–92.

Ridgeon, L. *Morals and Mysticism in Persian Sufism: A History of Sufi-*futuwwat *in Iran* (Abingdon, Oxon: Routledge, 2010).

Toorawa, S.M. "Defining *Adab* by (Re)defining the Adīb: Ibn Abī Ṭāhir Ṭayfūr and Storytelling", in ed. P.F. Kennedy, *On Fiction and Adab in Medieval Arabic Literature* (Wiesbaden: Harrassowitz, 2005), 287–308.

al-Munīriyya, 1369/1949–50), 38 (the whole book is indeed the lament of this renowned Ḥanbalī scholar for the loss of the true original state of Islamic teachings).

[104] See, e.g. Heck, "Mysticism as Morality", 254.

PART II

MEDIEVAL SUFISM

5

Antinomian Sufis[1]

Ahmet T. Karamustafa

BETWEEN SUBLIMATION AND SUBVERSION: DIVERGENT ATTITUDES TOWARDS SOCIAL NORMS AND THE SHARĪʿA IN EARLY SUFISM (850–1200)

Several different, albeit interconnected, modes of mystical piety emerged in the Muslim communities around the Mediterranean as well as West and Central Asia between the third/ninth and seventh/thirteenth centuries. The practitioners of these forms of piety occupied a range of positions in society along the spectrum of socio-economic, political and cultural belonging, and, given the heterogeneity of the mystical modes of piety in origin and approach, some early Muslim mystics were situated at the margins or even outside the boundaries of the "social and political mainstream" of their local communities on account of their beliefs and practices, while others occupied the centre stage of that mainstream.

The early mystics of Baghdad and Basra in lower Iraq, for instance, harboured some antisocial and iconoclastic tendencies side by side with socially and legally conformist ones. Celibacy, vegetarianism, avoidance of gainful employment, withdrawal and seclusion, as well as a certain proclivity for outlandish behaviour on the part of some mystics, must have raised eyebrows, even though these practices were not adopted by all or even most mystics. Other characteristic practices and beliefs – notably *samāʿ* of the Sufis of Baghdad, which was a blend of music, poetry and dance – may have been legally and theologically suspect in the eyes of some traditionalist Muslims.

1 This article draws upon two earlier publications by the author: *Sufism, the Formative Period* (Edinburgh: University Press, 2007 and Berkeley: University of California Press, 2007), especially 155–66; and *God's Unruly Friends: Dervish Groups in the Islamic Later Middle Period, 1200–1550* (Salt Lake City: The University of Utah Press, 1994; reprint: Oxford: Oneworld, 2006).

Nevertheless, the fact remains that we do not know what the central charge was against the Baghdad Sufis in the first documented (albeit unsuccessful) attempt to prosecute them in 264/877. Elsewhere, in Nishapur in northeast Iran, members of the Path of Blame, the Malāmatiyya, were almost certainly social and legal conformists, since blending into society was the hallmark of their piety.[2]

But side by side with mystics like the Sufis of Baghdad, and the Path of Blame in Nishapur who saw their piety as a deepening or expansion of legalistic observance and/or viewed the *sharīʿa* as an indispensable precondition and a steady companion of their religiosity, apparently there were others who had a conflictual relationship with the religious law, hence also with the social mainstream in large urban centres, where the religious scholars of various stripes were rapidly gaining the status of religious authorities. An early example is the "pneumatics" (*rūḥāniyya*), as documented by Abū ʿĀṣim Khushaysh ibn Aṣram al-Nasāʾī (d. 253/867):

> They are so called because they believe that their spirits see the *malakūt* ["the divine dominion"] of the heavens, that they see the pasture of paradise, and further, that they have sexual intercourse with the houris. Furthermore, they believe that they wander with their spirits in paradise. They are also called *fikriyya* ["meditationists"] because they meditate and believe that in their meditation they can reach God in reality. Thus they make their meditation the object of their devotions and of their striving towards God. In their meditation they see this goal by means of their spirit, through God speaking to them directly, passing his hand gently over them, and – as they believe – looking upon them directly, while they have intercourse with the houris and dally with them as they lay upon their couches, and while eternally young boys bring them food and drink and exquisite fruit.[3]

al-Nasāʾī then proceeded to report on other groups of mystics:

> Other mystics teach that when love of God has supplanted all other attachments in the heart (*khulla*), legal bans are no longer valid (*rukhaṣ*). And some teach a method of ascetic training (especially of the diet) that so

[2] For documentation on the incident in 264/877, see Karamustafa, *Sufism, the Formative Period*, 32, n.45. A concise discussion on the Path of Blame, with references, can be found in the same work, 48–51.

[3] Bernd Radtke, "How can man reach the mystical union: Ibn Ṭufayl and the divine spark", in *The World of Ibn Ṭufayl*, ed. Lawrence I. Conrad (Leiden: Brill, 1996), 189. Radtke's translation is from Khushaysh's *Kitāb al-istiqāma fi'l-sunna wa al-radd ʿalā ahl al-ahwā* (*The Book of Sound Tradition and Refutation of Dissenters*), which is printed on the margins of Abu'l-Ḥusayn al-Malaṭī, *al-Tanbīh wa al-radd ʿalā ahl al-ahwāʾ wa al-bidaʿ*, ed. Sven Dedering (Leipzig: Biblioteca Islamica, 1936), 73 ff.

> mortifies yearnings for the flesh that when the training is finished the "ascetic" gains license to everything (*ibāḥa*). Another group maintains that the heart is distracted when mortification becomes too vigorous; it is better to yield immediately to one's inclinations; the heart, having experienced vanity, can then detach itself from vain things without regret. One last group affirms that renunciation (*zuhd*) is applicable only to things forbidden by religious law, that enjoying permitted wealth is good and riches are superior to poverty.[4]

It is, of course, possible to question whether, and to what extent, the mystics al-Nasāʾī described actually existed – after all, heresiographers could be somewhat too zealous in sniffing out heretics. Yet, it is noteworthy that accusations of *ibāḥa* ("permissivism and antinomianism") and *ḥulūl* ("incarnationism or inherence of the Divine in the material world, especially in human form") appear very early in the sources, concomitantly with the emergence of mystical forms of piety. And, criticism came not only from the outside – thus the Muʿtazila and Shīʿa in particular piled on the charges of obscurantist anti-rationalism, making "false claims" to work miracles as well as rash dismissal of discursive learning against the mystics – some very prominent Sufi authors themselves joined the chorus to hold forth against libertines and antinomians who, they argued, should be differentiated from the true Sufis. It is difficult to argue that all these internal and external critics of libertine and antinomian mystics were simply fighting a chimera, and the inevitable conclusion is that there were indeed many mystics, increasingly all called Sufis, who were heedless or critical of the social mainstream and the emerging religio-political establishments of their societies and who found themselves branded as antinomians by Sufis and non-Sufis alike.

Who exactly were the libertines and antinomians associated with Sufism that were universally rejected by many Sufis and non-Sufi observers? It is difficult to trace these shady characters, but Abu Naṣr al-Sarrāj (d. 378/988) gave a full listing of them in the "Book of Errors" of his *The Book of Light Flashes on Sufism* (*Kitāb al-lumaʿ fī'l-taṣawwuf*), under the heading "On those who erred in fundamentals and were led to misbelieve."[5] These included the following: (1) those who thought that once mystics reached God they should

[4] Louis Massignon, *Essay on the Origins of the Technical Language of Islamic Mysticism*, trans. Benjamin Clark (Notre Dame, IN: University of Notre Dame Press, 1997), 80, paraphrasing from Abu'l-Ḥusayn al-Malaṭī, *al-Tanbīh wa al-radd ʿalā ahl al-ahwāʾ wa al-bidaʿ*, ed. Sven Dedering (Leipzig: Biblioteca Islamica, 1936), fols. 160–7 (I omitted personal names).

[5] Abu Naṣr al-Sarrāj, *Kitāb al-lumaʿ fī'l-taṣawwuf*, ed. Reynold A. Nicholson (London: Luzac & Co., 1914), 410–35; *Schlagrichter über das Sufitum*, trans. Richard Gramlich (Stuttgart: F. Steiner, 1990), 584–602.

be called "free" instead of "Godservants"; (2) a group of Iraqis who thought that the Godservant could not achieve true sincerity unless he ceased to pay attention to how others viewed him and who thus proceeded to ignore social norms in his actions, whether these were right or wrong; (3) those who placed sainthood above prophecy on account of their baseless interpretation of the Qur'ānic story of Moses and Khiḍr (Qur'ān, 18.60–82); (4) those who argued that all things were permitted and that prohibition applied only to excessive license taken with others' property; (5) those who believed in divine inherence in a person; (6) those who understood discourse of "passing away" (*fanā'*) as the passing away of human nature; (7) a group in Syria and a group in Basra (ʿAbd al-Wāḥid ibn Zayd is named) who believed in vision of God with the heart in this world; (8) those who believed that they were permanently and perfectly pure; (9) those who believed that their hearts contained divine lights that were uncreated; (10) those who sought to avert blame from themselves when they incurred the punishments laid down by the Qur'ān and violated the custom of the Prophet by arguing that they were compelled by God in all their actions; (11) those who surmised that their closeness to God exempted them from observing the same etiquette that they followed prior to achieving proximity to the Divine; (12) a group in Baghdad who thought that in passing away from their own qualities they had entered God's qualities; (13) a group in Iraq who claimed to lose all their senses in ecstasy and thus to transcend sensory phenomena; (14) those who erred in their beliefs concerning the spirit (*rūḥ*), with many versions of this error listed, most notably the belief in the uncreatedness of the spirit and the belief in transmigration of spirits.

Sarrāj did not claim to have personally seen all these groups, but there is little doubt that they existed (although their detractors no doubt exercised their imagination in their descriptions of them) and that they were generally linked with Sufism. A contemporary of Sarrāj, al-Muṭahhar ibn Ṭāhir al-Maqdisī, who composed an historical work called *Kitāb al-bad' wa'l-ta'rīkh* around 355/966 gave the names of four Sufi groups he came across as Ḥusniyya (*ḥusn* means "beauty"), Malāmatiyya, Sūqiyya/Sawqiyya (which probably should be amended to Shawqiyya [*shawq*: "longing"]), and Maʿdhūriyya (*maʿdhūr*: "excused"), and made the following observation about them:

> These are characterized by the lack of any consistent system or clear principles of faith. They make judgments according to their speculations and imagination, and they constantly change their opinions. Some of them believe in incarnationism (*ḥulūl*), as I have heard one of them claim that His habitation is in the cheeks of the beardless youth (*murd*). Some of them

> believe in permissiveness (*ibāḥa*) and neglect the religious law, and they do not heed those who blame them.[6]

Such somewhat generic accusations against Sufis continued to be aired even later, as evidenced by two critical chapters in the *Tabṣirat al-ʿawāmm fī maʿrifat maqālāt al-anām* ("Instructions for the Common People concerning the Knowledge of Human Discourses") of the Twelver Shīʿī Jamāl al-Dīn al-Murtaḍā al-Rāzī (lived first half of 6th/12th century). In his hostile review of the Sufis, Jamāl al-Dīn al-Murtaḍā mentioned antinomians called *Wāṣiliyya* (the "Attainers"), who thought that they attained union with God and thus saw no need to observe religious duties, as well as others who were against books and learning, and still other Sufis who cared only for sensual pleasures such as eating, dancing, and wearing nice clothes.

Noteworthy, however, is Maqdisī's use of the name "Malāmatī" for those who neglected the law and were not concerned with public blame. The term Malāmatī was initially used to refer to the movement known as the "Path of Blame" in Nishapur during the fourth/tenth century. The followers of this latter movement, as documented by Abū ʿAbd al-Raḥman al-Sulamī (d. 412/1021), appear to have understood "blame" primarily to mean "self-censure" rather than "public censure", and they certainly did not neglect the law. Nor is there strong evidence that they sought to discipline the lower self by subjecting it to public blame through commission of deliberate and conspicuous acts that violated social norms.[7] After all, attracting public blame would have been contrary to their goal of attaining complete public anonymity in an effort to conceal their true spiritual state from all others and thus deny the lower self, *nafs*, the opportunity to gloat in public attention of any kind. It appears, however, that sometime during the ascendancy of Iraq-oriented Sufism in Khurasan during the fourth/tenth century, the term Malāmatī came to be applied (perhaps first by Sufis who did not think very highly of the Path of Blame?) increasingly to real or imaginary libertines, who justified their social and legal transgressions, genuinely or in dissimulation, either as "indifference to public blame occasioned by true sincerity" (number 2 in Sarrāj's list of errors above) or as "disciplining the lower self by abasing it through public blame". Maqdisī's usage certainly reflects this different use of

6 Sara Sviri, "Ḥakīm Tirmidhī and the Malāmatī Movement in Early Sufism", in *Classical Persian Sufism from Its Origins to Rumi*, ed. Leonard Lewisohn (London: Khaniqahi Nimatullahi Publications, 1993), 591, translating from *Kitāb al-badʾ wa'l-taʾrīkh* (Paris 1899), 5: 147. Sviri gives the reading "Ḥasaniyya" and translates *ibāḥa* as "promiscuity".

7 Christopher Melchert, "Sufis and Competing Movements in Nishapur", *Iran* 39 (2001): 237–47.

the term outside Nishapur, and other independent evidence corroborates his observation. In a work written by the Caspian Zaydī Imam Aḥmad ibn al-Ḥusayn al-Mu'ayyad bi'llāh (d. 411/1021) that apparently is "the earliest extant Zaydī literary reaction to Sufism", the author referred to some Sufis who called themselves "the people of blame" (*ahl al-malāma*) and stated, "They claim that by involving themselves in evil situations and committing reprehensible acts they abase their ego, yet in reality they fall from the state of repentance and may well revert to being offenders (*fussāq*)."[8]

Abū 'Abd al-Raḥman al-Sulamī, who was a contemporary of al-Mu'ayyad bi'llāh, is oblivious to this use of the term Malāmatī to designate libertines and portrays the members of the Path of Blame as law-abiding mystics, but in spite of Sulamī's attempts at preserving the good name of this Path, the name Malāmatī comes to be used during the fifth/eleventh century to refer to antinomians who are indifferent to the *sharī'a*. Not surprisingly, Abu'l-Qāsim al-Qushayrī (d. 465/1072), whose conception of Sufism was carefully circumscribed by adherence to the religious law, mentioned the Malāmatīs of Nishapur only in passing in three entries in the biographical section of his *Risāla* ("Treatise"), possibly because the term Malāmatī was already tainted with antinomianism in his eyes, but 'Alī ibn 'Uthmān al-Hujwīrī (d. between 465/1073 and 469/1077) devoted a whole chapter of his *Uncovering the Veiled* (*Kashf al-maḥjūb*) to the question of "blame", which is packed with interesting information.[9] Referring to the Qur'ānic locus of the concept of blame – Qur'ān 5.54, which refers to the Prophet and his companions, "they struggle in the path of God and do not fear the blame of any blamer" – Hujwīrī reminded his readers that "God's elect [that is, prophets and saints] are distinguished from the rest by public blame" and that "public blame is the sustenance of God's friends".[10] He then proceeded to differentiate the different meanings of the concept with admirable clarity:

> Blame is of three kinds: (1) [blame attached] to following the right path, (2) blame [incurred] intentionally, (3) [blame attached] to abandoning [the law]. Blame is attached to following the right path when one who minds his own business, practices religion and abides by the rules of social interaction, is blamed by the people; this is the way people behave towards him but he is

[8] Wilferd Madelung, "Zaydī Attitudes to Sufism", in *Islamic Mysticism Contested: Thirteen Centuries of Controversies and Polemics*, eds. F. de Jong and Bernd Radtke (Leiden: Brill, 1999), 126.

[9] 'Alī ibn 'Uthmān al-Hujwīrī, *Kashf al-maḥjūb*, ed. Valentin Zhukovsky (Tehran: Kitābkhāna-i Ṭahūrī, 1378/1999), 68–78; *Revelation of the Mystery* (Kashf al-Mahjub), trans. Reynold A. Nicholson (Accord, NY: Pir Press, 1999 [1911]), 62–9.

[10] Hujwīrī, *Kashf*, 69–70 / *Revelation*, 62–3.

> indifferent to all that. Intentional blame is when one attracts great public esteem and becomes a center of attention, and his heart inclines towards that esteem and grows attached to it, yet he wants to rid himself of the people and devote himself to God, he incurs public blame by dissimulating a [blameworthy] act that is not against the law so that people would turn away from him. Blame is attached to abandoning the law when one is gripped in his nature by infidelity and misbelief so that people say that he abandoned the law and prophetic custom, while he thinks that he is walking the path of blame.[11]

Hujwīrī explained and endorsed the first two kinds, citing examples for them, and rejected the third, decrying it as a ploy to win fame and popularity. The proponents of this last kind often justified their actions as a deliberate attempt on their part to abase the lower self, and while Hujwīrī thought that public blame could certainly have that therapeutic effect – he proffered an example from his personal experience about how being pelted with melon skins by formalist Sufis saved him from a spiritual snare that had seized him – he could not countenance such flagrant violation of the religious law.[12]

Hujwīrī's attitude towards blame was shared by other fifth/eleventh century and, later, sixth/twelfth century figures who discussed the concept. Like Hujwīrī, Abū Ḥāmid Ghazālī (450–505/1058–1111) objected to those who contravened the law in the name of *malāma*, but accepted shocking though licit acts in order to repel public attention and along with it the desire for fame or good name (*jāh*); Ghazālī cited an unnamed renunciant who began to eat voraciously when he was visited by the political ruler in order to avert this latter's attention from himself.[13] The Ẓāhirī traditionist and Sufi Muḥammad ibn Ṭāhir al-Maqdisī "Ibn al-Qaysarānī" (448/1058–507/1113) criticized the Malāmatīs of his time as antinomians.[14] Muḥammad ibn Munawwar, the biographer of Abū Saʿīd-i Abu'l-Khayr (357/967–440/1049) who wrote towards the end of the sixth/twelfth century, quoted Abū Saʿīd as having said, "The Malāmatī is he who, out of love of God, does not fear whatever

[11] Hujwīrī, *Kashf*, 70–1 / cf. *Revelation*, 63–4.

[12] Hujwīrī, *Kashf*, 77–8 / *Revelation*, 69.

[13] Abū Ḥāmid Ghazālī, *Kīmiyā al-saʿādat*, ed. Ḥusayn Khidīvjam (Tehran: Shirkat-i Intishārāt-i ʿIlmī va Farhangī, 1364/1985), 2: 199; idem, *Iḥyāʾulūm al-dīn* (Beirut: Dār al-Kutub al-ʿIlmiyya, 1996), 3: 304–5; Fritz Meier, *Abū Saʿīd-i Abū l-Ḥayr (357–440/967–1049): Wirklichkeit und Legende* (Tehran: Bibliothèque Pahlavi, 1976), 497.

[14] Naṣr Allāh Pūrjavādī, *Du mujaddid: Pizhūhishāyī dar bāra-i Muḥammad-i Ghazzālī va Fakhr-i Rāzī* (Tehran: Markaz-i Nashr-i Dānishgāhī, 1381/2002), 147, reporting from Ibn al-Qaysarānī's *Ṣafwat al-taṣawwuf* (Beirut, 1416/1995), 473. On this figure, see Joseph Schacht, 'Ibn al-Ḳaysarānī,' *The Encyclopaedia of Islam*, 2d. ed., 3: 821a.

happens to him and does not care about blame."[15] At around the same time as Ibn Munavvar, the Ḥanbalī preacher and writer ʿAbd al-Raḥmān ibn ʿAlī Ibn al-Jawzī (510/1126–597/1200) decried Malāmatīs in much the same way as Hujwīrī and Ghazālī, though in more caustic terms:

> Certain Sufis, who are called the Malāmatiyya, plunged into sins and then said, "Our goal was to demote ourselves in the public eye in order to be safe from the disaster of good name and hypocrisy." They are like a man who fornicated with a woman and impregnated her, and when he was asked, "Why didn't you practice *coitus interruptus* (*ʿazl*?)" he replied, "I had heard that *ʿazl* is reprehensible." Then they told him, "And you had not heard that fornication is prohibited?" These ignorant people have lost their standing with God and have forgotten that Muslims are the witnesses of God on earth.[16]

Ibn al-Jawzī was in principle against intentional blame, and he stated unequivocally, "it is no religious act for a man to humiliate himself in public".[17] He narrated with disapproval what he considered clear examples of outrageous behavior, mentioning specifically Abu'l-Ḥusayn al-Nūrī (d. 295/907) and Abū Bakr al-Shiblī (d. 334/946), though he was mostly silent about similar behavior of Sufis closer to his own time. Like Hujwīrī and Ghazālī, however, he had no qualms about pious exemplars repelling public attention for the right reasons and repeated the anecdote about the renunciant who pretended to be a glutton in front of the political ruler with approbation.[18]

Were there really many libertines around who claimed to be Malāmatīs during the fourth/tenth and fifth/eleventh century? This question is rendered more complex by the emergence, at this period, of other terms that in time came to represent libertinism, notably *darvīsh* (Persian: "pauper, beggar") and *qalandar* (Persian: "uncouth"). Although the linguistic origins of these terms as well as the history of the social types they designate are obscure, it is likely that these terms were initially used equally for regular beggars as well as itinerant renunciants who practiced extreme *tawakkul* ("trust in God"). Some of the latter accepted charitable offerings without, however, actively seeking

[15] Muḥammad ibn Munavvar, *Asrār al-tawḥīd fī maqāmāt al-Shaykh Abī Saʿīd*, ed. Muḥammad Riżā Shafīʿī Kadkanī (Tehran: Mu'assasa-i Intishārāt-i Āgāh, 1366/1987), 1: 288; *The Secrets of God's Mystical Oneness*, trans. John O'Kane (Costa Mesa, CA: Mazda Publishers, 1992), 436; I have changed O'Kane's "does not think of it as reproach" to "does not care about blame".

[16] ʿAbd al-Raḥmān ibn ʿAlī Ibn al-Jawzī, *Talbīs Iblīs*, ed. ʿIsām Ḥarastānī and Muḥammad Ibrāhīm Zaghlī (Beirut: Al-Maktab al-Islāmī), 468; see also 478.

[17] Ibn al-Jawzī, *Talbīs*, 468.

[18] Ibn al-Jawzī, *Talbīs*, 201–2.

after charity, while others no doubt survived through active begging or, at least, were commonly perceived as beggars. It is, therefore, reasonable to see a confluence of voluntary and involuntary poverty, of wandering renunciants and the destitute, in the origin of *darvīsh*s and *qalandar*s, even though the etymologies of the two terms remain uncertain.[19]

During the fifth/eleventh and sixth/twelfth centuries, *darvīsh* seems to have mostly retained its primary meaning of "poor, beggar", but the term must have already started to assume the added connotation of a particular kind of piety characterized by itinerant mendicancy in this period, since the use of the term in this sense and the image of a wandering dervish – complete with his hallmark accoutrements of a begging bowl (*kashkūl*), a trumpet made from the horn of a ram or deer (*nafīr* or *būq*), a hat of felt (*tāj*), a short axe or hatchet (*tabarzīn*), a patched bag (*chanta*), a gnarled staff (*ʿaṣā*), an animal skin (*pūst*), and a rosary (*tasbīḥ*) – is well attested from the late fifth/eleventh century onwards.[20] The term *qalandar* may have had similar origins, but, unlike *darvīsh*, it came to be associated with libertinism from very early on, primarily because of the emergence of the *qalandar* as a peculiar literary type in Persian poetry during the late fifth/eleventh and early sixth/twelfth century – significantly, at the same time as the appearance of the *ghazal* as a new poetic form. More properly, one should talk of the emergence of a cluster of images organized around the central character *qalandar*. This cluster, which finds its first full-fledged expression in the poetry of Majdūd ibn Ādam Sanā'ī (d. 525/1131), sometimes jelled into a separate genre called *qalandariyyāt*, but more commonly it existed as a free-floating bundle of imagery found most conspicuously in lyric poetry but also in other poetic genres. It was composed of several sets of images connected, most notably, to the central themes of wine-drinking, sexual promiscuity, gambling as well as playing games of backgammon and chess, and entering into non-Islamic (especially Zoroastrian and Christian) cults, all located at the *kharābāt* (literally meaning "ruins" but with the very real connotation of "tavern" and "brothel"). Through the use of this provocative cluster woven around the figure of an unruly libertine, a highly positive spin was given to the *qalandar*'s way of life as the epitome of true piety cleansed of all dissimulation and hypocrisy, and the *qalandar* (along with his "look-alikes", *rind* ["heavy

19 Cf. Hamid Algar, "Begging, ii. In Sufi Literature and Practice", *Encyclopedia Iranica* 3: 81–2. For the latest attempt to discern the etymology of the word *qalandar*, see Muhammad Riżā Shafīʿī Kadkanī, *Qalandariyya dar ta'rīkh* (Tehran: Sukhan, 1386sh/2007), 36–49.

20 Hamid Algar, "Darvīš, ii. In the Islamic Period", *Encyclopedia Iranica* 7: 73–6. For an early attestation of mendicant dervishes, see Hujwīrī, *Kashf*, 432–79, esp. 449–53 / *Revelation*, 334–66, esp. 345–7.

drinker"] and *qallāsh* ["rascal"]) was portrayed as the truly sincere devotee of God unconcerned with "the blame of blamers" – in other words, as the real Malāmatī.[21] In this way, the term *qalandar* was brought within the orbit of the term Malāmatī.

The complexity of the issue of Sufi antinomianism during the sixth/twelfth century is best documented in a long chapter contained in Ibn al-Jawzī's (510/1126–597/1200) polemical work *The Devil's Delusion* (*Talbīs Iblīs*). In that chapter, Ibn al-Jawzī specifically denounced the following Sufi practices: *samā*ʿ; ecstasy; dance and hand-clapping; gazing at beardless youths; an excessive concern for cleanliness and ritual purity; dwelling in lodges; celibacy; giving up property; wearing *fuwaṭ* ("aprons") and *muraqqaʿa* ("patched cloak"); investiture with the cloak; refraining from eating meat; rejection of trade and employment; withdrawal from society through solitude and seclusion; abandoning marriage and desire for children; travelling without provisions with no particular destination, sometimes in solitude and walking at night; avoiding medical treatment; refusal to mourn the death of close companions; and abandoning scholarship. Ibn al-Jawzī also took the Sufis to task for the following beliefs: distinction between *ʿilm al-bāṭin* ("inner knowledge") and *ʿilm al-ẓāhir* ("outer knowledge"), this latter equated with *ʿilm al-sharīʿa* ("knowledge of the *sharīʿa*"); "loving God passionately" (*ʿishq*); vision of angels, jinns, demons, and even God in this world.[22]

All these practices and beliefs were indeed associated with Sufism, even though no single Sufi accepted all of them. Ibn al-Jawzī rejected them as reprehensible innovations (*bidʿa*, pl. *bidaʿ*) and attempted to prove his case with the help of reliable *ḥadīth*.[23] He was most unhappy with how the Sufis, in his eyes, undermined the supremacy of the *sharīʿa* by their claim to possess an

21 J. T. P. de Bruijn, "The *Qalandariyyāt* in Persian Mystical Poetry, from Sanāʾī Onwards", in *The Legacy of Medieval Persian Sufism*, ed. Leonard Lewisohn (London: Khaniqahi Nimatullahi Publications, 1992), 75–86; J. T. P. de Bruijn, *Persian Sufi Poetry: An Introduction to the Mystical Use of Classical Persian Poems* (Richmond, Surrey: Curzon, 1997), 71–6.

22 Ibn al-Jawzī, *Talbīs*, 211–487 (chapter 10); the last pages of this chapter (487–96) contain passages from an unidentified work of Ibn ʿAqīl (431/1040–513/1119). Chapters 9 and 11 also contain material relevant to Sufis. An English translation by D. S. Margoliouth appeared serially in *Islamic Culture* 9 (1935)–12 (1938) and 19 (1945)–22 (1948); I have used this in making my own translations.

23 The standard Sufi responses to the charge of *bidʿa* was (1) to deny the accusation and to prove that the practice in question was instead "recommended" (*sunna*) – this, for instance, was the strategy adopted by most Sufi authors who discussed the question of *samaʿ* though they carefully circumscribed the practice with qualifications; for brief overviews, see Jean During, "Samāʿ, 1. In Music and Mysticism", *The Encyclopaedia of Islam*, 2d ed., 8: 1018a–19b as well as Arthur Gribetz, "The *Samāʿ* Controversy: Sufi vs. Legalist", *Studia Islamica* 74 (1991): 43–62; and (2) to accept that the practice under discussion was an innovation but to cast it as an

"inner knowledge". The distinction that the Sufis drew between *sharīʿa* and *ḥaqīqa* ("reality"), he argued, was patently wrong since the two were completely identical, and contrary to Sufi views, inspiration (*ilhām*) was not a separate means of communication with God but was simply the result of genuine knowledge (*ʿilm*). It was clear to Ibn al-Jawzī that the Devil had succeeded in deluding the Sufis mainly by diverting them from discursive knowledge.[24]

Remarkably, Ibn al-Jawzī's criticism of the Sufis in particular sounded like the self-critical remarks of such eminent Sufi authors as Sarrāj, Hujwīrī, and Abū Ḥāmid Ghazālī. Particularly telling in this regard is Ibn al-Jawzī's account of "libertines" who discredited the Sufis.[25] According to Ibn al-Jawzī, certain antinomians and libertines had infiltrated Sufism and assumed Sufi identities in order to protect themselves by masking their true identities. These fell into three classes: (1) outright infidels; (2) those who professed Islam but followed their shaykhs without asking for any evidence or even "specious arguments" (*shubha*) about the legal-theological status of the acts they were asked to perform; and (3) those who did produce "specious arguments" for their actions but were deluded by the Devil into thinking that their false arguments were sound. Ibn al-Jawzī reviewed and rejected six such "specious arguments", all quasi-theological props for libertinism and abolition of the *sharīʿa*, some of which recall the heresiographical observations by al-Nasāʾī quoted above. According to him, some justified their hedonism through predestinarian arguments; some argued that God did not need our worship; some took refuge in God's infinite mercy; others gave up the effort to discipline the lower self as an unattainable goal; still others claimed to have transcended the law by having successfully tamed their lower selves or by having experienced clear signs of God's approval of their behavior in the form of miraculous occurrences or visions and dreams.

In his decision to exclude libertines from the body of Sufism, Ibn al-Jawzī was in agreement with most Sufi observers of the Sufi landscape, who also sought to domesticate or eliminate the antinomian trends interwoven into their tradition of piety. It is noteworthy that the scope of Sufism as it was viewed by its most powerful critic largely coincided with its scope as it was understood by its most astute "insider" observers from Sarrāj to Hujwīrī. Ibn

"acceptable innovation" and not a reprehensible one; this option was adopted especially in the cases of wearing patched frocks, building *khānaqāhs*, and extended seclusion: see Fritz Meier, "A book of etiquette for Sufis", in *Essays on Islamic Piety and Mysticism*, trans. John O'Kane (Leiden: Brill, 1999), 52–3.

24 Many early Sufis, on the other hand, saw the *sharīʿa* as a secure foundation for their spiritual endeavours; see Berndt Radtke, "Warum ist der Sufi orthodox?" *Der Islam* 71 (1994): 302–7.

25 Ibn al-Jawzī, *Talbīs*, 479 ff.

al-Jawzī rejected the practices and beliefs that he associated with Sufism, while the Sufi authorities evaluated them critically, endorsing many and ruling out others, but outsider critics and insider "experts" alike agreed on the boundaries of the form of piety that they picked out for review.

In his attempt to refute the whole of Sufism as antinomianism plain and simple, Ibn al-Jawzī relied directly on the views of the eminent scholar-Sufi Abū Ḥāmid Ghazālī. In his discussion of libertines in particular, Ibn al-Jawzī reproduced materials that can be traced back to the works of "the Proof of Islam". Indeed, since all six of the specious arguments and their correct answers given by Ibn al-Jawzī in his *Delusions* appear in a Persian treatise of Ghazālī titled *The Idiocy of Antinomians* (*Ḥamāqat-i ahl-i ibāḥat*), it is certain that Ibn al-Jawzī had access to an Arabic version of Ghazālī's treatise or another Arabic text that reproduced this latter's content.[26] For his part, Ghazālī naturally did not write *The Idiocy of Antinomians* as a refutation of Sufism; instead, he meant it as an attack against antinomians who masqueraded as Sufis. While Ghazālī debunked such "false" Sufis and expostulated the necessity of obeying the *sharīʿa* in several of his other works, the *Idiocy* was his most extensive and vehement criticism of "permissivists" (*ibāḥīs*).[27] In this treatise, Ghazālī decried antinomians as the worst of all people. Misled by lust and laziness, these had dropped all prescribed ritual observances and embraced total sexual promiscuity. In so doing, they had allowed themselves to become mere toys in the hands of Satan, who used them to misguide others. Deprived of any critical faculty, they had accepted Satan's insinuation that scholarship was but a veil for true seers such as themselves and had turned into venomous critics of scholars. While admittedly not all such antinomians were "Sufi-pretenders" (*ṣūfī-numā*), Ghazālī focused on these pretenders, for whom he reserved his most acerbic tone. Like the Sufis, these impostors dressed in blue gowns or wore the patched cloak, shaved their moustaches, carried prayer-rugs and toothbrushes but, unlike the Sufis, they freely consumed wine, used illicit funds without shame and availed themselves of all bodily pleasures. Ghazālī discussed in some detail eight "specious arguments" (*shubhāt*) that the Sufi-pretenders produced and refuted them one by one (the two that were not directly reproduced by Ibn

[26] An excellent recent edition of the *Ḥamāqat* is in Pūrjavādī, *Du mujaddid*, 153–209; this now replaces the earlier published edition in Otto Pretzl, *Die Streitschrift des Ġazālī gegen die Ibāḥīja* (Munich: Bayerischen Akademie der Wissenschaften, 1933), 63–118. The overlap between this work and Ibn al-Jawzis *Delusions* is also pointed out by Hamid Algar in "Ebāhīya", *Encyclopedia Iranica* 7: 653–4.

[27] See, for instance, his Persian letter on the same subject in Pūrjavādī, *Du mujaddid*, 139–45; Pūrjavādī discusses the contents of the letter on pages 126–38.

al-Jawzī were the denial of afterlife and the argument that true poverty meant the absence of all knowledge, including knowledge of good and bad deeds or of paradise and hell!). Irked beyond measure by these would-be Sufi libertines and their hostile attitude towards scholarship, Ghazālī the scholar-Sufi declared them, in no uncertain terms, beyond the pale of Islam and advised political rulers to ruthlessly exterminate these thoroughly incorrigible sinners.

It is very likely that the libertines and antinomians decried by Ghazālī and Ibn al-Jawzī included not only those who were criticized by Sarrāj (i.e., those whom Ghazālī called the "Sufi-pretenders") but also the nascent *qalandar* and *darvīsh* types who had already begun to enter the social stage during the sixth/twelfth century. Some of the practices denounced by Ibn al-Jawzī – specifically rejection of employment, withdrawal from society, abandoning marriage, and itinerancy without any provisions – would seem to point to mendicant dervishes. But, on the whole, there is little non-literary evidence about the *qalandar*s and *darvīsh*es as social types before the seventh/thirteenth century.[28]

Apart from the issue of whether the literary *qalandar* corresponded to some real libertines in Persian-speaking Muslim communities, however, the flowering of the *kharābāt* cluster gives rise to another significant question: could this new and potent poetic imagery be read as a literary commentary on the state of Sufism during the time period under consideration? More specifically, did the web of images spun around the figure of the *qalandar* constitute a criticism of the new Sufi communities that had taken shape under the leadership of powerful training masters? Indeed, the emergence of the *kharābāt* imagery in Persian poetry was most likely the literary counterpart of Qushayrī and Hujwīrī's theoretical critique of the formalism that was so evident in the new Sufi social enterprises built around increasingly more authoritarian training shaykhs resident in their lodges. Whether it had an actual social base or not, the *kharābāt* complex was the poetic response to the Sufi lodge (*khānaqāh*) and the *qalandar*s emerged as the authentic Sufis who were willing to sacrifice absolutely everything for the sake of God, while those *khānaqāh*-residents actually called "Sufis" were transformed in poetry to mere "exoterists" who had abandoned the search for God in their greed for this world and thus had turned Sufism into a profitable social profession. In this sense, the so-called Sufis of the lodge communities were indistinguishable from all the other social types, such as the *ḥadīth*-experts or the jurists of the *madrasa*s, that for most mystics exemplified a compromise, even a

[28] See Meier, *Abū Saʿīd-i Abū l-Ḫayr*, 494–516; Kadkanī, *Qalandariyya dar taʾrīkh*; and Karamustafa, *God's Unruly Friends*, 31–8 for more extended discussions.

corruption, of true piety because of their willingness to translate their expertise in religion to social, economic, and political power. It was for this reason that in the "strange looking glass" of the *kharābāt* complex, "the norms and values of Sufi piety [were] all reversed", and the *qalandar* was elevated to the role of the genuine mystic.[29] This complete role-reversal suggests that whether real or imaginary, the antinomian, nonconformist edge of Sufism always functioned as an indispensable mirror in which Sufis could look to see a critical reflection of their true place in society and on the spiritual path.

In addition to the nascent phenomenon of mendicant dervishes who began to function as "living commentary" on socially respectable, conformist Sufism, there was another social type whose ascendancy from the fifth/eleventh century onwards contributed to the growing popularity of antinomian Sufis. At around the same time as the appearance of the *qalandar* type, the "wise fool" (collectively referred to as *ʿuqalā al-majānīn* in Arabic), came to the surface as a prominent social type of medieval urban culture and gradually found a place in Sufi thought and practice as "the one captivated by God" (*majdhūb*). The wise fools lived beyond the pale, violating all social conventions, yet they were tolerated, even admired, especially on account of their total disregard for this world and their readiness to admonish their fellow citizens, particularly the wealthy and the powerful, against negligence of the hereafter.[30] In time, the wise fool came to be identified with the mystic who lost all self-consciousness in the encounter with God and became totally bewildered. The overpowering effect of divine intimacy had been described by the earliest Sufis, such as Abū Saʿīd al-Kharrāz (d. 286/899 or a few years earlier) and Abu'l- Ḥusayn al-Nūrī, and the bewilderment that resulted from such intimacy had been, at least to certain extent, exemplified in the lives of Nūrī and Abū Bakr al-Shiblī. About two or three generations after Shiblī, as Sufism became established in Khurasan during the second half of the fourth/century, certain wise fools now appeared in Sufi garb as "holy fools". Most notable were Muḥammad Maʿshūq of Ṭūs and Luqmān of Sarakhs. These figures were widely considered to have been freed of all constraints, including "reason", and, as madmen, they were not expected to abide by the law. Abū Saʿīd-i Abu'l-Khayr (357–440/967–1049) reportedly venerated Muḥammad Maʿshūq, and about Luqmān he observed, "No one is more unconnected and unattached and more pure than Luqmān. He has no ties whatsoever with

[29] The quotes are from Bruijn, *Persian Sufi Poetry*, 76.

[30] Michael W. Dols, *Majnūn: The Madman in Medieval Islamic Society* (Oxford: Oxford University Press, 1992), 349–65; Ulrich Marzolph, "ʿUqala' al-majānīn", *The Encyclopaedia of Islam*, 2d ed., Supplement: 816b–17a

anything, not with this world or the hereafter, and not with the self." Luqmān himself is supposed to have said, "Thirty years ago the True Sultan conquered my heart and since then no one else has dared exercise dominion over it and dwell therein."[31] The holy fools were not particular to Khurasan; in Syria and Egypt, for instance, where they were better known under the name *muwallah* ("one madly enamored of God"), Qaḍīb al-Bān of Mosul (471–573/1078–1177) was an early representative of this type. Qaḍīb al-Bān, who reportedly "was heedless of urine on his garments and legs and used to be immersed in mud", does not appear to have been clearly associated with Sufism, but by the seventh/thirteenth century, prominent Damascene *muwallahs* such as Yūsuf al-Qamīnī (d. 657/1259) and ʿAlī al-Kurdī had already come into the orbit of Sufism.[32] From this point onwards – well into the twentieth century – practically all regions where there were sizeable Muslim communities produced such enraptured saints, who often lived in liminal spaces in and around major urban centres and who were widely perceived as Sufi figures. The same phenomenon, that of the absorption of enraptured saints into Sufism, appears to have been at work also in rural environments, as exemplified in the way a rural *majdhūb* of the Nile delta, Aḥmad al-Badawī (d. 675/1276), gradually became a major Sufi saint of Egypt by the early Ottoman period.[33] Sufism thus came to be inextricably laced with antinomian dervishes and enraptured saints.

BETWEEN FAME AND NOTORIETY: DERVISH PIETY (1200–1900)

Antinomian and nonconformist Sufis may have had murky beginnings, but they surfaced with a vengeance, starting in the seventh/thirteenth century, in the form of itinerant bands of mendicants who roamed the countryside and inhabited liminal spaces around towns and villages as well as solitary

[31] Muḥammad ibn Munavvar, *Asrār*, 199 and 264/ Secrets, 306 and 400. Muḥammad Maʿshūq is discussed in detail in Naṣr Allāh Pūrjavādī , *ʿAyn al-Qużāt va ustādān-i ū* (Tehran: Asāṭīr, 1374/1995), 55–94; on Luqmān, other than *The Secrets*, see Hujwīrī, *Kashf*, 234 / *Revelation*, 189.

[32] For discussions of the *muwallahs* in Syria during the seventh/thirteenth century and after, see Joseph Meri, *The Cult of Saints among Muslims and Jews in Medieval Syria* (Oxford: Oxford University Press, 2002), 91–100 (the discussion and the quote on Qaḍīb al-Bān are on 97–8); Louis Pouzet, *Damas au VIIe-XIIIe siècle: vie et structures religieuses d'une métropole islamique* (Beirut: Dar el-Machreq, 1988), 222–6; Michael Chamberlain, *Knowledge and Social Practice in Medieval Damascus, 1190–1350* (Cambridge: Cambridge University Press, 1994), 130–3; and Eyüp Öztürk, "Muvelleh Kavramı Üzerine", *Ankara Üniversitesi İlahiyat Fakültesi Dergisi*, 53 (2012): 35–53.

[33] Catherine Mayeur-Jaouen, *Al-Sayyid Aḥmad al-Badawī: un grand saint de l'islam égyptien* (Cairo: Institut Français d'Archéologie Orientale, 1994), esp. 263–67.

enraptured saints who lived at the margins of urban society. The proliferation of dervish groups and *majdhūb* saints coincided with the growing popularity of some outlandish, shocking ritual practices, such as walking on fire, biting snakes and scorpions, and piercing the body with sharp iron skewers, by some otherwise socially integrated Sufis.

Dervish groups as identifiable social collectivities first appeared as two widespread movements: the Qalandariyya, which first flourished in Syria and Egypt under the leadership of Persian-speaking figures, most notably Jamāl al-Dīn Sāvī (d. ca. 630/1232–33), and the Ḥaydariyya, which took shape in Iran as a result of the activities of its eponymous founder Quṭb al-Dīn Ḥaydar (d. ca. 618/1221–22).[34] Both movements rapidly spread from their respective places of origin to India in the east and to Asia Minor in the west.

By way of example, it might be helpful to provide a brief review of the life of one of these key figures. Jamāl al-Dīn was born towards the end of the sixth/twelfth century, probably in the Iranian town of Sāva, situated just to the southwest of present-day Tehran. There is some evidence that he may have studied to become a religious scholar, since in at least one account he is said to have issued legal opinions without consulting any books, and in other sources he is reported to have studied the Qurʾān as well as religious sciences and to have written at least a partial Qurʾānic exegesis. As a young man, he travelled to Damascus to continue his studies, where he became affiliated with the Sufi hospice of ʿUthmān Rūmī located at the foot of the Qāsiyūn mountain to the northwest of the city. Soon, his allegiance to ʿUthmān Rūmī gave way to extreme asceticism through his encounter with a remarkable young ascetic named Jalāl Darguzīnī. Jamāl al-Dīn shaved his face and head and began to spend his time sitting motionless on graves with his face turned in the direction of Mecca, speechless and with grass as his only food. Another tradition of reports in the sources attributes Jamāl al-Dīn's turn to ascetic practices to his scrupulous endeavour to preserve his chastity, in a way reminiscent of one part of the Qurʾānic story of Yūsuf (the Qurʿān, 12:21–35). Jamāl al-Dīn was soon accosted by a group of disciples and eager followers. In order to preserve his solitude, he left Damascus and spent the last years of his life in total social isolation in a cemetery in Damietta in Egypt, where a hospice was later built around his tomb.

Jamāl al-Dīn was first and foremost an uncompromising renouncer. He was stringent in his rejection of this world, as evidenced by his penchant for residing in cemeteries, in both Damascus and Damietta, as well as by the

[34] See Karamustafa, *God's Unruly Friends*, 39–46 for detailed accounts on these two figures. The summary biography of Jamāl al-Dīn Sāvī that follows is adopted from this work.

extreme care he took to dissociate himself from all established patterns of social life through such practices as shaving the head and all facial hair, donning woollen sacks, and refusing to work for sustenance. Presumably, he was also celibate. He shunned all kinds of attention and preferred to lead the life of a complete recluse. It is not possible to determine the nature of his attitude towards the religious law. While there is no sign that he deliberately eschewed prescribed religious observances or clearly violated legal prohibitions, reports on his life leave the impression that conformity to the *sharīʿa* was not a major issue in his career. The unmistakable message of his personal example was total rejection of society.

The examples of Jamāl al-Dīn Sāvī and Quṭb al-Dīn Ḥaydar proved to be infectious. Qalandarī hospices appeared within decades after Jamāl al-Dīn's death, in Damascus, Damietta, Cairo and Jerusalem, and groups of "sack-wearing" Qalandars fanned out from the Arab Middle East to Anatolia in the west and to Iran, Central Asia and India in the east, where prominent early representatives included ʿUthmān Marandī, better known as Laʿl Shāhbāz Qalandar of Sehwan (d. 673/1274) and Bū ʿAlī Qalandar of Panipat. Ḥaydarīs, with their distinct iron paraphernalia and short sleeveless cloaks, also spread in these same regions. Before the end of the seventh/thirteenth century, other dervish groups similar to the mendicant Qalandars and Ḥaydarīs began to take shape. The followers of Baraq Baba (d. 707/1307–8) in Asia Minor and western Iran, followed by Abdāls of Rūm, Jāmīs, Bektāşīs, and Shams-i Tabrīzīs in Asia Minor and Madārīs and Jalālīs in Muslim South Asia were other representatives of this new wave of religious mendicancy.[35]

The itinerant dervishes bands considerably expanded the repertoire of unconventional and anti-*sharīʿa* behavior of previous antinomian Sufis by adopting a host of openly antisocial practices. They welded mendicancy, itinerancy, celibacy and self-mortification with striking forms of socially transgressive behavior, which they viewed as the ultimate measure of true religiosity. They actively violated prevalent social norms by adopting such shocking practices as nudity or improper clothing, shaving all bodily and facial hair, wearing iron chains, rings, collars, bracelets and anklets, as well as using hallucinogens and intoxicants. Not content with avoidance of gainful

[35] For a general history of the dervish groups until about the tenth/sixteenth century, see Karamustafa, *God's Unruly Friends*; Ahmet Yaşar Ocak, *Osmanlı İmparatorluğunda Marjinal Sufilik: Kalenderîler (XIV–XVII Yüzyıllar)* (Ankara: Türk Tarih Kurumu, 1992) also contains much information and analysis concerning dervish groups in the Ottoman Empire. On Laʿl Shāhbāz Qalandar, see Michel Boivin's *Le soufisme antinomien dans le sous-continent indien: Laʿl Shahbāz Qalandar et son heritage, XIIIe-XXe siècle* (Paris: Cerf, 2012), and on Baraq Baba, Ahmet T. Karamustafa, "Baraq Baba", *The Encyclopaedia of Islam three.*

employment, family life, indeed most forms of social association, they moved from mere nonconformist behavior to active rejection and destruction of established social customs. In this way, the dervish groups were striking in their deliberate and blatant rejection of the social mainstream as well as their apparent disregard for most strictures of the *sharīʿa*.

This new dervish piety was not homogeneous, and it manifested itself in the form of solitary mendicants, wandering bands and partially settled dervish communities. While mendicancy and itinerancy remained the norm, the attraction of settled community life sometimes prevailed, and some began to practice mendicancy and itinerancy on a part-time, mostly seasonal, basis. Wandering and begging in a state of extreme poverty most of the year, these dervishes returned to their hospices for the rest of the year, where they enjoyed the relative comfort of settled life. Throughout such diversity, however, antisocial, unconventional behavior remained a constant.

The penchant of the dervishes for distancing themselves from the established social and religious order was visible also in their adoption of controversial and radical beliefs and doctrines, even though it is extremely difficult to tease these out from the available sources, which are often biased and outright hostile towards the mendicants. It appears that the dervishes applied radical interpretations to central religious (in particular mystical) concepts such as passing away of the self (*fanāʾ*), poverty (*faqr*), theophany (*tajallī*) and sainthood (*walāya*). Indeed, they viewed their antinomianism as the natural result of the "correct" interpretation of these concepts. Thus, rejection of society was often justified as the passing away of the self, which was expressed in the language of death. The dervish was one who voluntarily chose death and "died before dying". The alleged *ḥadīth*, saying of the Prophet Muḥammad, *mūtū qabla an tamūtū* ("die before you die") supplied the prophetic sanction for this attitude. Technically, therefore, the dervish considered himself to have the status of a dead person. He often physically demonstrated the utter seriousness of this conviction by dwelling in cemeteries in the proximity of the dead. The implication was that he was not bound by social and legal norms. The latter applied to "legal persons" of clear social standing. The dervish, however, having shattered the confines of society, had no social persona: he functioned in a territory that was above and beyond society.

Similar interpretations of the concepts of poverty, theophany and sainthood always yielded the same rejectionist conclusion. Poverty literally meant absolute poverty. Theophany implied the presence of God in all his Creation, and thus the meaninglessness of legal prescriptions and proscriptions. Sainthood meant the existence of saints, the dervishes themselves, who were exempt from social and legal regulations. The underlying message was one and the same: the dervish had to implement an absolute break with his social past and to devote himself solely to God by means of radical renunciation.[36]

Even though the dervishes were united in their total rejection of society, it is important to emphasize that there were significant differences among the different dervish groups, in both external appearance and behavior. The uncontrolled ecstasy of the Abdāls of Rūm, with their boisterous communal rituals marked by music, dancing, consumption of hashish and self-laceration, diverged considerably from the learned gaiety of the Jāmīs with their carefully-crafted matted hair and belts studded with bells, while both of these groups stood quite apart from the fierce asceticism of the "heavy-metal" Ḥaydarīs and the clean-shaven, sack-wearing Qalandars. There were also linguistic factors that worked to render them distinct: the Qalandars and Jāmīs were overwhelmingly Persian-speakers, while Abdāls of Rūm and probably also Ḥaydarīs mainly spoke vernacular Turkish. These groups remained essentially separate for several centuries, at least until around the tenth/sixteenth century, even though it is likely that they heavily influenced each other. Outsider observers, Muslim and non-Muslim, frequently confused these groups with each other, yet the same cannot be said for the dervishes themselves, who appear to have been highly conscious of their own distinctive group identities.

Other dervish groups that took shape in this period distinguished themselves not by practicing renunciant mendicancy, but by incorporating shocking practices into their communal rituals. Most prominent in this regard were the Rifāʿī dervishes, who achieved notoriety by their practices of fire-walking, snake-biting and body-piercing. In contrast with the earlier Sufi practices of *samāʿ*, tearing the cloak in ecstasy, and searching for manifestations of God in the creation (most notoriously in the form of "gazing at beardless youths") – all of which had come under fire by critics of Sufism, but were nevertheless practiced widely – the new repertoire of outrageous ritualistic activity of the Rifāʿīs such as biting live snakes and scorpions, swallowing broken glass, sticking needles into the body and walking on fire, was positively scandalous. Nevertheless, such "miracle performances" became popular, and the Rifāʿiyya and its branches rapidly spread from their origins in lower Iraq to Syria, Egypt, Anatolia and eventually the Balkans. In the Maghrib, similar practices appeared much later, when two new groups took shape in Morocco: the Ḥamādisha (Ḥmādsha in the local pronunciation), whose spiritual lineage

[36] For a fuller account, see Karamustafa, *God's Unruly Friends*, 13–23.

is traced back to two obscure Moroccan saints of the late eleventh/seventeenth and early twelfth/eighteenth centuries, Sīdī Abū l-Ḥasan ʿAlī b. Ḥamdush (d. 1131/1718–9 or 1135/1722–3, known popularly as Sīdī ʿAlī) and Sīdī Aḥmad Dghughī (dates unknown), and ʿĪsāwa (Aïssaouas), founded during the early tenth/sixteenth century by Muḥammad b. ʿĪsā l-Sufyānī l-Mukhtārī (d. 932/1526). These groups were well-known for the activities associated elsewhere with the Rifāʿīs, as well as for slashing their heads with knives or axes and beating their heads with hard objects.[37]

The establishment of the regional empires of the Ottomans, Ṣafavids, Üzbeks and the Mughals during the tenth/sixteenth century led to changes in the organization of the dervish groups. In many regions, the loose social collectivity of the previous few centuries was assimilated into an older one, or, rarely, transformed into a new, institutionalized Sufi path. In Ottoman Asia Minor and the Balkans, the Bektāşiyye emerged as a major new Sufi path that carried the legacy of the earlier Qalandars, Ḥaydarīs, and Abdāls of Rūm, while in India the Qalandars formed associations with the socially respectable Sufi paths (*ṭarīqas*), which led to the emergence of "hyphenated" paths like the Chishtiyya-Qalandariyya. The Khāksār in Iran probably came into being as a distinct path through a merger of different movements such as the Ḥaydariyya and Jalāliyya. Not all of the earlier dervish groups survived into the early modern period, however, and some simply disappeared altogether, as evidenced by the case of the Jāmīs in the Ottoman Empire.[38]

But new dervish saints continued to appear with regular frequency in the early modern period. In Asia, such figures were generally identified as *qalandar*, *dīvāne* (Central Asia) or *malang* (South Asia), but the term *qalandar* no longer denoted allegiance to the specific example of Jamāl al-Dīn Sāvī. The stories of these saints believed to have been pulled out of society directly by God vary considerably in this era, but there are recurring patterns and common features that can be noted. Some *majdhūbs* were presumably not integrated into society even from childhood and grew up as misfits of one kind or another, as in the example of the Central Asian *qalandar*

[37] Clifford E. Bosworth, "Rifāʿiyya", *The Encyclopaedia of Islam*, 2d ed. (8: 525–26); ʿVincent Crapanzano, "Ḥamādisha", *The Encyclopaedia of Islam THREE*, and Sossie Andézian, ʿAïssaouas (ʿĪsāwa),ʾ *The Encyclopaedia of Islam THREE.*

[38] On the Bektaşis, see Hamid Algar, ʿBektāšīya,ʾ *Encyclopedia Iranica* 4:118–122 for a concise but comprehensive treatment; the early phase of the path is well-covered in Zeynep Yürekli, *Architecture and Hagiography in the Ottoman Empire: The Politics of Bektashi Shrines in the Classical Age* (Farnham, Surrey: Ashgate, 2012), chapter 1. For the Khāksār, see Zahra Taheri, ʿḴāksār,ʾ *Encyclopedia Iranica* 15: 356–59.

poet Bābābrahīm, known as Mashrab (1640–1711 CE).[39] Others evidently underwent conversion experiences as adults that threw them off course from socially respectable life trajectories into the "social wilderness" at the heart of urban society. The Punjabi poet and saint Shah Ḥusayn of Lahore (1539–99 CE), for instance, was a Qādirī Sufi until he experienced a dramatic spiritual transformation at the age of 36 when he heard his Sufi teacher recite the verse "The life of the world is nothing but play and pleasurable distraction" (Qur'an 6.32), which led him to cast aside his previous social identity and start living beyond the pale, drinking wine in public and singing and dancing in the streets.[40] Still others, like Muḥammad Ṣiddīq Ẕalīlī (1676–1753 CE) and 'Abd Allāh Nidā'ī (1688–1760 CE) of Central Asia, had complex but continuous relationships with an established Sufi path (in their case the Naqshbandiyya).[41] Conversion from a respectable social status, especially from the ranks of religious scholars and Sufis, continued to be a common trope in hagiographic and literary accounts of enraptured saints in the age of the regional empires, though in some cases such conversion did not necessarily mean a complete rupture in the relationship between antinomian dervishes and mainstream Sufi paths.

The antinomian and antisocial repertoire of *majdhūb* saints of the early modern era mirrors that of the earlier dervish groups, but it is in the historical accounts of the former that we come across clear evidence of transgression and even inversion of prevalent gender roles, for which the historical record of the late medieval dervish groups remains inconclusive. Abū Bakr ibn Abi'l-Wafā' of Aleppo (1503–83), for instance, who spoke in the Arabic vernacular only, addressed "his male interlocutors in the feminine grammatical gender", thus inverting gender hierarchy by demeaning adult Muslim males.[42] Shah Ḥusayn of Lahore, mentioned above, not only often "spoke in the voice of a woman" in his Punjabi poetry, but openly lived with his Brahmin lover Madho in an homoerotic relationship in defiance of prevalent heteronormative custom.[43] Mūsā Sadā Sohāg (d. 1449 CE), originally a Chistī Sufi from

[39] Alexandre Papas, *Mystiques et vagabonds en islam: portraits de trois soufis qalandar* (Paris: Cerf, 2010), 31–136.

[40] Scott Kugle, *Sufis and Saints' Bodies: Mysticism, Corporeality, and Sacred Power in Islam* (Chapel Hill: University of North Carolina Press, 2007), 185.

[41] Papas, *Mystiques et vagabonds en islam*, 137–257.

[42] Heghnar Zeitlian Watenpaugh, "Deviant Dervishes: Space, Gender, and the Construction of Antinomian Piety in Ottoman Aleppo", *International Journal of Middle East Studies* 37 (2005), 547–49. Also see Khaled El-Rouayheb, "Heresy and Sufism in the Arabic-Islamic World: Some Preliminary Observations", *Bulletin of the School of Oriental and African Studies* 73 (2010): 357–80.

[43] For a full account, see Kugle, *Sufis and Saints' Bodies*, 181–220; the quote is on 201.

Gujarat, went even further by completely inverting gender roles when he decided to take on the persona of a woman: "he donned the red clothes of a bride awaiting her groom and adopted the nickname Sada Sohag 'the Eternal Bride'".[44] It appears, therefore, that transgression of gender roles was a persistent feature of saints captivated by God, and in South Asia their shrines exercised a special attraction to transgendered individuals (*khusras*) until recent times, as in the case of the Punjabi saint ʿAbd al-Laṭīf Shāh, known as Barrī Imām (d. 1120/1708).[45]

The dervish groups and unaffiliated individual enraptured saints survived well into late colonial times, but they gradually petered out in the era of modern nation states, except in South Asia.[46] The attitudes of the colonial authorities as well as the political elites of the new nation states towards the dervishes and the challenges that these latter presented to both colonial and national establishment agendas of "modernization" form fascinating subjects of study.[47] In some instances, the "wild and unruly" dervishes of the medieval and early modern times have retroactively been "tamed" into symbols of national/regional religious identity, with major shrine complexes honouring their "historic" legacy, as in the cases of Laʿl Shāhbāz Qalandar in Sehwan Sharif, Pakistan and Aḥmad al-Badawī in Tanta, Egypt.[48] The formation of

[44] Scott Kugle, "Dancing with Khusro: Gender Ambiguities and Poetic Performance in a Delhi *Dargah*", in *Rethinking Islamic Studies From Orientalism to Cosmopolitanism*, eds. Carl W. Ernst and Richard C. Martin (Columbia, SC: University of South Carolina Press, 2010), 254–56; the quote is on 255.

[45] M. Azam Chaudhary, "Barrī Imām", *The Encyclopaedia of Islam, THREE*. Jürgen Wasim Frembgen; 'The *Majzub* Mama Ji Sarkar,' in *Embodying Charisma: Modernity, Locality, and Performance of Emotion in Sufi Cults*, eds. Pnina Werbner and Helene Basu (New York: Routledge, 1998), 140–59, is a study of a late-twentieth century majdhūb associated with Barrī Imām.

[46] There is no comprehensive historical overview of the dervish groups for the early modern and modern periods, but for many leads and references, see Jürgen Wasim Frembgen, *Journey to God: Sufis and Dervishes in Islam*, trans. Jane Ripken (Oxford: Oxford University Press, 2008), and Alexandre Papas, "Dervish", *The Encyclopaedia of Islam*, THREE.

[47] For an exemplary anthropological study based on fieldwork in Lahore, Pakistan, that includes much coverage of qalandars, see Katherine Pratt Ewing, *Arguing Sainthood: Modernity, Psychoanalysis, and Islam* (Durham, NC: Duke University Press, 1997).

[48] The former shrine is admirably studied by Michel Boivin in *Artefacts of Devotion: A Sufi Repertoire of the Qalandariyya in Sehwan Sharif, Sindh, Pakistan* (Karachi, Pakistan: Oxford University Press, 2011) and *Le soufisme antinomien dans le sous-continent indien*, and the latter by Edward B. Reeves, *The Hidden Government: Ritual, Clientelism, and Legitimation in Northern Egypt* (Salt Lake City: University of Utah Press, 1990). Kumkum Srivastava's *The Wandering Sufis: Qalandars and their Path* (Bhopla: Indira Gandhi Manav Sangrahalaya, 2009) includes information on the current state of affairs at the shrines of Abū Bakr Tusi Haydari Qalandari (Matkey Shah) in Delhi and Bu Ali Shah Qalandar in Panipat (chapters 4–6).

cultic activity around the shrines of antinomian dervishes as well as their poetic and hagiographical legacy preserved and cultivated in the various vernaculars of Muslim peoples constitutes a significant chapter in the Islamization of the common masses everywhere, which is a topic that still awaits its researchers.

How should we explain the somewhat sudden upsurge of antinomian dervish activity during the thirteenth century and its lasting popularity in Muslim communities from that point onwards until well into the twentieth century? To a large extent, the formation of dervish piety appears to have been a reaction to the increasing institutionalization of Sufism from the twelfth century onwards. The dervish groups rejected the basic institutions of society, but their living critique was pointed specifically towards socially well-integrated Sufis, who formed widespread patron–client networks that controlled much property and wielded immense political and social power. The dervishes viewed these respectable Sufis as cop-outs who had forsaken the basic mandate of the Sufi path – which was selfless and total devotion to God – for the comfort of social acceptance built on cultivation of a spiritualized (albeit socially pliable) subjectivity. In this sense, it is possible to see dervish piety as a real-time running commentary – mostly vehemently critical – on socially domesticated Sufi paths. The dervishes functioned as the social and religious conscience of socially mainstream Sufis.

This inextricable though largely conflictual bond between antinomian dervishes and socially mainstream, law-abiding Sufis partly explains the emergence and durability of dervish piety in medieval and early modern times when mainstream urban Muslim religiosity everywhere assumed an unmistakable Sufi colouring. Where there were Sufis – and no place was devoid of them – there were dervishes. Yet, it is important to realize that, quite apart from its ties to mainstream Sufi paths, antinomian dervish piety had its own independent appeal to large numbers of ordinary believers, particularly in the countryside, where it seems to have impacted the everyday piety of many, often newly Islamized, Muslims in a formative way. The dervishes spoke in the vernacular as opposed to the learned idiom of the cultural elite, and they were not normally cluttered with – and thus were not compromised by – ties of clientage with power holders (though there were exceptions, such as Baraq Baba); as such, it appears that they were often perceived as the very personification of total devotion to God – in other words, as the true saints. Their social distance from the cultural elites and their real closeness, especially in terms of poverty and everyday language, to the common people evidently rendered them viable candidates for popular sainthood. Their exemplary piety informed the daily religiosity of rural and urban masses, at times in a defining manner.[49] In some cases, there even appears to have been real blending between mendicant dervishes and actual communities of itinerant beggars, musicians, and bards.[50] The enduring popularity and lasting legacy of dervish piety should be understood in the light of the popular appeal it has had among the common people from its origins in the seventh/thirteenth century until well into the modern period.

[49] For the argument that *abdals* of *Rūm*, for instance, played a formative role in the emergence of Alevi piety in Anatolia and the Balkans, see Ahmet T. Karamustafa, "Kaygusuz Abdal: A Medieval Turkish Saint and the Formation of Vernacular Islam in Anatolia", in *Unity in Diversity: Mysticism, Messianism and Construction of Religious Authority in Islam*, ed. Orkhan Mir Kasimov (Leiden: Brill, 2013), 329–42.

[50] Frembgen, *Journey to God*, 115–20; Anna L. Troitskaja, 'Des anciens qalandar et maddāh d'Ouzbekistane,' translated from the original Russian in Pappas, *Mystiques et Vagabonds en Islam*, 269–312 ['Iz proshlogo kalandarov i maddakhov v Uzbekistane,' in *Domusulmanskie Verovanija i Obrjady v Srednej Azii* (Moscow: Nauka, 1975), 191–223].

6

Mysticism in Medieval Sufism

Lloyd Ridgeon

INTRODUCTION

In this essay I shall attempt to tease out the extent to which there is truth in Martin Lings' statement that "Sufism is nothing other than Islamic mysticism."[1] Undertaking this investigation is perilous because the key terms of the study are far from clear. Indeed, the term "Sufism" is discussed in various ways by those who have called themselves Sufis, resulting in emic authors investigating the derivation of the term or citing a range of definitions in their treatises from "past masters" of the tradition.[2] Moreover, some Western academics have simply labelled Sufism with the term "mysticism", even though the meaning of this word is greatly contested and its suitability for non-Christian traditions is suspect.[3] An example of the pitfalls that are encountered when defining mysticism becomes all too apparent when considering the attempt of Ninian Smart, who considered mysticism as "primarily consisting in an interior or introvertive

[1] Martin Lings served as Keeper of Oriental Printed Books and Manuscripts at the British Museum from 1970–3. The statement is found in his *What is Sufism* (London: George Allen & Unwin, 1975), 15.

[2] For Sufis discussing the derivations of the term, see: *Kashf al-Maḥjūb of al-Hujwiri: The Oldest Persian Treatise on Sufism*, trans. R. A. Nicholson (London: Luzac & Co, 1911), 30–1. For those citing definitions from past masters see *Al-Qushayri's Epistle on Sufism (Al-Risala al-qushayriyya fi 'ilm al-tasawwuf)* translated by Alexander Knysh (Reading: Garner, 2007), 288–92.

[3] See for example, R.A. Nicholson, *The Mystics of Islam* (London: George Bell & Sons Ltd, 1914); Annemarie Schimmel, *The Mystical Dimension of Islam* (Chapel Hill: University of North Carolina Press, 1975); and Alexander Knysh, *Islamic Mysticism: A Short History* (Leiden: Brill, 1999). Unfortunately, some of my own works have also used the term rather uncritically: see Lloyd Ridgeon, *Morals and Mysticism in Persian Sufism* (London: Routledge, 2012). "Mysticism" is a term that is difficult to define due to various understandings that have been offered by those that claim to have experienced something that transcends the usual state of consciousness. This essay is not a discussion about the "reality" of mysticism. I have refrained from dressing the word "mysticism" (and associated terms) in speech-marks which would highlight the tendentious nature of the term, although readers may envisage speech-marks there should they wish.

quest, culminating in certain interior experiences which are not described in terms of sense-experience or of mental images".[4] Smart's definition fails to correlate with the way that many Sufis described encounters of the ultimate reality through what they called the "imaginal" sense,[5] and which were cloaked in sensory forms that made what they understood as the divine more comprehensible. This was not a case of Sufis witnessing what Rudolph Otto called the *numinious*;[6] it was not a terrifying, wholly other, awe-inspiring deity, but a beautiful beloved with whom the Sufi wanted to unite. In short, Smart's definition cited above is too restrictive. In this essay I use the term mysticism in the Islamic tradition to refer to the belief among some Sufis that experience of some form of intimacy with God was possible in their own lifetimes (whether it was an apprehension of ontological unity or else a vision of ultimate reality), which went beyond the piety of many Muslims who engaged in "normative" Islamic ritual activity and who accepted "orthodox" forms of belief.

To answer the question of whether Sufism is Islamic mysticism, and, if so, which kind of mysticism is being discussed, I shall commence by analysing the kinds of subjects that the Sufis included within their literature, and in this fashion indicate the extent to which mysticism was a significant concern. Subsequently I shall investigate the thought of several Sufis who discuss the notion of mystical unity and experience. My main source in this article is the first chapter of a work called *The Book of the Descent* (*Kitāb-i tanzīl*)[7] by ʿAzīz Nasafī, a Sufi from the Persian-speaking world of the thirteenth century. His views will be compared with alternative Sufi voices of a similar timeframe, which offer different perspectives to demonstrate the heterogeneous nature of Sufi ontological and mystical beliefs. It is vital to stress this diversity, simply because it is problematic to discuss a single Sufi tradition. Steven Katz has argued convincingly that the experience of the mystic is in no small measure influenced by preconceptions, prejudices and expectations – that is to say, there no such thing as "pure unmediated experience".[8] From this perspective,

4 Ninian Smart, "Interpretation and Mystical Experience", *Religious Studies* 1(1), (1965): 75.

5 A good explanation of the imaginal sense is offered by William Chittick, *Imaginal Worlds* (Albany: Suny Press, 1994).

6 Rudolph Otto, *The Idea of the Holy*. trans. John W. Harvey (Oxford: University Press, 1923).

7 The manuscript for this text that I use is actually called *The Explanation of the Descent* (*Bayān-i tanzīl*); however, Hermann Landolt convincingly argues that this manuscript is virtually the same as six other manuscripts which are called *Kitāb-i tanzīl*. (See his "Nasafī and the *Bayān al-tanzīl*", in *Bayān al-tanzīl*, edited by S.A.A. Mīr Bāgherī Fard (Tehran: Tahuri, 2000). The manuscript of *Kitāb-i tanzīl* that I have used for this chapter is in the John Rylands Library, University of Manchester, C112, folios 38–84. It is henceforth referred to as *K.T.*

8 Steven T. Katz, "The Conservative Character of Mystical Experience", in Steven T. Katz (ed.), *Mysticism and Religious Traditions* (Oxford: University Press, 1983), 3–60.

it follows that, of necessity, a Sufi baggage is so unique that it is difficult to speak of an essential Sufi worldview and concomitant practice that shaped the mystical experience of all Sufis. At best, a constructivist Katzian argument would run that Sufis were influenced by a broad tradition, both generally Islamic and specifically Sufi, which is sufficiently wide and challenging to define.[9] This challenge has been taken up in Pnina Werbner's chapter in this volume (Chapter 12), as she focuses on the practice of Sufi regional cults to "construct a comparative framework to differentiate Sufi cults or shrine-focused orders from one another". She demonstrates that there are many similarities in shrine complexes in regions as far apart as Indonesia, the Indian sub-continent and North Africa. Werbner's concern is with practice, but this chapter focuses upon belief, particularly the different kinds of ontological relationships (or explanations for mystical encounters) between God and creation that the Sufis of the medieval period discussed. Although the focus is primarily upon the medieval period, the discussion will examine contemporary ways in which the phenomena of mysticism have been understood. It is striking that the three main ways of accounting for mystical encounters from the medieval period are still discussed in the modern period, by both believers and academic commentators.

In this chapter it is possible to give only a sample of the various ways in which Sufis accounted for mystical experience. The sheer diversity of Sufism does not mean that we are left meandering aimlessly in the realm of words, for the analysis of terms such as "Sufism" and "mysticism" is not necessarily negative, as it opens up new landscapes in which the limits and possibilities of these terms are realised, and appropriate neologisms may be coined to reflect the changing horizons.

CONCERNS OF EARLY AND MEDIEVAL SUFIS

A survey of the early and medieval Sufi literature reveals diverse interests among practitioners of the tradition; indeed, treatises on what may be termed mystical experience represent just one element among many that interested Sufis. As Muslims, Sufi authors were concerned to investigate sacred scripture, and it is not surprising that they composed works on the Qur'ān, *ḥadīth* and theology.[10] In addition, much literature is of an ethical and spiritual

[9] Pnina Werbner in this volume (Chapter 12), as she attempts to identify common elements of practice in Sufi regional cults.

[10] See, for example, the commentary on the Qur'ān by Sahl Tustarī (d. c. 896) which has been translated into English by Annabel Keeler as *Tafsīr Al-Tustarī* (Fons Vitae, 2008). For a more general work on the importance of the Qur'ān among Sufis and their methods of

nature, which suggests that the tradition was an attempt to adopt a way of life that was God-centred. The point is that the Sufi was not necessarily a mystic, but that a pious life, sincerity, considerable self-reflection and the performance of additional devotions that have come to be associated specifically with various forms of Sufism were all prerequisites of the "path" (*ṭarīqa*). This, of course, was in addition to the "normative" confirmation of belief and standard Islamic practice. A pious life was one that was firmly grounded in society, and much of the Sufi tradition was focused on imitating the life of the prophet Muḥammad, who was believed to have established an ethical Muslim community. Therefore, many early Sufis composed treatises in which ethics were a prime consideration, typified by the writings of ʿAbd al-Raḥmān Sulamī (d. 1021), who described how the individual could both engage in society and focus his or her attention upon God.[11] Sufi works on ethics continued to abound after Sulamī, so similar concerns are paramount in the treatises of celebrated masters including Qushayrī (986–1072), Hujwīrī (d. 1071), Ghazālī (d. 1111) and Abū Ḥafṣ ʿUmar Suhrawardī (d. 1234).[12]

Aside from ethics, another genre of Sufi literature reflected upon ritual activity, and these writings examined the conditions and regulations that the individual needed to observe in the total ritualistic lifestyles of Sufis (generally to ensure the observance of the *sharīʿa*). The most well known of these rituals is the *dhikr*, or the remembrance of God – the continual repetition of one of his so-called ninety-nine beautiful names.[13] Other rituals included particular fasts, spiritual isolation for periods of forty days, introspection and the

interpretation see Kristin Sands, *Sufi Commentaries of the Qur'ān in Classical Islam* (London, Routledge, 2008). For the relationship between *ḥadīth* and early Sufism see Christopher Melchert, "The Piety of the Hadith Folk", *International Journal of Middle East Studies* 34 (2002), 425–39.

11 See, for example, Abū ʿAbd al-Raḥmān Sulamī, *A Collection of Sufi Rules of Conduct* [a translation of his *Jawāmiʿ al-ādāb al-ṣūfiyya*] by Elana Biagi (Cambridge: Islamic Texts Society, 2010); ibid., *The Book of Sufi Chivalry* [a translation of Sulamī's *Kitāb al-futuwwa*] by Sheikh Tosun Bayrak al-Jerrahi al-Halveti (London: East West Publications, 1983).

12 For Qushayrī see *Al-Qushayri's Epistle on Sufism*, which is divided into three sections. One of these was devoted to the "stations" (*maqāmāt*) that are acquired by the effort of the individual, and reflect the various character traits and the impact these have on ethical concerns, such as "repentance", "striving", "fear of God", and "scrupulousness", to mention four of the first five. For Hujwīrī, see *Kashf al-Maḥjūb of al-Hujwiri*. This manual of Sufism included discussions that were essentially of an ethical import. Thus chapters 15–25 examine the way that Sufis understood normative Islamic faith and practice, the ethical implications of which are pronounced. Ghazālī's works, such as *Iḥyā ʿulūm al-dīn* and *Kīmīyā-yi saʿādat*, also contain long discussions about the communal nature and ethical import of Sufism. For Suhrawardī, see Erik Ohlander, *Sufism in a Time of Transition* (Leiden: Brill, 2008).

13 On the ninety-nine names of God and its theological significance see *Al-Ghazālī: The Ninety-Nine Beautiful Names of God* [a translation by David Burrell and Nazih Daher of his *al-Maqṣad al-asnā fī sharḥ asmāʾ Allāh al-ḥusnā*], (Cambridge: Islamic Texts Society, 1992).

examination and analysis of each and every thought, the *samā'* (or listening and sometimes dancing to devotional music – typified best by the Sufis of the Mevleviyya order),[14] and travelling from one location to another in search of the perfect spiritual guide. There were also specific rituals for communal living in Sufi convents. Works pertaining to rituals were not merely directed to the "fully-blown" members of Sufi orders, but also to the more lay-orientated groups, which included individuals known as *akhīs* or *javānmardān*, who appear almost as "second-class" Sufis in Anatolia and Iran respectively and who flourished in post-Mongol times.[15] It is also necessary to include the more extreme manifestations of devotional ritual (which were considered by some Sufis to be beyond the pale of the tradition), such as the body-piercing of Rifā'iya Sufis and the shaving of all facial hair by Qalandar Sufis.[16]

Perhaps to reinforce the guidelines offered in ethical treatises and those on Sufi ritual activity, some Sufis took to recording anecdotes and sayings of individuals from the previous generations of exemplars of the tradition, and so biographies of famous "Sufis" are included in the writings of Sulamī, Qushayrī, Hujwīrī, Ansārī (d. 1089) and 'Aṭṭār (d. c. 1220)[17]. Such works also functioned to legitimise the emerging tradition by appropriating as Sufis those who were generally respected within the Islamic tradition at large.[18] This form of literature may be compared to the larger hagiographical tradition in which works were devoted to the life of a single Sufi, or else the lives of several individuals within the same order or brotherhood.[19]

[14] On which see William C. Chittick, "Rumi and the Mawlawiyyah", in S.H. Nasr (ed.), *Islamic Spirituality: Manifestations II* (London: SCM Press, 1991), 105–26.

[15] On the *akhīs* and *javānmardān*, see Lloyd Ridgeon, *Morals and Mysticism in Persian Sufism* (London: Routledge, 2010), 61–91.

[16] On the Rifā'īya, see John Renard, "Rifā'īya", in *Historical Dictionary of Sufism* (London: The Scarecrow Press, 2005), 202. On the Qalandars see Lloyd Ridgeon, "Shaggy or Shaved?" *Iran and the Caucuses*, 14.2 (2010): 233–64.

[17] See Sulamī, *Ṭabaqāt al-ṣūfiyya*, Nūr al-Dīn Shurayba (ed.) (Cairo: Maktaba al-Khānjī, 1372/1953); *Al-Qurayshi's Epistle on Sufism*, 17–74; *Kashf al-Maḥjūb of al-Hujwiri*, 70–171: for Ansārī, see *Ṭabaqāt al-Ṣūfiyya*, by M. S. Mawlā'ī (ed.) (Tehran, Tahuri, 1376/1997–8); for 'Aṭṭār, see Paul Losensky (translated) *Farid Ad-Din 'Attar's Memorial of God's Friends* (New York: Paulist Press, 2009).

[18] See Suleiman Ali Murad, *Early Islam between Myth and History: Al-Ḥasan al-Baṣrī (d. 110H/728CE) and the Formation of his Legacy in Classical Islamic Scholarship* (Leiden, Brill, 2006).

[19] These include hagiographies of Abū Sa'īd Abī'l-Khayr. *Kashf al-Asrār*, translated by John O'Kane as *The Secrets of God's Mystical Oneness* (Costa Mesa: Mazda, 1992); the anonymous hagiography of Awḥad al-dīn Kirmānī, entitled *Manāqib-i Awḥad al-Dīn Kirmānī* (Tehran: Bungāh-i Nashr-i Kitāb, 1969); and Aflākī's biography of Sufis of the Mevleviyya order, *Manāqib al-'ārifīn*, translated by John O'Kane as *The Feats of the Knowers of God* (Leiden: Brill, 2002).

All of this serves to indicate that the Sufi tradition was certainly not a mystics-only club. However, from the ninth century onwards the tradition was not devoid of mystical content: the ecstatic statements (*shaṭḥiyāt*) of Sufis, including most famously those of Bāyazīd Basṭāmī (d. 877) and Manṣūr al-Ḥallāj (d. 922), reflect the growing tendency to express experiences that have been understood in a mystical nature.[20] By the thirteenth century the form of mystical literature was becoming increasingly diverse, for Sufis such as Najm al-Dīn Kubrā (d. 1220) composed an autobiographical account of his encounter with God, the voluminous works of Ibn 'Arabi (d. 1245) presented a profound philosophy that illustrated his view of the ultimate reality that has been termed the unity of existence (*waḥdat al-wujūd*),[21] while Persian poets such as 'Aṭṭār and Jalāl al-Dīn Rūmī (d. 1273) portrayed the underlying unity of creation and God.[22]

Mysticism, in the sense of claims of communion with God, or the experience of the ultimate reality, has been an important component of the Sufi tradition. Sufis held that there could be no guarantee that an individual who embraced Islamic theology, engaged in Sufi rituals and reflected upon the various ways to perfection as manifested through Sufi history would experience the divine while alive in this world. Yet at the same time, it *was* argued by many Sufis that such an experience was the pinnacle of the Sufi path, and, as such, represented the ultimate level of awareness that transcended knowledge derived from sense perception and rational reflection. Our chief representative of the Sufi tradition in this article, 'Azīz Nasafī, expresses this in his treatise *Kitāb-i Tanzīl*:

> Oh dear friend! One must not trust in reason (*'aql*) alone [to acquire] gnosis (*ma'rifat*) of things. It is clear that the limit of human reason [is the realisation] that nothing is actualised other than confusion if one steps beyond one's limit . . . There is a path, and traversing that path by starlight is insufficient. Moonlight is required. And there is another path, and traversing that path by moonlight is insufficient. Sunlight is required. Starlight is like sense perception, moonlight is like the light of reason, and the sunlight is like God's light.[23]

[20] See Christopher Melchert, "The Transition from Asceticism to Mysticism at the Middle of the Ninth Century C.E.", *Studia Islamica*, 83, (1996): 51–70.

[21] See William Chittick, *The Sufi Path of Knowledge* (Albany: SUNY Press, 1989), xii–xv. Ibn 'Arabī claimed that his writings were based on his mystical unveilings.

[22] For Kubrā, see *Die fawā'iḥ al-ĝamāl wa fawātiḥ al-ĝalāl des Naĝm-uddīn Kubrā*, edited by Fritz Meier (Weisbaden, 1957); for Ibn 'Arabī, see William Chittick, *The Sufi Path of Knowledge*; for 'Aṭṭār, see H. Ritter, *Ocean of the Soul* (Leiden: Brill, 2012); for Rūmī, see Franklin Lewis, *Rumi Past and Present, East and West* (Oxford: Oneworld, 2000).

[23] *K.T.* folio 38b.

TYPES OF SUFI MYSTICAL EXPERIENCE

Within much of the Western literature that attempts to summarise or popularise Sufism there has been a tendency to associate the tradition with mysticism. Yet some scholars are reticent to use the word, to the extent that William Chittick has claimed, "In my own writings, I have always avoided the word 'mysticism'." In a number of publications he has elaborated upon the reasons for this: firstly, there is the desire to avoid negative connotations of mysticism as being vague speculation at best and "mindless mush" at worst; a second reason is that much Sufi literature is not mystical (as we have seen), and is therefore denigrated by those who approve of mysticism.[24] Other academics, typified by Carl Ernst, have pointed out the "orientalist-baggage" that sometimes comes with mysticism when it is linked with Sufism.[25] This is typified by the attempts of some nineteenth-century orientalists to divorce Sufism (and therefore mysticism) from its Islamic heritage, and so Islam was associated with the Semitic Arabs while Sufism was characterised by its Aryan lineage. A good example of this occurs in the preface to the earliest English translation of one of Nasafī's works, as the English translator states, "in . . . a future work . . . I hope to prove that Sufism is really the development of the Primaeval Religion of the Aryan race."[26] A similar sentiment appears to be echoed in the influential work of William James (who is discussed below) when he remarked, "The Sufis have existed in Persia from the earliest times, and as their pantheism is so at variance with the hot and rigid monotheism of the Arab mind, it has been suggested that Sufism must have been inoculated into Islam by Hindu influences."[27] And in the late nineteenth century the famous French philosopher Ernst Renan expressed sympathy for the Aryans over the Semitic persuasion of Islam and the Arabs when he approvingly described Jamāl al-Dīn al-Afghānī as belonging to "those energetic races of Iran, near India, where the Aryan spirit lives still so energetically under the superficial layer of official Islam".[28] Although most scholars now reject this view, vestiges of such a perspective surface on occasions.[29]

[24] William C. Chittick, "Mysticism in Islam." A lecture delivered at the David M. Kennedy Center for International Studies, Brigham Young University, May 2003. See http://meti.byu.edu/mysticism_chittick.html (accessed 08/10/2012). See also ibid., *Faith and Practice of Islam* (Albany: SUNY Press, 1992), 168–73.

[25] Carl Ernst, *The Shambhala Guide to Sufism*, 8–18.

[26] E.H. Palmer, "Introduction", *Oriental Mysticism* (first published 1867, reprinted London: Octogon Press, 1974), p. vi.

[27] William James, *The Varieties of Religious Experience* (London: Longmans, 1902), 402.

[28] Cited in Nikki R. Keddie, *An Islamic Response to Imperialism* (Berkeley: University of California Press, 1983), 92.

[29] See, e.g., G.A. Lipton, "Secular Sufism: Neoliberalism, Ethnoracism, and the Reformation of the Muslim Other", *Muslim World*, 101.3 (2011), 427–40.

Another criticism of Western scholarship on Sufism has come from Omid Safi, who has demonstrated the drawbacks of applying a term steeped in a Western, Protestant tradition to Sufism. Safi highlights a tendency among some Western academics to "borrow theoretical frameworks which relegate mysticism to a privatised realm, focusing on 'mystical experience' ".[30] His point is that such post-Enlightenment and Christian tendencies (which privilege the individual and private religiosity) stand in contrast to the Sufi tradition in which Sufi masters are reported in hagiographical literature to be deeply involved in society, influencing the immediate community and powerful individuals such as kings, princes and other authoritative figures. Whether this is historically true or not is irrelevant for Safi, for the followers of Sufi masters certainly perceived the active engagement of the spiritual élite in society to be a necessary component of the Sufi path. While Safi's plea for more historically grounded studies that demonstrate the nature of medieval Sufism is well founded, it is also the case that an examination of Sufi portrayals and explanations of mystical experience reveals the benefits and limitations of Western scholarship on mysticism, as carried out by the likes of James, Zaehner and Smart, the views of whom are discussed in this chapter. Surveys of mystical experience therefore do not necessarily further the post-Enlightenment, Protestant worldview.

Thus far we have skirted around the word mysticism due to difficulties that an analysis of the term inevitably involves. In the West one of the first serious attempts to investigate mysticism was made by William James, who delivered the Gifford Lectures at Edinburgh University; these lectures formed the basis of *The Varieties of Religious Experience* which was published in 1902.[31] James included a chapter on mysticism in this work, and he viewed common qualities within the mystical dimensions of the world's major religious traditions including Islam, Christianity, Hinduism and Buddhism.[32] These common qualities were the ineffability of the experience, its noetic nature, its transiency and lastly the passivity of the subject (meaning that ultimately the experience is bestowed by God rather than acquired by the individual). James'

[30] Omid Safi, "Bargaining with Baraka: Persian Sufism, 'Mysticism' and Pre-Modern Politics", *The Muslim World*, vol. 90 (2000), 260.

[31] William James, *The Varieties of Religious Experience*. Lectures XVI–XVII (379–429) are entitled "Mysticism".

[32] James' sources on Sufism were limited. He focused on Ghazālī and cited the work of D.B. MacDonald, "The Life of Al-Ghazzali", *Journal of the American Oriental Society*, 1899, vol. xx. A second source on Ghazālī that James cites is A. Schmölders, *Essai sur les Ecoles Philosophiques chez les Arabes* (Paris: 1842).

four qualities of mystical experience are applicable to the Sufi tradition with varying degrees of compatibility.[33]

James's first quality is the ineffability of the experience, and it is perhaps the very nature of this quality that Sufis have largely refrained from explicating in detail. King has observed that mystical literature shows that it is not the ineffable experience itself that mystics describe, rather that their works pay more attention to the portrayal of the ineffable nature of ultimate reality itself.[34] Our example from the Sufi tradition, ʿAzīz Nasafī wrote several works that typify this tendency; his treatises concentrate on ontology, whereas the focus of mystical experience and its ineffability are peripheral to the extent that it is valid to question whether he had any mystical experience of his own or was simply reporting about a phenomena for which he had much liking. Nasafī very briefly mentions mystical visions in which the spirit leaves the body and witnesses heaven and the circumstances individuals will experience after death;[35] he also speaks of the ability to see into the past and future,[36] and refers in passing to the mysterious spiritual guide (*shaykh al-ghayb*).[37] It is more common for Nasafī to describe the mystical knowledge of the underlying unity of existence. He portrays God, usually in the abstract form of existence, through the views of other groups (most commonly the People of the Holy Law (*ahl-i sharīʿat*), the Philosophers (*ahl-i ḥikmat*) and the People of Unity (*ahl-i waḥdat*)). However, there were some Sufis of his era who left depictions of a recognisable and anthropomorphic God who appeared in mystical visions, sometimes in beautiful forms, and at others in a terrifying fashion.[38]

[33] It is worth stating at the very start that such qualities and the terms used to denote them may be employed to describe a completely different reality. As Katz observes, the atheist may experience the ineffability of the dread and absurdity of the cosmos, which is obviously different from the ineffability felt by a theist before God. See Steven T. Katz, "Language, Epistemology, and Mysticism", in Steven T. Katz (ed.), *Mysticism and Philosophical Analysis* (London: Sheldon Press, 1978), 48. See also Sviri, "Sufism: Reconsidering Terms", in G. Gobillot (ed.), *Les Mâitres Soufis et Leurs Disciples des III–V siècles de l'hégire* (Paris: Presses de l'Ifpo, 2013), who describes how the term "Sufi" was used in number of ways to denote different realities.

[34] Richard King, "Mysticism and Spirituality", in John Hinnels (ed.), *Routledge Companion to the Study of Religion* (London: Routledge, 2005), 327.

[35] ʿAzīz Nasafī, *al-Insān al-kāmil* (Tehran : Institut Français d'Iranologie de Téhéran, 1990), 108.

[36] Ibid., 89–90.

[37] See, e.g., *al-Insān al-kāmil*, 241; *K.T.*, 47a. The kinds of visionary phenomena that Nasafī mentions were regarded by other Sufis, such as Najm al-Dīn Rāzī (whose ideas are discussed in this chapter), as indications of a particular spiritual attainment rather than proof of reaching the ultimate goal (or God).

[38] Of note in this respect are the visions of Rūzbihān Baqlī. See Carl W. Ernst, *Ruzbihan Baqli* (Richmond: Curzon Press, 1996); see also Rūzbihān Baqlī, *The Unveiling of Secrets*, trans. Carl Ernst (Chapel Hill: Parvardigar Press, 1997).

James' second quality, the noetic nature of the experience, certainly has a clear resonance in the Sufi tradition. This noetic quality is a form of knowledge not grounded in everyday reason, and is termed "tasting" (*dhawq*) in the Sufi tradition. In the following quote, Nasafī plays with the term so that it conveys both its mystical and mundane sense:

> Whoever hears that there is a thing in the world called sugar is never equal with someone who knows there is a plant called sugar-cane which is extremely sweet, and that both sugar and cane is produced when that plant is cut and beaten, and the water is extracted from it and the residue is left to thicken. Whoever knows how sugar is made is never equal to someone who sees how it is made and [then] places sugar in his mouth. First is the level of hearing concerning the gnosis of sugar, second is the level of knowledge, and third is the level of tasting.[39]

James' third quality, which is the transiency of the experience, in one sense mirrors the mystical experiences described by Nasafī. For example, the latter remarks that mystical experience can last for several hours, yet his own spiritual master enjoyed an experience in which his spirit spent up to thirteen days in the heavens while his body was like that of a dead person.[40] Yet it is difficult to describe the Sufi mystical experience as transient, for Nasafī claimed that the benefits of the noetic knowledge associated with the person who enjoyed the most perfect state of stability (*tamkīn*) were permanent and had lasting effects. Here the wayfarer is able to manifest whatever divine name or attribute s/he desires and this results in the individual adopting a lifestyle that "verified" the authenticity of the experience.[41] After reaching and recognising God

> ... nothing is concealed for the perfect person. S/he has reached and recognised God, and after recognising God s/he has understood and seen all the substances of things as they are. [After this] he does not regard any task or any obedience as equal to or better than bringing comfort to people. [The perfect person] does not consider any comfort better than engaging in perfecting [others] so that they obtain salvation in this and the next world when they listen and carry out that task. This is a blessing that the [perfect] perform ...[42]

39 ʿAzīz Nasafī, *K.T.* folio 72a.

40 Ibid., folio 40a.

41 See his discussion of *tamkin*, in Ridgeon, *Persian Metaphysics and Mysticism* (Richmond: Curzon 2002), 220; *Kashf al-ḥaqā'iq*, A. Dāmghānī (ed.) (Tehran: Bungāh-i tarjuman wa nashr-i kitāb, 1965), 141; see also Hujwiri, *Kashf al-Maḥjūb*, 370–3.

42 Lloyd Ridgeon, *Persian Metaphysics and Mysticism*, 51: (*Maqṣad-i aqṣā*, appended to Jāmī's *Ashiʿʿāt al-lamaʿāt*, edited H. Rabbānī, Tehran: Kitābkhāna-yi ʿilmiyya-yi ḥāmidī, 1352/1973), 217.

From this perspective at least, the mystic is permanently with God and renders problematic the notion of transiency because the experience cannot be completely differentiated from the noetic knowledge which may endure for a considerable time.

James' fourth quality, the passivity of the experience, is a result of God ultimately bestowing his grace on the individual. In the Sufi tradition, the experience in the form of a mystical state (s. *ḥāl*; pl. *aḥwāl*) is understood to come from God and is never acquired through the individual's own effort. This explains the discussions among Sufis of individuals known as *majdhūb*, who are those that God draws to himself without them having engaged in any of the Sufi rituals designed to promote devotion to God.[43]

One of the conclusions that James drew from his study of mysticism is that "[Mysticism] is optimistic, or at least the opposite of pessimistic",[44] which reflects much of the general Sufi perspective. For example, Nasafī remarks in *Kitāb-i tanzīl*, "Oh dear friend! Don't be pessimistic! Be optimistic because it is said [in the *ḥadīth qudsī*], '*My mercy takes precedence over my wrath.*'"[45] Such a position reflects the rapturous and ecstatic Sufi poetry that typifies the Persian Sufi tradition of the medieval period. However, James also concludes that there had been a tendency towards "pantheism" within all the religious traditions, and it is on this point that the limitations of such generalisations become glaringly apparent. The inappropriateness of applying the term "pantheism" in the sense of identity between the subject and object (creation and God) to Sufism may be illustrated by referring to the first chapter of Nasafī's *Kitāb al-tanzīl*. Nasafī observed that intelligence cannot comprehend the reality of God. The theism of this stance, the suggestion of duality implied in portraying God as ultimately transcendent from creation, is clear:

> Oh dear friend! The incomparable (*munnaza*) essence and holy face of the Truth (*ḥaqq*)[46] is so great that an individual's reason cannot encompass it. Rather [the Truth's] exalted self is higher than that anyone may discover It as

[43] Nasafī describes the *majdhūb* in a number of works. See his comments in Ridgeon, *Persian Metaphysics*, 60 (*Maqṣad-i aqṣā*, 226).

[44] James, *The Varieties*, 422.

[45] Nasafī, *K.T.* folio 80b. A *ḥadīth qudsī* is a saying attributed to Muḥammad in which the words of God are reported. This saying, "*My mercy takes precedence over my wrath*", was particularly popular among those Sufis who advocated the ideas of Ibn ʿArabī. (This *ḥadīth qudsī* is found in Bukhārī, *Tawḥīd*, 15, 35). To appreciate how this *ḥadīth qudsī* fits into the larger picture that is presented by Sufis see Sachiko Murata, *The Tao of Islam* (Albany: SUNY Press, 1992), 49–80. On this *ḥadīth* and its use by Ibn ʿArabī, see W. Chittick "Ibn ʿArabī's Hermeneutics of Mercy", in Steven T. Katz (ed.), *Mysticism and Sacred Scripture* (Oxford: University Press, 2000), 157–60.

[46] A term that typically refers to God.

> It really is . . . the extremity of man's knowledge is that point where he knows that he cannot know God as God really is.[47]

Nasafī's emphasis on describing a remote God at the start of his treatise stands in contrast to the lengthy and intimate portrayals of the Truth in the subsequent sections. This perspective reflects a common theological position among Sufis of his time, which was to balance God's similarity to humans with his utter incomparability.[48] This view is frequently attributed to Ibn 'Arabī, whose enigmatic phrase "He/not he"[49] is mirrored by Nasafī's own comment that, "It is correct if they say, 'It is we who were, are and will be,' and it is also correct if they say, 'It is not we who were, are and will be.' "[50] Similarity (*tashbīh*) was legitimised with reference to 32.9 of the Qur'ān (which speaks of God blowing of his spirit into Adam, the archetypal human being, which suggests that the human spirit in some way shares certain qualities of the holy spirit), while incomparability (*tanzīh*) was frequently read in verse 42.11, "Nothing is like him."[51] Pantheism, or monism, does not fully equate with this Sufi understanding of reality that from a rational perspective at least appears illogical, because this Sufi stance posits a God that is "closer than the jugular vein" (50.16) and one that at the same time is remote and unknowable.

In Nasafī's treatise *Kitāb-i tanzīl* the general and *tanzīh* introductory warning at the start of the treatise is very brief,[52] and indeed it is washed

[47] *K.T.* folio 32a.

[48] This was a typical theme among Sufis of the thirteenth century. An excellent poetic example of this is given by Rūmī, *Kulliyāt-i Shams*, edited by B. Furūzānfar (Tehran, Amīr Kabīr, third edition, 1363/1984–5), vol. II, no. 900, 202–3; English translation by A.J. Arberry, *Mystical Poems of Rūmī, 1* (Chicago: University Press, 1991), 100.

[49] William Chittick, *The Sufi Path of Knowledge*, 3–4.

[50] Nasafī, in *Zubdat al-ḥaqā'iq*, trans. Ridgeon in *Persian Metaphysics*, p. 156.

[51] For *tashbīh* and *tanzīh* see Sachiko Murata and William Chittick, *The Vision of Islam* (New York: Paragon House, 1994), 45–80. Islamic scholars categorised God's names under these two terms. Those which portrayed God as merciful and loving were considered *tashbīh* names, while those that emphasised God's independence and might were understood as *tanzīh* names.

[52] In other works Nasafī gives more extensive *tanzīh* warnings. The following quote is typical of the general tenor of his worldview:

> Know that the travellers in God's path have spent periods of time in the *madrasa* (seminary) at the service of the *'ulamā'* (clerics) in study and repetition. Then they went from the *madrasa* to the *khānaqāh* (convent) and spent time in the service of the shaykhs in ascetic discipline and religious effort. They supposed that they had become wise men and they wrote books on the gnosis of God and the gnosis of his creation. They took many students and were busy in training them. After all of this, they knew for sure that they had understood nothing and through verification they confirmed their ignorance and renounced those books. O dervish! Whoever has understood God as

away by wave after wave of *tashbīh* passages in which there are descriptions of various ontological arguments and their associated mystical moments. In one of these moments Nasafī claimed that:

> The sign of whoever reaches God's essence is that he sees himself as an expanded, unlimited and infinite light, and it has no beginning or end. Another sign is that all the eyes, ears, tongues and hands of this world's creatures are his. He sees through all the eyes, listens through all the ears, speaks through all the tongues and gives through all the hands because the eyes, the ears, the tongues and the hands of all the [creatures of the] world are God's. [God] sees through all the eyes, listens through all the ears, speaks through all the tongues and gives and takes through all the hands.[53]

The difficulty of defining the kind of Sufi positions that Nasafī articulated suggests that the current religious terminology in the West (such as "pantheist") is simply inadequate to delineate this "reality". As a result, neologisms have been coined, most notably by Henry Corbin, who used the expression "theo-monist".[54] This term captures the seeming irrationality of depicting a God that is both *tashbīh* and *tanzīh*, a position that rests comfortably with either/or, and yes/no, and rejects reified and dogmatic perspectives. Like so many other Sufis of his time, Nasafī uses the term "bewilderment" to denote this irrationality:

> The final task of the wise man is bewilderment (*ḥayrat*) in the gnosis of God and the gnosis of the world. The greater the bewilderment, the greater [the wise man] engages in spectating (*niẓāra kardan*), because knowledge (*'ilm*) is the cause of bewilderment and bewilderment is the cause of spectating . . . Oh dear friend! If someone fancies that he has understood whatever can be understood and has discovered whatever can be found, this fancy is his idol, and [such] a wretched person becomes an idol worshipper.[55]

"Spectating" in the above quotation pertains to both the mystical experience itself and to post-experience interpretation. The final task is bewilderment because the experience enables the individual to oscillate between the multiplicity and unity inherent in existence; in other words, the wayfarer spectates at the *tashbīh* dimension of God, but remains aware of the concept of *tanzīh*.

God really is cannot have understood [the *ḥadīth*] "*incapacity to attain comprehension is comprehension itself*". The person whose realisation and knowledge reaches the point that he knows 'the things as they are' cannot be known in truth is a wise man. (Nasafī in *Maqṣad al-aqṣā*, translated in Ridgeon, *Persian Metaphysics*, 126–7).

53 Nasafī, *K.T.* folio 49a.

54 Henry Corbin, *History of Islamic Philosophy* (London: Kegan Paul International, 1993), 294–5.

55 *K.T.* folio 38b.

That is to say, the traces of the noetic quality remain with the bewildered wayfarer, who can only spectate, or look at the ultimate reality in a way that defies logical constructs of either/or. Nasafī himself seems to be speaking from his own experience, as in a rare biographical aside he stated, "After abandonment, this helpless one has spent long periods in seclusion, satisfaction [with fate] and anonymity, and also after renunciation long periods in satisfaction, surrender and spectating."[56]

Another interesting dimension to Nasafī's presentation of mystical experience is that it appears that groups which did not advocate identical epistemology or ontology could ultimately enjoy similar experiences. The discussion of mystical experience is scattered in the six stations of his first chapter of *The Book of the Descent*, which reflects various ontological understandings of reality.[57] So, in the first station God is comprehended in a fashion in which creation is completely separate from God's essence, but connected to him through his attributes. In effect, Nasafī's first station typifies the position of a group that in other treatises he names the *ahl-i sharī'at* ("the people of the Holy Law"), and "*'ulama*",[58] and who occupy an inferior position in the spiritual hierarchy due to their reliance on sense perception. In the second station God is positioned above the sensual, spiritual and divine worlds, yet he is with them all through essence and attribute. In his other works the ideas of this group pertain to a group he calls the *ahl-i ḥikmat* and "people of reasoning", who utilise reason and demonstration as the foundation of their epistemological insights.[59] The subsequent four stations reflect the varying ways in which the *ahl-i waḥdat* (the group with which Nasafī appears to have most sympathy) present their ontological beliefs. But perhaps the most significant station is the fifth, in which Nasafī likens all existence to God

[56] Nasafī, *al-Insān al-kāmil*, 10. Spectating, or gazing, has a mystical meaning in the Qur'ānic commentary attributed to Ja'far al-Ṣadiq. See *Spiritual Gems*, trans. and annotated Farhana Mayer (Louisville, KY: Fons Vitae, 2011), lxi, 156.

[57] For a discussion of the first chapter of *Kitāb-i tanzīl*, see Lloyd Ridgeon, "'Azīz Nasafī's Six Ontological Faces", *Iran* (1996), 85–99; Hermann Landolt, "Le Paradoxe De La 'Face De Dieu', *Studia Islamica*, 25 (1996) 163–192. "Stations" (s. *maqām*, pl. *maqāmāt*) which are usually understood as spiritual stages in which knowledge is acquired, and the moment (*waqt*) or experience which is bestowed by God.) The moment (*waqt*) is a mystical term of the Sufis which has meaning of a time when all concerns for past and present are obliterated and one focuses or concentrates solely upon the present time. At such times, a state (*ḥāl*) may descend upon the wayfarer. The *ḥāl* and the *waqt* are not volitional. During the *waqt* one of the many different states may descend upon the wayfarer, thus the experiences may be different from one person to the other. See Hujwiri, *Kashf al-Mahjub*, pp. 367–70. Nasafī does not appear to make a distinction between *waqt* and *ḥāl*.

[58] *K.T.* folio 39b. Compare with *Persian Metaphysics*, 86 (*Maqṣad-i aqṣā*, 247).

[59] *K.T.* folios 40a–40b. Compare with *Persian Metaphysics* pp. 87–9. *Maqṣad-i aqṣā*, 247–8).

through an analogy of the existence of water: there is the essential or general form of water, the form of water within an individual plant and the comprehensive form which reflects the reality of water within all plants.[60] Here we have a God who is intimate and the priority is the *tashbīh* dimension of God. Despite these ontological differences, Nasafī portrays the experience of the mystical moment to be one and the same. He remarks that the first wayfarer (the individual who is among the *ahl-i sharīʿat* and who perceives only through sense perception) forgets his individual existence and does not know or see anything other than God, which is the station of "annihilation of annihilation" (a typical Sufi idiom, which for Sufis of Nasafī's ilk denoted the obliteration of creaturely attributes and the eradication of any awareness of the concept that creaturely attributes have been annihilated).[61] In other words, there is no consciousness of the creaturely nature of the individual. The second wayfarer (who is the individual within the *ahl-i ḥikmat* and apprehends realities through pure reason) reaches a stage through "ascetic discipline and spiritual effort", and it is in this "moment" that "the soul of the soul, the hearing of the hearing, the sight of sight sees, listens and speaks in [the wayfarer]".[62] Thus, the two wayfarers who from a Sufi perspective stand on the least secure epistemological grounds enjoy profound moments where the distinctions between man and God are blurred. And likewise, the moment of the wayfarer in the fifth station reflects the experience of pure unity:

> . . . when the wayfarer does not refrain from ascetic discipline and spiritual effort and perseveres and persists in the task, and when he is completely cleansed of blameworthy attributes and unpleasant character traits and may be described and characterised with praiseworthy attributes and pleasant character traits, and when he becomes translucent, reflective and glass-like . . . then the real light – which is God's essence – becomes like one thing with this wayfarer's existence . . . in such a way that one cannot distinguish the light from the glass or the glass from the light. It is just like a glass goblet that is extremely translucent and reflective, and which has a very fine and pure wine poured in to it. It is not possible to distinguish the goblet from the wine or the wine from the goblet. This is because the two things are like one. From this perspective the prophets said, "*Our spirits are our bodies and our bodies are our spirits.*" Each cry that comes from the wayfarer such as, [Bāyazīd Basṭāmī's] "*There is nothing in my cloak except God!*" and [Ḥallāj's] "*I am the Truth*" is in this station.[63]

[60] *K.T.* folios 46b–49a.
[61] *K.T.* folio 40a.
[62] *K.T.* folio 43a.
[63] *K.T.* folio 48b.

From a reading of the *Kitāb-i tanzīl* one would be forgiven for assuming that the mystical experience of God for the *ahl-i sharī'at*, the *ahl-i ḥikmat*, and the *ahl-i waḥdat* are one and the same, even if their epistemological and ontological groundings are different. From a survey of all of Nasafī's known works, however, it is possible to understand how he reached such a conclusion. Mystical insight or gnosis, according to Nasafī, was not always the result of the individual engaging in Sufi training and exercises and leading a pious life. He composed chapters in his *al-Insān al-kāmil* in which he claimed that knowledge of the unseen could appear on plain and untarnished hearts. He elaborated further and said that such a condition did not apply to belief or unbelief (*kufr*), as such knowledge could appear for the pious person or the lewd person, and it could even occur in animals.[64] Such a view also needs to be considered with his views related to the *majdhūb* (mentioned above) – that is to say, God draws to himself whomsoever he pleases and causes rapture in these individuals. Therefore, according to Nasafī's worldview, even the *ahl-i sharī'at* and the *ahl-i ḥikmat* actually experience God – but it is the interpretations of these groups that are incorrect. Nasafī appeared to endorse the view that all of creation was made existent through the first thing that God created (whether this occurred in time or was an eternal emanation is beyond our discussion), and he stated:

> Many great men among the Shaykhs have reached this first intelligence and they stayed with it . . . they believed that perhaps it was God. And they worshipped it for a while until the favour of the Truth Most High came to them . . . At that time it became clear for them that it was God's caliph, it was not God.[65]

The important point here is the recognition of erroneous belief, although in quote above that belief or interpretation is rectified. His ecumenical position does, however, distinguish between the worship of different aspects of God:

> Whoever reaches God's face (*wajh*) and has not reached the essence has become an unbeliever [lit. – an associator of others with God (*mushrik*)], and whoever has not passed on from God's face and does not reach God's essence is an unbeliever (*mushrik*). Whoever passes on from God's face and reaches the essence is a unitarian (*muwaḥḥid*). So whoever worships something worships nothing except God, and whoever turns to something turns to nothing except God: "*wherever you turn, there is the face of God.*" [2.115] Although all the *mushriks* have turned to God's face and worship God, they

[64] *al-Insān al-kāmil*, chapter 18.3.
[65] Ibid., chapter 17.2.

were limited to one face and turned their backs on the other faces. Consenting to some and denying others is not acceptable, so the Prophets called them from the limited God to the non-delimited God, and they said, "God is one. Whatever you have turned towards, it is all one God that you have worshipped." The *mushriks* were surprised at this and denied the words of the Prophets, but they marvelled, "*What! Has he made the gods one God? This is indeed a marvellous thing*!" [Q. 38.5].[66]

Nasafī's sympathy for the views of the *ahl-i waḥdat* must have contributed to his relative "non-partisan" writing style, which emphasised the positive elements in diverse beliefs to convey a teaching. He was prepared to include in his treatises the views of groups that were most likely non-Muslim to express their belief, for at one point he endorsed the views of the Indians (*ahl-i hind*)[67] and those who believed in the transmigration of souls.[68] He also recounted the famous story of the blind men and the elephant in which each blind man touches a different part of the animal and claims to have ultimate knowledge of the creature, but in reality has only a portion of the truth.[69] Only once in his treatises does he mention why in all of his works he steps back and adopts an "objective" voice that allows others the opportunity to present their worldviews: "Now I do not reveal my own opinions, so they cannot accuse me of infidelity. I relate and I say, 'The *ahl-i waḥdat* say this and the Sufis say that'."[70] Nasafī's form of Sufism, in which fuller moments may be enjoyed as the wayfarer progresses on the path, resembles the *philosophia perennis*. In the West such an ecumenical pluralism has been advocated by Aldous Huxley. In 1944 Huxley argued that there is an essential core within the world's religions.[71] It is noteworthy that the perennial philosophy was adopted by a number of leading scholars, including Frithjof Schuon, the author of *Islam and the Perennial Philosophy*,[72] and Seyyed Hossein Nasr (both of whom are discussed by Geaves in this volume: see Chapter 10). In response to the perennial philosophy F.C. Happold published *Mysticism: A Study and an Anthology* in which he provided a classification of

[66] *K.T.*, 48a.
[67] *Al-insān al-kāmil*, 24–7.
[68] Ibid., 408–20.
[69] Nasafī, *K.T.* folio 51a-b. Maria Subtelny, "An Old Tale with a New Twist: The Elephant and the Blind Men in Rūmī's Masnavī and Its Precursors." In *No Tapping around Philology: A Festschrift in Celebration and Honor of Wheeler McIntosh Thackson, Jr's 70th Birthday*, edited by Dan Sheffield and Alireza Korangy (Wiesbaden: Harrassowitz, 2014) [page range tbc].
[70] Ridgeon, *Persian Metaphysics*, 119 (*Maqṣad-i aqṣā*, 277).
[71] *The Perennial Philosophy*, 1944.
[72] *Islam and the Perennial Philosophy* (London: World of Islam Festival Publishing Company, 1976).

nature-mysticism, soul-mysticism and God-mysticism.[73] Resembling Happold's classification was the work of R.C. Zaehner, the Spalding Professor of Eastern Religions and Ethics at Oxford University.[74] Zaehner argued that there were three basic types of mystical experience, but that a clear hierarchy existed among them. At the top of the hierarchy was the theistic (and dualistic) variety, followed by monistic mysticism (which conveyed the idea that the individual realised the self or spirit beyond time and space as the Absolute), and nature mysticism in which there was no reference to a God. In short, Zaehner argued against the essentialists of the perennial philosophy and posited real differences of experience. In his view, Islam was fundamentally theistic, but it had been distorted as a result of the teachings of early mystics such as Bāyazīd Basṭāmī, who (argued Zaehner) had a Hindu teacher whose monism transformed the Sufi message.[75]

Zaehner's methodology has been criticised by several leading scholars,[76] however, his theory relating to mysticism is worth considering further because his negative views of "monistic" experience bear some similarity to the arguments of a hierarchy of mystical experience that was suggested by some thirteenth- and fourteenth-century Sufis. One of these was Najm al-Dīn Rāzī (1177–1256), whose *Mirṣād al-ʿibāḍ* included sections that delineate a clear progression of mystical unveilings. Indeed, he builds a structure of five levels of unveiling.[77] Rāzī believed that the aim was to reach the pinnacle, and was critical of those Sufis such as Ḥallāj, whom he positioned in the fourth

[73] F.C. Happold, *Mysticism: A Study and Anthology* (London: Penguin, 1963).

[74] See, e.g., *Mysticism: Sacred and Profane* (Oxford: Clarendon Press, 1957), and *Hindu and Muslim Mysticism* (London: Athlone Press, 1960).

[75] For a rejection of Zaehner's thesis relating to Bāyazīd Basṭāmī, see A.J. Arberry, "Bistamiana" *Bulletin of the School of Oriental and African Studies*, 25 (1962), 28–37.

[76] See Philip C. Almond, *Mystical Experience and Religious Doctrine* (Berlin, Walter de Gruyter, 1982), 23–42. It is not hard to see why some scholars and Muslims would take offence at Zaehner's work in light of his view that "Muslim mysticism is entirely derivative. Its beginnings are unmistakeably borrowed from Christianity ... and with Abū Yazīd [Bāyazīd Basṭāmī] in the ninth century we find Indian monism invading the Muslim mystical world." (*Mysticism: Sacred and Profane*, 160–1). A number of scholars have highlighted the Sufis' primary focus and concentration on *Islamic* scripture and practice rather than on Hindu or Christian sources. It does, however, appear true that Sufis have argued for different levels or degrees of mystical experience, but this does not justify the conclusion that "Muslim mysticism is a source of confusion". Zaehner's position has been neatly summarised in the following fashion: "We learn from this book [*Hindu and Muslim Mysticism*] that Zaehner is in fundamental sympathy with orthodox Islam, but is greatly irritated by the monistic trends in Islam", F. Staal, *Exploring Mysticism* (University of California, 1975), 74.

[77] These are *kashf-i naẓarī*, *kashf-i shuhūdī*, *kashf-i rūḥī*, *kashf-i sirrī*, and *kashf-i maʿnawī* (*Mirṣād al-ʿibād*, 182–3: This work has been translated by Hamid Algar as *The Path of God's Bondsmen from Origin to Return* (New Jersey, Islamic Publications International, 1980), 305–9.

level, which he termed "spiritual unveiling."[78] Rāzī's ambivalence to Ḥallāj may be related to the former's stress on correct training and obedience to a spiritual guide, elements that have been the subject of debate in relation to Ḥallāj.[79] Indeed, Rāzī even accused him of egotism (*anāniyat*),[80] claiming that he had achieved only partial unveiling.[81] This criticism of Ḥallāj has been taken up in more recent times by Zaehner, who was at pains to demonstrate the superiority of a mystical experience in which the subject/object dichotomy was maintained over and above what he considered to be the Godless and monistic mysticism of the spirit of the Indian Vedanta tradition and which he believed had infiltrated Sufism. Claiming that Rāzī was castigating Ḥallāj on this very point, Zaehner concluded that "Najm al-Dīn Rāzī once again exposes what he considers to be the error of the monists, and he did this in defence of orthodoxy."[82] He approved of Rāzī's description of how the divine flame burns each and every tree and brings out its particular scent, and paraphrased Rāzī's view that "the scent of each kind of wood differs as the personalities of different men differ." However, the "orthodoxy" that Zaehner read into Najm al-Dīn Rāzī is rather contentious. While Zaehner is correct to highlight the differences in mystical experience as portrayed by Rāzī,[83] his belief that the Sufi's description of ultimate unity accords with the subject/object dichotomy is hard to justify. Rāzī's portrayal of those who attain the pinnacle of mystical experience, typified in his words cited below, appears "monistic" (to use Zaehner's term) and could quite easily have been uttered by the likes of Nasafī (particularly in his presentation of the views of the *ahl-i waḥdat*). Rāzī uses the imagery of a moth diving into a candle flame to depict the ultimate reality:

78 For the original Persian, see *Mirṣād al-ʿibād min al-mabdāʾ ilāʾl-maʿād* (Tehran: Sinānī, 1373/1994–5), 177. *The Path of God's Bondsmen*, 313.

79 Ḥallāj was a hugely controversial figure, even among the Sufis themselves, to the extent that some Sufi authors ignored him in the biographical entries to their works. See Jawid Mojaddedi, "Ḥallāj, Abu'l-Moḡiṯ Ḥosayn" *Encyclopedia Iranica* (2003), volume XI, fasc. 6, 589–92.

80 On the need for the spiritual guide and the formal dimension of Sufism, see Najm al-Dīn Rāzī, *The Path of God's Bondsmen*, 281–5. See also his comments on p. 239, which are positioned in a chapter entitled "The Need for a Shaykh". This passage is cited by Zaehner, *Hindu and Muslim Mysticism*, 182. Najm al-Dīn Rāzī's accusation of egotism is found in *The Path of God's Bondsmen*, 331 (*Mirṣād al-ʿibād*, 3.20 (189)).

81 Najm al-Dīn Rāzī *The Path of God's Bondsmen*, 305–6 (*Mirṣād al-ʿibād*, 172); 312–4 (*Mirṣād al-ʿibād*, 175–84), 361–2 (*Mirṣād al-ʿibād*, 210).

82 Zaehner, *Hindu and Muslim Mysticism*, 183.

83 Rāzī explained the differences as a result of deficient practices, adherence to the intellect rather than the divine law, which results in incomplete unveiling, a weakening of the spiritual quest, arrogance and fantasy.

> [The moth] flies into the existence of the flame, just as [the Qur'ān 50.51] says, "*flee unto God*". It flees from itself and surrenders [its existence] in [the flame]. It becomes non-existent in it, and non-existence is mixed in existence. And when [the moth] surrenders its own existence in that [of the flame] it loses both fear of hell and hope of heaven.[84]

This is not an isolated incidence of "monism", for in another place Rāzī describes the highest spiritual stations in which there is either the unveiling of divine beauty (representing *tashbīh*) or divine majesty (representing *tanzīh*). With regard to the names of divine beauty, Rāzī outlines a phenomenon that is similar to Nasafī's presentation of *tamkīn*, for he states that the wayfarer is either adorned with one of the divine names and reflects the unity of the manifestor and the manifested, or he is attributed with all of the names. With regard to the names of divine majesty, "neither name nor trace, unity nor multiplicity, witness nor witnessed, unveiler nor unveiled . . . remain. The Truth remains! The Truth remains! The Truth remains!"[85] Such passages, which may very readily be understood in a theo-monist fashion, probably account for Zaehner's observation that Rāzī is "not always consistent".[86]

Had he focused on the mystical worldview of 'Alā' al-Dīn Simnānī (d. 1336), Zaehner would most likely have adopted him as an advocate of preserving God's ultimate transcendence and thus the duality between created and creator.[87] Like Rāzī, Simnānī was critical of Ḥallāj, as the former believed that at the final level of the mystical encounter the individual became mirror-like, and was thus able to manifest God in a complete fashion, while not himself being God. In this fashion the statement "I am God's secret" [not Ḥallāj's "I am God"] shows that the "divine Being cannot exist without me, nor I exist without Him".[88] Moreover, Simnānī believed that the wayfarer reached a stage "in which even the image of the Mirror was ultimately abolished".[89] Whether or not Simnānī fully endorsed the theo-monist position as described by Nasafī, or whether he misunderstood the position of Sufis

84 *The Path of God's Bondsmen*, 374–5 (*Mirṣād al-'ibād*, 218).
85 *Mirṣād al-'ibād*, 175: *The Path of God's Bondsmen*, 368–9. Algar's translation differs from the *Mirṣād* I have used. The latter is an edition prepared by Shams al-'Urafa, whereas the former is based on an edition prepared by Dr. Rīyāḥī.
86 Zaehner, *Hindu and Muslim Mysticism*, 182.
87 For Simnānī, see Jamal J. Elias, "A Kubrawī Treatise on Mystical Visions: The *Risāla-yi nūriyya* of 'Alā' ad-dawla as-Simnānī", *Muslim World*, 83 (1993), 63–80.
88 Henry Corbin, *The Man of Light in Iranian Sufism* (New York: Omega Publications, 1994), 127–8.
89 Landolt, "Simnani on *wahdat al-wujud*", in H. Landolt and M. Mohaghegh (eds), *Wisdom of Persia*, 4, (Tehran: La Branche de Teheran de L'institut des Etudes Islamique de L'universite McGill, 1971), 96.

who argued this perspective, remains inconclusive, and, given the confines of this chapter, cannot be investigated further.[90]

A radical difference of opinion from Nasafī, Najm al-Dīn Rāzī and Simnānī, and seemingly coming from within the Sufi tradition, is observable in the thought of Ibn Taymiyya (d. 1328). There has been some controversy as to whether he should be considered a Sufi, although George Makdisi has pointed to the inclusion of Ibn Taymiyya within a Sufi *silsila* (spiritual genealogy) in medieval manuscripts, his preference for *ilhām* (Sufi inspiration) over weak *ḥadīth* as a source of authority and his burial in a Sufi graveyard, all of which suggest that he was inclined to the tradition.[91] Yet in a treatise entitled *al-Ṣūfiya wa-al-fuqarā'* ("The Sufis and the Poor"), Ibn Taymiyya was reluctant to allow any mystical experience with God. Although he admitted the possibility for Muḥammad, Ibn Taymiyya domesticated the experience by arguing that the prophet was in full control of his reason. This stands in contrast to his discussion of *fanā'*, which he described as "things among the afflictions which cause the intellect to vanish".[92] And, in another

[90] It is interesting to compare the worldviews of Nasafī and Simnānī, especially as some scholars have associated the former with Ibn 'Arabī and the school of *waḥdat al-wujūd*, and the latter has been considered as a forerunner of the school of *waḥdat al-shuhūd*. Contemporary scholars have attempted to distinguish and categorise the two. For example, Louis Massignon described Ibn 'Arabī's worldview as "static existential monism", whereas the unity of witnessing was termed "dynamic testimonial monism". (See W. Chittick, "Rūmī and *waḥdat al-wujūd*", in A. Banani, R. Houannisian and G. Sabagh (eds), *Poetry and Mysticism in Islam* (Cambridge: University Press, 1994), 90. Chittick states that Massignon "had a well-known personal preference for the love mysticism of al-Ḥallāj and a deep aversion to Ibn al-'Arabī's approach" (p. 90). Chittick proceeds to add that Ibn 'Arabī's worldview was indeed dynamic because of the infinite and never repeating manifestations of God (110, n. 69), an idea that is also repeated by Nasafī (folios 47a–47b). More recently, the static/dynamic classification was repeated by Hermann Landolt, in "Simnani on *wahdat al-wujud*", 199, and his "Two Types of Mystical Thought in Muslim Iran", *Muslim World*, 68, (1978): 187–204. Landolt likens 'Ayn al-Quḍāt Hamadānī with Ibn 'Arabī (198–9), and he also describes his "static quality". This is in contrast to Sufis such as Simnānī and Suhrawardī (*shaykh al-Ishrāq*) as "dynamic" (203).

[91] For Ibn Taymiyya's critique of the Sufis who advocated forms of ontological unity, see chapter 4 of Alexander D. Knysh, *Ibn 'Arabī in the Later Islamic Tradition* (Albany: SUNY Press, 1999), 87–112. For George Makdisi's views, see his "Ibn Taymiyya: A Ṣūfī of the Qādirīya Order", *American Journal of Arabic Studies*, 1 (1973), 118–129. Others have pointed out that he is best viewed as a "neo-Sufi" (see Fazlur Rahman, *Islam* (Chicago, University Press, 1979, 206). Many modern Salafis refute any association between Ibn Taymiyya and Sufism, a view that is easily found when searching the internet. The scope of this article has not permitted an investigation into modern forms of Sufism, yet one very interesting development is the emergence of Salafi-Sufis who claim to be the inheritors of Ibn Taymiyya's legacy and appropriate the ethical teachings (as opposed to the metaphysical teachings) of the likes of Ghazālī, and reject the type of Sufism associated with discussions of ontological unity. See Richard Gauvain, *Salafi Ritual Purity* (London: Routledge, 2012), in particular part II, 79–92.

[92] Th Emil Homerin, "Ibn Taymiyya's *al-Ṣūfīyah wa-l-fuqarā'*", in *Arabica*, 32/2 (1985): 226.

passage, Ibn Taymiyya understood *fanā‘* as a state in which "one has no feeling of oneself":[93] there is no mention of experiencing God. Sarrio has observed that Ibn Taymiyya denied the "view of *fanā'* as the perfect absorption of the self in the deity, with the imperfect attributes of the creature being replaced by God's perfect attributes . . . [but he] proposes a notion of *fanā'* as a fusion of wills (*fanā' irādī*)".[94] Michot has portrayed Ibn Taymiyya's opposition to the worst kinds of *fanā'*: *fanā' al-wujūd* (or the annihilation of existence), which consists "in bearing witness that there is nothing existing but God, that the existence of the Creator is the existence of the created, and that there is no difference between the Lord and the servant – this is the extinction of the adepts of straying and heresy, who fall into the doctrines of indwelling and union".[95] Ibn Taymiyya advanced a preference for a form of ascetic and pious practice in which reason is maintained, and he attributed this understanding of Islam with the Companions (*salafīs*) and the very early generations of pious Muslims. As an example, he noted that those who receive divine inspiration (*muḥaddathūn*) such as ‘Umar (the Companion and second Caliph) "would always submit anything he received by inspiration to the judgement of the Prophet's message, and willingly retract his opinions when appropriate".[96]

It should come as no surprise that Ibn Taymiyya was a fierce opponent of the doctrines commonly associated with Ibn ‘Arabī.[97] Alexander Knysh has conveniently summarised four of Ibn Taymiyya's treatises that critique the worldview of the unity of existence (*waḥdat al-wujūd*).[98] What was disturbing for Ibn Taymiyya was the similarity of Ibn ‘Arabī's teaching with the doctrines of "mainstream Christian theology, especially the Melkites, who hold that divine and human natures form one substance with two different hypostases".[99] Likewise, in one *fatwa* he compared the doctrines commonly ascribed to Ḥallāj with those of the Nazarenes[100] – doctrines which could have applied to the portrayal of the state of the wayfarer that Nasafī offered ("He speaks through all the tongues . . . "). Ibn Taymiyya stated that:

[93] Ibid., 228.
[94] Diego R. Sarrio, "Spiritual Anti-Elitism: Ibn Taymiyya's Doctrine of Sainthood (*walāya*)", *Islam and Christian-Muslim Relations*, 22:3 (2011): 287.
[95] Yahya Michot, "Ibn Taymiyya's Commentary on the Creed of al-Ḥallaj", in Ayman Shihadeh, *Sufism and Theology* (Edinburgh: University Press, 2007), 132.
[96] Ibid., 281.
[97] Ibn Taymiyya was also opposed to the type of Sufis associated with Ḥallāj and Bāyazīd Basṭāmī. (See Knysh, *Ibn ‘Arabī in the Later Islamic Tradition*, 90, 93.)
[98] Alexander D. Knysh, *Ibn ‘Arabī in the Later Islamic Tradition*, 88–96.
[99] Ibid., 95.
[100] Michot, "Ibn Taymiyya's Commentary on the Creed of al-Ḥallaj", 126.

> Whoever says that God spoke by the tongue of al-Ḥallāj, that the words that were heard from al-Ḥallāj were words of God, and that it is God who, by his tongue said "I am God" is an unbeliever – the Muslims are agreed on that. God indeed does not indwell in humanity and does not speak by the tongue of a human but sends the Messengers with His words. [The Messengers] then say on his behalf what He ordered them to communicate and he thus says, by the tongues of the Messengers, what He ordered them to say.[101]

In short, what the pinnacle of mystical experience was for the likes of Nasafī is nothing but delusion. Knysh eloquently paraphrased Ibn Taymiyya's opposition to this kind of Sufism: "On the whole, both the Christian theologians and the supporters of unificationism share one thing in common: their argumentation throws them into the state of permanent perplexity and confusion (*hayra*), [or bewilderment] which Ibn 'Arabi indeed continually invoked in his writings."[102]

CONCLUSION

With Ibn Taymiyya we return to the very start of this essay: Is Sufism nothing other than Islamic mysticism? Mystical experience in the sense of some form of intimacy with the divine was possible for Ibn Taymiyya,[103] yet discussions of ontological identity were strictly off limits. His views are representative of one extreme of Sufi thinking, while those of Nasafī, – in which all individuals (Muslims and non-Muslims alike) may share – typify the opposite extreme. Ibn Taymiyya's perspective resembles the kind of salafi spirituality that is exemplified by the Deobandi school (as mentioned in Werbner's chapter in the present volume: Chapter 12), while Nasafī's ontology resembles the perennialism of some contemporary Sufi thinkers. Located between these two are Rāzī and Simnānī, whose positions endorse the perspective argued by Zaehner, and also those modern Muslims who wish to focus less on God's *tashbih* dimension. What should be highlighted in these emic accounts is the difficulty of separating purely descriptive accounts of experience from interpretation. This may explain why Nasafī believed that the experiences of the *ahl-i sharīʿat* and the *ahl-i ḥikmat* could be genuine and the same as those of

[101] Ibid.

[102] Alexander D. Knysh, *Ibn 'Arabī in the Later Islamic Tradition*, 95.

[103] "The existence and efficacy of what Ibn Taymiyya calls the 'misericordial states' (*ḥāl raḥmānī*) given by God to those following His path – i.e., His friends, the saints (walī), and the believers, who fear Him – can therefore not be denied." Yahya Michot, "Between Entertainment and Religion: Ibn Taymiyya's Views on Superstition", *Muslim World* (2009), 99.1, 12.

the *ahl-i waḥdat*, yet he rejected their ontological interpretations and epistemology. Moreover, it is possible that his ecumenical perspective was also driven by his fear of being labelled an unbeliever. Rāzī's ambivalence to Ḥallāj may have been a result of his commitment to a form of Sufism that prioritised strict adherence to the path's rules and courtesies (*adab*). The extent to which these factors had a bearing of the mystical unveilings of the Sufis in question is difficult to assess, but certainly historical conditions, as Safi has indicated, are vital for a more comprehensive perspective of Sufis and their tradition.

This chapter has also addressed the ways in which mysticism has been studied in the modern West. While the Western attempt to understand the phenomenon of Sufism has advanced considerably from the nineteenth century, when attempts were made to link the tradition with Aryanism, the theories of Western academics such as James, Zaehner and Smart have serious limitations. It has been argued that Sufism is not simply mysticism, and that a more careful application of terms is necessary to reflect the nuances of mysticism within the Sufi tradition. Corbin's term "theomonism" appears to be as good as any advanced so far, and it does indeed capture the way that *wujūdī* Sufis portrayed their vision of reality.[104] Moreover, it is not simply a matter of using inappropriate descriptive terms, for the preferences of some scholars (typified in this chapter by Zaehner) have completely misrepresented the worldviews of some Sufis in an attempt to promote a certain universal understanding of the mystical phenomenon.

The chapter has also suggested that the indiscriminate use of the word "mystic" to describe a Sufi should be challenged. While I am not denying the possibility that there were some Sufis who had experiences that seem to be of a mystical nature, I am questioning the fashion in which all Sufis appear as mystics who are in touch with God on a regular basis. Nasafī's treatises are a point in case. His works do not easily lead to the conclusion that he himself had undergone any kind of mystical encounter, and yet it would be incorrect to include him among the ranks of the "vulgar mass of sober intellectualising Sufis",[105] the numbers of whom seem to have been substantial in his time. It would seem that during the medieval period it was not necessary to be a Sufi to receive teaching about specifically Sufi knowledge, as Chittick has observed: "It is highly likely that Ibn 'Arabī himself taught his own works both to initiated Sufis and to those who were intellectually attracted to Sufism but had not taken the practical step of swearing allegiance to a shaykh."[106]

[104] The term has been used by some scholars, see for example, Hermann Landolt, "Two Types", 198.
[105] See Lewisohn in this volume, Chapter 7, p. 158.
[106] W. Chittick, "Ibn 'Arabī and His School", in S.H. Nasr (ed.), *Islamic Spirituality*, 54.

The significance of works such as Ibn ʿArabī's or Nasafī's has been highlighted by Michael Sells, who discusses how it is not necessary to focus on whether this kind of literature reflected an actual mystical encounter by the author of the text. What is important is the effect these works had on their readers, and it is the move beyond the subject–object dichotomy (which he terms the "meaning event") that nurtures a kind of intellectual mystical union. Sells says, "The meaning event is the semantic analogue to the experience of mystical union. It does not describe or refer to mystical union but effects a semantic union that re-creates or imitates the mystical union."[107] Sells argues from the perspective of performative reading in which "the emphasis [is] on language rather than experience [which] reflects the view that mystical texts primarily set out to convey beliefs not experiences".[108]

FURTHER READING

Algar, H. *The Path of God's Bondsmen from Origin to Return* (New Jersey, Islamic Publications International, 1980).
Almond, P.C. *Mystical Experience and Religious Doctrine* (Berlin, Walter de Gruyter, 1982).
Homerin, Th Emil, "Ibn Taymiyya's *al-Ṣūfīyah wa-l-fuqarā'* ", in *Arabica*, 32/2 (1985)
James, W. *The Varieties of Religious Experience* (London: Longmans, 1902).
Landolt, H. "Le Paradoxe De La 'Face De Dieu', *Studia Islamica*, 25 (1996) 163–192.
Ridgeon, L. *Persian Metaphysics and Mysticism* (*Richmond*: *Curzon* 2002).

107 Michael Sells, *Mystical Languages of Unsaying* (Chicago: Chicago University Press, 1994), 9.
108 Louise Nelstrop, *Christian Mysticism: An Introduction to Contemporary Theoretical Approaches* (London: Ashgate, 2009), 37.

7

Sufism's Religion of Love, from Rābi'a to Ibn 'Arabī

Leonard Lewisohn

One day in pre-eternity a ray of your beauty
Shot forth in a blaze of epiphany.
Then Love revealed itself and cast down
A fire which razed the earth from toe to crown.[1]

Ḥāfiẓ

"The religious conscience of Islam is centred upon a fact of meta-history" wrote Henry Corbin,[2] referring here to the pre-eternal covenant mentioned in the Qur'ān (7.172), where God asks the yet uncreated souls of Adam's off-spring, "Am I not your Lord?" and the souls in their pre-creational state, reply "Yes (*balā*)", thus acknowledging Him as their Lord. The entire mythopoetic romance of Sufism developed out of this primordial, pre-eternal covenant (*mithāq*)[3] between man and God.[4] Apropos of this verse, one of the greatest theoreticians of the Sufi erotic religion, Rūzbihān Baqlī (d. 606/1210), was thus to comment how "the spirits of the prophets and saints became intoxicated from the influence of hearing the divine speech and seeing the beauty of majesty. They fell in love with the eternal beloved, with no trace of temporality".[5]

1 Ḥāfiẓ Shīrāzī, *Dīwān-i Khwāja Shams al-Dīn Muḥammad Ḥāfiẓ*, ed. Parvīz Nātil Khānlarī (Tehran: Intishārāt-i Khawārazmī 1359 A.Hsh./1980), 2 vols, ghazal 148: 1. Translation by Leonard Lewisohn.

2 Cited by Paul Nwyia, *Exègése Coranique et Langage Mystique* (Beirut: Dar El-Machreq 1970), 46.

3 Ali Hassan Abdel-Kader, *The Life, Personality and Writings of Al-Junayd* (London: Luzac & Co. Ltd., 1976), 76–80; Louis Massignon, *The Passion of al-Ḥallāj: Mystic and Martyr of Islam*, trans. Herbert Mason (Princeton: Princeton University Press 1982), III, 105 ff.

4 Martin Lings, "The Koranic Origins of Sufism", *Sufi*, 18 (1993), 5–9.

5 Rūzbihān Baqlī. *Kitāb 'Abhar al-'āshiqīn*, H. Corbin and M. Mu'īn (eds) (Tehran/Paris: Institute Français de Recherche en Iran 1958; reprint edition, Tehran: Intishārāt-i Manūchihrī 1365 A.Hsh./1981), 132; cited by Carl Ernst, "The Stages of Love in Persian Sufism, from Rabi'a to Ruzbihan", in L. Lewisohn (ed.), *The Heritage of Sufism*, vol. 2: *Classical Persian Sufism from Its Origins to Rumi* (Oxford: Oneworld 1999), 435–56.

Referring to another Qur'anic verse, "He loves them and they love Him" (5.54), another key Sufi theorist, Aḥmad Ghazālī (d. 520/1126), would compare God's love for mankind ("them") to a seed sewn in pre-Eternity sprouting up in the tree of "they love Him". There is only one love that pervades the hearts of men according to Ghazali, for all love is ultimately spiritual, all love ultimately originating in the "Spirit's Court".[6]

Sufis know that to experientially understand God's love for humankind one must practice works of devotion, leading to "proximity caused by supererogotative works of worship" (*qurb al-nawāfil*), as encapsulated in the famous *Ḥadīth qudsī*, often referred to as the *ḥadīth* of "intimacy with God":

> My slave draws near to Me through nothing I love more than that which I have made obligatory for him. My slave never ceases to draw near to Me through supererogatory acts until I love him. And when I love him, I am his hearing by which he hears, his sight by which he sees, his hand by which he grasps, and his foot by which he walks. And when he approaches a span, I approach a cubit and when he comes walking I come running.[7]

The idea of God's pre-eternal passionate love (*'ishq*) expressed in this *ḥadīth*, the above-cited verses (as well as many other passages) from the Qur'ān, infiltrated the spirituality of Islam from the very earliest period. In this chapter I have endeavoured to sketch the basic contours of the theories and doctrines of Sufi erotic theology, which later became known as the "Religion of Love" in Islam. My discussion of love begins with one of the key founders of early Sufi ascetic theology, Rābi'a Adawiyya (d. ca. 162–176/788–92), who figures as supreme mistress of the Sufi Religion of Love, before chronologically surveying the Sufi theosophy of eros and the erotic in Sufism over the ensuing five hundred years. The chapter ends with the final blossoming and culmination of Islam's "religion-of-love mysticism" in the thought of Ibn 'Arabī (d. 638/1240).

EIGHTH- AND NINTH-CENTURY LOVE MYSTICISM: HASAN AL-BAṢRĪ (D. 110/728), RĀBI'A AL-'ADAWIYYA (D. 185–801) AND ABŪ JA'FAR AL-ṢĀDIQ (145–765)

In the first two centuries after the death of the Prophet, the various doctrines of love encapsulated in various verses of the Qur'ān and *ḥadīth*, including

[6] Aḥmad al-Ghazālī, *Sawāniḥ al-'ushshāq*, "The Lovers' Experiences", *Sawāniḥ: Aphorismen über die Liebe*, edited by H. Ritter (Istanbul: Staatsdruckerei 1942; reprt.: Tehran: Tehran University Press 1368 A.Hsh./1989), 82 ff.

[7] al-Bukhārī. *Ṣaḥīḥ al-Bukhārī* (Riyadh: Maktaba Dar-us-Salam, 1996/1417), no. 2117.

those cited above, were adopted and elaborated by a number of mystical theologians and thinkers.

One of the first Sufis to speak of God's passionate love (*ʿishq*) was Ḥasan al-Baṣrī (d. 110/728).[8] ʿAbd al-Wāḥid ibn Zayd transmitted the following *ḥadīth qudsī* from Ḥasan:

> As soon as My dear servant's first care becomes the remembrance of Me, I make him find happiness and joy in remembering Me. And when I have made him find happiness and joy in remembering Me, he desires Me and I desire him (*ʿashiqanī wa ʿashiqtuhu*). And when he desires Me and I desire him, I raise the veils between him and Me, and I become a cluster of knowable things (*maʿālimā*) before his eyes.[9]

Among ascetics of the generation following Ḥasan al-Baṣrī was Rābiʿa of Basra (d. ca. 162–176/788–92), who belonged to the second ascetic school of Basra. Rābiʿa figures as a founder of early Sufi ascetic theology in general, and the unrivalled exponent of all later Sufi doctrines of love in particular. Her views on divine love infused "the doctrines of Sufism for centuries to come",[10] and as Ibn al-ʿArabī remarked, "she is the one who analyzes and classes the categories of love to the point of being the most famous interpreter of love".

Rābiʿa's theoerotic position that love (*ḥubb* or *maḥabba*) implied exclusive concentration on God was famously expressed in her dictum: "I have not worshipped Him from fear of His fire, nor for love of His garden, so that I should be like a lowly hireling; rather, I have worshipped Him for love of Him and longing for Him". She distinguished between the "two loves" – a selfish love seeking Paradise, and a selfless love seeking God's pleasure – a distinction which underlies all discussion of love in later Sufism.[11] The latter type of love she termed *ḥubb al-hawā* (love of passion) in her poetry,[12] for which the Sufis

8 For a good overview of his place in Sufism, see Javad Nurbakhsh, *Ḥasan Baṣrī: pīr-i payravān-i ṭarīqat va rāhnamā-yi javānmardān* (London: Khānaqāh-i Niʿmatu'llāhī 1375/ 1996); for a more scholarly, far less mystical treatment, see Sulieman Ali Mourad, *Early Islam Between Myth and History: Al-Ḥasan al-Baṣrī (d. 110H/728CE) and the Formation of his Legacy in Classical Islamic Thought* (Leiden: Brill 2006). For a good overview of Ḥasan's mystico-ascetic views, see Louis Massignon, *Essai sur les Origines du Lexique Technique de la Mystique Musulmane* (Nouvelle edition, Paris: J. Vrin 1954), English trans. by Bemjamin Clark as *Essay on the Origins of the Technical Language of Islamic Mysticism* (Indiana: University of Notre Dame Press 1997), 131–35.

9 Cited by Massignon, *Essay on the Origins*, 135.

10 Gavin Picken, *Spiritual Purification in Islam: The Life and Works of al-Muḥāsibī* (London: Routledge 2011), 25.

11 See Ernst, "The Stages of Love", 438.

12 Abū Ḥāmid al-Ghazālī, *The Book of Love, Longing, Intimacy and Contentment*, trans. Eric Ormsby (Cambridge: Islamic Texts Society 2011), 52. See also Jalāl Sattārī, *ʿIshq-i*

were later to substitute the term *'ishq* (passionate love, *eros*). The exclusive focus of Rābi'a on God as the sole object of devotion was a kind of praiseworthy excess and extravagance that the Sufis admired. Although Rābi'a flourished only a century and a half after the Prophet's death, there was already considerable controversy in her day about whether it was valid for the lover of God to aspire for Paradise, understood to be "something besides" (*ghayr*) God. This negative view of Paradise, advocated by most Sufis of her day, was enunciated in Rābi'a's maxim: "First the neighbour, then the house" (*al-jār thumma al-dār*).[13] One finds a similar sentiment expressed a century later in Bāyazīd Bisṭāmī's (d. 261/875) saying: "If the eight paradises were revealed to me in my hut, and the dominion of both the worlds and all their environs were given to me, I still would not wish them in place a single sigh that rises at morning tide from the depth of my soul recalling my yearning [*yād-i shawq-i ū*] for Him."[14]

An important originator of early Sufi love mysticism was Rābi'a's contemporary, the sixth Shi'ite Imām Abū Ja'far al-Ṣādiq (d. 145/765), whom 'Aṭṭār in his *Memoirs of the Saints* (*Tadhkirat al-awliyā'*) lauds as being "the pathmaster of the people of love (*pīshvā-yi ahl-i 'ishq*)."[15]

The love mysticism found in the esoteric Qur'ān commentary ascribed to Ja'far al-Ṣādiq is remarkable. In particular, his interpretation of the verse: "Blessed is He who placed in the sky stellar constellations", (25.61), merits citation:

> Heaven is called "heaven" due to its loftiness. The heart is a heaven, since it rises by means of faith and gnosis without any limit or end. Just as God – the Known One – has no finite limit, likewise gnosis of Him has no end. The zodiacal signs of heaven comprise the orbits of the sun and moon, and they are Aries, Taurus, Gemini, Cancer, Leo, Virgo, Libra, Scorpio, Sagittarius,

ṣūfiyyāna (Tehran: Nashr-i Markaz 1374 A.Hsh./1995), chapter 5 (96–97) for a good discussion of her poetry and its place in later Sufi mysticism.

13 Ghazālī, *Iḥyā' 'ulūm al-dīn* (Beirut: Dār al-Fikr, n.d., rprt of Cairo 1352/1933 edition), vol. 4, 313. Ghazālī contextualizes this statement by explaining that Rābi'a felt that "within her heart there was no concern for the Garden but rather, for the Lord of the Garden". Ghazālī, *The Book of Love, Longing*, 61.

14 Farīd al-Dīn 'Aṭṭār, *Tadhkirat al-awliyā'*, ed. R. A. Nicholson (London: Luzac & Co.: 1905; rprt. Tehran; Dunyā-yi Kitāb, n.d. [2 vols]), I, 159.

15 'Aṭṭār, *Tadhkirat*, edited by M. Isti'lamī (Tehrān: Zawwār, 1372 A.Hsh./1993 [7th edition]), 12. For further studies on Rābi'a, see Margaret Smith, *Rābi'a the Mystic and Her Fellow-Saints in Islām* (Cambridge: Cambridge University Press 1928; repr. 2010); Nurbakhsh, *Sufi Women*, translated by Leonard Lewisohn (New York: Khaniqahi Nimatullahi Publications, 1983; repr. 2004), 12–52. As John Taylor ("Ja'far al-Ṣādiq: Spiritual Forebear of the Ṣūfīs", *Islamic Culture*, XL/1, (1966) 112) pointed out: "In many senses, the entire love-mysticism of Sufism can be traced back to Ja'far who was said to have interpreted the Qur'ānic verse *ihdina al-sirat al-mustaqim* [guide us on the Straight Path] to mean *urshudna ila mahabbatika* [guide us to your love]."

> Capricorn, Aquarius, and Pisces. In the heart there are zodiacal signs or mansions (*burūj*), and they are:
> 1. The mansion of faith (*īmān*);
> 2. The mansion of gnosis (*maʿrifa*);
> 3. The mansion of intellect (*ʿaql*);
> 4. The mansion of certainty (*yaqīn*);
> 5. The mansion of submission (*islām*);
> 6. The mansion of beneficence (*iḥsān*);
> 7. The mansion of trust in God (*tawakkul*);
> 8. The mansion of fear (*khawf*);
> 9. The mansion of hope (*rajāʾ*);
> 10. The mansion of love (*maḥabba*);
> 11. The mansion of yearning (*shawq*);
> 12. The mansion of enravishment (*walah*).
>
> It is by these twelve zodiacal mansions that the heart remains sound, just as it is by the twelve zodiacal signs, from Aries and Taurus to the end, that the evanescent realm and its people are sound.[16]

As can be seen from this schema, *maḥabba* and its sister expressions are used to denote the heights of mystical love. Throughout his commentary, "the negative connotations of passionate love (*ʿishq*) . . . bespeak an early period because in later Sufism, when *ʿishq* became part and parcel of Sufi common vocabulary, it is used positively with reference to the deep love of God".[17]

In his *Etiquette of Devotion* (*Ādāb al-ʿibādāt*), Shaqīq al-Balkhī (d. 194/810), who belonged to the next generation of mystics after Jaʿfar al-Ṣādiq, describes the mystics who dwell in the station of "longing for paradise" as possessing the penultimate degree among the adepts in sincerity (*ahl al-sidq*),[18] their level only being transcended by those who rely exclusively on the love of God without intermediary:

> The stages where the *ahl al-ṣidq* halt are four: the first is Renunciation (*zuhd*), the second is Fear (*khwaf*); the third is Yearning for paradise

[16] My translation from Paul Nwyia's edition of the Arabic text largely follows that of Ernst, "The Stages of Love", 437; and Farhana Mayer (trans.), *Spiritual Gems: The Mystical Qur'ān Commentary Ascribed to Jaʿfar al-Ṣādiq* (Louisville, KY: Fons Vitae 2011), 102.

[17] Farhana Mayer (trans.), *Spiritual Gems*, translator's introduction, xxiii. For further study of this passage, see ibid., lxiii–lxv. The question of the reliability of the ascription of this commentary to the Imām, first raised by Louis Massignon in his *Essay on the Origins*, trans. Clark, 138 ff, is beyond the scope of this chapter.

[18] It should also be noted that Shaqīq was nearly unique among his Sufi contemporaries in endorsing the positive spiritual value of anticipating the delights of Paradise.

(*al-shawq ilā-l-janna*); and the fourth is Love for God (*maḥabba li-Lāh*).[19]

In Shaqīq's hierarchy of spiritual states, love replaces enravishment (found in Ja'far al-Ṣādiq) as the supreme stage of realization. Ultimately, due to God's grace, the mystic is advanced to the highest grade – love of God – the radiance of which fills his heart, supplanting the previous three stages, just as sunlight eclipses starlight.[20] Shaqīq's hierarchial schema of Renunciation →Fear →Yearning →Love permeates the entire subsequent history of Ṣūfī love theory in general.

"The most authentic and ancient comprehensive work to discuss love [*maḥabbat*] from a Ṣūfī point of view which has reached us today"[21] is the *Book of Love* (*Kitāb al-maḥabba*) by Ḥarīth al-Muḥāsibī (d. 243/857). In this work he describes "the love of God for His saints, and the signs by which these lovers of God may be known while they dwell in this world among men. To such lovers is granted the Vision of God and that communion with Him, which is the aim of the mystic, the in-dwelling of the human by the divine".[22] According to Muḥāsibī, love of God comprises "an intensity of yearning (*al-shawq*). This is because yearning in essence is the recollection of the vision of the beloved in the heart (*inna al-ḥubbu'llāh huwa shadda al-shawq* ... *wa dhalaka inna al-shawq fī nafsihu tadhakāra al-qulūb bi-mushāhada al-ma'shūq*)".[23] Muḥāsibī is also famed for a Sufi definition of love: "love is for your heart to be in agreement with what your beloved wills".[24]

A number of important Sufi doctrines of love can be traced back to Muḥāsibī's contemporary Dhū'l-Nūn al-Miṣrī (d. 245/859).[25] Perhaps his most famous saying, cited repeatedly by Sufis over the ensuing centuries, is "Whoever becomes an intimate of God becomes intimate with every beautiful thing (*shay' malīḥ*), every beautiful face (*wajh ṣabīḥ*), every beautiful

[19] Cited by Nwyia, *Exègése Coranique*, 215–16. See Shaqīq's *Ādāb al-'ibādāt*, in ed., *idem.*, *Trois Oeuvres Inédites de Mystiques Musulmans: Shaqīq al-Bakhī, Ibn 'Aṭā, Niffarī* (Beirut: Dar El-Machreq 1986), 12–22.

[20] Nwyia, *Exègése Coranique*, 226–27.

[21] N. Pūrjavādī, "Qibla-yi shawq", *Nashr-i dānish*, XIV/5, 1994, Part II, 17. Selections from the *Kitāb al-maḥabba* are cited by Abū Nu'aym Iṣfahānī, *Ḥilyat al-awliyā'* (Cairo: 1932), X, 76 ff.

[22] Margaret Smith, *Al-Muḥāsibī: An Early Mystic of Baghdad* (London: Sheldon Press 1935), 57–58; cited by Picken, *Spiritual Purification*, 90.

[23] *Ḥilyat*, X, p. 78.

[24] Abū'l-Ḥasan 'Alī b. Muḥammad al-Daylamī, *Kitāb 'aṭf al-alif al-ma'lūf 'alā al-lām al-ma'ṭūf*, translated by Jean-Claude Vadet, *Le Traité d'Amour Mystique d'al-Daylami* (Paris: Librairie Champion/ Geneva: Librairie Droz, 1980), para 155, 85. *A Treatise on Mystical Love*, translated by Joseph Bell and Hassan Mahmoud Abdul Latif Al-Shafie (Edinburgh: Edinburgh University Press 2005), 68.

[25] Nicholson, "A Historical Enquiry", p. 324.

form and every delectable fragrance (*rā'iḥa ṭayyiba*)".[26] The following lines from Rūzbihān Baqlī's commentary on this saying are worth quoting as they illustrate an idea prevalent in later Persian love mysticism – the doctrine of the "game of glances" (*naẓar-bāzī*, found in Ḥāfiẓ in particular) – that spiritual understanding and love can be amplified by ocular means:

> At the spiritual station of love, such contemplation has been said to amplify one's insight into divine knowledge, insofar as [the *ḥadīth* relates], "Gazing upon fair faces amplifies one's vision" (*al-naẓar ilā al-wajh al-ḥasana yuzīda fi al-baṣar*). That pure and pious lady, the truthful daughter of Abū Bakr – may God be pleased with her – declared, "That superior man [the Prophet] loved fair faces." Oh friend! Do not let equivocal ambiguity of [the *ḥadīth* that relates] "Three things have been beloved to me in this world of yours: women, perfume, and prayer" blur the beauteous countenance of Eternity – for when the lightning flash of the two stars of Ursa Minor in the heaven of the invisible world drinks the wine of divine Majesty with the Jupiter of Beauty, it was far removed from the nature of passionate sensuality and incarnationism (*az tab'-i shahwat u ḥulūl birūn būd*).[27]

Abū Sa'īd al-Kharrāz (d. 277/890 or 286/899) was another important Sufi in whose thought love (*maḥabba*) played a central role. In his *Book of Separation* (*Kitāb al-farāgh*), which delineates three stations of the mystical quest, he writes that:

> The fruits of the light of gnosis in the heart are longing (*shawq*) for the Known, repentance (*ināba*) towards the Lord, and love for Him (*maḥabba*). The fruits of longing consist of poems composed in the language of the lovers which the mystic never ceases to intone whether during the darkness of the night or the radiance of the day; the fruits of repentance consist in his supplication to be freed from sin, while the fruits of love consist in the opening of the heart to the recollection of the Beloved.[28]

[26] *Kitāb 'aṭf al-alif al-ma'lūf 'alā'l-lām al-ma'ṭūf*, trans. Vadet, *Le Traité d'Amour Mystique d'al-Daylami*, n. 244, 118. Also cited by Carl Ernst, "Rūzbihān Baqlī on Love as 'Essential Desire' ", in A. Geise & J. C. Bürgel, *God is Beautiful and He loves Beauty: Festschrift in honour of Annemarie Schimmel* (Berlin: Peter Lang, 1994), 184, who gives an extended commentary on later Sufis' reaction and interpretation of this saying. This saying was commented upon in Persian by Rūzbihān Baqlī of Shiraz, who translated it as: "Whoever gains intimacy with God, gains intimacy with all good things, with every bright and beautiful fair face, with every sweet voice, and with every sweet fragrance."

[27] Rūzbihān Baqlī, *Sharḥ-i shaṭḥīyyāt*, edited by Henry Corbin (Tehran: Bibliothéque Iranienne 12; Departement D'iranologie de l'Institut Franco-Iranien 1345 A.Hsh./1966), no. 86, 150 f.

[28] Cited by Nwyia, *Exègése Coranique*, 250.

However, for the development of Sufi erotic theology, Sumnūn al-Muḥibb ("the Lover", d. 298/910–11) is a much more important figure than Kharrāz. "They called him 'Sumnūn the Lover', but he called himself 'Sumnūn the Liar' " states 'Ali b. 'Uthmān Jullābī Ḥujwīrī (d. 463/1071), who also extolled him as being "the Sun in Love's Heaven (*aftāb-i āsimān-i maḥabbat*)".[29] In Sumnūn's erotic theology love is considered to be the supreme spiritual abode which has neither decline nor diminution. Hujwīrī draws our attention to the centrality of love and erotic imagery in his teachings:

> Among the Sufi masters, Sumnūn holds his own particular faith and doctrine (*madhhabī u mashrabī dārad makhṣūṣ*) and he asserts that love is the foundation and principle of the way to God Almighty. All the various mystical states and spiritual stations (*aḥwāl u maqāmāt*) are of a low degree, and every abode that the seeker may abide in is susceptible to decline and diminution except the abode of love (*maḥall-i maḥabbat*) which in no circumstance whatsoever ever admits of decline nor diminution as long as the way itself remains in existence.
>
> All the other Sufi masters are in total concordance with him concerning this idea. However, because of the fact that love is quite a common and well-known term, they wished to conceal this idea from people, so they switched the terms. Thus, when it came to experiential verification of the existence of the idea of the purity of that love (*ṣafā-yi maḥabbat*), instead of calling it "love" they simply named it "purity" (*ṣafwat*), and the lover (*muḥibb*) they called a "Sufi". Some others employed the word *faqīr* (poor mendicant) to denote the lover's abandonment of his own will whilst affirming of the will of the beloved, and thus called the lover a *faqīr*, insofar as the least degree of love is concordance (*muwāfiqat*), and concordance with the beloved's will is contrary to opposition to it.[30]

Hujwīrī's semantic speculations about Sufism (*taṣawwuf*) being synonymous with love (*maḥabbat*) and purity (*ṣafā*) communicates to us that the romantic and erotic elements in Sufism pertain to the quintessence of both its theory and practice. Writing some two hundred and fifty years later, in his description of Sumnūn's beliefs, 'Aṭṭār repeats the first part of this statement, but puts Sumnūn's doctrine of love in the context of the debate between love and knowledge by adding that "He preferred love (*maḥabbat*) over gnosis (*ma'rifat*), whereas most of the masters have preferred gnosis over love."[31] This is of course *exactly the opposite* of what Hujwīrī had said, since it pits the

[29] 'Alī Hujwīrī, *Kashf al-maḥjūb*, ed. V.A. Zhukovskii (St. Petersburg 1899. Reprinted, Leningrad 1926), 172.
[30] Hujwīrī, *Kashf*, pp. 398–99.
[31] 'Aṭṭār, *Tadhkirat*, ed. Isti'lamī, 510.

virtuoso wild romantic Lover-Sumnūn against a vulgar mass of sober intellectualising Sufis, which perhaps says more about 'Aṭṭār's mystical milieu than about Sumnūn's theoerotic doctrine.

There are two other important doctrines of love associated with Sumnūn: one being that love is the supreme subtlety, and the other that love is always of necessity intimately associated with adversity. Regarding the first, Sumnūn said: "A thing can be explained only by means of something more subtle than itself, and since there is nothing subtler than love, by what, then can one explain it?"[32] Perhaps Ḥāfiẓ's riddle-in-verse had this saying in mind:

> The jealousy of love has severed the tongues of all
> The gnostics. How could it be that the mystery of His grief
> Has settled down to the people walking along the street?[33]

Regarding the second, Sumnūn was asked, "Why has love always been bound up together with adversity (*balā*)?" He replied, "It is so that each and every ignoramus will not lay claim to love, and being confronted with adversity, they will be forced to retreat."[34] Sumnūn's vaunting of love-as-adversity and adversity-in-love became a distinct poetic topos in the Persian Sufi poetry of 'Aṭṭār and Rūmī.[35] Again, as Ḥāfiẓ put it:

> The waiting station of pleasure and delight
> Always includes suffering. In Pre-eternity
> The souls bound themselves to that tragedy.[36]

THE TENTH-CENTURY SUFI SCHOOL OF BAGHDAD

From the tenth century onwards, with the rise of the Baghdad School of Sufism, theoerotic themes (love as *maḥabba*, *ḥubb*, and *'ishq*) took centre

[32] Cited by Daylamī, *A Treatise on Mystical Love*, 19; Hujwīrī, *Kashf al-maḥjūb*, 172–74. On this saying, also see 'Aṭṭār's commentary, *Tadhkirat*, p. 513.

[33] *Dīvān-i Ḥāfiẓ*, ed. Khānlarī, ghazal 107: 4. Trans. Robert Bly and Leonard Lewisohn, *The Angels Knocking on the Tavern Door* (New York: Harper Collins, 2008), 57.

[34] *Tadhkirat al-awliyā'*, 513.

[35] Jalāl al-Dīn Rūmī, *The Mathnawí of Jalálu'ddín Rúmí*, translated and edited by R. A. Nicholson (London: E.J.W. Gibb Memorial Trust 1924–40), III: 4466.

[36] See Bly and Lewisohn (trans.), *The Angels*, 59. The poet here refers to the Qur'ānic verse (7: 172) cited at the outset of this essay. As Annemarie Schimmel explains: "the theme of Affliction, *balā'* is ingeniously combined with the word *balā*, 'Yes', that the souls spoke at the Day of the Covenant, thus accepting in advance every tribulation that might be showered upon them until Doomsday"; *Mystical Dimensions of Islam* (Chapel Hill: University of N. Carolina Press 1975), 136–37. For further discussion of this topos, see A. A. Seyed-Gohrab, "The Erotic Spirit: Love, Man and Satan in Ḥāfiẓ's Poetry", in Lewisohn (ed.), *Ḥāfiẓ and the Religion of Love in Classical Persian Poetry* (London: I.B. Tauris 2010), 113–14.

stage in Sufi mystical literature and terminology. Amongst the key members of this school was Abū'l-Ḥusayn al-Nūrī (d. 295/907), who was famous for his belief that *maḥabba* is higher than *'ishq* and for being the first Sufi to speak of "passionate love" (*'ishq*) in reference to the love of God. His use of *'ishq* for this love was denounced by the Ḥanbalites, "who declared him a heretic as the word *'ishq* was not permissible to express the relation between man and God in the Arabic language; but for Nūrī the term *maḥabba* (from the root that occurs in the Qur'ān, 5.59) denoted a higher stage than *'ishq*".[37]

Nūrī notoriously claimed to be a lover (*'āshiq*) of God, and the legend of his passionate death (transported in a flight of ecstasy during *samā'*, he ran into a reed-bed, cut his feet and so bled to death) was later adduced by Abū Ḥāmid Ghazālī as the supreme example and "greatest cause of love of God, the dearest and rarest of all kinds of love".[38] Nūrī's treatise on *The Stations of the Heart* (*Maqāmāt al-qulūb*), which has been compared by Annemarie Schimmel and Luce López-Baralt to St. Teresa's *Interior Castle*, delineates the four types of fire which are found in the gnostic's heart:

> The fire of Fear (*nār al-khawf*), the fire of Love (*maḥabba*), the fire of Gnosis (*ma'rifa*) and the fire of Yearning (*shawq*) . . . The fire of Fear burns away the pleasure found in transgressing the Law; the fire of Love burns away the sweetness found in [performing acts of] obedience; the fire of Gnosis burns away attachments [to the world] and the fire of Yearning burns away all peace (*rawḥ*) in order to unite [the seeker] at last with the Beloved.[39]

It was typical of Nūrī's passionate temperament to wish to burn off the delights found in Paradise (to which the Koranic term *rawḥ* here alludes). His view of the supreme Object of "longing" as comprising a "burning away" of all paradisiacal superfluities in order to unite the mystic with God alone reflected the attitude of the primacy of the love of God that prevailed in all later Sufism, which "succeeded in excluding the desire for paradise as a legitimate goal of mysticism; henceforth, longing [*shawq*]can only be directed toward God".[40]

37 Adopted from Schimmel, "Abū'l-Ḥusayn al-Nūrī: 'Qibla of the Lights,' " in L. Lewisohn, (ed.), *The Heritage of Sufism, I: Classical Persian Sufism: from Its Origins to Rūmī* (Oxford: Oneworld 1999), 62.

38 Ghazālī, *Iḥyā' 'ulūm al-dīn*, IV, 307.

39 *Maqāmāt al-qulūb*, in P. Nwyia (edited) *Textes mystiques inédits* (Beirut: Mélanges de l'Université Saint-Joseph 1968).

40 Ernst, "The Stages of Love", 440. Ghazālī's commentary on the following Sufi couplet typifies the negative attitude towards longing for paradise found in the later history of Persian Sufism: "*Separation from Him is more terrible than His fire; / attaining Him is sweeter than Paradise.* By this they [the Sufis] mean to express a preference for the heart's pleasure in knowing God over the pleasures of food, drink and sex. Paradise is the source of the pleasure of the senses but the heart takes its pleasure in the encounter with God alone." (Ghazālī, *Love, Longing*, 54).

One of Nūrī's key doctrines was that love demands revelation and eschews concealment. Thus, he said, "Love (*maḥabba*) is to rend the veils and unveil the secrets", upon which saying Rūzbihān wrote a fascinating and long exegesis.[41] In the beginning of *Yūsuf u Zulaykhā*, Jāmī set Nūrī's aphorism to verse when he commented that the Godhead "played the melodies of lovers to Himself alone, gambling like a lover with Himself. But since it is the custom of those with pretty faces that they feel constrained when they are compelled to curtain themselves away. No pretty woman can bear to veil herself. Shut the door in her face and she'll peek her head out the window."[42]

The acknowledged leader of the School of Baghdad[43] was Abū'l-Qāsim Junayd (d. 297/910), who utilized Muḥāsibī's terminology and perfected his orthodox teachings. Some of the key definitions of the meaning of passionate love or eros in the Sufi lexicon derived from Junayd, who had endorsed the idea that *ʿishq* was the supreme degree of love (*maḥabba*),[44] reasoning that *ʿishq* is etymologically derived from *ʿashaq*, the peak and highest point of a mountain, such that *ʿishq* rises to the supreme heights of love where it attains "fullness of its being".[45]

Another important member of the Baghdad school of Sufism was Abū Bakr al-Shiblī (d. 334/945), renowned, like Rabīʿa, for an extravagant emphasis on the jealous exclusivity of divine love. Thus, Hujwīrī commented that

> *Maḥabbat* (love) is derived from *ḥubb*, which means a jar completely brimful of water such that nothing more can be poured into it. In the same fashion, when love is collected within the seeker's heart, it fills it to the point of saturation, so that only the sayings of the beloved object can be contained in his heart. . . . And it was to this meaning that Shiblī alluded when he said, "Love (*maḥabbat*) is called *maḥabbat* because it obliterates from the heart everything but the beloved".[46]

41 *Sharḥ-i shaṭḥīyyāt*, 176–77.

42 Jāmī, ʿAbd al-Raḥmān, *Mathnawī-yi Haft awrang*, edited by Ḥ. Aʿlākhān Afḍaḥzād, Aḥmad Tarbiyat (Tehran: Nashr-i Mīrāth-i maktūb 1378 A.Hsh./1999, 2 vols), vol. 2, 35, vv. 315–17.

43 The doctrines of love which were later popularized in Sufism were largely opposed by the teachers of the anti-ascetic ninth-century Sufi School of Khurāsān, most of who reviled the idea of passionate love (*ʿishq*). For instance, Abū ʿAlī Daqqāq (d. 412/1021), who was the father-in-law of Abū'l-Qāsim al-Qushayrī's (d. 465/1074), argued that the idea of *ʿishq* (passionate love, eros) implies "an overstepping of limit in love but God may not be characterised as one who oversteps a limit. . . . God may not be characterised as having passionate love, nor may man in his ascription to God, for He negates passion. There is no way to attribute this to God, neither on God's part for man, nor on man's part for God." Cited (from Zabīdī's *Itḥāf*), in Ghazālī, *Love, Longing*, 100.

44 Ibid., 52.

45 Cited by Daylamī, *A Treatise on Mystical Love*, 27.

46 *Kashf*, 394.

Like Nūrī, Shiblī questioned whether yearning for Paradise is a legitimate goal for the Sufi lover. He was fond of quoting from the *Isrā'īliyyāt*, a genre of literature consisting of alleged quotations from the Bible. He thus narrated that "God revealed to David (peace be upon him), 'O David, remembrance of Me belongs to those who remember while paradise belongs to those who are obedient; visiting Me belongs to those who yearn; but I belong exclusively to those who love.' "[47]

The association of love with risk[48] appears vividly in the life and writings of the most sensational figure of the Baghdad School of Sufis, Manṣūr al-Ḥallāj (d. 309/922), whose love theory had a huge impact on later Sufi erotic theology. Ḥallāj listed the spiritual states required of any mystic who lays claim to attaining any stage as follows: "One who claims (i) fear (*khwaf*) needs (ii) agitation (*inzi'āj*); one who claims hope (iii) (*rajā'*) needs (iv) quietude (*ṭama'nīna*); one who claims (v) love (*maḥabba*) needs (vi) yearning (*shawq*); one who claims yearning needs (vii) ravishing (*walah*); one who claims ravishing needs (viii) *Allāh*".[49] As Massignon pointed out, the last six terms in this list are identical with the last six terms in Ja'far's constellations of the heart. The linked sequence "*maḥabba* → *shawq* → *walah* → *Allāh*" in this list, based on Ja'far al-Ṣādiq's mystical theology, is used by Ḥallāj to emphasize "the supreme position that love holds among the spiritual degrees".[50]

Ḥallāj's mystical theories were preserved in a long fragment, extant in no other source, in the *Kitāb 'aṭf al-alif al-ma'lūf 'alā'l-lām al-ma'ṭūf* ("The Book of the Inclination of the Familiar Alif toward the Inclined Lām"), described as "the oldest complete and extant mystical book on love"[51] by Abū al-Ḥasan al-Daylamī (*fl.* 10th century). Daylamī's *Treatise on Mystical Love* set the stage for all later philosophical treatments of love influenced by Sufism. Daylamī's own theory of ten stations of love, which was based on Ḥallāj's speculations, used the distinctive Sufi term "spiritual station" (*maqām*) to describe them, as follows: 1. *ulfa* or familiarity → 2. *uns* or intimacy → 3. *wudd* or affection → 4. *maḥabba ḥaqīqiyya dūna al-majāziyya* or real love without metaphorical (i.e. physical) love → 5. *khulla* or friendship → 6. *sha'af* or excessive love → 7. *shaghaf* or infatuation → 8. *istihtār* or recklessness → 9. *walah* or ravishing

47 Ghazālī, *Love, Longing*, 192.

48 In his life, Ḥallāj echoed Nūrī's doctrine that "Love, so long as it hides, feels itself in great danger, and is only reassured by exposing itself to risk." Massignon, *The Passion of al-Ḥallāj*, trans. Mason, I, 347.

49 Cited by Massignon, *Essai sur les origines*, 428–29.

50 Ernst, "The Stages of Love", 443.

51 L. A. Giffen, *The Theory of Profane Love among the Arabs: the Development of the Genre* (New York: NYU Press, 1971), 66.

→ 10. *hayamān* or bewilderment. These ten categories are completed by an eleventh – *'ishq* or passionate love – as a comprehensive term for exclusive devotion to the beloved.[52]

Ḥallāj was known for the doctrine of essential union (*ittiḥād*) of lover and beloved, expressed in famous verses beginning: "I am the one I love, and the one I love is I."[53] In terms of metaphysics, Ḥallāj's most important contribution to the development of love theory in Islam was his original conception of love as constituting the divine Essence itself.[54] It was above all Ḥallāj who had been – as Daylamī pointed out – the first to conceive of love as the divine Essence.[55] Daylamī comments that Ḥallāj's originality

> lies in his treating Love (*'ishq*) as an attribute of the Essence in the Absolute just as he does the loci of the Absolute's epiphanies. Other masters have demonstrated this [love theory] in respect to the love of the beloved and lover and their arriving at the height of ecstasy in this feeling, such that the whole of the lover is annihilated in the beloved. But they have not professed any view about the divine nature (*lāhūt*) and human nature (*nāsūt*). Indeed, they have equally maintained that God's love for the saints is pre-eternal and that their love for Him comes from the effects [of that pre-eternal love] which He leaves in their hearts without fusion [of the two natures], but with union of the faithful believer [to his God] to the point where he becomes annihilated in Him, so there appears to be no one left but Him.[56]

The 'Grand Master' (*Shaykh-i kabīr*) Abū 'Abdullāh Muḥammad ibn Khafīf Shīrāzī (d. 371/981) is extremely important for the role he played in transmitting Ḥallāj's teachings on love. Although hailing from Fars and thus not geographically speaking a member of the School of Baghdad, he authored two short works and a tract on love which are no longer extant.[57] A rather austere figure despite having a multitude of wives, Ibn Khafīf did permit contemplation of the beautiful as a reminder of the divine which is clear, as

[52] Ernst, "The Stages of Love", 444; Daylamī, *A Treatise on Mystical Love*, 31–37.

[53] For the entire passage, see Daylamī, *A Treatise on Mystical Love*, 168.

[54] Not Aḥmad Ghazālī – as N. Pūrjavādy asserts (*Sulṭān-i ṭarīqat: Sawāniḥ-yi zindigī u sharḥ-i athār-i Khwāja Aḥmad Ghazālī* (Tehran: Intishārat-i Āgāh 1358 A.Hsh./1979), 90). See Ernst, "Rūzbihān Baqlī on Love as 'Essential Desire' ", in A. Geise and J. C. Bürgel, *God is Beautiful and He loves Beauty: Festschrift in honour of Annemarie Schimmel* (Berlin: Peter Lang, 1994), 181–89. See also Massignon, *The Passion of al-Ḥallāj*, trans. Mason, III, 100–4; Daylamī, *A Treatise on Mystical Love*, chap. 5.

[55] See Jean-Claude Vadet (trans.), *Le Traité d-Amour Mystique d'al-Daylami*, 87–88, nos. 162–66; see also Daylamī, *A Treatise on Mystical Love*, trans. Bell and Al-Shafie, liii.

[56] My translation here is based on Daylamī's original Arabic text, as well as Claude Vadet's French translation (87–88; paragraphs 163–66); Bell and Shafie's translation of Daylamī, *A Treatise on Mystical Love*, 70–72; and Massignon's *The Passion of al-Ḥallāj*, I, 366–67.

[57] Bell and Shafie's introduction to their translation of Daylamī's *Treatise on Mystical Love*, xxiii.

Schimmel observes, from his view that the spirit takes pleasure in three things: a sweet smell, a beautiful voice, and looking (*naẓar*),[58] recalling Dhū'l-Nūn al-Miṣrī's dictum mentioned above.

THE RELIGION OF LOVE FROM AVICENNA (D. 428/1037) TO ʿAYN AL-QUDĀT HAMADĀNĪ (D. 526/1132) AND QUṬB AL-DĪN ARDISHĪR AL-ʿIBBĀDĪ (D. 547/1152)

Adopting the term *ʿishq* from Sufis of Ḥallāj's school,[59] in his *Treatise on Love* (*Risāla fī al-ʿishq*) the great Muslim Peripatetic thinker Abū ʿAlī ibn Sīnā (Avicenna, d. 428/1037) described God as the First Beloved (*maʿshūq-i awwal*), speaking of Him as being Loved, Lover and Love at once.[60] Avicenna's ontological eroticism (he maintained that Being's emanation is itself erotic, taking place by way of yearning, *ʿalā sabīl al-tashawwuq*[61]) and theory of the ontological unity of Lover, Love and Beloved had a great influence on later Sufi theoerotic theories. But the notion of erotic yearning is even more mystical in Avicenna, because it is man who becomes the beloved for whom God-the-lover yearns. In the following passage, Avicenna speaks the language of theoerotic mysticism to express his own philosophical outlook on love:

> Every single being loves the Absolute Good (*al-khayr al-muṭlaq*) with an inborn love, and that Absolute Good (*al-khayr al-muṭlaq*) manifests Himself to all those that love Him. However, the capacity of the latter to receive this manifestation (*tajallī*) differs in degree, and so does the connection (*ittiḥād*) they have with Him. The highest degree of approximation to It is the reception of Its manifestation in Its full reality, i.e. in the most perfect possible way, which is what the Sufis call unification (*ittiḥād*).[62]

A separate section of Avicenna's treatise on love was consecrated to the notion of the love of gallant youths for fair faces, where he argues that love

[58] Abū'l-Ḥasan al-Daylamī, *Sīrat Abū ʿAbdullāh İbn al-Ḫafīf aş-Şīrāzī*, Introduction, 31 (text 214); cited by Bell and Shafie (trans.), Daylamī, *A Treatise on Mystical Love*, xxxix.

[59] Giffen, *Profane Love*, p. 146; Joseph Norment Bell, "Avicenna's *Treatise on Love* and the Nonphilosophical Muslim Tradition", *Der Islam*, Band 63 (1986), 80. He also accepted the use of the word *ʿishq* to describe man's love of God and that God may be described as loving man, citing Ḥasan al-Basrī's so-called *ḥadīth-i qudsī*: "He loves me with *ʿishq* and I love him with *ʿishq*." Ibid., 78.

[60] Etin Anwar, "Ibn Sīna's Philosophical Theology of Love: A Study of *Risālah fī al-ʿishq*", in *Islamic Studies*, XLII/2 (2003), 341.

[61] One can note here Avicenna's adoption of the terminology of the early Sufis such as Shaqīq al-Balkhī and later Abū'l-Ḥasan Nūrī, both of who spoke of the fire of yearning uniting man with God, the Absolute Beloved.

[62] Cited by Bell, "Avicenna's *Treatise on Love*", 78; see also Anwar, "Philosophical Theology", 343.

of beauty is innate in refined people, demonstrating their proximity to the First Object of Love.[63]

The geographical centre for the development of Islamic erotic theology during the eleventh and twelfth centuries was Khurāsān, where a flourishing of antinomian love mysticism occurred. In this context, the Persian Sufi quatrains of Abū Saʿīd ibn Abī'l-Khayr of Nishapur (357/967–440/1048), one of the first Sufis to use secular love poetry to illustrate his mystical teachings, are extremely significant.[64] Abū Saʿīd's older contemporary, the Ḥanbalite Sufi Khwāja 'Abdullāh Anṣārī of Herāt (396/1006–481/1089), is another key figure in the erotic spirituality of Iranian Islam[65] who played a paramount role in the development of the theoerotic lexicon of Persian Sufism.[66]

Anṣārī is justly celebrated for his two treatises: *Stages of the Sufi Wayfarers* (*Manāzil al-sā'irīn*)[67] and *The Hundred Fields* (*Ṣad maydān*, written in Persian in 448/1056), each of which itemized the Ṣūfī path into some 100 stages of spiritual progress. In each stage of the *Manāzil*, apparently following ternary structure initiated by Abū Manṣūr Iṣfahānī's (d. 417/1026) *Nahj al-khāṣṣ*,[68] Anṣārī categorizes his subjects in triparite form. *Maḥabba* is placed in the seventh chapter (*bāb*) on the "mystical states" (*aḥwāl*) experienced by the wayfarer in the following order: 61. Love (*maḥabba*) → 62. Zeal (*ghayra*) → 63. Yearning, (*shawq*) → 64. Disquiet (*qalaq*) → 65. Thirst (*'aṭash*) → 66.

[63] Bell, "Avicenna's *Treatise on Love*", 77.

[64] Terry Graham, "Abū Saʿīd ibn Abī'l-Khayr and the School of Khurāsān", in Leonard Lewisohn (ed.), *The Heritage of Sufism*, vol. 1: *Classical Persian Sufism from Its Origins to Rumi* (Oxford: Oneworld 1999), 83–135.

[65] See Lewisohn, "Divine Love in Islam", in *Encyclopædia of Love in World Religions*, ed. Yudit Greenberg, (New York: Macmillan Reference & Thomson Gale 2007), vol. 1, 163–65.

[66] See Lewisohn, "Preface: Anṣārī and Early Persian Erotic Spirituality", in Nahid Angha (trans.), *Ansari's* Hundred Fields: *An Early Persian Treatise on the Sufi Way* (London: Archetype 2010), 1–16. See also Annabel Keeler, "Maybudī's love mysticism and the heritage of Anṣārī", in her *Sufi Hermeneutics: the Qur'an Commentary of Rashīd al-Dīn Maybudī* (Oxford: Oxford University Press 2006) 111–16. At the same time that the doctrines of love were developing in the tenth century School of Baghdad, "the ecstatic tradition of love and intoxication that had been associated with Bāyazīd [Bisṭāmī, d. ca. 261/875] was continuing in Khurāsān", Keeler informs us. In this respect Anṣārī represents the most important link in "the ecstatic tradition of love and intoxication that had been associated with Bāyazīd [Bisṭāmī] . . . in Khurāsān". Keeler, ibid., 109. Bāyazīd's school, however, was radically ascetic in temperament, and although characterized by rapture (*ghalabat*) and intoxication (*sukr*), it should be strictly distinguished from the school of love associated with Anṣārī that developed two centuries later in the same area. Bāyazīd's boast, "God made a woman and a wall seem the same to me" ('Aṭṭār, *Tadhkirat*, ed. Istiʿlāmī, [6th edition], 349) is more typical of the arid, ascetic spirit of Byzantine hesychastic spirituality than that of Sufi love mysticism.

[67] *Manāzil al-sā'irīn*, Arabic text edited with Persian trans. by Ravān Farhādī (Kabul: 1971).

[68] Abū Manṣūr Iṣfahānī, *Nahj al-khāṣṣ*, ed. N. Purjavādī, in *Taḥqīqāt-i islāmī*, (1367 A.Hsh./1988), nos. 1&2.

Ecstasy (*wajd*) → 67. Consternation (*dahash*) → 68. Infatuation (*hayamān*) → 69. Lightning (*barq*) → 70. Heart-savour (*dhawq*).

In his *Ṣad maydān*, Anṣārī also itemized the Sufi path into a different series of one hundred stages, here describing the final ten spiritual stages (91–100) as culminating in a supreme hundred-and-first stage which is Love: 91. The Metaphysical Moment (*waqt*) → 92. Breath (*nafas*) → 93. Unveiling (*mukāshafa*) → 94. Rejoicing (*surūr*) → 95. Intimacy (*uns*) → 96. Consternation (*dahshat*) → 97. Contemplation and Witnessing (*mushāhada*) → 98. Observation (*mu'āyana*) → 99. Annihilation (*fanā'*) → 100. Subsistence in God (*baqā'*). He concludes the treatise by underlining the all-comprehensive nature of love: "Now, these Hundred Grounds are all drowned in the [101] Ground of Love (*maḥabba*)", which he describes as "the Ground of Friendship (*dūstī*). God Almighty declares: '... a people whom He loves and they love Him' (5.54) and, 'Say: If you love God ...' (3.31) Love has three stages: First of all, Uprightness; at midway, Intoxication, and finally, Annihilation – and praise be to God, the First and the Last!"[69] To expound the one-hundred-and-first station of Love (*maḥabbat*), Anṣārī composed a separate *Book of Love* (*Maḥabbat-nāma*), the structure of which is similar to *The Hundred Fields*.[70]

In Anṣārī's mysticism, love thus assumes the supreme place in the hierarchy of Sufi stages. Within less than a century of his death, his sayings and works became one of one of the mainstays of the Sufi school of thought known as the "Religion of Love" (*madhhab-i 'ishq*) in classical Persian poetry.[71] Anṣārī's Sufi doctrines of love appear most clearly in his renowned *Supplications* (*Munājāt*), his "most love-oriented text"[72] that "won him the greatest admiration ... in which he pours out his love, longing and his advice".[73]

Anṣārī's foremost disciple, Rashīd al-Dīn Maybudī (d. 520/1126), expanded and elaborated these doctrines of love in great depth and detail, replacing the neutral term *maḥabba* with "passionate love" (*'ishq*) – a term never used by

[69] *Ansari's Hundred Fields: An Early Persian Treatise on the Sufi Way*, trans. Nahid Angha (London: Archetype 2010), 134–40 (I have modified her translation).

[70] According to Muḥammad Sarvar Mawlā'ī, the *Maḥabbat-nāma* constitutes an extended meditation on that 101st station: see his edition of *Majmū'a-yi Rasā'il-i fārsī-yi Khwāja 'Abdu'llāh-i Anṣārī* (Tehran: Intishārāt-i Tūs 1377 A.Hsh./1998), clxv.

[71] As Keeler (*Sufi Hermeneutics*, 111) notes, this movement or school "embraced different interpretations of the concept of love and distinct approaches to the mystical path". For a thorough introduction into this distinct Sufi tradition of sacral eroticism in Islam, see Lewisohn, "Prolegomenon to the Study of Ḥāfiẓ, 2 – The Mystical Milieu: Ḥāfiẓ's Erotic Spirituality", in Lewisohn (ed.) *Hafiz and the Religion of Love*, 31–73.

[72] Joseph Lumbard, "From *Ḥubb* to *'Ishq*: the Development of Love in Early Sufism", *Journal of Islamic Studies*, 18/3 (2007), 353.

[73] Schimmel, *Mystical Dimensions*, 90–91.

Anṣārī – all throughout his monumental multi-volume Qur'ān commentary written in Persian, entitled *The Revelation of Mysteries* (*Kashf al-asrār*).[74]

However, the most elaborate elucidation of the doctrine of love that became fully established in Khurāsān during the early sixth/twelfth century[75] is found in the writings of two of Islam's great mystical theologians: Abū Ḥāmid Muḥammad al-Ghazālī (d. 505/1111) and his younger brother Aḥmad Ghazālī (d. 520/1126).[76]

Standing squarely in the centre of the both the Khurāsānian and Baghdādian schools of Sufism, Aḥmad Ghazālī was the teacher of two important figures in the history of Sufism in particular: Abū'l-Najīb al-Suhrawardī (d. 563/1168), who was in turn the master of his nephew Shihāb al-Dīn Abū Ḥafṣ 'Umar Suhrawardī (d. 632/1234), founder of the Suhrawardī order, famed as the "Mother of Sufi Orders". He was also the master of the enigmatic mystical theologian 'Ayn al-Quḍāt Hamadānī (executed 526/1132), author of the *Tamhīdāt*, a voluminous commentary on his master's *The Lovers' Experiences* (*Sawāniḥ al-'ushshaq*).[77] In the writings of Aḥmad Ghazālī the influences of both Bāyazīd Bisṭāmī and Abū'l-Ḥasan Kharaqānī (d. 426/1034) as well as Ḥallāj and Junayd are clearly visible.

Aḥmad Ghazālī's *Sawaniḥ* is a short work on the spiritual psychology of divine love couched in the terminology of human erotic relationships. In this work, Ghazālī followed Ḥallāj in identifying Love with the Absolute as well as with the divine Spirit (*rūḥ*). The main subject of Ghazālī's philosophy is passionate love (*'ishq*), which, formally speaking, is not "philosophy" – *Falsafa* – but rather comprises a sort of "erotic theosophy" apprehended by intuitional means (*dhawq*), based on contemplative experience rather than rational meditations and deliberations.

In Ghazālī's metaphysics of love there seems to be little or no differentiation between human and divine love, so it is virtually impossible to distinguish between the metaphysics of the spirit and the erotics of the flesh. His use of an explicitly erotic vocabulary couched in symbolic allusions (*ishārāt*) to describe the experience of love, whether sexual or sacral, did not go as far as that of some of his later Sufi followers, such as Rūzbihān Baqlī

[74] "Maybudī has no hesitation in using the word *'ishq*, applying it to the mystic's love of God, to the Prophet's love for God, and even to God's love for man. . . . [He] illustrates the theme of love with numerous poems and allegories, and he interprets numerous passages of the Qur'ān in the light of the doctrine of love." Keeler, *Sufi Hermeneutics*, 116.

[75] Keeler, *Sufi Hermeneutics*, 110.

[76] See Leonard Lewisohn, "Sawanih", in *Encyclopædia of Love in World Religions*, ed. Yudit Greenberg (New York: Macmillan Reference & Thomson Gale 2007), II, 535–38.

[77] *Sawāniḥ: Aphorismen über die Liebe.*

(d. 606/1210) and Awḥad al-Dīn Kirmānī (d. 635/1238), who held that human love formed a bridge, across which every seeker necessarily must fare to reach the farther – divine – shore.[78] Human love can only been described as being a bridge to divine love (according to the renowned adage: "The fictional is a bridge to Reality" or "the unreal form is a bridge to the supra-formal Reality", *al-majāz qantarat al-ḥaqīqat*), as Ghazālī states, if and when the mystic has already found union with the divine source. Once having attained annihilation in God (*fanā'*), from the standpoint of Eternity, the adept casts his regard back on the realm of created beings, beholding the radiance of human beauties reflecting the eternal beauty back at him.[79]

He maintained that these various forms of love (*ʿishq*) differ only in degrees of intensity, not in kind; love is a single reality composed of various analogical graduations of intensity and weakness. Nonetheless, in the *Sawāniḥ*[80] he states that human love (*ʿishq-i khalq*) is finite and limited, and seldom – or, rather, never – penetrates the heart's deepest core, for it proceeds from the outward and goes inward (towards God), in contrast to the pre-eternal love of the "divine covenant" which proceeds from within (God) and goes out. By "within", Ghazālī refers here to the pre-eternal covenant mentioned in the Qur'ān (7.172), where God asks the yet uncreated souls of Adam's offspring, "Am I not your Lord?" and the souls in their unconscious, uncreated state, reply: "yes (*bala*)", thus establishing their on-going colloquy with God.

All love is ultimately spiritual, since all love ultimately originates from the "Spirit's Court" (*bargāh-i jān*). Love hails from Eternity (*qidam*), having descended down from a state of intimate converse with God into the temporal realm of being (*wujūd*), where it is incarnated in two forms: (i) the beloved (*maʿshūq*), who is described as the "instrument of union" (*sāz-i wisāl*) and who is a manifestation of beauty, and (ii) the lover (*ʿāshiq*), who is described as the "instrument of separation" (*sāz-i firāq*), one who apprehends and contemplates beauty and who has personally verified the reality of divine Unity (*tawḥīd*) on the psychospiritual level of the Spirit.[81] Yet in its own essence, Love itself "is independent of all of these attachments and causes [that is, the beloved and the lover]".[82]

Love is also described as "an intoxication (*sukr*) in the very organ of apprehension, which is itself an obstacle to obtaining perfect apprehension". This intoxication initially exalts but ultimately inhibits the lover's

78 Pūrjavādī, *Sulṭān-i ṭarīqat*, 57.
79 Ibid., 63–64.
80 Sawāniḥ: Aphorismen über die Liebe, 53–54.
81 Pūrjavādī, *Sultan-i tariqat*, 197.
82 *Sawāniḥ: Aphorismen über die Liebe*, 61.

apprehension (*idrāk*) of the beloved, since his giddy vision of her qualities impedes his deeper comprehension of her Essence. Although this does remind one of Socrates' prayer "that those things that pertain to the body may not impede the beauty of the soul" (*Phaedrus*, 279b-c), Ghazālī's doctrine of intoxication alludes to something more profound – being in fact the central theme of Sufi epistemology – that he sums up in a Sufi adage: "the inability to apprehend apprehension comprises apprehension" (*al-'ijz 'an darak al-idrāk idrāk^an*).[83] That is to say, the summit of knowledge lies in a kind of drunken inapprehension, which is a type of apprehension without any of the limitations of subjective consciousness (one recalls San Juan de la Cruz's poem: "*no saber sabiendo . . . toda sciencia trascendiendo*"[84]).

Knowledge (*'ilm*) is unable to grasp love (*'ishq*). Ghazālī compares the former to the shore of the sea and the latter to a pearl in an oyster submerged in its lowest depths. Forever shore-bound in immanence, neither dry reason (*'aql*) nor barren knowledge (*'ilm*) can access or apprehend the transcendent truths of Love's apophatic teachings. The dry bank of love's ocean remains the farthest reach of knowledge. Knowledge is also likened to a moth and love to a candle: any "knowledge" that the moth possesses of flame is purely exoteric and external, since all its understanding is consumed away and vanishes once that "knowledge" enters the fire. Who then can relate anything about love? Since love is beyond knowledge, it is also supra-ontological, or "beyond being". Ghazālī paradoxically describes this understanding of love that is "beyond knowledge" as being a kind of surmise or conjecture (Arabic: *zann*; Persian: *gumān*). This conjectural wisdom is higher than certainty (*yaqīn*), for it is only that surmise or conjecture that can swim Love's ocean to dive under in pursuit of its pearl.[85]

Despite its strange, transcendent nature, Love can be discerned intuitively through the faculty of imagination. In chapters 37–38 of the *Sawāniḥ*, Ahmad Ghazālī explains that

> Sometimes [Love] makes an appearance through the curl (*zulf*), sometimes by the down (*khāṭṭ*), sometimes by the beauty-spot or mole (*khāl*), sometimes by the lofty stature (*qadd*), sometimes by the eye (*dīda*), sometimes by the face (*rū'y*), sometimes by the coquettish glance (*ghamza*), sometimes by the beloved's laugh and sometimes by her reproach. Each of these spiritual realities (*ma'ānī*) is a sign testifying to the quest of the lover's soul.

83 Ibid., 74–75.

84 "Entréme donde no supe", in *The Poems of Saint John of the Cross: English Versions and Spanish Originals*, trans. Willis Barnstone (New York: New Directions Publications 1972), 58–59.

85 *Sawāniḥ: Aphorismen über die Liebe*, 11–14.

Among later important works of erotic spirituality composed in the same vein as the *Sawāniḥ*, and penned in imitation of its style, vocabulary and terminology, which copied its topoi and themes, may be mentioned the *Divine Gleams* (*Lawāyiḥ*) of Qāḍī Hamīd al-Dīn Nagūrī (d. 643/1245), the *Divine Flashes* (*Lama'āt*) of Fakhr al-Dīn 'Irāqī (d. 688/1289), the *Commentary on Divine Flashes of the Divine Flashes [of 'Irāqī]* (*Sharḥ-i Lama'āt*) by Shāh Ni'matu'llāh (d. 835/1437), the *Radiant Rays from the Divine Flashes [of 'Irāqī]* (*Ashi''āt al-Lama'āt*) by 'Abd al-Raḥmān Jāmī (d. 898/1492), and the *Ḥaqq al-yaqīn* of Mahmud Shabistari (d. after 741/1340). Due to the erotic mysticism of his *Sawāniḥ* and the many works of imitation that it spawned, Aḥmad Ghazālī is today generally regarded as the foremost metaphysician of love in the Sufi tradition as well as celebrated as the founder of the literary topos and mystical persuasion known as the "Religion of Love" (*madhhab-i 'ishq*) in Islam.

Book 37 of the great Sunni mystical theologian Abū Ḥāmid al-Ghazālī's monumental *Revivification of the Religious Sciences* (*Iḥyā' 'ulūm al-dīn*), which is entitled *The Book of Love, Yearning, Intimacy and Contentment* (*Kitāb al-maḥabbat wa' l-shawq wa' l-uns wa' l-riḍā*) constitutes a comprehensive monograph on the philosophico-theological premises underlying the mystical understanding of the varieties of divine and worldly love. Abū Ḥāmid al-Ghazālī asserted that the various types of love can be reduced to five: [1] self-love, or the instinct for survival; [2] love of beneficence from others which abet one's survival; [3] love of a benefactor for himself even if his benefaction doesn't affect one personally; [4] the love of everything beautiful in itself, whether that be an external or internal beauty; [5] love that is aroused by concordance, affinity and compatibility of nature.[86]

Despite this fivefold multiplicity of causes, the different sources of love are all illusion, for in reality there is no object of love but God – the ultimate source of love. The principle that God is the ultimate source of both [1] the instinct for survival and [2] beneficence, Jalāl al-Dīn Rūmī (d. 672/1273) was later to versify in the *Mathnawī*.[87] Ghazālī argues (in respect to 3) that humankind harbours an innate love of goodness and knowledge and an innate repugnance and hatred of injustice and wickedness, and since "God is the benefactor to the totality of creatures",[88] ultimately no one but God is loved. Man is merely the temporal occasion of love, God the final cause.

86 Ghazālī, *Love, Longing*, 22–41.
87 *Mathnawī*, ed. Nicholson, III; 3352 ff.
88 Ghazālī, *Love, Longing*, 29.

Regarding the fourth type of love, Ghazālī reiterates that love of both external (physical) and internal (spiritual) beauty is ingrained and innate in man. When one loves a prophet or saint, one actually loves a quality of theirs lying behind their actions "at the source of their deeds".[89] That beauty of quality or character that animates our love of spiritual heroes and great personalities is ultimately reducible to three things: knowledge, power, and perfection. However, it is clear that nobody can compete with God or rival the Almighty in respect to these things.

According to Ghazālī, the "first principle of love (*al-ḥubb*) is that it cannot occur without interior knowledge or gnosis (*maʿrifa*) and perception (*idrāk*)".[90] According to this epistemological theory – the love of beauty is in essence a love of *qualities* (i.e. divine attributes) that are imperceptible to the senses but visible through the enlightened vision of the heart (*nūr baṣīra al-bāṭina*)[91] – gnosis (*maʿrifa*) is shown to be the basis of love, a Ghazālian doctrine later adopted by Rūmī in his *Mathnawī*.[92]

Further underlining the centrality of gnosis, he affirms that "love (*al-maḥabbat*) increases in exact proportion to gnosis".[93] Although the common denominator of all believers is their mutual love (*al-maḥabbat*), their variation in degree before God derives from different degrees of gnosis – combined with their respective passion or dispassion towards the world.[94] It thus follows that two "causes" serve to increase Love: i) Detachment from the world, for "one of the main causes which decreases love of God is love of the world".[95] Such detachment sustains the second "cause", which is the strength of gnosis (*maʿrifa*) of God which overpowers and purifies the heart, making it a receptacle for the "science of divine unveilings (*ʿilm al-mukāshafat*)" (equivalent in Ghazālī's lexicon here to *maʿrifa*). Such an epistemological bias towards the noetic understanding of *ʿishq* – love's dependence upon intimate knowledge of God (*maʿrifa*) – is reaffirmed by Ghazālī here (as throughout this chapter). "*Maʿrifa* gained in this world is like a seed which turns into vision (*mushāhida*) in the next."[96] "Whoever does not enjoy the pleasure of *maʿrifa* here in this world cannot enjoy the pleasure of [divine] vision (*al-naẓar*) in the Next."[97] He exclaims: "The ocean of *maʿrifa* has no

89 Ibid., 31.
90 Abū Ḥāmid al-Ghazālī, *Iḥyāʾ ʿulūm al-dīn*, IV: 296, also cf. 321.
91 Abū Ḥāmid al-Ghazālī, *Iḥyāʾ ʿulūm al-dīn*, IV: 299.
92 *Mathnawī*, ed. Nicholson, II: 1532.
93 Ghazālī, *Iḥyāʾ*, IV, 317.
94 Ibid., 319.
95 Ibid., 316.
96 Ibid., 312.
97 Ibid., 314.

shore."[98] (IV: 315) Ultimately, *ma'rifa* arouses *ḥubb*, and *ḥubb*, when quickened to an excess, is transformed into *'ishq*. (IV: 316).[99]

In the generation following the great Ghazālī brothers' speculations on love, another Persian Ṣūfī to integrate love into a comprehensive schema of mystical pedagogy was Quṭb al-dīn Ardishīr al-'Ibbādī (d. 547/1152), who in his Persian work *Refinement of the Sufis' Mystical States* (*Al-Taṣfiya fī aḥwāl al-mutasawwifa*[100]) accords *'ishq* a very prominent position. *Al-Taṣfiya* is structured in four chapters, each representing a diffferent key "pillar (*rukn*)" of Islamic spirituality: i) the Path, (*ṭarīqat*); ii) the Law (*sharī'a*); iii) works (*a'māl*), and iv) "mystical states" (*aḥwāl*), with a concluding chapter on technical terms and expressions (*iṣṭilāḥāt*). In this schema he discerns six levels of love. Discussing the fourth pillar of the "inner mystical states" (*aḥwāl-i bāṭin*), he records:

> When intimate knowledge (*ma'rifa*) of someone is confirmed, this is called ardent affection (*mawadda*). When one adopts someone exclusively as one's friend, this is called familiarity (*khulla*). When one's friendship (*dustī*) is cleansed of all aberrations and becomes totally devoted to obtaining the satisfaction of one's friend, it is called loving-kindness (*maḥabba*). When friendship is melted in the crucible of adversity and turns towards annihilation (*fanā'*), then it is called passionate love (*'ishq*).[101]

'Ibbādī's schema recalls Sarrāj's and Ghazālī's similar observations, but his love theory (*shawq* → *ma'rifa* → *mawadda* → *khulla* → *maḥabba* → *'ishq*) is unique in its emotionalism: "*Shawq* is for beginners; *khulla* for those midway on the Path and *maḥabba* for the adepts. Now if anyone realize the perfection of love (*'ishq*), he will see what he sees – for the reality of love cannot be related."[102]

SUFI EROTIC THEOLOGY FROM SHIHĀB AL-DĪN YAḤYĀ SUHRAWARDĪ (D. 587/1191) TO IBN 'ARABĪ (D. 638/1240)

The infusion of eros into Avicenna's ontology pervaded the metaphysics of later Islamic thought, whether in the form of theomonist doctrines of the Akbarian thinkers of Ibn 'Arabī's school or the Ishrāqī thinkers. The founder of the latter school, '*Shaykh al-Ishrāq*' Shihāb al-Dīn Yaḥyā Suhrawardī

[98] Ibid., 315.
[99] Ibid., 316.
[100] Quṭb al-dīn Ardishīr al-'Ibbādī, *Al-Taṣfiya fī aḥwāl al-mutasawwifa*, ed. Gh. Yūsufī, (Tehran: 1989).
[101] *Al-Taṣfiya*, 170–71
[102] Ibid., 173.

(d. 587/1191), in his *Treatise on the Reality of Love* (*Risāla fi ḥaqīqat al-ʿishq*) considered Love (*maḥabbat*) and Strife (*munāzaʿat*) to be the first two emanations from the Intellect. The world is created by the conflict between the three offspring of Intellect: Beauty, Love and Grief. From Love the upper heavenly or celestial realm down to the sphere of the moon (*ʿālam-i ʿulwī*) arose and from Strife everything in the lower, terrestrial realm (or sublunar sphere). First Love infused himself into Adam, then into Beauty, causing the angels to prostrate themselves to him (Adam thus acting as exemplar of Beauty/Love). Beauty then infuses himself into Joseph, here playing the role of Sufi master (*pīr*), with Love and Grief featuring as two disciples who, being rejected by Beauty, set out in different directions: Love travelling to Egypt and entering into Zulaykha (who immediately falls "in Love" with Joseph), and Grief travelling to Canaan and afflicting Jacob. In Suhrawardī's erotic ontology, Beauty is in reality the Active Intelligence (*ʿaql- faʿʿāl*) of al-Fārābī and Avicenna.[103] This allegorical tale had a huge impact on all subsequent Persian Sufi poetry of love.[104]

Rūzbihān Baqlī was an extremely important theoretician of love whose writings offer "the most striking articulation of the stages of love in early Persian Sufism"[105] and "constitute a vast synthesis and rethinking of early Islamic religious thought from the perspective of pre-Mongol Sufism".[106] His *Jasmine of the Lovers* (*Abhar al-ʿāshiqīn*) was highly influenced by Daylamī's *ʿAṭf al-alif*, drawing on much of its terminology.[107] In this work, Rūzbihān's schema of the stations of love is similar to the mystics of the classical period, from Jaʿfar al-Ṣādiq to Shaqīq down to Sarrāj. Like Ghazālī,[108] Rūzbihān held that "the end of *ʿishq* is the beginning of gnosis and in gnosis *ʿishq* reaches

[103] N. Pūrjavādī, "*Mūnis al-ʿushshāq*-i Suhrawardī va ta'thīr-i ān dar adabiyāt-i fārsī", *Nashr-i Dānish*, XVIII/2 (1380/2001), 7.

[104] The Persian poet ʿArabshāh Yazdī composed a 2000-line *mathnawī* poem in 781/1379 modelled on Suhrawardī's *Treatise on the Reality of Love*, a little less than half of which was a direct versification of Suhrawardī's prose allegory, although Yazdī is unfaithful to Suhrawardī's philosophical genealogy, attacking the philosophers as well as Ibn ʿArabī in this poem (Pūrjavādī, "*Mūnis al-ʿushshāq-i Suhrawardī*, 10). In the 908/1502, a Sufi named Ḥusayn Gāzurgāhī at the court of Sulṭān Ḥusayn Bāyqarā wrote a treatise called *The Assemblies of Lovers* (*Majālis al-ʿushshāq*), containing accounts of fabulous and legendary love affairs conducted by a number of famous Sufis, beginning with Jaʿfar al-Ṣādiq. The introduction to this work was modelled on sections of Suhrawardī's *Risāla fī ḥaqīqat al-ʿishq* (ibid., 13–14). Likewise, The *Risāla-yi ishq va rūḥ* ("Treatise on Love and the Spirit"), composed in Persian by the Turkish poet Fuzūlī Baghdādī (d. 963/1556), adopted many themes and ideas from Suhrawardī's treatise.

[105] Ernst, "The Stages of Love", 448.

[106] Ernst, *Ruzbihan Baqli: Mysticism and the Rhetoric of Sainthood in Persian Sufism*, x.

[107] Ernst, "The Stages of Love", 449.

[108] cf. Ghazālī, *Iḥyā'*, IV: 312–19.

perfection".[109] In a chapter on "*maḥabba* as the introduction to *'ishq*", Rūzbihān states that "when *maḥabba* attains perfection, that is *shawq*, and when *maḥabba* reaches the reality of immersion [in the divine] it is called *'ishq*".[110] Elsewhere, he identifies *maḥabba* and *'ishq* as one, enjoining the reader not to be "mislead by words".[111] Whereas passionate love (*'ishq*) is an ocean, yearning (*shawq*) is a riverlet flowing into it, yet

> ... The ocean of passionate love (*'ishq*) and the ocean of yearning (*shawq*) both dry up in the divine Essence which is the Eternity's Essence. For when the lover is united with the Beloved whom is left to yearn for? And whom beside oneself does one love? For passionate love in the verse: "And they measure not God's power with true measure" (Qur'ān 6.91) is all duality. Yearning is the steed of passionate love, of which passionate love the rider, who, mounted on the steed of yearning, can go no further than [the shore of] the sea of Unity (*tawḥīd*). Should they set foot therein neither yearning nor love would remain. Love is augmented through yearning, since only through yearning will its ship reach the shores of contemplation.[112]

Rūzbihān's immersion in classical Ṣūfī love theory from Rabī'a to Daylamī is evident throughout this treatise.[113] His privileging of passionate love (*'ishq*) was typical of almost all Sufis in the post-Ghazālī-brothers' period, as is visible in his replacing of *walah* with *'ishq* as the final stage of the *Jasmine of the Lovers'* ladder of love: [1] servanthood (*'ubūdiyyat*) → ([2] sainthood (*wilāyat*) → [3] meditation (*murāqabat*) → [4] fear (*khawf*) → [5] hope (rajā') → [6] ecstasy (*wajd*) → [7] certainty (*yaqīn*) → [8] nearness (*qurbat*) → [9] unveiling (*mukāshafa*) → [10] contemplation (*mushāhada*) → [11] love (*maḥabbat*) → [12] yearning (*shawq*) → [13] universal passionate love [*eros*] (*'ishq-i kullī*).[114] Rūzbihān's stages of love resemble those of Ja'far al-Ṣādiq, but his main innovation, as Carl Ernst points out, was to stress, under the influence of Manṣūr al-Ḥallāj, "the centrality of the notion of God's essence as Love".[115]

Islam's supreme mystical theoretician Muḥyī al-Dīn Ibn 'Arabī of Spain (d. 638/1240) was, more than any other Sufi, responsible for showing that "it is irrelevant to place the way of love and the way of knowledge in opposition".[116]

109 *'Abhar*, 145: 6–7.
110 Ibid., 115: 6–7.
111 Ibid., 138: 8.
112 Ibid., 137–38.
113 For an excellent overview of his doctrine of love, see Ernst, "The Stages of Love", 448–54.
114 Adopted with some modifications from Ernst, "The Stages of Love", 450–51.
115 Ernst, "Rūzbihān Baqlī on Love as 'Essential Desire'", 182.
116 Claude Addas, "The Experience and Doctrine of Love in Ibn 'Arabī", *JMIAS*, XXXII (2002), 26. This is contrary to what Louis Massignon thought [*La Passion d Hallāj* [Paris: 1975], II, 414), as Addas (25) notes.

His most famous collection of poetry, *The Dragoman of Erotic Yearning* (*Tarjumān al-ashwāq*), celebrates his love for a learned Isfahanī girl Niẓām,[117] whose fascinating beauty, intellect and sensuality he extols in highly erotic imagery, appended to which he penned a recondite metaphysical commentary to explain the spiritual realities embodied in his sensual expressions.[118] His most celebrated treatise is the *Bezels of Wisdom* (*Fuṣūṣ al-ḥikam*), comprising 27 chapters, each of which is devoted to the divine wisdom revealed in a particular prophet and specific divine word. For nearly five hundred years this work was the most frequently commented upon work in Sufi and theological circles in the Middle East, Central Asia, and India.

In his major work *The Meccan Revelations* (*al-Futūḥāt al-makkiyya*) he consecrated a special chapter (178) to the "Knowledge of the Station of Love and its Mysteries".[119] While admitting that love was too subtle to be defined (echoing Sumnūn al-Muḥibb's statement to this effect),[120] he declared that the "Station of Love" has four names ([1] *ḥubb*, [2] *wadd*, [3] *'ishq* and [4] *hawā*), each with different connotations. The first is original or "seminal/seed-love", since *ḥubb* derives from *habba* (grain, seed). The second is strong affection or attachment, since *wadd*, from whence the Divine Name *al-Wadūd* (the All-Loving) derives, also means "peg", "post", or "stake", denoting rooted, faithful love. The third is passionate, extreme, distraught love, being derived from bindweed or convolvulus (*'ashaqa*), which winds itself in a spiral around another tree and smothers it.[121] Fourthly and lastly is the term "passion", which is derived from the word for air, and also signifies "falling from above to below", denoting a sudden surge of amorous inclination.[122] However, he speaks of *hawā* not as sensual desire but in the meaning of

[117] Sadiyya Shaikh, *Sufi Narratives of Intimacy: Ibn 'Arabī, Gender, and Sexuality* (Chapel Hill: University of North Carolina Press, 2012), 102–4.

[118] *The Tarjumán al-Ashwáq: A Collection of Mystical Odes*, ed. and trans. R. A. Nicholson, (London: Theosophical Publishing House 1978).

[119] Also translated into French by M. Gloton as *Traite de l'amour* (Paris 1986).

[120] Ibn 'Arabī noted: "Definitions of Love have been proposed, but I do not know anyone who has been able to define what it is in itself. One cannot even imagine that it is worthwhile giving them." (M. Gloton [trans.] *Traite de l'amour*, p. 54); cited by Maurice Gloton, "The Quranic Inspiration of Ibn 'Arabi's Vocabulary of Love: Etymological and Doctrinal Development", *JMIAS*, XXVII (2000), 40.

[121] Cf. the striking similarity of imagery in Elizabeth Barrett Browning's sonnet:

> I think of thee! – my thoughts do twine and bud
> About thee, as wild vines, about a tree
> Put out broad leaves, and soon there's nought to see
> Except the straggling green which hides the wood.

[122] Gloton, "The Quranic Inspiration", 41–43.

"passionate love" – *eros, 'ishq* – which he characterizes a "total annihilation of the will in the Beloved".[123]

In the final chapter of the *Fuṣūs al-ḥikam*, which is dedicated to the wisdom of the Prophet Muḥammad, he elucidates the idea that man can best contemplate God in the form of a woman. What makes Ibn 'Arabī's erotic theology so unusual is his interpretation of the *ḥadīth*: "Three things have been made beloved to me in this world of yours: women, perfume, while the coolness of my eye was placed in ritual prayer." Whereas Ghazālī had simply summed up this *ḥadīth* to mean that prayer was more worthy of love than women,[124] for Ibn 'Arabī the Prophet's reference to love of women in the *ḥadīth* had a much deeper spiritual significance. Because man's witnessing of God cannot take place outside of matter, he argued, contemplation necessarily finds its grandest and most complete summation in woman:

> When man loves woman, he desires to conjoin and unite with her, and when the act is consummated pleasure overtakes all parts of his body, and it is as if he were annihilated in her. Thus, God is jealous for his servant, He orders him to perform a full ablution in order that he be cleansed of "other" and return to observing Him in the one in whom he has been annihilated, i.e. woman. God has cleansed man by complete ablution because he has to witness God in woman, because it is a witnessed of God as actor and acted-upon simultaneously.[125]

Knowledge of the place of woman is of central spiritual significance for the male Sufi, since the possibility of

> Perfect contemplation of the Reality is present in them [women]. Contemplation of the Reality [God] without formal support is not possible, since God, in His Essence, is far beyond all need of the Cosmos. Since, therefore, some form of support is necessary, the best and most perfect kind is the contemplation of God in women. The greatest union is that between

[123] Claude Addas, "The Experience and Doctrine of Love in Ibn 'Arabī", 29.

[124] Ghazālī imagined that the Prophet's love of women was something superficially sensual, stating "he termed women loveable even though only sight and touch partake of them, but not smell or hearing. He termed prayer 'the apple of his eye' and declared it most worthy of love, even though, as is obvious, the five senses play no part in prayer; on the contrary, it involves a sixth sense whose seat is the heart and he alone perceives it *who possesses such a heart* [XXXIV: 3]." Ghazālī, *Love, Longing*, 12. For Ghazālī, any notion that God could be contemplated through medium of a mortal being, whether male or female – aside from his condoning the use of erotic metaphors relating to female beauty to refer to God in Sufi poetry for meditation during *samā'* under particular circumstances (on which see Leonard Lewisohn, "The Sacred Music of Islam: *Samā'* in the Persian Sufi Tradition") – was complete anathema.

[125] Souad al-Hakim, "Ibn 'Arabī's Twofold Perception of Woman, *JMIAS*, XXXIX (2006), 10.

> man and woman, corresponding as it does to the turning of God towards the one He created in His own image, to make him His viceregent.[126]

In short, for Ibn 'Arabī the contemplation of God by males through the female form represented a spiritual experience of the highest order, since he conceived of sexual union as "based on a deep existential love . . . [and] as having the potential to be the greatest self-disclosure of God".[127] Men are needy and must actively seek out women in order to know both themselves and God,[128] and women were made lovable to men to bring them closer to God:[129]

> Love does not absorb the lover entirely unless his beloved is the Real [*al-Ḥaqq*] or someone of his own kind or a slave girl (*jāriyya*) or slave boy (*ghulām*). Except for what has been mentioned, the love for anything else cannot fully absorb him. We say this because the human being in his complete essence does not conjoin with anything except one that is of his own form. When he loves that person, there is no part of him that doesn't have a [corresponding] likeness in the other. Then there remains nothing left over of him by which he can be sober for a single instant. He is enraptured, his outer form in the other's outer form, and inner being in the other's inner being.[130]

Ibn 'Arabī's theories about concerning the divine roots of romantic love, the celestial sources of beauty and love, and the sacred origins of human sexuality appear developed to their utmost refinement and theosophical sophistication in the eminent Kubrawī Shaykh Muḥammad Lāhījī's (d. 912/1507) exegesis[131] of Maḥmūd Shabistarī's (d. after 737/1337) lovely short *mathnawī* poem entitled *Garden of Mystery* (*Gulshan-i rāz*), a major section of which is devoted to the issue to witnessing beauty and the 'Witness of Beauty'

[126] *Ibn al-'Arabī: The Bezels of Wisdom*, trans. Austin, (New York: Paulist Press/ SPCK, 1980), 275. See also Shaikh, *Sufi Narratives of Intimacy*, 162–67, 176–92 for excellent discussions of the implications of these ideas for gender relations between man and woman.

[127] Shaikh, *Sufi Narratives of Intimacy*, 188. For a more elaborate discussion, see Sachiko Murata, *The Tao of Islam: A Sourcebook on Gender Relationships in Islamic Thought* (Albany: SUNY, 1992), 183–96.

[128] Shaikh, *Sufi Narratives of Intimacy*, 176–77.

[129] Ibid., 185–86.

[130] Ibn 'Arabī, *Al-Futūḥāt al-makkiyya* (Cairo: N.p., 1911; repr. Beirut: Dār Ṣādir, n.d.) III, 325; cited by Shaikh, *Sufi Narratives of Intimacy*, 191.

[131] Muḥammad Lāhījī, *Mafātīḥ al-i'jāz fī sharḥ-i Gulshan-i rāz*, ed. Muḥammad Riḍā Barzgār Khāliqī and 'Iffat Karbāsī (Tehran: Zawwār 1371 A.Hsh./1992); Lāhījī's own doctrine of love is found in his *Mathnawī-yi Asrār al-shuhūd* (ed. B. Zanjānī. Tehran: Intishārāt-i Amīr Kabīr 1365 A.Hsh./1986), 67–68: on "*shawq* and *'ishq*, the mystical states and levels (*aḥwāl va aṭwār*) of lovers who forego their souls, and those who yearn (*mushtāqān*) with fervor and humble neediness".

(*shāhid*). In a prose treatise, written under the influence of Aḥmad Ghazālī's *Sawāniḥ*, Shabistarī wrote:

> Romantic "unreal" love (*'ishq-i majāzī*), which constitutes an excess of loving-kindness (*maḥabbat*), cannot be configured and formed except through the beauty of the epiphanic form of man/woman (*maẓhar-i insānī*) – for his/her heart's mirror (that heart which is endowed with spacious breadth of "My Heaven and earth contain me not, but the heart of my faithful servant contains me"[132]) is never absorbed [in an experience of romantic love] except by medium of a form of absolute beauty. Now, it is (only) this sort of love which, when overwhelmed by the figure of the human beloved (*ma'shūq-i majāzī*), enables the lover to burn away the delimiting individuality of form (*ta'ayyun*) so that, undisturbed by the illusory veils of "other-than-itself" (*aghyār*), of his own accord he may engage in love's play. It is at this point that 'love' becomes divine/real (*ḥaqīqī*). '(God will bring a people) whom He loves and they love Him'. (Qur'ān, 5.54)[133]

At the same time, these ideas received their most beautiful elaboration in the romantic-gnostic poetry of Sa'dī (d. ca. 691/1292) and Ḥāfiẓ (d. 791/1389). By the mid-thirteenth century onwards, most of the Sufi gnostic poets and the romantic poets who used the vocabulary and lexicon of Sufism, especially all those influenced by Ibn 'Arabī's radical erotic theology, had largely ceased to divide love into "romantic human"and "divine spiritual" types. Khwājū Kirmānī (d. after 753/1352), summed up their vision when he stated in verse: "In way of spiritual reality, fictional romantic love (*'ishq-i majāzī*) is all real, divine – although to adepts in spiritual truth, romantic love is never simply fiction (*'ishq rā majāz nīst*)."[134]

The Sufis following Aḥmad Ghazālī largely conceived of love as a unitary reality manifesting itself in diverse levels and degrees – so that it would be possible to move from earthly to heavenly love simply by focusing one's attention upon the divine source, thus making the world of Appearance (*majāz*) a bridge to the realm Reality (*ḥaqīqat*). This teaching is summed up in the famous Arabic adage "the phenomenal is a bridge to the real" (*Al-majāz qanṭaratu al-ḥaqīqat*), an idea that Rūmī epitomized as an epigram in the following verse: "If loss you suffer in love's way, know it to be God's

[132] *Aḥādīth-i Mathnawī*, ed. B. Furūzānfar, (Tehran: Amīr Kabīr 1361 A.Hsh./1982), 26. See also Nurbakhsh, *Traditions of the Prophet, Traditions of the Prophet*, vol. 1, trans. Leonard Lewisohn (New York: KNP 1981), I, 25.

[133] Maḥmūd Shabistarī, "Risāla-yi Ḥaqq al-yaqīn", in *Majmū'a-i āthār-i Shaykh Maḥmūd Shabistarī*, ed. Ṣamad Muwaḥḥid (Tehran: Kitābkhāna-i Ṭahūrī 1965 A.Hsh./1986), 303.

[134] Khwājū Kirmānī, *Dīwān-i Khwājū Kirmānī*, ed. Sa'īd Qāni'ī (Tehran: Intishārāt-i Āftāb 1374 A.Hsh./1995), 214.

grace, for fictional romantic love is but a bridge one treads across – the shore beyond is love divine."[135]

CONCLUSION

From the meta-history of the pre-eternal covenant of God with man to the theophany of the Sophianic Feminine in Ibn ʿArabī's *Fuṣūs al-ḥikam*, *Eros* has been the constant preoccupation of Muslim mystics. As this study has demonstrated, during half a millennium of dialogue of man with the divine and the Absolute with the finite, the passionate romantic intoxication of love (*ḥubb*, *maḥabbat*, *ʿishq* ...) has always been regarded as Sufism's supreme station of contemplation and the ultimate aim of mystical self-realization.

For this reason, none of the great mystics of Islam surveyed above would disdain to second the refrain of Shāh Qāsim al-Anwār's (d. 837/1433) *ghazal*:

> In pagoda and mosque, in Kaʿba and tavern,
> The God of Love is the sole aim;
> All the rest are just moonshine.[136]

It is in this sense that the ecumenical affirmation that all the various faiths and sects of mankind are but multiple expressions of a single ideal-Beloved still remains, in the words of Shaykh Bahāʾī, the heart of the Sufi theoerotic imagination:

> I visited the hermitage of pietists and priests;
> I witnessed they all knelt in awe and reverence
> Before her visage there. Since in the winecell of the monk
> And in the chapel of the pietist I was
> At home, it's there I dwell. At times I make my residence
> The mosque, at times the cell: which is to say, it's you
> I seek in every place, both in the tavern and the church.
>
> Whatever door I knock upon, the Lord within
> The house is always you, and every place I go
> The light that shines therein is always you.
> The One beloved in bodega and convent you:

[135] *Kulliyāt-i Shams yā Dīwān-i kabīr az guftār-i Mawlānā Jalāl al-Dīn Muḥammad mashhūr bi Mawlavī, ba taṣḥīḥāt wa ḥawwashī*, ed. Badīʿ al-Zamān Furūzānfar (Tehran: Sipihr 1363 A. Hsh./1984, 10 vols in 9), I, *ghazal* 28, vv. 336–37.

[136] Qāsim-i Anwār *Kulliyāt-i Qāsim-i Anvār*, ed. S. Nafīsī (Tehran: Kitāb-khāna Sanāʾī 1337 A.Hsh./1958), 281: 4621.

From Ka'ba or pagoda all my quest and aim
Again, is you. You, *you*, are what I seek therein:
The rest – pagoda or the Ka'ba – all is but a ruse.[137]

Likewise, few Sufis would take umbrage at 'Urfī Shīrāzī's (d. 1000/1591) antinomian celebration of Sufism's transcendental Religion of Love:

The lover's drunk and senseless; he
Knows neither Islam or infidelity.
He's like a moth empassioned over fire
So one appears to him the burning pyre
Outside the Hindu's pagoda
Or candle burning in the Ka'ba.[138]

Nor would Rūmī's intuition in a quatrain that the lover is neither exoterically "Muslim" nor actually "infidel" be a heresy that Sufis of any place or age would disdain to plight their faith:

Know it for certain that the lover's not a Muslim
For in the creed of love there's neither infidelity
Or faith; since once you fall in love, you have no body,
No soul, no heart, no mind: who ain't like this, ain't nothin.[139]

In the same sense, from Hyderabad to Jalalabad, from Shiraz to Samarqand, and Baghdad to Bukhara, few Muslim mystics can be found who would disagree with either the mood or message of Ḥāfiẓ's famous verse:

Whether we are drunk or sober, each of us is making
For the street of the Friend. The temple, the synagogue,
The church and the mosque are all houses of love.[140]

For teleologically speaking, this cosmopolitan vision of a "Religion of Love" as being the universal faith of mankind[141] encapsulates – to cite two other of Ḥāfiẓ's verse-epigrams to this effect – the quintessence of all faith:

[137] Translation mine. From al-'Āmilī, *Kulliyāt-i ash'ār va āthār-i fārsī Shaykh Bahā'ī*, ed. 'Alī Kātibī (Tehran: Nashr-i Chakāma, n.d.), 348.

[138] Cited by Khaliq Ahmad Nizami, *Akbar and Religion* (Dehli: Idarah-i Adabiyat-i-Dehli, 1989), 210. Translation mine.

[139] Rūmī, *Kulliyāt-i Shams*, VIII, 130, Quatrain 767. "*Āshiq tu yaqīn dān kay musalmān nabvad. Dar madhhab-i 'āshiq kufr u īmān nabvad. / Dar 'ishq, tan u 'aql u dil u jān nabvad. Har kas kay chinīn nagasht ū ān nabvad.*"

[140] *Dīwān-i . . . Ḥāfiẓ*, Khānlarī, ghazal 78: 3. Trans. Robert Bly and Leonard Lewisohn.

[141] On which, see Husayn Ilahi-Ghomshei, "The Principles of the Religion of Love in Classical Persian Poetry", in L. Lewisohn (ed.), *Hafiz and the Religion of Love in Classical Persian Poetry*, 77–106.

Both human beings and spirits take their sustenance
From the existence of love. The practice of devotion
Is a good way to arrive at happiness in both worlds.[142]

Become a lover; if you don't, one day the affairs of the world
Will come to an end, and you'll never have had even
One glimpse of the purpose of the workings of space and time.[143]

FURTHER READING

Chittick, William. *Divine Love: Islamic Literature and the Path to God.* New Haven: Yale University Press 2013.

Ernst, Carl W. "The Stages of Love in Persian Sufism, from Rabi'a to Ruzbihan", in *The Heritage of Sufism, vol. 2: Classical Persian Sufism from Its Origins to Rumi* ed. Leonard Lewisohn. Oxford: Oneworld 1999, 435–56.

Ghazālī, Abū Ḥāmid al-. *The Book of Love, Longing, Intimacy and Contentment.* Trans. Eric Ormsby. Cambridge: Islamic Texts Society 2011.

Ghomshei, Husayn Ilahi-. "The Principles of the Religion of Love in Classical Persian Poetry". In L. Lewisohn (ed.), *Hafiz and the Religion of Love in Classical Persian Poetry.* London: I.B. Tauris 2010, 77–106

Lumbard, Joseph. "From Ḥubb to 'Ishq: The Development of Love in Early Sufism", *Journal of Islamic Studies*, 18/3 (2007), 345–85.

Paz, Octavio. *The Double Flame: Essays on Love and Eroticism*, trans. from the Spanish by Helen Lane. London: Harcourt 1996.

Sattārī, Jalāl. *'Ishq-i ṣūfiyya.* Tehran: Nashr-i Markaz 1374 A.Hsh./1995.

Schimmel, Annemarie. "Eros – Heavenly and not so Heavenly – in Sufi Literature and Life". *Sufi*, 19 (1996), pp. 30–42.

Shah-Kazemi, Reza. "God, 'The Loving' ". In Miroslav Volf, Ghazi bin Muhammad and Mellisa Yarrington (eds), *A Common Word: Muslims and Christians on Loving God and Neighbour.* Grand Rapids, Michigan: Wm. B. Eerdmans 2010 88–109.

Shaikh, Sadiyya. *Sufi Narratives of Intimacy: Ibn 'Arabī, Gender, and Sexuality.* Chapel Hill: University of North Carolina Press 2012.

[142] *Dīwān-i Ḥāfiẓ*, ed. Khānlarī, ghazal 443: 1. Trans. Bly and Lewisohn, *The Angels*, 53.
[143] Ibid., ghazal 426: 5. Trans. Bly and Lewisohn, *The Angels*, 49.

PART III

SUFISM IN THE MODERN AGE

8

Nana Asma'u: Nineteenth-Century West African Sufi[1]

Beverly Mack

Nineteenth-century Nana Asma'u lived a scholarly, activist life in what is now Nigeria. She was an accomplished multilingual scholar who considered the education of illiterate masses to be as important as her own communication with other scholars in her community and across the Sahara to Mauritania and Timbuktu. She promoted education through the use of her poetry, which included texts about Islamic ethics, Islamic histories, and clear approaches to Islamic daily practices. Until recently Asma'u's work has been far less discussed than that of her famous father, Shehu Usman 'dan Fodio, leader of the Sokoto Jihād which began in 1804,[2] and the Fodio family's Sufi profile has

[1] This chapter contains technical terms and names from a number of different languages, and it is impossible to reflect the sometimes conflicting methods of transliteration. For this reason the usual dots and dashes have been omitted in most cases. Hausa has several implosive sounds often indicated in print by hooks appended to the letters b, d, k, and y. These diacriticals are not as readily accommodated by presses as standard Arabic diacriticals. Therefore, for this publication, words with hooks are indicated by the insertion of an apostrophe in place of the hook, as in *'dan Fodio*. In this case *'dan* is the Hausa word for the Arabic "ibn", meaning "son of". Other examples are the terms: *'Dan Yalli, Mo'dibo, Fa'dima, Wa'kar, Al'kammu, A'kilu, 'Yan Taru.*

[2] The Shehu's life and times have been discussed extensively, but principally by Murray Last and Mervyn Hiskett [Murray Last, *The Sokoto Caliphate* (Ibadan, Nigeria: Longman, 1967); Mervyn Hiskett, *The Sword of Truth* (London: Oxford University Press, 1973)], both of whom drew heavily on the Arabic writings of the Shehu himself, along with works by his younger brother Abdullahi, his son Muhammad Bello, and son-in-law, Gidado 'dan Laima. What is known to date about Nana Asma'u and her active role in the history of her times is found in a biography and four recently published books: the text and translations of her collected works, and three other books on Asma'u's life and times:Jean Boyd, *The Caliph's Sister* (London: Frank Cass, 1989); Jean Boyd and Beverly Mack, *The Collected Works of Nana Asma'u, Daughter of Usman 'dan Fodiyo (1793–1864)* (East Lansing, Michigan: Michigan State University Press, 1997); Beverly Mack and Jean Boyd, *One Woman's Jihad: Nana Asma'u, Scholar and Scribe* (Bloomington, Indiana: Indiana University Press, 2000); and Jean Boyd and Beverly Mack, *Educating Muslim Women: The West African Legacy of Nana Asma'u (1793–1864)* (Oxford: Interface Publications, 2013). These five volumes constitute the principal

been discussed less often than the historical effect of its jihād. As Qādiriyya Sufis, the Fodios were intellectually engaged; they eschewed overt demonstrations of ecstatic engagement like dancing or large public *dhikr* sessions. This chapter addresses Nana Asma'u's writings and activism as they represent the Fodio clan's Sufi identity and, as a part of that philosophy, their perspectives on gender-equity. Asma'u's poetic works and social welfare activities demonstrate the extent to which she and her associates were quietly, and thoroughly, immersed in Sufi belief and practice.

HISTORICAL CONTEXT: THE FODIO FAMILY IN WEST AFRICA

Nana Asma'u bint Usman 'dan Fodio (1793–1864) was born into a family of Muslim scholars in the region now known as northwestern Nigeria, in the community of Degel, which no longer exists. Degel was, in its day, a lively centre of scholarly interests. It was home to several thousand scholars, many of whom were *ḥuffāz*, imams, muezzins, and panegyrists, some with nicknames indicating their origins: *al-Maghribī, al-Sūdanī, Malle.*[3] The Sokoto Jihād, a struggle of Islamic reform led by Asma'u's father, Shehu Usman 'dan Fodio, saw the decline of Degel and the rise of Sokoto as a thriving urban centre in the aftermath of the Jihād's series of conflicts.[4] The Jihād constituted a watershed of religious reform that permanently altered the social fabric of what was to become Africa's most populous contemporary nation, Nigeria; social relations there occasionally still echo the Jihad's Hausa-Fulani confrontations, even after two centuries of integration and intermarriage.[5]

By the eighteenth century, literacy and intellectual exchange across the Maghreb was central to the way of life and communications among West

sources for this chapter. I am grateful, as always, to Jean Boyd for her careful reading, comments, and suggestions for revisions on this chapter.

3 Boyd notes that the document listing scholars living at Degel can be found in Gidado's 1838/39 manuscript, *Majmu Khisal al Shaikh* (Last, *The Sokoto Caliphate*, xxxvi and 250); Last, *The Sokoto Caliphate*, 18–20.

4 The tombs of both Nana Asma'u and the Shehu are in the Fodio family compound (H. *hubbare*) in Sokoto.

Capitalization of "jihad" in this chapter indicates reference to the Sokoto Jihad in particular, as distinguished from other jihads of the time, or jihad behavior in general. The Sokoto jihād was the most far-reaching and effective of a series of several nineteenth century West African jihads. Sokoto continues to be a thriving urban centre, but it retains its small-town atmosphere and spiritual ambience in the twenty-first century, about which Murray Last has written (*African Studies Review* Vol. 56, No. 2 (September 2013), 1–20).

5 Since the nineteenth century in northern Nigeria, Hausa-Fulani ethnicity has been a source of both unity (with much intermarriage), and conflict, with political rivals blaming ethnicity for certain disparate points of view and political affiliations.

African Fodio clan members, both women and men. What is known about the Fodio family's nineteenth-century conditions and philosophies comes from their own writings; hagiographic perspective about them originates in their own impressions of their historical roles, which were overtly aimed at creating a lifestyle that followed the *sunna*. The foundational principles of Islam – Qur'ānic ethics, adherence to the pillars, expectations of equality – were their avowed ethical guidelines. Sufi tenets were integral to the intentions of the Jihādists in their efforts at resocialization that followed jihād battles. This effort was significantly orchestrated by women's roles in teaching Sufi values.

The Fodio family was known as ethnic Toronkawa for their origins in the Futa Toro region (Senegal) of West Africa. Their antecedents emigrated eastward in the sixteenth century, from Futa Toro to Konni, the border region of what is now northwest Nigeria and Niger, led by their patriarch, scholar Musa Jokollo.[6] Eleven generations after the clan settled there at the border of Bornu and Songhai, Shehu Usman 'dan Fodio's great-grandfather, Muhammad Sa'd, shifted the family to the town of Maratta, in the Konni region, to escape persecution that prevented his freedom to teach. Sa'd's son (the Shehu's father, Muhammad) was a scholar there, and the Shehu's mother was from Maratta. Muhammad subsequently moved his own family further into the bush, to Degel, where they settled, continuing to work as scholars.[7] It is believed that the Shehu was born in Maratta, in 1754, either before his father moved the family, or because his mother had returned to her own family for the birth. He grew up in Degel. His mother Hawwa's lineage is significant in the family's Islamic identity, for her line of descent is "linked to the branch of the family most noted for its learning";[8] she traced her descent directly from the Prophet Muḥammad's daughter Fāṭima. The family's Islamic identity was demonstrated in their given names, their scholarly heritage was evident in their surname, and their Sufi affiliation was indicated in a lineage connection to the Prophet's family.

The Shehu's father Muhammad became known by the name "Fodio/Fudi", the Fulfulde term for "learned", in recognition of his scholarship.[9] This

6 This and the following historical information from Last, *The Sokoto Caliphate*, lxxiii.

7 This is the region on the main road to Birnin Kebbi and Gobir, the route from Agadez, Ingall, Birinin Konni; the connection to Niger is strong.

8 Although Last notes that the Shehu never mentioned this in his writings, others have documented Hawwa's descent as: "Hawwa bint Muhammad b. Ahmad al-Sharif b. b. Ali al-Yanbu'i b. 'Abd al-Razzaq b. al-Salih b. al-Mubarak b. Ahmad b. Abi'l-Hasan al-Shadhali b. 'Abdullah b. 'Abd al-Jabbar b. Hurmuz b. Hatim b. Qusay b. Muhammad b. al-Hasan b. Fatima, daughter of the Prophet." (Last, *The Sokoto Caliphate*, 4, n. 9)

9 This has been spelled as variants "Fodio", "Fodiyo", and "Fudi".

became the surname for him and his descendents. Muhammad Fodio instructed his son, as did the Shehu's mother Hawwa, and her mother, the Shehu's maternal grandmother Rukayya.[10] Traditions about the Shehu's education confirm the ethnic pattern of mothers and grandmothers as children's first instructors in these communities. The Fodios' mode of scholarship followed traditional models, in which a student studied with a credible scholar to the point of earning an *ijāza* – a license to teach a particular book that one had mastered under that tutelage – conveying scholarship that was couched in terms of both practical and mystical understandings of the world.

QĀDIRIYYA SUFISM AMONG THE FODIO FAMILY IN WEST AFRICA

The Sufi character of the Fodio family was clear in their self-identification as Kadirawa, adherents of Qādiriyya Islam, a Sufi brotherhood which originated in the teachings of Persian scholar 'Abd al-Qadir al-Jilānī (d. 1166, Baghdad) and took its name from him.[11] Al-Jilānī is revered as a saint and *sayyid*; he traced his lineage to both Ḥasan and Ḥusayn, sons of Fāṭima and 'Alī, the Prophet Muḥammad's daughter and son-in-law. Born in Persia, al-Jilānī was a preacher, teacher, and writer, and one of the most revered among Sufi notables. He promoted the Ḥanbalite doctrine of Sufism that conformed to the foundational precepts of Islam, rejecting the imposition of esoteric beliefs that threatened violation of Islamic traditions rooted in the tradition of the Qur'ān and the *sunna*. al-Jilānī was known as *Muḥyi ad-dīn*, the "reviver of religion",[12] and was revered by even as great a saint as Abu Madyan (1126–1198) of Tlemcen, who studied with al-Jilānī in Makkah; Abu Madyan is revered in his own right as an ascetic saint of the Maghreb.[13] Another Sufi

10 The Shehu's early life is recounted in Last, *The Sokoto Caliphate*, Hiskett, *The Sword of Truth*, and in accounts contemporary to the Shehu, including *al-Kashf wa'l-bayan* and *Raud al-jinan* by Gidado 'dan Laima, *'ida' al-nusukh* an *tazyin al-waraqat* by Abdullah b. Muhammad Fodio. Jean Boyd's *The Caliph's Sister* is a wealth of information about the Shehu's family with a focus on Asma'u and her life.

11 His full name is Al-Sayyid Muḥyi al-dīn Abu Muḥammad 'Abd al-Qādir Al-Jilānī al-Hasanī Wal-Husaynī, (1077–1166 CE), born in the town of Na'if, district of Gilan, Iran, and died in Baghdad, Iraq. He was a famous Ḥanbali Salafiyyah jurist and Sufi based in Baghdad. He is also referred to as al-Qadir, al-Gilani, or al-Jelani.

12 Annemarie Schimmel, *The Mystical Dimensions of Islam* (Chapel Hill, North Carolina: University of North Carolina Press, 1975, 247) discusses the legend that accounts for this sobriquet.

13 Abu Maydan was born in Andalusia, studied in Fes, and established a *zāwiya* in Bejaia on the Algerian coast. He is associated with Tlemcen, near where he is buried, and he is known for his rejection of the material trappings of the world.

figure, Ibn Qayyim al-Jawziyya (d. 1350), documented Ḥanbalite Sufism; his writings were supported by an outpouring of works that confirmed the conformity of Sufism to "'orthodox' Sunni creeds ... rooted in the Qur'ān and the precedent of the Prophet and the first Muslims".[14] The writings of the Fodio family reflect these Qādiriyya views on practical asceticism and reliance on the example of the original Muslim community; their inclination towards Ḥanbalite Sufism is reflected in the Shehu's preference for promoting the primacy of Qur'ānic ethos and rejection of local inclination towards syncretism.

Sufism was a prime means of spreading Islam beyond its place of origin, especially in sub-Saharan Africa, through "the untiring effort of Sufi preachers who manifested in their lives the basic obligations of Islam",[15] and used vernaculars to spread the veneration of the Prophet. From the tenth to the nineteenth century C.E., Sufi preachers were increasingly active in the Maghreb through trans-Saharan networks of commerce and scholarship, which facilitated interchange from Arabia to North Africa and throughout sub-Saharan Africa. Islamic scholars travelled and wrote to one another across the entire region, and Sufi concepts were transmitted widely. By the late eighteenth and early nineteenth centuries, a West African surge of interest in the Qādiriyya order may have been caused by the confluence of the decline of the Ottoman Empire, the rise of European imperialism, and the appearance of the Wahabī movement seeking reform in Islamic communities; added to these influences, the revival of Sufi thought at al-Azhar in Cairo promoted Qādiriyya activity among orders throughout the Maghreb and West Africa.[16] In the Fodio family, Muhammad Bello cites evidence of sixteenth century Sufi presence in the region in the name of a scholar of the Saharan kingdom of Ahir (c. 1543) called al-'Aqib b. 'Abdullah al-Ansamuni al-Massufi, and in the writings of Abdullahi Sikka, a Kano (Nigeria) scholar of that same period.[17] It is safe to say that by the nineteenth century, Sufi activity in the region was active and widespread.

Family accounts indicate that Asma'u's education, like that of her siblings, followed the pattern of her father's classical grounding in Qur'ān memorization early in his life, followed by the study of *tafsīr* and *sīra*, including the Moroccan mystic Abu 'Ali al-Ḥasan b. Ma'sūd al-Yusī, al-Fazzāzī's panegyric

[14] Toby Mayer, "Theology and Sufism", in *The Cambridge Companion to Classical Islamic Theology*, Ed. Tim Winter. New York: Cambridge University Press, 2008, 268.

[15] Schimmel, *The Mystical Dimensions of Islam*, 240.

[16] Hiskett, *The Sword of Truth*, 61–63.

[17] Ibid., 60; this is from *al-'Atiyya lil-mut'I*, cited in Hiskett's PhD dissertation, I, 91.

to the Prophet "The Twenties" (*al-'Ishrīniyyāt*),[18] and Berber al-Busīrī's *Burda* ("The Cloak"), both of which discuss the Prophet Muḥammad's miracles.[19] The Shehu's education also included *fiqh*, *ḥadīth* (relying on ninth century al-Bukhārī's *Saḥīḥ*), his most comprehensive guide to an understanding of the Prophet's life, astronomy, and Sufism:[20]

> In all of this the Shehu became learned, through the study of certain Arabic texts which had become standard works among the scholars of his community, and he encouraged his daughter Asma to acquire such knowledge. His son Bello was also an expert in this study and so, no doubt, were his other children.[21]

Hiskett cites his source for this information as "WKS, p. 83, i.e. *Wa'kar Karomomin Shehu*" ("Song of the Shehu's Miracles") by Malam Isa 'dan Shehu (the Shehu's son, Asma'u's brother).[22] This was a Hausa verse form of the longer Arabic prose account of the Shehu's life, *Raud al-Jinān* (Meadow of Paradise), written by the Shehu's son-in-law, Gidado 'dan Laima.[23] Gidado was Bello's best friend, who fought beside him in the Jihād battles, and Asma'u's husband. It is clear from these writings that they were all immersed in scholarly pursuits and felt it important to document their intellectual activities.

For his early education the Shehu's teachers were his uncles 'Uthman Binduri and Muhammad Sambo, who were both accomplished scholars and known as pious men of "magisterial reforming zeal".[24] The Shehu's son, Muhammad Bello, wrote that his father's grounding in Qādiriyya Sufism came from the Shehu's Tuareg teacher, Shaikh Jibril b. 'Umar, who conferred on the Shehu *salasil* in Qādiriyya, Shādhiliyya, Khalwatiyya, and several other licenses from Jibril when Jibril returned from Egypt, where he himself received them from Muhammad Murtada b. al-Husaini al-Wasiti. Jibril's enthusiasm for reform of local practices underlined perspectives that

18 Asma'u's "Remembrance of the Prophet" (*Mantore* Arande, F. 1843) and "Yearning for the Prophet" (*Begore*, F. n.d.) reflect these influences (see Boyd and Mack 1997:188–189, 304–345).

19 Hiskett, *The Sword of Truth*, 37.

20 Ibid., 37–39.

21 Ibid., 39.

22 See Mervyn Hiskett, "*The Song of the Shaihu's Miracles*: A Hausa Hagiography from Sokoto", in *African Language Studies* XII (1971), 71–107.

23 Boyd notes that in *Raud al-jinān* Gidado has listed everyone who was close to the Shehu: children, wives, aunts, uncles, servants, judges, imāms, *waziris*, and disciples. Children are listed in birth order, with Bello fourth in order of sons, and Asma'u height in order of daughters (personal communication 11/14/13).

24 Hiskett, *The Sword of Truth*, 39–40; Last, *The Sokoto Caliphate*, 5.

the Shehu had learned from his previous teachers.[25] Other influences may have been a Degel resident Sufi, Muhammad Koiranga, who is reported to have facilitated the Shehu's mystical experiences,[26] and Sidi al-Mukhtar al-Kunti, whose active preaching in the regions west of Degel coincided with and acknowledged the Shehu's preaching and activism.[27] Whether these scholars were influenced by disciples of Abū Madyān or al-Jawziyya is not known, but the active nature of the trans-Saharan trade routes from West Africa through the Sudan to Cairo make the prospect feasible. Through his teaching, Shaikh 'Umar's commitment to the Qādiriyya brand of Sufism passed to the Shehu, along with privileged knowledge about Sufi secrets of litanies, prayers, and religious exercises leading to ecstatic states;[28] many of these were said to have been conveyed directly to the Shehu by the saint al-Jilānī himself in the Shehu's mystical experiences.

Thus, by the time the twenty-year-old Shehu's missionary career began in 1774, he had not only spent many years studying Islam, but had also engaged in spiritual practices like retreats and extended prayer sessions. He continued to study throughout his life, as was the custom among scholars of the time. The Shehu's wives Aisha, Hauwa (Bello's mother), and Maimuna (Asma'u's mother) were confirmed Sufi mystics, as were other women of the community, described in Asma'u's "Sufi Women" (discussed below; see p. 207); his household was one in which his immersion in mystical experiences was common.[29] Thus, Asma'u absorbed the wholly Sufi nature of the family, the only context that she knew, through her studies, daily discourse, and the influence of family members. The Shehu wrote books in Arabic, and long Fulfulde poems on *tafsīr*, *tawḥīd*, *fiqh*, and Sufi tenets. His preaching was in the Hausa vernacular of the region.[30] The Shehu's sermons, written down by

25 Last (*The Sokoto Caliphate*, 6) and Hiskett (*The Sword of Truth*, 60) culled this information from Muhammad Bello's *Infaq al-maisur*.

26 Last (*The Sokoto Caliphate*, 20), notes that there were more than seven Sufi students of the Shehu at the time. This information is culled from Gidado's nineteenth-century *Raud al-Jinān*.

27 See Batran, Abdal-Aziz, "An Introductory Note on the Impact of Sidi al-Mukhtar al-Kunti (1729–1811) on West African Islam in the eighteenth and nineteenth centuries." *Journal of the Historical Society of Nigeria*, 6, No. 4 (June 1, 1973), 347–352. Batran notes that al-Kunti regarded the Shehu as a Sufi saint, and was aware of Abdullahi b. Fodio and Muhammad Bello's writings and activism. I am grateful to Professor Yacine Daddi-Addoun for pointing out this reference.

28 Hiskett, *The Sword of Truth*, 61.

29 Ibid., 64. Boyd confirms that Hauwa, Bello's mother, and Maimuna, Asma'u's mother, were confirmed mystics. These and other women are mentioned in the poem "Sufi Women" in Boyd and Mack (1997) (personal communication, 14 November 2013).

30 Last, *The Sokoto Caliphate*, 9.

his son Muhammad Bello, confirmed the importance of upholding the obligations of the pillars of Islam, and discussed Sufi concepts of the soul's tendencies towards either destructiveness or salvation, depending on one's inclination towards ego-fulfilment or selfless purity.[31] Asma'u was born when the Shehu, in his late thirties, had just returned from five years of preaching and having mystical visions in Faru, in nearby Zamfara. He had written a book on the *sunna* (*Ilyā' al-sunna*) that marked him as an important scholar of his time.[32] The association of Faru with the Shehu's mystical visions and emphasis on following the *sunna* endowed Faru with importance as a Sufi site.[33]

The Qādiriyya emphasis on adherence to the *sunna* is clearly evident in the manner that the Shehu sought to emulate the life and jihād of the Prophet. Asma'u describes this aim in several of her works.[34] The Shehu's immersion in Sufi learning is further reflected in the library holdings of the family, to which he would have turned during his education. For example, he studied Ibn Arabī's "Meccan Revelations" (*al-Futūḥāt al-makkiya*), and al-Ghazālī's well-known "Revivification of the Sciences of the Faith" (*Iḥyā ulūm al-dīn*), which was likely the inspiration for the Shehu's own work, "Revivification of Orthodoxy" (*Iḥyā al-Sunna*).[35] It is clear that the Shehu understood himself to be a reviver of religion in the Degel region, following the historical example of al-Jilānī himself.

Although the early years of the Shehu's preaching were non-confrontational, change in leadership brought difficulty. Over a period of thirty years (1774–1804) the Shehu became increasingly at odds with local Hausa leaders concerning religious matters. The Sokoto Jihād aimed at reform of local non-Islamic religious practices and resistance to local prohibitions on preaching and teaching of Islam. The Shehu was not a restrictive fundamentalist in the Wahabi sense, but he did advocate conformity to orthodoxy within the

31 Hiskett, *The Sword of Truth*, 42 et passim.

32 Boyd, *The Caliph's Sister*, 3. Boyd also notes that the Shehu lived for four years in Faru east of Bakura, Zamfara, where he had the mystic experiences as described in his *Wird* 1204–1208 (personal communication 14th November 2013).

33 This accounts for its significance as the place from which Sarkin Musulmi Attahiru 1st said farewell after setting out from Sokoto for Makkah in 1903; this was an important assertion of resistance of the Caliphate leaders to British colonial incursions.

34 Her works "The Journey" (*Filitago*, F. / *Wa'kar Gewaye* H. 1839, /840) and "The Story of the Shehu" (*Ko'iwi Shehu*, F. / *Labaran Shehu*, H. 1841/1864) (CW 131–153 and 156–175) have been discussed by Beverly Mack in "Imitating the Life of the Prophet: Nana Asma'u and Shehu Usman 'dan Fodiyo" in *Tales of God's Friends: Islamic Hagiography*, Ed. John Renard (Berkeley, California: University of California Press, 2009), 179–196, and will be addressed below.

35 Hiskett, *The Sword of Truth*, 60–61.

Qādiriyya Sufi context. Political resistance to his efforts to secure the right to practice Islam without persecution led him to launch the Jihad in imitation of the Prophet.

In the two decades between 1774 and 1794 the Shehu gained a significant following. Prior to this time his preaching had been well received by local kings, but as local leadership changed, the Shehu found himself increasingly at odds with kings who sought to control or subdue the rising numbers of Qādiriyya Muslims in their midst. Although the Gobir ruler declared himself a Muslim, the Shehu objected to his methods of rule, which favoured local traditions in conflict with Islamic ideals and codes of behaviour.[36] New laws against sartorial expressions of Islam, demands for the reversal of conversions to Islam, and increased aggression towards Muslims fuelled the need to mount a jihād of resistance and reform.[37] It was at this time (1793–1794 C.E.), that the Shehu began having mystical experiences, including dreams in which the saint 'Abd al-Qādir al-Jilānī spoke to him about making a *hijra*, which was the beginning of plans for a jihād.[38] He later wrote about these experiences in his work *Wird* ("The Litany").[39]

It was also at this time that his wife Maimuna gave birth to twins. It has long been a tradition among Muslims to name twins after the Prophet's (non-twin) grandsons, Ḥasan and Ḥusayn. In 1793 the Shehu duly named his son Hasan, but instead of Husseina, he chose the name Asma'u for his twin daughter. Some speculated that she was named after the daughter of the Prophet's Companion Abu Bakr. Odd as this seemed at the time, the only sense that could be made of the Shehu's choice was that he had foreknowledge of the girl's destiny to play a significant role in her father's work, as did the historical Asma in aiding the Prophet's and Abu Bakr's *hijra* out of Makkah. As history has demonstrated, Asma'u did indeed play a significant role as a scholar, teacher, and confidante to her father the Shehu, her brother Caliph Bello, and her husband Lieutenant Gidado during the Sokoto jihād and its aftermath.

The Sokoto Jihād battles were precipitated by a local king's reversal of his father's earlier conciliatory attitudes. Prohibitions on public prayer,

[36] Last notes the Shehu's concerns about issues of jurisprudence, taxation, conscription, political appointments, music, and women's activities, as cited in *Kitab al Farq* (Last, *The Sokoto Caliphate*, lxviii).

[37] Last (*The Sokoto Caliphate*) and Hiskett (*The Sword of Truth*) provide many more details about the prelude to the jihād, but that is not this chapter's focus.

[38] Last (*The Sokoto Caliphate*, 10, 20) explains the details of his mystical encounters as described by the Shehu in his *Wird*. Hiskett (*The Sword of Truth*, 63. et passim) discusses the Sufi nature of the Shehu's learning and teaching.

[39] Hiskett, *The Sword of Truth*, 64–67.

conversion, wearing turbans and veils, and the selling of some Fulani as slaves, all increased to breaking point.[40] From her infancy, Asma'u had known nothing but the struggle to defend what her family perceived to be an Islamic way of life, against opposition they considered to be parallel to that of the original community of Muslims more than a millennium earlier.

ASMA'U'S SUFI UPBRINGING

By the time Nana Asma'u was born, her scholarly family was already at the centre of social conflict. She knew her father as a devout Sufi whose mystical encounters were the likely source of her unexpected name, and whose long years of fraught existence confirmed his belief in the spiritual imperative of his reformist mission. Eleven years old when the Jihād battles began, Asma'u had studied the classics from her father's library, internalized Qādiriyya tenets of belief, and understood her father to be striving to emulate the Prophet. Her written works and activist behaviour throughout the rest of her life are consistent with this grounding in Qādiriyya spirituality. It is no surprise that her work is infused with Sufi concepts and advocacy.

The Shehu's Sufi practices combined voluntaristic and gnostic approaches.[41] When he was nearly forty, his gnostic encounters merged with his worldly endeavours in dreams in which he met the eponymous founder of the Qādiriyya order who fostered promotion of the Jihad in order to put Sufi behaviour into practice in the community.[42] The Islamic reform the Shehu sought through the Jihad was one that secured for the average person the opportunity to practice Islam and gain access to deeper spiritual experiences, as in the Prophet's jihād. In this the Fodio clan's Sufi tenets were "both generated and ... illustrated out of Muhammad's own mysticism".[43] The Fodios demonstrate in their writings – as a rationale for the Jihād – the importance of following the *sunna* and encouraging such behaviour on the part of others.[44] Asma'u's poetic descriptions of her father confirm his intention to imitate the Prophet, and echo the tradition that

[40] Last, *The Sokoto Caliphate*, 11–13.

[41] Schimmel suggests that it is often the case that the tendency is towards one of these over the other (*The Mystical Dimensions of Islam*, 6).

[42] Hiskett (*The Sword of Truth*, 66–67) discusses the Shehu's dreams (recounted in Abdullahi's writings) in which al-Jelani robed the Shehu in symbolically Sufi garb and also handed him the "sword of Truth", saying "Verily to make ready weapons is *Sunna*."

[43] Schimmel *The Mystical Dimensions of Islam*, 9, quoting F.A.D. Tholuck in his 1821 volume on Sufism.

[44] Schimmel (*The Mystical Dimensions of Islam*, 9, 24, 27) confirms the origins of Sufism in the life and behavior of the Prophet and Qur'ānic inspiration.

"a Sheikh in his group is like the prophet in his people".[45] The hagiographic nature of the family's descriptions of Shehu Usman 'dan Fodio are meant to endow his life's story, and therefore his reformist aims, with credibility, as well as to demonstrate reverence for him.[46] The Shehu's confidence that his jihād was destined to be successful was based on his belief in the intersession of saints who would aid Muslims in overcoming unbelievers.[47] He understood his mission of reform as progress on the Sufi path, providing service to his community.[48]

EDUCATION AND GENDER EQUALITY

The pursuit of education was incumbent on both women and men among the Fodios. Asma'u was educated in her early years by her mother and grandmother, as was her father. As an adult, she taught classes of young men as well as separate classes of women, and communicated freely with male scholars across the wider Maghreb region. The Shehu is known for having admonished local Hausa men for not encouraging the women of their families to leave the house for the purpose of education whenever that instruction was available locally. He said that preventing women's education was antithetical to appropriate Islamic behaviour,[49] and the number of scholarly women in the Fodio family attests to the practical application of that belief in the importance of education and enlightenment, regardless of gender. If the estimate of more than a thousand male scholars among the Shehu's followers is accurate, it can be assumed there were among them a goodly number of women scholars as well.[50] Judging from what is known about women scholars in the Fodio family, and from the testimony of contemporary Sufi shaykhs

[45] Schimmel, *The Mystical Dimensions of Islam*, 101.

[46] See Carl Ernst's commentary on hagiography in his *The Shambhala Guide to Sufism* (Boston, Massachusetts: Shambhala Publications, 1997, pp. 63, 65–68, 137). The works mentioned above – Hausa poem *Wa'kar Karomomin Shehu* ("Song of the Shehu's Miracles") by Malam Isa 'dan Shehu (the Shehu's son) and Arabic prose account of the Shehu's life, *Raud al-Jinān (Meadow of Paradise)* by Gidado 'dan Laima – are explicitly hagiographic.

[47] Schimmel, *The Mystical Dimensions of Islam*, 203 discusses saints as the "governors of the universe", granting blessings from rainfall to victory over oppression.

[48] Ibid., 229, notes that this is a characteristic aim of Sufi striving.

[49] See Boyd, *The Caliph's Sister*, 4–6, in which she cites passages from the Shehu's Fulfulde works that criticize men's unfair and unkind treatment of their wives. Asma'u reiterates this in her Hausa poem "A Warning" (1856). She also criticized women's bad treatment of their husbands. This even-handed view is in keeping with the Qur'ān's consistently egalitarian treatment of the genders; see 24:3, and 24:26, for examples.

[50] This number is cited by Last, *The Sokoto Caliphate*, lxxvi, who drew it from Gidado's *Raud al-Jinān*.

that they are unlikely to marry women who are not their equals,[51] it must be assumed that there were significant numbers of women scholars in the Sokoto Caliphate community.

Asma'u's own education involved personal instruction from family members who drew from a corpus of works in the Shehu's library of manuscripts, which numbered in the thousands. These included not just the books the Shehu had written – those were more than three hundred – but also many Arabic manuscripts of classical Islamic literature, some dating back to works by twelfth-century authors. Evidence of these is clear in Asma'u's own poetry, which includes her reworkings of earlier authors' classical works, according to literary custom.

In contrast to Asma'u's rigorous education, there were in the region increasing numbers of uneducated, non-Muslim slave women captured in Jihad battles whose new positions as wives or servants were potentially disruptive to community welfare. A shared understanding of Islamic values was crucial to unity in the incipient Caliphate. To this end, Asma'u organized a corpus of educated Muslim women capable of reaching uneducated rural women to instil in them the essentials of Islam. Asma'u's model of extension education was called the *'Yan Taru* ("The Associates").[52] Its teachers were older women and young girls – those without child-care responsibilities – who would first study with Asma'u, and then, once trained, travel together in groups on foot to remote areas to instruct rural women. *'Yan Taru* lessons included poetic works that described normative Qādiriyya Sufi values, as well as practices that ranged from the quotidian (how to pray, how to dress) to the esoteric (ethics, tenets of belief). The rationale for this organization of women teachers was that early marriage and domestic obligations militated against young girls being at liberty to leave their communities and travel with a Shaykh for study as boys did, but women should not be deprived of enlightenment because of their domestic obligations; thus, the *'Yan Taru* could bring education to them in their homes. The value of this organization is evident in the fact that it has remained active from its inception – throughout colonization, post-colonial times, and into independence – into the twenty-first

[51] This perspective has been conveyed to me numerous times in Morocco and Nigeria; in Morocco individuals have testified to the logic of marrying one's intellectual equal, while the prevalence of women in the Sokoto Caliphate is evident in genealogies that pre-date the jihād (listed in Jean Boyd's notebooks) and in the lists of women *'Yan Taru* teachers from the period of the jihād to the present, as documented in the appendix in Boyd and Mack, *Educating Muslim Women*.

[52] The *'Yan Taru* movement has been discussed in Boyd, *The Caliph's Sister*, and Boyd and Mack, *Educating Muslim Women*.

century, when contemporary women continue to educate one another in a Qādiriyya context using the methods and materials begun by Asma'u in the 1820s.[53]

EVIDENCE OF SUFISM IN ASMA'U'S STYLE: POETIC FORM, ORALITY, VERNACULAR LANGUAGE

Asma'u's collected works present the strongest evidence of immersion in Sufi tenets: first, these are poems, not prose; second, they lend themselves to oral recitation; and third, they are composed in the vernacular as well as in more scholarly languages. Although other members of the Fodio clan wrote prose and treatises, Asma'u's works are in poetic form, the perennial mode of communication of Sufi themes. The importance of poetry to Sufis is derived from its Arabic linguistic origins, in which ever-deepening esoteric meanings can be implied most economically in poetic form.[54] Asma'u's poems are Sufi in content. They express the importance of emulation of the Prophet, commentary on the *sunna*, discussion of miracles, belief in the guidance provided in the Qur'ān, ethical behaviour, adherence to practices prescribed in the pillars, affirmation of the benefit of wisdom over knowledge (*ma'rifa* v. *'ilm*), and the superiority of moral obligation to the community over conquest. Other topics of Asma'u's that reflect constant Sufi concerns include detailed parallels between the Shehu's life and the Prophet's, comparisons between their inspirations for jihād and the jihād battles (set over a millennium apart), attention to miracles, and reference to Sufi figures in history.

These concepts are conveyed in poetic works whose mnemonic qualities facilitate their being internalized through oral repetition and memorization. Each of Asma'u's works, while written, lends itself to memorization and oral recitation for use as a lesson plan in the *'Yan Taru* context. Oral expression is characteristic of Islamic devotions, as is evident in daily prayer, and repetition of prayerful words and phrases in the process of *dhikr*. Sufis have long acknowledged the value of oral transmission of spirituality, understanding that repeated oral prayer allows for the internalization of the word, which transforms the human vessel in ways that writing cannot: Sufis say they write their prayers on the heart, where they cannot be destroyed. In Sufism's early years, attention to the oral communication of gnosis was recommended:

53 There also exist North American chapters of the 'Yan Taru, as discussed in Boyd and Mack, *Educating Muslim Women* (chapter 6), and in Beverly Mack's "Nana Asma'u's Instruction and Poetry for Present-day American Muslimahs" in *History in Africa*, 38, (2011), 1–16.

54 Schimmel, *The Mystical Dimensions of Islam*, 13.

"[t]rue gnosis . . . is not attained through books . . . 'to break the ink-pots and tear the books' was considered by some mystics the first step in Sufism".[55] The respectability of illiteracy in this context is inherent in the Prophet having been called *ummī*, (Qur'ān 7:157), a word implying mystical associations in a man who was pure spirituality, untouched by worldly intellectuality; "[t]he heir of the Prophet is he who follows the Prophet with his actions, not he who blackens the face of paper".[56] Although Asma'u was not without her inkpot, this perspective underlines the value afforded oral communication in her community. Western scholarship has long since endowed the written form with greater credibility than the oral form, but among nineteenth-century Sufis oral communication remained a respectable means of conveying important concepts.

Asma'u's poems were intended to be recited in Fulfulde and Arabic among her family members and other scholars, and in Hausa among the masses. Inherent in that practice was her reliance on the vernacular, which facilitated the spread of Sufism from its inception.[57] Early Sufis composed in vernaculars to make esoteric concepts clear to non-Arabic speakers, and thus developed vernaculars into poetic languages of new literary modes.[58] Sufi teaching circles are vibrant centres of learning around the world, where they combine oral instruction in local languages with communal *dhikr* in Arabic.[59] Asma'u was quadrilingual, but wrote in only three of these languages: Arabic, Fulfulde, and Hausa,[60] depending on which language was understood by her audience. This practice was in keeping with Prophetic instruction to teach to the level of the student, and served the practical needs of the Caliphate following the Jihad, during years of integration of refugees.

For example, one of Asma'u's Hausa poems – "The Qur'ān" – contained all 114 names of Qur'ānic chapters in a mere 30 couplets.[61] Its brevity facilitated its memorization by rural women, while the itinerant teachers were qualified to unpack the work, explaining the import of each Qur'ānic chapter (discussed more fully below; see p. 209). "The Qur'ān" is interesting for its having

55 Schimmel, *The Mystical Dimensions of Islam*, 17.

56 Ibid., 218, 222.

57 Schimmel gives examples of the use of Persian, Turkish, and Indo-Muslim languages as vehicles for the spread of spiritual concepts that could not be understood by the masses in classical Arabic (*The Mystical Dimensions of Islam*, 33).

58 Schimmel, *The Mystical Dimensions of Islam*, 33.

59 Personal experience in visiting women's *zāwiya* meetings throughout Morocco (2001–2008) indicate the efficacy of the use of *darija* Arabic for discussions.

60 Asma'u also spoke the Berber language Tamachek, although she did not compose in it.

61 All references to Asma'u's poems in the following discussions are from Boyd and Mack, *The Collected Works*. The interested reader may refer to it for details.

been composed first in Fulfulde (1829), then in Hausa (1838), and finally in Arabic (1850). Hiskett noted its Arabic title, *Qasīda fī'l munāja*, while mentioning that it was of "little literary interest".[62] As a listing of Qur'ānic chapter titles, it is certainly not compelling in a literary way, but its function was one of educational value. Asma'u composed it first in Fulfulde – towards the end of the period of Jihad battles – perhaps as an exercise, and for review and commentary by her family members. Its Hausa composition in 1838 was a deliberate effort to create a lesson plan that was succinctly composed and transparent in intention to serve the needs of reconstruction, in which *'Yan Taru* instruction was instrumental.

ASMA'U'S POETRY: SUFI IDEALS IN ARABIC, FULFULDE AND HAUSA

Asma'u's collected works include over sixty originals. Of these, eighteen are elegies of family members primarily written in Fulfulde; one is in Hausa, two are in Arabic. Among the rest of the poems, seven (11 percent) are in Arabic, thirteen (21 percent) are in Hausa, and the majority, twenty (33 percent), are in Fulfulde, her first language, and that of the scholars of her community. Each poetic work, especially among the elegies, is composed in a context of Sufi values, with a focus on the importance of the *sunna* and cultivating Sufi character traits of humility, piety, and active social welfare behaviour. Because the language of the work indicates the audience to whom she was speaking, these poems will be discussed here as compositions that seek to communicate Sufi concepts to particular groups of listeners.

ARABIC WORKS

In 1820, when she was in her mid-twenties, Asma'u wrote her first composition, "The Way of the Pious", in Arabic. This inaugural piece was Asma'u's presentation of the tenets she had learned, as well as an example of her facility with the poetic style. In this four-part work she clarifies the importance of expending one's energy in support of the Islamic community through good works such as visiting the sick, and cultivating character traits such as humility and modesty, which reflect values she will extol in those she eulogizes later in her life. Like all her works, this first poem is well organized and moves logically from difficulty to resolution: part one lists barriers between humans and heaven (death, difficulties of the grave, resurrection); part two

[62] Mervyn Hiskett *A History of Hausa Islamic Verse* (London: SOAS, 1975), 44.

explains personal traits that lead to damnation (eight in number); part three lists redeeming habits (also eight in number), and part four lists ways in which a human can exemplify the Prophet (and thus demonstrate love of God) in daily life. All of this is information she would have absorbed from her studies and from listening to her father's sermons.

The next composition that Asma'u wrote in Arabic came many years later, in 1839, and after she had written many other poems in Fulfulde and Hausa. *Tabshīr al-ikhwān* is literally "A Message to the Brethren", but it was addressed to those who specialized in *ṭibb an-nabī*, medicines of the Prophet. The Shehu barely mentioned this kind of spiritual healing, except to say it was *sunna* (in his *iḥyā al-sunna*). This work of Asma'u's addresses many women's health issues referenced in the Qur'ān, such as childbirth (*sura* 56), pregnancy (*sura* 69), weaning (*sura* 85), desire for a male child (*sura* 89) and protection of newborns (*sura* 90). That Asma'u composed it in Arabic indicates that it is not meant for consumption by the masses, but for scholars who could use this information to counter the growing tendency of post-Jihād communities turning to Hausa non-Muslim *bori* spirit-possession-curing cults for these problems. The Jihād battles were fought for the reform of syncretistic practices; the remedies described in this work were meant to prevent back-sliding, and to offer acceptable solutions to health dilemmas. Writing this in Arabic would ensure that only responsible individuals, well versed in *sunna* practices, would have access to the information in it.[63]

Several other Arabic works are included among Asma'u's collection: a prayer for recovery, missives to foreign scholars, and three elegies. Asma'u's "Thanksgiving for Recovery" also was composed in 1839, but its date is not as important as its focus, which echoes historical Sufi Rābi'a al Adawiyya's prayer for recovery from a broken wrist. The implications of drawing a parallel with Rābi'a are evident; other Arabic speakers would have known about the iconic "first Sufi".[64] The three Arabic communiques in Asma'u's collection have no dates, but indicate that Asma'u was accustomed to being in touch with scholars well beyond her home. "Welcome to the Mauritanian Scholar" is addressed to a foreign scholar, Alhaji Ahmad b. Muhammad al-Shinqiti. Asma'u calls him "brother" and refers to olfactory manifestations

63 What remains a mystery is the reason that Asma'u chose to focus on Qur'ānic chapters 44–108. Boyd notes that this is a section from a work written by an earlier scholar or maybe the Egyptian physician who visited Bello and passed medical books to Asma'u for her use (personal communication 14 November 2013).

64 Reference to Rābi'a's prayer is given in Dr. Javad Nurbaksh's *Sufi Women* (London: Khaniqahi-Nimatullahi Publications [1st ed. 1983, 2nd ed. 1990]), 15.

of his grace; clearly these two scholars knew one another through communications across the desert, and respected one another's intellectual capabilities. Her greeting represents a continuation of their long pattern of exchange in Arabic, the lingua franca of Islamic scholarship. Another communique includes messages from her kinsman Shaikh Sa'ad, in which each of them praises the accomplishments and character of the other, citing *aḥādīth* to illustrate their points. It is clear by this exchange that Asma'u was a respected scholar among her peers. The third example, "Poems Exchanged Between Asma'u and Aliyu", is replete with metaphoric language in a refutation of the claim by some Tijāniyya adherents that the Shehu had left the Qādiriyya brotherhood and embraced Tijāniyya affiliation late in his life. Commenting on the awkward situation of Tijāniyya Shaikh 'Umar having overstayed his welcome in Qādiriyya-dominant Sokoto, a poet named Aliyu b. Ibrahim writes to Asma'u, describing the situation as comparable to being wooed by "girls in flowing robes ... daughters of a noble lady", and challenged by the appearance of two other "girls garbed in lovely clothes, prancing ... their sloe-eyes flashing and their bodies beautifully perfumed." Thus, he personifies poems that describe these two competing brotherhoods: the "daughters of a noble lady", that is Asma'u's poems, he implies, represent the Qādiriyya, and the other poems come alive as rival allures, representing the Tijāniyya. His poem sets up the tension between them. Asma'u replies to his imagery with graciousness, praising his poetic skills, and yet deftly refraining from commentary on the subject matter itself. Their several exchanges end with wishes for mutual goodwill "the scent of which is like the perfume that wafts from wine", bringing to mind the metaphoric image of ecstatic intoxication rendered by divine love in Sufi poetry.

The three Arabic elegies that Asma'u's wrote were two lamentations for her close friend and life-long companion 'Ayesha, and one for her brother Bello, which appeared in Fulfulde as well as in Arabic. Asma'u was extremely close to her brother Bello, whose best friend was Asma'u's husband, Gidado. 'Ayesha and Bello were married; Asma'u's close companionship with 'Ayesha is no surprise. The use of Arabic for remembrances of 'Ayesha and Bello accomplishes three aims: first, it indicates the esteem in which Asma'u held them both; second, it indicates that the scholarly language was suitable for them in death as in life; and third, it allows Asma'u to speak of qualities of their characters that reflect immersion in a *sunna* context. These Arabic remembrances remain more widely accessible than any written in Fulfulde or Hausa. Asma'u's grief at their loss is deep, and she means to respect their memory through her use of Arabic, making the sterling qualities of their spirits known on as wide a scale as possible.

FULFULDE WORKS

In 1822, just two years after completing her first composition, Asma'u was inspired to write her second work, which was to be her first in Fulfulde. Prior to a jihād battle, as Asma'u and her close friend 'Ayesha were steeling themselves for the beginning of the battle, Asma'u's brother Bello, aware of his sister's and wife's anxiety about the danger, hastily composed a fourteen line work in acrostic form, which he had delivered to Asma'u as she sat with 'Ayesha in 'Ayesha's house.[65] Its acrostic line is the Qur'ānic verse *Fa'inna ma'a al-'usrin yusra* (94:5): "so verily with every difficulty there is relief". His poem includes commentary from this *sura*, including the questions, "Are you apprehensive, knowing that your Lord is powerful?" (v. 6); "do you think He would neglect one who is hopeful of Him?" (v. 14). It also advises, "Do not be despondent, but anticipate His bounties, God's affairs are according to plan … Joyful relief will come soon" (vv. 7–8), and "Despairing from His mercy is a loss – nay, it is a disbelief leading to Hell" (v. 11). With the war drums sounding just over the hill, Asma'u had to have replied hurriedly. Her skill was such that she was able to reply aptly, in a new poem with the same acrostic line; she included a prayer "for victory and that the rebellion of [the enemy] may be overcome" (v. 9). This is the first known literary collaboration of the siblings.

In 1826, having seen years of Jihād battles wear down communities on both sides, Asma'u, like many, was desperate for an end to the fighting. She composed "Give Us Victory", her second Fulfulde poem, as an urgent prayer for God's help in resolving the conflict in the Jihādists' favour. She appeals to God for the overthrow of the enemy, seeking it "For the honor, the board and the pen, and what was written/For the honor of the Qur'ān, the most excellent of books, and the Old Testament books of Psalms and the words of Jesus/ For the honor of all holy books of God, religion, and insight of precious Belief/ For the honor of the Prophet and other Envoys of God" (vv. 11–14). The poem is unfinished, but her belief in the validity of the Jihād's promotion of the *sunna* is evident in this fragment. Those who were able to understand it would have been familiar with her referents, having been educated in Islamic works as she was.

Asma'u's belief in the credibility of her father's mission is evident in the extent to which she draws parallels between the Shehu's life and times and those of the Prophet Muḥammad in two closely related Fulfulde works: she

[65] An acrostic poem uses the letters in a word or phrase as the beginning of each line. Read vertically, the first letters comprise a phrase that defines the topic of the completed poem.

describes the details of the Shehu's mission in her Fulfulde poem "The Journey" (1839) and gives biographical details about the Shehu and his family in "The Story of the Shehu" (1841). Her audience of Fulfulde-speaking clanspeople would have been fully apprised of the events of both Jihāds, so the intention of the first poem is to emphasize similarities between the Shehu's mission and that of the Prophet Muḥammad, drawing parallels between their respective metaphysical missions, struggles, and battles. In the second of these works, modelled on Prophetic *sira* compositions, her dense history of the Shehu's family members and associates was but one of several such works being composed at around the same time by Asma'u's husband Gidado and uncle Abdullahi. Attention to all these works in relation to one another is interesting because it allows for examination of their differences: Asma'u's poem, unlike Gidado's prose work on the topic, includes fewer names in a more compressed length, which allows for easier memorization. She mentions individuals who would have been known to the audience: for example, reference to the "scholar of Al'kammu" (v. 60) referred to the Shehu's close friend Umaru, the father of 'Ayesha, Bello's wife and Asma'u close friend. The next line mentions "the scholar from Jenne who knew divine mysteries". The talismanic qualities of such images would have given rise to discussion about their roles in the community, the Shehu's own personality, and each individual's contribution to the mission of the Caliphate. These were individuals whose Sufi affiliations were taken for granted by those in the community, so discussing their poetic descriptions would have provided opportunity to affirm the credibility of their actions.[66]

In 1833 Asma'u turned her versification to both education and introspection. Her 1833 Fulfulde work "A Warning" is a straightforward, twenty-six line explanation of the behavioural obligations incumbent upon Muslims and the reverence for the Prophet that they should exhibit. It appears to have been created for students who would be using this material in their own classrooms; its clarity and brevity are intentional. In the same year Asma'u produced a deeply personal poem called "Forgive Me" that appears to have resulted from her having spent time in *khalwa*. This was written when she was forty, about the same age as her father was when he began to have mystical experiences, like several other family members: her own mother Maimuna and her (half-)brother Bello's mother Hauwa were known for their frequent spiritual retreats, as was Bello's sister Fa'dima. In participating in a mystical retreat, Asma'u was seeking to strengthen her spirituality and character. She describes seeking assistance in overcoming self-will ("it is my own will which

[66] Both these works were later translated into Hausa by Asma'u's brother Isa.

has control, help me to overrule it", v. 2), expresses inadequacy in feeling penitence for her sins (v. 3), and mentions the Prophet's "religious duties in the cave" (v. 15) as exemplary. Most noteworthy is her reference to her own blameworthy faults. She would have understood these through her father's explication of blameworthy qualities in a Sufi context, which she had enumerated in her very first composition, "The Way of the Pious". These two poems, "A Warning" and "Forgive Me", produced during the same year, represent the two most active aspects of Asma'u's personality: the drive to educate, and the desire to deepen her spirituality.

Several of Asma'u's Fulfulde works describe for the Fulfulde-speaking clan significant Jihād events. "The Victory at Gawakuke" and "The Battle of Gawakuke" demonstrate Asma'u's active involvement in Jihād events. The first was written in 1836, immediately after the victory, which was a turning point for the Jihād forces. In this work Asma'u's identified both the Shehu and his son Bello as saints ("Great blessings were obtained through this saint [*waliyyi*] of God, son of God's saint" v. 19). Asma'u not only calls Bello himself a saint, and son of a saint, but she also describes the miracle of the pouring forth of water as being parallel to such an event during a Prophetic battle in the historic Tabura campaign. This poem is evidence that the Shehu and Bello were considered to be Sufi saints at the time of the Jihād, which itself was understood to be a military campaign in the tradition of Islam.[67] Bello died the year after this poem was completed. The second poem was written decades later, in 1856, and included far more details about the battle. By the time she wrote it, she was well known to have followed her father and brother in their degrees of scholarship, piety, and *baraka*.[68] In this second poem on Gawakuke she sought to commemorate Bello as a charismatic leader who had grown up in a pious family, had demonstrated personal *baraka*, had been profoundly studious, and as someone who had demonstrated therapeutic gifts and miracles. Asma'u explains his accomplishments in theology, jurisprudence, medicine, mathematics, and *ḥadīth* (v. 6); notes his familiarity with the esoteric as well as the exoteric (vv. 7–8, noting ability in *kashf*); confirms that he followed the *sunna*, as did the Shehu (vv. 10, 18), and demonstrated justice, generosity and mercy (vv. 10–15); cites oaths of loyalty to Bello from followers

[67] See Donal B. Cruise O'Brien and Christian Coulon, Eds. *Charisma and Brotherhood in African Islam* (Oxford: Clarendon Press, 1989:17) (quoted in Boyd and Mack, *The Collected Works*, 64n) for a (mistaken) argument that the Fodio community did not regard the Shehu and Bello as saints until much later and only in response to challenges by the late-coming Tijaniyya members in the region.

[68] Bello's nature is confirmed by European travellers who met him, such as Heinrich Barth (1859 III: 108, 117, quoted in Boyd and Mack, *The Collected Works*, 230).

of al-Jilānī (v. 32); describes the miracles Bello performed in bringing forth water (vv. 35–38);[69] and explains how he defeated non-Muslims (vv. 52–54). It may be that by this time, twenty years after the battle and nearly as long after Bello's death, the Caliphate was in need of reinforcement; Asma'u sought to make this second poem on Gawakuke a vivid reminder of what they had fought for, and encouragement of the ideals that needed to be upheld.

Ten years after admonishing the community to attend to the maintenance of their hard-won Islamic community, Asma'u wrote "Islam, Sokoto, and Wurno" in Fulfulde in 1849 because she saw that people were disinterested in maintaining Sokoto and Wurno as had been intended. She was by this time an authority in the community. She explained that she knew the Shehu had "seen" the fortress town of Wurno before it was built ("The Shehu pointed eastward from where they were and said, 'There is your town. Everything about it has been revealed'." v. 8), and understood that its purpose was to give light to the region; its aim was to defend the Caliphate. The Shehu had prayed for the (newly built) Sokoto to be an exemplary community, while Wurno was "likened to a lamp giving our light to Sokoto" (vv. 11–12). Those who knew the Qur'ān would have understood this immediately as an allusion to *ayat al-nūr* (24:35). She intended that the poem would spur them to support what had been built.

A few years later, Asma'u was distressed about the new threats to the community raised by the advances of enemies from without and within. The urgency she felt is evident in her poems "Destroy Mayaki" (1853), "Destroy Bawa" (1861), and "'Dan Yalli" (1863). The first two focus on enemies who continued, despite years of Jihād battles, to plague the security of Islamic communities; the third, written the year before her death, criticizes the misgovernment that Asma'u sees among her own people. All three begin in urgency, omitting the customary opening doxologies. In the first (Mayaki) Asma'u urges community leaders to "destroy those who have set out to destroy religion ... [and] give victory to those who have learned from their religion ... strengthen the hearts of Muslims to fight the Jihād" (vv. 10–11, 13). The aim of this activity is to bring prosperity in a community in which people can practice Islam: "bless Muslims with food and clothing, bless herdsmen with good pastures ... open the routes in all directions so that communications ... will

[69] As discussed in Boyd and Mack, *The Collected Works*, 237n, Asma'u says of this miracle "I saw it with my own eyes". This may be an indication of her mystic capabilities, or perhaps she was actually on horseback at the battlefield; she was known to have ridden horses often, and knew about the historical Aisha's propensity for involvement in battle. H. Clapperton *Journal of a Second Expedition into the Interior of Africa* (Philadelphia, PA: Carey, Lea, and Carey 1829: Vol. 2, 177) notes women in Gidado's entourage.

be easier ... give us fat cattle, goats, sheep and camels" (vv. 16–18). Thus, she sought to inspire men to fight to protect what they had, giving them a vision of the security they should be seeking, and specifying the work they had before them. Similarly, in the poem about Bawa, she calls on God for help: "[they seek] to eradicate religion, May God eradicate them" (v. 4). Just as she named the enemy in these first two works, in the third she names her kinsman, 'Dan 'Yalli, criticizing his unlawful behaviour, which she saw as detrimental to the welfare of the newly formed Caliphate. In all three works she calls on the spirit of the Shehu, the miracles of Qādiriyyya 'Abd al-Qādir, and Sufi saints Shaykh Aḥmad al-Rifā'ī (d. 1122), Shaykh Aḥmad al-Badawī (1199–1276, Egypt), and Shaykh Ibrāhīm al-Dasūqī (1246–1277?) for aid. This is a mark of her authorship.[70] Especially at the end of her life, Asma'u was unafraid of speaking her mind, and confident in her estimation of what was right. She had spent years immersed in study, prayer, and contemplative retreat. At this point she felt compelled to speak the truth with the urgency of one who knows that there is little time for politesse. These poems were written in a language the enemy would not have understood, but certainly her kinsman would have heard the criticism that she was ready to direct towards them whenever necessary.

"Remembrance of the Shehu" is an 1854 Fulfulde composition that exemplifies the collaborative composition process that is a signature of Asma'u's time. She wrote it to honour the style and content of one of her father's Sufi litanies, called "*Afalgimi*",[71] said to have been written when he was ten years old. Although both his poem and her imitation of it are simple litanies outlining the obligations of the pillars and requesting guidance and strength to follow the *sunna*, perform ablutions, and be generous in *zakat*, nevertheless the focus of each is the saintly nature of the Shehu. It might have been presumptuous for anyone else to write a poem in imitation of the Shehu's own work and to state clearly in it "I have copied the style from the Shehu" (v. 10), but Asma'u was 62 years old when she wrote this, her father was long dead, and she was, after all, her father's daughter. The fact that verse three opens with three untranslatable words is likely the fault of we who presented Asma'u's material in English,[72] or perhaps an error in copying, but it is an

[70] Boyd says Waziri Junaidu told her that the inclusion of Shaykhs in a work aids in identification of a work as hers. "Elegy for Bukhari" (v. 2) may be the earliest time in which she included them (personal communication 14 November 2013).

[71] *Falgimi*, "visitation"; *Afalgimi*, "you have visited me" (F.). I am grateful to Malama Nafisa Gusau and her mother, Hajiya Hanatu A'kilu for confirming a definition of this term.

[72] Of course, we also enlisted the aid of several Fulfulde speakers, who were also unable to make sense of the words.

intriguing conundrum that bears comparison with the untranslatable letters that preface several Qur'ānic verses.

Finally, Asma'u's Fulfulde "Fear This" (n.d.) is a terrifying, 99-quintain poem based on a poem in couplets by Mamman Tukur. To his poem Asma'u added her own *takhmis*, a three-line addition to an existing couplet, maintaining original rhyme and metre, creating a new poem in quintains, whose original author nevertheless would be well known. This was a standard means of creating new poetic works that honoured earlier ones through their evident association, and added new information to each verse; often it was a pious exercise. Based on Qur'ānic descriptions of Hell, this is a stern reminder to listeners of the horrifying punishments awaiting those who stray from the path. Its detailed content demonstrates Asma'u's thorough grounding in the Qur'ān through both memorization and exegesis. In addition to this detailed work, she also composed in 1860, in both Fulfulde and Hausa, a work of similar import called "Fear of the Hereafter", whose 54-couplet form was much more readily memorized for dissemination in instructional *'Yan Taru* classes in its Hausa form.

HAUSA POEMS

The Hausa masses, having had no training in Qur'ānic study or *sira* works, could not be expected to know the details of either. To provide an educational basis for this knowledge, Asma'u created poems of her own composition and also translated into Hausa certain effective works by others. The horrors of everlasting damnation certainly got people's attention. In discussing Hell in her Hausa works "Fear of the Hereafter" (above), and "Signs of the Day of Judgment" (n.d.), she was able to explain what she understood to be the fate of those who ignored the obligations of Islam and refused to follow the *sunna*. These two works, at 54 and 75 couplets, respectively, were readily memorized by both teachers and students in the *'Yan Taru* movement. The latter work not only spoke of the pains of Hell, but also explained the need to follow the *sharī'a*, making a logical connection between the law of the community based on Qur'ānic interpretation and divine law.

Having got her audience's attention by scaring them, Asma'u also offered listeners accounts of the exemplary lives of both the Prophet and the Shehu in two works that represent a wealth of such panegyric composition by many others in her community, a mark of Sufism in a community.[73] Asma'u translated into Hausa Muhammad Tukur's Fulfulde poem "Yearning for

[73] Hiskett, *A History of Hausa Islamic Verse*, 43.

the Prophet" (n.d.), a detailed 316-couplet work aimed at educating the masses about the Prophet's life and times.[74] Another of her works, her 1839 poem "Ahmada", presents the Prophet's life in 55 couplets – perhaps easier for learners to memorize than the longer one. It is a panegyric in the *madih* eulogy style. Both works have a rhyme scheme that depends on the frequent use of the terms *Ahmada* and *Muhammada*, emphasizing the Arabic root ḤMD, "praise".[75] Asma'u was familiar with thirteenth-century works on the topic, such as al-Busīrī's *Burda*, al-Fazzāzī's *al-qasā'id al-witriyya*, and al-Tawzarī's *simt al-hudā*, which are commonly known in the region.

In 1831, with the Jihād battles well over and the populace striving to resume a semblance of normalcy, Asma'u composed a formidable work in Hausa for use by the *'Yan Taru* instructors in rural areas among Hausa speaking women. "Be Sure of God's Truth" discusses the concept of *ḥaqīqa*, Divine Truth, in informing people at all levels of their obligations in a community based on Islamic principles. The Shehu, his brother Abdullahi, and his son Bello had organized the new Caliphate on the classical concepts of State developed by the Abbasids (circa eighteenth century). Each wrote a book advising that the viability of a community rested on the morality of its leader. These books are, respectively: *Bayān Wujūb al-hijra*, 1806 ("Communication of What is Necessary Concerning the Jihād"), *Diyya al-Ḥukkām*, 1821 ("Light for Governors/the Brilliance of Wisdom"), and *al-Gaith*, 1821 ("The Abundant Downpour: Regarding the Behavior of the Just Imam").[76] Asma'u's Hausa poem is based on her father's 1812 Fulfulde poem on the same topic, which he wrote to remind the ruling elite, flush from jihād victories, to keep in mind a focus on divine law in the process of establishing an administrative order. In her poem Asma'u has added a *takhmis* to each verse of his original poem. Asma'u's composition in Hausa is meant for mass consumption, reminding people of the reciprocal responsibilities between the ruled and the rulers, all of whom answer to God's ultimate authority. The poem's refrain, *Tabbat Hakika* ("Be sure of God's Truth") holds both esoteric and exoteric meaning. As shown in *sura* 69, *al-Ḥaqq* is one of God's 99 names; the end-line refrain is the Hausa form, *hakika*. The dual exoteric Prophetic and the esoteric mystic messages are clear throughout the poem: "Whoever seeks a position of

[74] See Mack 2009 for details about "Sufi Women", "Yearning for the Prophet", and "The Journey" in a Sufi hagiographic context.

[75] Hiskett, Mervyn, *Some to Mecca Turn to Pray: Islamic Values and the Modern World* (St. Albans: Claridge Press, 1993), 293.

[76] Shaykh Muhammad Sharif maintains a rich Web site on which his translations of these and many other Fodio-related works are given. See the library listings on the Web site of the Sankore Institute (http://siiasi.org).

authority/So that he can get rich or powerful/Or slyly allies himself with wrong-doers/And those who buy titles of authority/Without doubt will burn ... be sure of God's Truth (v. 8). Asma'u's poetic explanation of the need for the rulers and ruled to work together for a higher good has become famous in the region and continues to be popular in contemporary times. Its perennial message is as important now as it was when it was first composed.

Asma'u's Hausa poem "A Warning" (1856) differs significantly from the one she wrote in earlier in Fulfulde; the Fulfulde poem describes Islam's pillars and obligations, with no mention of gender issues, presumably because the active participation of Fulfulde-speaking women in scholarly endeavours made gender a non-issue. For Hausa listeners, however, Asma'u stated clearly that "Women may leave their home freely for [education]" (v. 21). The poem contains information about the *sunna*, describes the esoteric nature of God ("He knows all mysteries" v. 3), clarifies the importance of following the pillars, and explains the use of prayer beads, a mainstay of Sufi devotions. The following year Asma'u composed "A Prayer for Rain" as a critique of non-Islamic customs, like drumming, which is associated with *bori* spirit possession cult activities. The point of the message was that relief from drought should only be sought from God, with the aid of saints: the Shehu, al-Jīlānī, Rifā'ī, Badawī, and Dasūqī (vv. 9–10). She invokes the importance of following the *sunna*, and describes (rain) water in the same way as the Prophet has been described: as a mercy to the world (v. 5).

"Reasons for Seeking God" (1861) is meant as a straightforward lesson plan for Hausa speakers explaining why and how one should seek God. Like her very first poem, this one is based on her father's sermons. Its brevity (35 couplets) allows for easy memorization. This work includes instruction in following the *sunna*, instruction on prayer and the other pillars, and reiterates the "forbidden behaviours" that the Shehu had described in his writings on Sufism. Asma'u includes in this work mystical numbers, noting that God's messengers number 313, and His prophets 4,120. As in other poems, she calls on the support of saints like al-Jīlānī, Rifā'ī, Badawī and Dasūqī.

ASMA'U'S TRANSLATIONS OF HER OWN WORKS

Asma'u translated several of her own poems to make them available to different audiences. Some works, written originally in Hausa, presumably for use in *'Yan Taru* classes, she then translated into Fulfulde for dissemination among her clanspeople. For example, "Sufi Women" (Hausa, 1836; Fulfulde 1837) is Asma'u's version of a classic work that dates back to as-Sulamī's tenth century work of the same name, which was recomposed by Ibn al-Jawzī in the twelfth century.[77] The Shehu likely had a version of the classical "Sufi Women" among his library holdings, on which Asma'u's brother Muhammad Bello modelled his own prose work of the same name in 1836.[78] Bello asked Asma'u to write versified translations into both Hausa (1836) and Fulfulde (1837), into which she incorporated names of contemporary women of the community. The aim of her translations was to make his news on the topic widely available, because it was needed by both women and men. On the one hand, it appeared that the significant numbers of Hausa women war refugees who had been put into concubinage by the Jihādists between 1810 and 1835 were unfamiliar with and disinterested in Islamic women's roles. At the same time, the men of their households were failing to provide re-education programs and social support for these women. Bello and Asma'u sought to bolster women's social roles by educating both genders about the importance of Sufi women, both historically and in their own community. Thus the aim of offering the "Sufi Women" poem in Arabic, Hausa, and Fulfulde was to be sure that everyone heard, in his or her own language, examples of ways in which women were important to society, and the names of particular historical and contemporary individuals whose roles were valued. What distinguishes Asma'u's Hausa and Fulfulde versions of this work is her addition of the names and attributes of women of the Sokoto Caliphate. By adding them to this classic praise of Sufi women in history, she elevates their standing to that of those earlier women, thereby adding them to the chronicles of those to be revered in Sufi history.

Asma'u wrote some works in both Hausa and Fulfulde at the same time, intending to reach both her brethren Fulfulde speakers and the Hausas masses with the same news: "Caliph Aliyu's Victory" (Hausa and Fulfulde, 1844) and "Fear of the Hereafter" (Hausa and Fulfulde, 1860). "Caliph Aliyu's Victory" explains the defeat of non-Muslim Kebbi forces. It is spare, a news bulletin, but the delivery of the same information is different in tone between the two renderings. The Fulfulde version is more subdued, explaining the expectedness of the outcome, given the unbeliever status of the Kebbi forces: "Anyone who leaves the community of the Shehu has left the *sunna* and is doomed (v. 12)". The Hausa version is more direct and didactic: "of the Kebbi people no one is left/ They are in profound trouble/They rebel because of their worldliness/ They are beyond reach and will not go to Heaven" (vv. 10–12).

[77] Abu 'Abd al-Rahman as-Sulamī, *Early Sufi Women: Dhikr an-niswa al-muta 'abbidat as sufiyyat*, Trans. Rkia Cornell (Louisville, KY: Fons Vitae, 1999). Historian and Ḥanbalī jurist (d. 1200) Abu al-Faraz ibn al Jawzī's work is *Safwat al-Safwa*.

[78] At this writing, Bello's Arabic version remains untranslated.

Yet both works explain the defeat, and confirm the importance of following the *sunna* and eschewing worldliness if one is to hope for heaven.

The work that was chronologically Asma'u's third was the Fulfulde version of "The Qur'ān". This represents a unique example of her translations of her own works for the purposes of instruction. In 1829 she composed this succinct, 30-couplet poem that included the names of all 114 chapters of the Qur'ān. To have written this in Fulfulde indicates that she was concerned to test it on her family members – Fulfulde speakers – to be sure that it was comprehensive and clear. None of them would have needed instruction in the names of Qur'ānic content, but they surely could have commented on the efficacy of her presentation of this information. By 1829 the Jihād battles – two and a half decades after their start – were nearly over. At this time she would have been well aware of the effects of warfare and the need for resocialization. The '*Yan Taru* movement had begun, so in 1838 she translated this work into Hausa, for use by '*Yan Taru* teachers. It was brief enough so that it could be memorized; the '*Yan Taru* who taught it would have been intimately familiar with the import of the chapters, which they could explain during their teaching residence in a village. By the time the '*Yan Taru* teachers left the village, the women villagers would have the memorized poem as an internal index of Qur'ānic contents, and would remember what had been conveyed about each chapter in the lessons they had received. Late in her life, in 1850, Asma'u translated this work into Arabic, making it more widely available to Islamic scholars in the Maghreb region.[79]

THE ELEGIES

Nearly all Asma'u's elegies were in Fulfulde and were meant as consolation for her clanspeople and close friends. She wrote elegies for: her uncles Abdullahi and Na'Inna; brothers Caliph Bello and Buhari; husband Buhari; brother-in-law Mustafa; cousins Halilu and Mo'dibo; local man Malam Dandi; sister Fa'dima; close friend 'Ayesha; niece Fa'dima; neighbour Halima; local woman Zaharatu; '*Yan Taru* leader Hawa'u; and even an unnamed "youth" who had assisted her in her later years. Each work extols the qualities of the individual that are worthy of blessings: hospitality, piety, kindness, generosity, patience, respectfulness of others, diligence in helping, and a conciliatory nature. Some were praised as scholars, citing the ḥadīth "when a scholar dies, Islam is

[79] When this poem was published in 1997 (Boyd and Mack), the women of FOMWAN in Nigeria were quite interested in its use for educating contemporary women. (Boyd, personal communication 14 November 2013).

breached". The Sufi devotional nature of some was mentioned, commenting on their use of *tasbīḥ* and recitation of *Wird*. For each, Asma'u closes by calling on the blessings of the Prophet, his Companions and Followers, and the Shehu. For some she adds an appeal to a combination of the Sufi saints mentioned in her other works – al-Jilānī, the Shehu, Rifā'ī, Badawī, and Dasūqī. What is significant in these elegies is the variety of individuals remembered, from a "youth" and local man and woman who worked unceasingly for the benefit of the community, to significant historical individuals like the Shehu's brother Abdullahi, Caliph Bello, and Gidado. All three of these were individuals known to European travellers and active in Jihād warfare. They were important historical figures, but Asma'u's elegies are significant for what they omit: she did not discuss military campaigns, swordsmanship, international scholarly renown, miracle-working, or qualities of *baraka*. Every individual is evaluated in terms of non-worldly qualities that are significant in relation to their heavenly rewards, nothing more. Their statuses were measured against Sufi qualities of character, because that is what Asma'u believed to be the most important features of a person.

CONCLUSION

Asma'u's Sufi upbringing infused her poetic works with the tenets of Qādiriyya Islam. She was a scholar respected by her kinspeople at home and scholars across the Sahara. Asma'u was immersed in practices of *khalwa*, *dhikr*, *sunna*, Qur'ānic recitation, reliance on appeal to Sufi saints, and instruction of all these behaviours in a multiplicity of modes, including three languages and several poetic styles. She collaborated with her brother, Caliph Muhammad Bello, on several poetic works, and worked to organize the Shehu's library after his death: Asma'u was designated to catalogue the hundreds of volumes in it, and she enlisted the assistance of her husband Gidado.[80] Asma'u organized and wrote the material for a mass social welfare educational program for women, the '*Yan Taru*, to ensure the education and welfare of women no matter whether they came from town or village, and were of Muslim birth or otherwise. *Jaji*s, the women leaders, required that everyone set out with the right intentions, for every religious act must begin

[80] The Shehu's library was in the rooms of the Shehu's wives; Asma'u would have had access to these materials at any time. Gidado was adamant that the Shehu's books be preserved, and in many cases this required recopying of older manuscripts. See "Elegy for Gidado", vv. 17–20 (Boyd and Mack, *The Collected Works*, 201).

with the formulation of the *niyyah*, pious intention.[81] The '*Yan Taru* organization, with its Sufi foundation, has operated unabated from its inception in the nineteenth century, throughout the twentieth century colonial and post-colonial periods, and into contemporary times in the twenty-first century. All Asma'u's work and study were rooted in Sufi scholarship, and fuelled by her life-long devotion to Sufi tenets and practices that sustained her and her kinspeople through warfare, itinerancy, and the task of supporting an Islamic state against the human propensity to take the easier, instead of the right path.

FURTHER READING

Boyd, Jean. *The Caliph's Sister* (London: Frank Cass, 1989).

Boyd, Jean and Beverly Mack, *The Collected Works of Nana Asma'u, Daughter of Usman 'dan Fodiyo (1793–1864)* (East Lansing, Michigan: Michigan State University Press, 1997).

Boyd, Jean and Beverly Mack, *Educating Muslim Women: The West African Legacy of Nana Asma'u (1793–1864)* (Oxford: Interface Publications, 2013).

Hiskett, Mervyn. "*The Song of the Shaihu's Miracles*: A Hausa Hagiography from Sokoto" in *Language Studies* XII (1971), 71–107.

Hiskett, Mervyn. *The Sword of Truth* (London: Oxford University Press, 1973).

Hiskett, Mervyn. *A History of Hausa Islamic Verse* (London: SOAS, 1975:44).

Last, Murray. *The Sokoto Caliphate* (Ibadan, Nigeria: Longman, 1967).

Last, Murray "Contradictions in Creating a Jihadi Capital: Sokoto in the Nineteenth Century and Its Legacy" *African Studies Review* Vol. 56, No. 2 (September 2013), 1–20.

Mack, Beverly and Jean Boyd, *One Woman's Jihad: Nana Asma'u, Scholar and Scribe* (Bloomington, Indiana: Indiana University Press, 2000).

Mack, Beverly "Imitating the Life of the Prophet: Nana Asma'u and Shehu Usman 'dan Fodiyo" in *Tales of God's Friends: Islamic Hagiography*, Ed. John Renard (Berkeley, California: University of California Press, 2009), 179–196.

Mack, Beverly "Nana Asma'u's Instruction and Poetry for Present-day American Muslimahs" *History in Africa*, 38, (2011), 1–16.

[81] See "Elegy for Hawa'u" (Boyd and Mack, *The Collected Works*, 252–254 and fn 594, citing Annemarie Schimmel *Deciphering the Signs of God*, 199, 102 on *niyya*).

9

Sufism and Colonialism

Knut S. Vikør

The advent of European forces that took control over their lands was a shocking experience for all Muslim societies. Colonialism took many forms in the different regions that came under European control, but it always implied that at some level Muslim political power was set aside by a Christian power, and that new social structures were introduced from outside.

Like Muslims in general, Sufis reacted in different ways to the new conditions. Throughout history, some Sufi groups have been involved in power struggles or even formed states,[1] but the vast majority of Sufis had no such interest. In the encounter with colonial expansion, some Sufis did in the same way take on a political role, while the great majority of Sufis either ignored the new conditions to the best of their ability, or involved themselves as members of the Muslim society without bring their Sufi affiliations into it.

Thus, one cannot generalize and speak of "*the* Sufi response" to colonialism, only of the various ways that Sufi experiences interacted with political ones. However, the Europeans did make precisely such generalizations. Since *some* Sufi orders had played political roles in the past, and some brotherhoods or Sufi leaders had an active role in the resistance to the foreign invasion, they came to fear *all* brotherhoods, at least until the opposite was proven and each brotherhood, lodge or *shaykh* was properly categorized as either "docile" or "rebellious".[2]

In particular, this led the French colonial authorities, with their early colonial experiences in Algeria from 1830, to put great effort into mapping

1 For example, the Ṣafawī state that became Iran; R. S. Savory, *Iran under the Safavids* (Cambridge: Cambridge University Press, 1980), and Charles Melville (ed.), *Safavid Persia* (London: I.B.Tauris, 1996).

2 K. S. Vikør, *Sufi and Scholar on the Desert Edge. Muhammad b. ʿAlī al-Sanūsī and His Brotherhood* (London: Hurst, 1995), 6–13.

and cataloguing the Sufi organizations of the lands they came to control, since they feared the potential danger of these "secret societies".[3] For the modern historian, their diligent concern has been of great help, since many of these colonial reports were carried out by meticulous scholars who published them as monographs that we can now use as historical sources for the period. These works are a great asset in our understanding of Sufi brotherhoods, in particular in French North and West Africa.

But it is of course a tainted gift. The carefully tabulated surveys were made for the specific purpose of discovering what rebellious tendencies there were in the brotherhoods, and that coloured what they saw. Not only were they on occasion notoriously wrong, as we shall see below, but in most cases it also led to an over-emphasis on organization and structure, because that was where the danger could lie. Thus, relying too much on these French sources may lead us not only to falsely dichotomize the brotherhoods into "activist" and "quietist", but also to craft them into fixed structures of authority and delimitation that may in *some* cases be quite valid, but in others cover up a reality that was much more ad hoc and reliant on personal and contextual leadership than the sources would have us believe.[4] Not all *shaykhs* who were neatly added to the column of a *ṭarīqa* in the French sources necessarily had very much to do with that order's structure.

With these caveats, it cannot be denied that colonialism *did* have an impact, and that some Sufi organizations *did* play a role both in resistance to the colonialists, and in working with the new powers once they were in place. Muslims and Sufis encountered colonial powers in various ways from the Atlantic to the Pacific, in India, Russia and the Middle East.[5] But we may perhaps consider the African continent as a microcosm of the variety of Sufi responses to colonialism, and of how it changed over time. It can therefore be useful to look at a number of cases from Africa, north and south of the Sahara, as examples of the variety of Sufi reaction to the colonial phenomenon.

3 Such as Louis Rinn, *Marabouts et Khouan. Étude sur l'Islam en Algérie* (Alger: A. Jourdan 1884) and Octave Depont and Xavier Coppolani, *Les Confréries Musulmanes* (Alger: A. Jourdan, 1897), among many others.

4 Alexander Knysh, "Sufism as an Explanatory Paradigm. The Issue of the Motivations of Sufi Resistance Movements in Western and Russian Scholarship", *Die Welt des Islams*, xlii, 2 (2002), 139–73.

5 See, e.g., Alexander Knysh, *Islamic Mysticism* (Leiden: Brill, 2000), 289–300.

SUFI RESISTANCE

First Contact: ʿAbd al-Qādir and the French

Africa's first experience with colonial rule came when French troops landed in Algiers and caused the rule of the Turkish *dey* there to collapse.[6] The sudden disintegration of power that left the French in charge came as a bit of a surprise to all parties, and initially the French did not have the manpower to control more than a few cities on the coast. In the east of the province, the local Ottoman governor retained control, while in the western regions, the Moroccan sultan, not wishing to involve himself in a conflict that could provoke the powerful Europeans, asked a local *shaykh*, Muḥyī 'l-Dīn, to act on his behalf.[7] Muḥyī 'l-Dīn had acquired a following primarily for his work in spreading the Qādiriyya order, initiated there by his father Muṣṭafā. The Maghreb had by this time long been dominated by the Shādhiliyya order, although there had always been groups of Qādirīs as well as other brotherhoods there. Muṣṭafā and his successors' work for the order, however, created an important reinvigoration of the order. Muḥyī 'l-Dīn set up a centre in Guetna, not far from Mascara, and seems to have had considerable influence over the tribes in the region. However, he was around 60 years old when the French came, and he asked his followers to transfer their loyalty to his 25-year-old son, ʿAbd al-Qādir, rather than lead them himself. The latter thus received the *bayʿa* of most tribes in the region, and declared himself *amīr al-muʾminīn*, in preparation for the *jihād* against the French.

ʿAbd al-Qādir's resistance against the French colonial expansion, from his declaration in 1832 until his final defeat and exile in 1847, has caught the imagination of later times as a symbol of both the Algerian nation and a successful Arab and Muslim anti-colonial resistance.[8] He at times united much of western and central Algeria under his control and created a small state that was part tribal alliance, part an attempted modernization of the political structures of the region. But what part did his Sufi background play in his struggle?

6 Benjamin Stora, *Algeria 1830–2000. A Short History* (London: Ithaca, 2004); Charles-Robert Ageron, *Modern Algeria. A History from 1830 to the Present* (London: Hurst, 1991); and Knut S. Vikør, *The Maghreb since 1800. A Short History* (London: Hurst, 2012).

7 Raphael Danziger, *Abd al-Qadir and the Algerians. Resistance to the French and Internal Consolidation* (New York: Holmes and Meier, 1977), 51–62, and Bruno Étienne, *Abdelkader. Isthme des Isthmes (Barzakh al-barazikh)* (Paris: Hachette, 1994), 21–85.

8 Danziger, *Abd al-Qadir*, and Amira K. Bennison, *Jihad and Its Interpretations in Pre-colonial Morocco. State-Society Relations during the French Conquest of Algeria* (London: RoutledgeCurzon, 2002).

Overtly, not much. He is normally called the "emir", from the title he claimed, *amīr al-muʾminīn*, which is one of the titles of a caliph. He apparently never referred to himself as *shaykh* or other Sufi title, and in his political structures we can find no specific trace of Sufi-based authority.[9] At the same time, there is little doubt of his own Sufi convictions, even though it was only later in life, in exile in Damascus, that he was able to live this out fully. It is also clear that his initial legitimacy as leader of the resistance was inherited from his father and was based on the family's role as Sufi leaders at Guetna in the region. It was this that made the tribes accept the old man and his son as the natural persons to turn to, in this new situation when there was no one else. Thus, Sufi authority laid the foundation for the struggle, but, once it begun, ʿAbd al-Qādir could not or would not establish himself as political leader on that authority, and instead sought the more traditional and solidly founded role of "commander of the faithful" and leader of the *jihād*.

The Tijānī Jihād *in West Africa*

One major incident in ʿAbd al-Qādir's war that was clearly linked to his Sufi background happened during a two-year truce with the French forces, in 1839. During the lull in fighting the French, he turned his army south and attacked the headquarters of the Tijāniyya order in the oasis of ʿAyn Māḍī.[10] This brotherhood had refused to recognize ʿAbd al-Qādir's authority, no doubt because they would not be subservient to a rivalling *ṭarīqa* leader, and ʿAbd al-Qādir could not accept this division on the Muslim side.

This does not mean that the Tijānīs were active as a political opposition to ʿAbd al-Qādir. On the contrary, this order, which had recently been founded by Aḥmad al-Tijānī (d. in Fez 1815), stayed away from political strife (which led them to be classified as "friendly" by the French cataloguers) both in Morocco and Algeria. They did, however, have strained relations with other *ṭarīqa*s because of their exclusivist attitude: while most orders allowed brethren to "collect" multiple affiliations, joining the Tijāniyya meant leaving all others, which they considered inferior.[11] But this rivalry was mitigated by al-Tijānī and many of his followers preferring to withdraw to desert outposts such as ʿAyn Māḍī.

9 He did, however, work to set up some Qādirī lodges in his regions during its existence, but this does not seem to have been a major concern or to have had special impact; Danziger, *Abd al-Qadir*, 195–6.

10 Jamil M. Abun-Nasr, *The Tijaniyya. A Sufi Order in the Modern World* (London: Oxford University Press, 1965), 62–8.

11 Abun-Nasr, *Tijaniyya*, 27–57.

This was true for the Tijānīs in North Africa. But matters could not have been more different for the order south of the desert, at least at the time it first made its mark there. West Africa had since the middle of the eighteenth century seen a series of Islamic reform movements called the "Fulani *jihāds*", directed at existing local Muslim rulers who were considered insufficiently pure in their application of Muslim rules.[12] Most of these movements were dominated by scholars-activists from the Fulani people who live throughout West Africa. Some of these scholars had a background in the Qādiriyya order, but, again, the major religious framework of the movements was *jihād fī sabīl Allāh* and not Sufism.

These movements had dominated political life in Muslim West Africa for half a century when the young ʿUmar Tall from Futa Toro (today's southern Senegal) went on the *ḥajj* to Mecca in 1828–30.[13] The Tijāniyya had not yet gained a foothold in the south, but he had met some Saharan followers of the order before he left, and in Mecca he was appointed to "spread the Tijāniyya" in West Africa. On his return in the 1840s, he first established a Tijānī centre in Futa Jalon (today in Guinea), and later at Dinguiray (Mali), where he gathered young *talibés* (students). Studying religion and the tenets of the scholarly order, these students also trained for war, and, after six years, in 1852 *al-ḥājj* ʿUmar (as he was now called) launched his *jihād* against the "infidel" rulers of the west. Unlike earlier *jihād*ists, he did in fact spend much of his energy against pagan kingdoms, after having quickly disposed of the local Muslim kings, but he also fought against neighbouring Muslim centres of high renown, including rival *jihādī* (but not Tijānī) states.

By this time, the French had established themselves on the Atlantic coast of Senegal. They were of no great concern to ʿUmar, who had no designs on the coastal regions; his centre of attention was the upper regions of the Niger river. Thus, he did not set out on any *jihād* against the Europeans, and in fact approached them for a *modus vivendi*. The French, however, had grander plans and began to move up the Senegal river and thus eventually came into contact with ʿUmar's territory in the late 1850s. This was at the height of ʿUmar's expansion east and north, and he did not consider the French in the west a major challenge. He pulled back, and asked his supporters instead to move from enemy territory in a *hijra* (withdrawal) to the areas ʿUmar still

[12] The most famous ones came after that of Sokoto in Northern Nigeria, from 1804, but relevant here are also the early *jihāds* in the Futas, ʿUmar Tall's home region; David Robinson, "Revolutions in the Western Sudan" in Nehemia Levtzion and Randall L. Pouwels (eds), *The History of Islam in Africa* (Athens, OH: Ohio University Press, 2000), 133–7.

[13] B.O. Ọlọruntimehin, *The Segu Tukolor Empire* (London: Longman, 1972), and David Robinson, *The Holy War of Umar Tal. The Western Sudan in the Mid-Nineteenth Century* (Oxford: Clarendon Press, 1985).

controlled. The French, however, did not shy away from confronting the Muslim state and moved into what became a sustained conflict between the two. Before it had reached its apex, however, ʿUmar had himself already fallen on the battlefield, in a war against the Muslim state of Masina in 1864. His son and heir Aḥmad was weakened by internal dissension and was not able to stem the slow French advance towards the Niger. In 1890, the French conquered the ʿUmarian capital at Segu, and Aḥmad had to flee. Soon after, the French were in full control of the old *jihād*ist state.

ʿUmar's *jihād* had a much clearer Sufi character than those of his predecessors in West Africa.[14] He was the recognized leader of the Tijāniyya south of the Sahara, he used the brotherhood actively in spreading his authority before he started his war, and his fighting force – which later became the "aristocracy" of the state he set up – was the *talibés*, the Sufi brethren. ʿUmar was himself a renowned scholar: his work on Tijānī faith, the *Rimāḥ*, is central to all members of the Tijāniyya the world over, and may be one of the most influential works of Islamic scholarship produced in sub-Saharan Africa.[15]

On the other hand, he was "anti-colonialist" not by choice, but by force of circumstance. He began his political career long before colonial ambitions had made themselves known in his regions, and he thought for most of his own lifetime that he would not have to deal with the Europeans at all.[16] It was the French who made him into a resistance fighter, because they sought to conquer all of West Africa and must therefore overcome those who held power. ʿUmar and his successors could not submit, and so must be removed.

ʿUmar's anti-colonial Sufism therefore came about through a combination of several elements: that he began a *jihād* for spreading true Islamic understanding; that he used the Tijāniyya pattern as an important basis for this *jihād*, and that the success of his wars made him an enemy for the later French arrivals. He was not a *jihād*ist in spite of himself, but it was factors other than Sufism that produced his conflict with the colonialists.

Jihād *Imposed: The Sanūsiyya*

A different type of "Sufi-inspired *jihād* imposed from outside" can be seen a bit further east and north, in what today is Chad and Libya, in the first decades

14 K. S. Vikør, "Jihād in West Africa: A global theme in a regional setting" in Leif Manger (ed.), *Muslim Diversity. Local Islam in a Global Context* (Richmond: Curzon, 1999), 80–101.

15 B. Radtke, "Studies on the Sources of the *Kitāb Rimāḥ Ḥizb al-Raḥīm* of *al-ḥājj* ʿUmar", *Sudanic Africa* 6 (1995): 73–113.

16 Except as purveyors of arms – many of his firearms were bought from the French and British; Robinson "Revolutions in the Western Sudan", 141.

of the twentieth century. Like the Tijāniyya, the Sanūsī order was created in the nineteenth century.[17] Its founder, Muḥammad b. ʿAlī al-Sanūsī (d. 1859), came from the same Moroccan environment as Aḥmad al-Tijānī, although they were not intellectually related – while the two are grouped with several other contemporary orders as "Neo-Sufi", there is in fact little to connect them in contrast to other Sufi orders.[18] Al-Sanūsī was instead part of a group of closely related orders founded by students of the reformist Sufi teacher Aḥmad b. Idrīs (d. 1837), whom he met in Mecca,[19] and al-Sanūsī's intention was clearly to spread his master's vision rather than his own.

However, his focus was on improving the religious life of Bedouin of the desert, and when he decided to set up a structured brotherhood after his master's death, he left for North Africa looking for such an environment. He found it in Cyrenaica (today eastern Libya) and began building lodges in the close cooperation of the Bedouin tribes there.[20] While the brotherhood's aim and activity was, like any Sufi order, focused on the religious experiences and rituals of the initiates, it is its "external" and social activity that has caught the interest of the historians. The internal and external, work and prayer, went hand in hand for the Sanūsī. The brotherhood constructed their lodges in the oases of the desert edge, and later through the eastern Sahara desert, and where possible began cultivating gardens for their own needs and to provide food and services for the needy of the local Bedouin community. The lodges included schools for youngsters; most tribal leaders, who came to identify with the brotherhood and its lodge, sent their children to the lodge schools, while some also went to further education in the order's centre in the oasis-town of Jaghbūb.

All this was thus done with the full understanding of the tribal leaders, who ruled the desert-side with little or no interference from the Ottomans, the theoretical masters of Cyrenaica. The Sanūsī did not challenge the tribal authority, but did insist on the maintenance of peace between the tribes, which otherwise had a history of bloody rivalry. The brotherhood could

17 Muḥammad Fuʾād Shukrī, *al-Sanūsiyya, dīn wa-dawla* (Cairo: Dār al-fikr al-ʿarabī, 1948), Aḥmad Ṣidqī al-Dajjānī, *al-Ḥaraka al-Sanūsiyya: nashʾatuhā wa-numūwuhā fī ʾl-qarn al-tāsiʿ ʿashar* (Beirut: n.p. [Dār Lubnān], 1967) and Vikør, *Sufi and Scholar.*

18 See R. S. O'Fahey and Bernd Radtke, "Neo-Sufism Reconsidered," *Der Islam* lxxii, 1 (1993): 52–87.

19 Other orders were the Khatmiyya in the Sudan, the Rāshidiyya-Dandarawiyya of the Sudan and others; R. S. O'Fahey, *Enigmatic Saint. Ahmad Ibn Idris and the Idrisi Tradition* (London: Hurst, 1990), and Ali Salih Karrar, *The Sufi Brotherhoods in the Sudan* (London: Hurst, 1992).

20 E. E. Evans-Pritchard, *The Sanusi of Cyrenaica* (Oxford: Clarendon Press, 1949), and Emrys Peters, "The Sanusi order and the Bedouin," in *The Bedouin of Cyrenaica. Studies in Personal and Corporate Power* (Cambridge: Cambridge University Press, 1990), 10–28.

negotiate in potential conflicts between the tribes, but it was perhaps in particular the economic development of the latter half of the century that ensured cooperation and peace. At this time, the main trans-Saharan trade route shifted from the central Sahara (ending in Tripoli) to an eastern route that passed through Cyrenaica to Benghazi. The Sanūsī, who had lodges all along this route, supported and encouraged the trade, digging wells and letting their lodges be used as trade entrepôts. Of course the tribes, for their part, benefitted greatly from this trade as participants and protectors, but its success depended on the security for the traders and the absence of brigandage and conflict.[21]

Thus, the Sanūsīs were socially active, but not politically so. However, the suspicious French colonial authorities, far away in Algeria and West Africa, imagined the Sanūsīs as dangerous, anti-western and fanatical, partly because of their remote location in the desert, partly fuelled by stories from rivals and storytellers.[22] As far as we can see, the Sanūsī paid no particular attention to the encroaching European presence, and there are no comments on Christianity or other religions in their writings; if al-Sanūsī was critical of other theologies, it was the "orthodox Muslims" who had stifled the study of Prophetic *ḥadīth*, in particular in matters of religious ritual.

But when the French West African forces began to move east from the Niger past Lake Chad towards the north and east (what is now Chad), they came into contact with the Sanūsīs, who were expanding their religious activities southwards, building their southern-most lodge in Biʾr Alali in western Chad in 1900.[23] When the French came there the following year, a battle took place and the Sanūsī had to flee. The French claimed the Sanūsī had attacked them, but it was clear that the skirmish had caught the brotherhood quite unawares. All desert lodges had some arms for protection, but they were not prepared for battle, and it was the local Teda tribes who took up

[21] It was largely such unrest, after the expulsion of the Awlād Sulaymān tribe from Fezzan in south-western Libya, which had brought the central Saharan route to its end; Dennis D. Cordell, "The Awlad Sulayman of Libya and Chad: Power and Adaptation in the Sahara and the Sahel", *Canadian Journal of African Studies* ii (1985): 319–43. For the trade, see Glauco Ciammaichella, *Libyens et Français au Tchad (1897–1914). La confrérie Senoussie et le Commerce Transsaharien* (Paris: Éditions du Centre National de la Recherche Scientifique, 1987).

[22] The full story of this "creation of a legend" is described in Jean-Louis Triaud, *La Légende Noire de la Sanûsiyya. Une Confrérie Musulmane Saharienne sous le Regard Français (1840–1930)* (Paris, 1995).

[23] Jean-Louis Triaud, *Tchad 1900–1902: Une Guerre Franco-Libyenne Oubliée? Une Confrérie Musulmane, la Sanûsiyya, face à la France* (Paris: Éditions de la Maison des sciences de l'homme, 1987), 13–36, and *Légende Noire*, 611–42.

arms against the invaders.[24] But since the French identified the "Senoussistes" (Sanūsīs) as their enemy, the tribes began to claim that they fought to protect their Sanūsī order from the infidels. Thus, these southern lodges of the order became embroiled in the conflict. The French did not have the resources to follow the enemy into the desert except for a few raids in the following years, so the war remained low-key.[25] The Sanūsī leadership sent some of their *shaykhs* south to see what they could do, but advice from them on strategy was mostly ignored by the local tribal chiefs, so the resistance, such as it was, was still a local tribal warfare, although it was fought in the Sanūsīs' name. Still, in the public mind, also on the Muslim side, the two became intermingled, and the Sanūsīs began to acquire a somewhat undeserved glory for steadfast opposition to foreign invasion, just as the French had imagined them.

In 1911, Italy invaded the Ottoman provinces of Tripolitania and Cyrenaica.[26] They were met with immediate resistance – in Cyrenaica by local Bedouin tribes, spontaneously or in cooperation with the Ottoman force. However, the Balkan wars occurring at the same time forced the Ottomans to withdraw from Libya – as the Italians now called the province – signing a treaty with Italy in October 1912. The resistance was therefore left to fend for itself, and Cyrenaica separately from Tripolitania.[27] Given the renown the Sanūsīs had acquired, deserved or not, from the Saharan campaigns, many people wanted the Sanūsī to take leadership in this war. Several tribal leaders approached its then young leader Aḥmad al-Sharīf al-Sanūsī for this.[28] Al-Sharīf was a grandson of the founder of the order, and acceded to leadership when his uncle Muḥammad al-Mahdī died in 1902. Many of the Sanūsī council of elders opposed the idea of getting involved in the war, but al-Sharīf overruled them and threw the resources of the brotherhood into the resistance. The brunt of the fighting was still done by the Bedouin, and many commanders were tribal leaders each fighting on his own, but they were now joined by Sanūsī lodge *shaykhs*, and the

[24] The Teda (Toubou, Goranes) are an African people who inhabit northern Chad and the eastern Sahara, thus ethnically and linguistically distinct from the Arab Bedouin of the Sanūsī's Cyrenaican heartland; Jean Chapelle, *Nomades Noirs de Sahara* (Paris: Plon, 1957).

[25] They returned to the region in particular after the largest kingdom in the region, Waday, had fallen in 1909, and had mostly "pacified" the Sahara by 1913.

[26] John Wright, *Libya. A Modern History* (London: Croon Helm, 1983), 25–41; Ali Abdullatif Ahmida, *The Making of Modern Libya. State Formation, Colonization and Resistance, 1830–1932* (Albany: SUNY Press, 1994), 103–40, and Dirk Vandevalle, *A History of Modern Libya* (Cambridge: Cambridge University Press, 2006), 24–42.

[27] Attempts to unify their forces failed because of distrust over the ultimate aims each party might have had over the other.

[28] Abdulmola El-Horeir, "Social and Economic Transformations in the Libyan Hinterland during the Second Half of the Nineteenth Century," (PhD Thesis, UCLA, 1981), 224–6, and Triaud, *Légende Noire*, 782–3.

lodges were transformed into resistance centres. The order could thus provide some element of cohesion and structure to the Cyrenaican war, and they were more successful in keeping the Italians at bay than the Tripolitanians were. In 1915, when Italy joined the Entente in the World War and thus became an enemy of the German–Ottoman alliance, these two came to the aid of the Cyreanicans and provided the Sanūsī with weapons and material support, thus making their resistance a part of the global conflict.[29] While this helped the resistance considerably against Italy, the Germans asked that al-Sharīf should also join the common effort by attacking the British in Egypt. The Sanūsī had some support in the western Egyptian desert, but when they crossed the border in 1916, they were no serious match for the British forces. Forcing the Sanūsī back into Libya, Britain put an end to the German–Ottoman assistance and demanded that al-Sharīf should step down as leader of the order. He was replaced by his cousin Muḥammad Idrīs, son of the previous leader al-Mahdī. He had gained the friendship of the British in Egypt, and the latter, having thus dissociated the Libyan resistance from the global war, saw no reason to impose an Italian rule that Italy clearly did not have the means to enforce. Instead, the British brokered a deal, the Akrama accord in 1917, which in effect recognized the Sanūsī leader as the temporal authority in the interior of Cyrenaica, leaving the coastal region only to the Italians. Idrīs was given the title of emir and thus had the trappings of political power, although the autonomy and power of the tribes was still the reality on the ground.

The accords lasted until 1922, the year Mussolini came to power in Italy. Prior to his takeover, the Italians had already taken up the fighting again and brought Tripolitania under effective control, but Cyrenaica remained elusive. Italy was not able to overcome the resistance of the Sanūsī and the tribes. Idrīs – who, unlike his cousin, was not a war leader – went into exile in Egypt, but remained the head of the order. The war that followed was fought in his name by tribal guerrillas. The Sanūsī structure was now heavily integrated into the struggle, and both tribal leaders and Sanūsī lodge *shaykhs* led guerrilla bands. The most successful of these, who came to unite the various groups under his command, was the Sanūsī *shaykh* ʿUmar al-Mukhtār, a native of Cyrenaica, but a Sufi, not a tribal leader.[30] He worked as *al-nāʾib al-ʿāmm* (general representative) of Idrīs, and apparently in concert with

[29] Evans-Pritchard, *Sanusi*, 104–33.

[30] Ibid., 168, and Enzo Santarelli, Giorgio Rochat, and Romain Rainero, *Omar Al-Mukhtar* (London: Darf, 1986). ʿUmar became a heroic figure beyond Libya and was also the main character, played by Anthony Quinn, in the 1981 blockbuster movie *Lion of the Desert*.

him.[31] The war was thus both a tribal Cyrenaican war and one led by Sanūsīs, and the Italians came to consider it an anti-Sanūsī war. Hence, they targeted the order, their lodges and members. The Sufi brotherhood, which had already largely been transformed into a war machine, was in this way destroyed as a religious organization by the Italians, who, after nine years of intense fighting, with tremendous hardships for the local Bedouin who were forced into concentration camps and fenced in with barbed wire, forced the guerrillas to retreat. They captured al-Mukhtār at the end of 1931 and thus brought the war to an end. But only eleven years later, their time was up when Allied forces liberated Libya, and after the world war consecrated the Sanūsī's transformation from Sufi brotherhood to temporal power by making Idrīs the first and last king in the short-lived kingdom of Libya.

The "Mad Mullah": A Sufi Jihād*ist*

The last example of Sufi-related resistance was almost contemporaneous with that of the Sanūsī, and came from an order distantly related to theirs. The youngest of Aḥmad b. Idrīs's students was Ibrāhīm al-Rashīd (d. 1874), after whom the Rashīdiyya order was established in the Sudan in the 1870s, known in Egypt as the Dandarawiyya.[32] Al-Rashīd's nephew, al-Shaykh Muḥammad b. Ṣāliḥ (d. 1919) brought the order to Somalia, where it took the latter's name and became known as the Ṣāliḥiyya.[33] In Mecca, he recruited an activist Somali scholar, Muḥammad ʿAbd Allāh Ḥassān (1864–1920). On his return home in 1895, Abdille Hassan (as he was known) began spreading the order but also preached social reform, such as abstention from tobacco and qat. He also preached against the growing foreign presence in the region, and it seems intentional that he provoked a conflict with the British that four years after his return led to a full-scale *jihād* against them and the later Italian arrivals. Unifying the clans and at times playing on the divisions between the colonial powers, he was able to set up a small state that, however, came to an end when he died in 1920.[34]

31 Later historiography, in particular that of the Qadhāfī era, sought to depict a split between the "cowardly" Sufi hiding under British protection in Egypt and the "courageous" anti-imperialist hero of al-Mukhtār. Rather, the two played complementary roles, with Idrīs ensuring British sympathy for the war.

32 Mark Sedgwick, *Saints and Sons. The Making and Remaking of the Rashīdi Aḥmadi Sufi Order, 1799–2000* (Leiden: Brill, 2005).

33 O'Fahey, *Enigmatic Saint*, 163–5 and Karrar, *Sufi Brotherhoods*, 109–10.

34 I. M. Lewis, "Sufism in Somaliland: A Study in Tribal Islam" in Akbar S. Ahmed and D. M. Hart (eds), *Islam in Tribal Societies, from the Atlas to the Indus* (London: Routledge & Kegan Paul, 1984), 127–68, and A. S. Bemath, "The Sayyid and the Saalihiya

Abdille Hassan was thus another conscious *jihād* leader who sought to use Sufi authority both for his social reform before the *jihād* and in the struggle. However, he was only a local leader of the Ṣāliḥiyya, and he was repudiated by the head of the order in Mecca, dividing the Ṣāliḥiyya in Somalia into pro- and anti-*jihād* factions. He could not command the support of all of the Ṣāliḥī centres, many of which had been set up independently of him.

These examples of Sufi resistance to colonialism show that there is no single or direct link between Sufi organization and militant action. The actors all came to oppose colonial power in different ways, and the Sufi element in each of their struggles is different: ʿAbd al-Qādir sought the *jihād*, and used a pre-existing Sufi legitimacy inherited from his father and grandfather to establish his authority, but did not use the Sufi background any further in his struggle or in the state he tried to establish. The Sanūsī had the *jihād* thrust upon them by circumstances: it was largely the French who, through their mis-conception of them as a "secret society", pushed the Sanūsī into activism. But once they had thrown their weight into the struggle, they did use the Sufi structures for all that they were worth in their war against Italy, at the cost of destroying the brotherhood as a religious movement. *Al-ḥājj* ʿUmar also used his Sufi authority as representative of the otherwise fully "quietist" Tijāniyya for his *jihād*. This, however, was not an anti-colonialist effort, but one directed against previous Muslim rulers and neighbouring "pagan" kingdoms. He too had the anti-colonialist struggle pushed upon him by French advances, and it was primarily during his son's time at the helm that his *jihād* turned into anti-colonial resistance. Abdille Hassan, finally, was the one who most clearly conformed to the notion of a Sufi who intentionally sets out, on the basis of social and political reform, to lead a *jihād* based on Sufi authority. But he was disowned by his own Sufi superiors, and in effect, like all the others, ended up in leading a small short-lived state based as much on traditional local leadership and tribal alliances as on any particular Sufi ideal.

Sufism was not the only religious pattern for Muslim resistance to colonial advance. Equally widespread was the use of the *mahdī* conception.[35] The most famous and successful of the *mahdī* movements was that of Muḥammad Aḥmad in the Sudan, who in 1881–85 united most of what is now the republic of Sudan in a revolt against the British-supported Egyptian rule of his country and established a religious state that lasted more than a decade after his own

tariqa: Reformist, anticolonial hero in Somalia" in Said S. Samatar (ed.), *In the Shadow of Conquest. Islam in Colonial Northeast Africa* (Trenton, NJ: Red Sea Press, 1992), 33–47.

[35] The *mahdī* is the supernatural figure who, before the Day of Resurrections, shall lead the believers to victory and re-establish true religion.

death.[36] But he was far from the only *mahdī* of this time. Others sprang up in West Africa, and several arose in Algeria after the defeat of ʿAbd al-Qādir's larger movement.[37] Apart from the Sudanese Mahdi, they all failed, sometimes after surprising initial success. It would thus seem that Sufism and Mahdism were two alternative models to recruit an ad-hoc movement against foreign invasion, and they seem in particular to appear when the established Muslim state structures have either been crushed by the invaders or were never there in the first place.

Of the two, Mahdist movements are almost always overtly political and revolutionary. They spring up when a pretender's claim to the status of the expected *mahdī* is accepted by a sufficiently large number of people. It has the advantage that the *mahdī*, if he is believed, can guarantee victory and even, in cases, invulnerability against the enemy's bullets. This, and the speed of such a movement's rise, can give them rapid victories over a surprised enemy force, which further confirms the pretender's claims and extends his support. But it is a volatile support. The pretender's proof of his *mahdī*-hood is only his person and that he is always victorious. Once the enemy is able to gather enough strength to win one or more battles against him, the falsity of his claim to be *mahdī* is proven, and his supporters may desert him in the blink of an eye.

A Sufi resistance leader also bases his legitimacy and authority on his own personality as a friend of God and his acknowledged personal piety. It is these special qualities and his religious status that make his supporters willing to follow him. But these qualities are not dependent on constant victories in war. His Sufi legitimacy, be it individual as a *shaykh* or vested in a larger brotherhood, has a foundation outside the political field. Therefore, his movement can well support failures on the battlefield without losing support or legitimacy. In fact, the followers may not expect the Sufi to conduct or take part in the actual struggle; it is sufficient that he is the focus around which the battle is fought. Furthermore, if he is part of one of the more centralized Sufi brotherhoods, such as the Sanūsiyya or Tijāniyya (but not so much the loose Qādiriyya), there are direct organizational and networking resources such as "chains of command" that can be utilized in a protracted struggle. So, while a Sufi-based resistance movement may be less spectacular than a

[36] P. M. Holt, *The Mahdist State in the Sudan, 1881–98* (Oxford: Clarendon Press, 1979).

[37] Julia A. Clancy-Smith, *Rebel and Saint. Muslim Notables, Populist Protest, Colonial Encounters (Algeria and Tunisia 1800–1904)* (Berkeley: University of California Press, 1994), and K. S. Vikør, "Sufism and foreign rule in Africa: politics and piety" in Sato Tsugitaka (ed.), *Muslim Societies. Historical and Comparative Aspects* (London: RoutledgeCurzon, 2004), 9–28.

Mahdist one, and the religious elements in time become more subdued both in the propaganda (where traditional *jihād* conceptions will take priority) and in practice, it may prove more enduring and robust than that of a Mahdist revolt.

SUFI ADAPTATION

The Two Faces of the Fāḍiliyya

That the Sufis' choice of how to react to colonialism did not stem from their *ṭarīqa* ideas can be seen from the difference between the Tijāniyya's response to the French advance in North Africa and that of the Tijānī *al-ḥājj* ʿUmar, above. An even more clear example is that of the two leaders of the Fāḍiliyya brotherhood in the western Sahara.[38] The brothers Muṣṭafā and Saʿd Būh (d. 1917), who both inherited authority from their father, took diametrically opposing political views and yet remained united in their Sufi affiliation. Muṣṭafā, more known by his nickname Māʾ al-ʿAynayn, took up arms against the French in Western Sahara, Mauritania and southern Morocco, partly in alliance with the Moroccan sultan, and led the tribal resistance there until his death in 1910. His younger brother, on the other hand, who established himself further south, made close contact with the French. He may therefore be seen as a "collaborator" to the colonialists. However, the "collaboration" was not just an acquiescence, but rather an adaptation where the Sufi leaders tried to use the new political realities as resources to promote their ideals and Sufi aspirations. Thus, they were not "passivists", as they were seen by the colonial ethnographers and later nationalist ideologues, but were actively using the French or other political powers to promote their own agenda and interests.

Saʿd set up his centre in Trarza in southern Mauritania.[39] This is a fairly desolate region, but Saʿd gained a following on the more prosperous southern bank of the Senegal river and beyond. By frequently travelling there on "collection tours", he could gather material support from the brotherhood's followers, support that was extremely important for the survival for his community. Thus, he had to compose with the political masters of the region. Clearly the improved communications and stability in the region were also

38 David Robinson, "Saʿd Buh and the Fadiliyya and French Colonial Authorities," *Islam et Sociétés au Sud du Sahara*, 11 (1997): 129–48, and Rahal Boubrik, *Saints et Société en Islam. La Confrérie Ouest Saharienne Fâdiliyya* (Paris: CNRS Éditions, 1999).

39 David Robinson, *Paths of Accommodation. Muslim Societies and French Colonial Authorities in Senegal and Mauritania, 1880–1920* (Athens, OH: Ohio University Press, 2000), 161–93.

important in allowing him to travel regularly with much greater ease to a larger area and spread his *ṭarīqa*. He also came to disagree with his brother's use of *jihād*, a concept he believed was not applicable to the circumstances of the day. Thus, he published a religious critique of his brother's campaign, a pamphlet that the French evidently adopted and spread with great energy in those regions of Mauritania where Mā al-ʿAynayn was still active.[40]

The Tijāniyya Under French Rule

The premise for Saʿd's acceptance of French rule was clearly that it was an indisputable fact. By his time, the prospect of defeating the colonial power by military means had shown itself to be unrealistic. The same realization can be seen in the later development of the Tijānīs in the region. After the fall of the ʿUmarian state in the 1890s, the most important disseminator of the order was probably Mālik Sy (1855–1922).[41] He had a background in one of the smaller *jihād*ist states in Senegal, but by the time he had grown up, completed his education and joined the Tijāniyya, that state had been swept aside by the colonial power. Mālik had been influenced by ʿUmar's Sufi scholarship, but sought a separate initiation into the order, so as not to be an "ʿUmarian" Tijānī. He stayed away from any public appearance before he began to collect followers in his centre in Tiwawane, and it was only in 1910 that the French became aware of him. As he expressed his acceptance and support for the colonial regime, he was allowed to develop and prosper, and seemed not to have had any problems with the colonial regime; he also did not seek them out, but let them come to him if they needed to.

His branch of the Tijāniyya thus developed rapidly to become the largest of the three major branches of the order in Senegal. As they practiced a policy of acceptance, but at a distance, of the colonial power, the relation must mainly be described as one of polite remoteness.

Not so with the apparent heir to *al-ḥājj* ʿUmar's Sufi legacy in Senegal, at least in French eyes. The grand-nephew of the great *jihād* leader, Sayyid Nūru Tall (d. 1980), formed a close relationship with the authorities, toured the

[40] Dedoud ould Abdallah, "Guerre sainte ou sédition blâmable? *Nasiha* de shaikh Sa'd Bu contre le *jihad* de son frère shaikh Ma al-Ainin" in David Robinson et Jean-Louis Triaud (eds), *Le Temps des Marabouts* (Paris: Karthala, 1997), 119–54.

[41] L. A. Villalón, *Islamic Society and State Power in Senegal. Disciples and Citizens in Fatick* (Cambridge: Cambridge University Press, 1995), 67–8, 139–40; David Robinson, "Malik Sy: un intellectuel dans l'ordre colonial au Sénégal", *Islam et Sociétés au Sud du Sahara*, 7 (1993), 183–92; idem, *Paths of Accommodation*, 194–207; and "Malik Sy: Teacher in the New Colonial Order" in Jean-Louis Triaud and David Robinson (eds), *La Tijâniyya* (Paris: Karthala, 2000), 201–18.

country and region with a message of support and acceptance of the French order, and was in return showered with distinction and support by the authorities, as *grand marabout* – "head Sufi" – in the region.[42] His political views must be considered opportunistic in that they were based on support for the power-that-be, whichever it was. Thus he argued for the Vichy government when it held the power in Senegal, but was one of the important elements of the Free French supporters when they took over the colony in 1942, and he was a pillar of president Senghor's rule after independence.

Clearly, however, the relation was not one-sided. During his many travels for the authorities, Nūru Tall was also actively working to spread his branch of the Tijāniyya, and formed many local groups. While this ʿUmarian branch remained smaller than those of his two rivals, Mālik Sy in Tiwawane and Ibrāhīm Niasse of Kaolack,[43] it was clear that Nūru used his relationship with the French as a method to spread his Sufi organization and promote its ideas.

The French did not just support the "friendly" Sufis indirectly by allowing them to travel in the country and to collect followers; they also gave material assistance, financing the building of mosques and other enterprises. It was to the benefit of the colonialists to have the religious experience organized in a manner they could oversee, but it was also to the benefit of the Sufis that the colonial authorities allowed them to form solid and nationwide networks of Sufi authority. That the various Sufi brotherhoods were in competition, both the various branches of the Tijāniyya and other brotherhoods, also played a role. Each of them needed to accumulate supporters both for religious status and authority, but also because followers translated into economic support. In this competition, access to the political power of the day was not without importance and had to be utilized.

Sufism and Peanuts: The Murīdiyya

The other large *ṭarīqa* in Senegal, the Murīdiyya, followed a parallel development of building up a rich and powerful economic and social structure within the colonial framework.[44] While earlier Sufis had based their economy on

[42] Sylvianne Garcia, "Al-Hajj Seydou Nourou Tall, 'Grand marabout' tijani: L'histoire d'un carrière (v. 1880–1980)" in Robinson and Triaud, *Le Temps des Marabouts*, 247–76.

[43] On the Niassiyya branch, see Villalón, *Islamic Society and State Power*, and Rüdiger Seesemann, *The Divine Flood. Ibrāhīm Niasse and the Roots of a Twentieth-Century Sufi Revival* (Oxford: University Press, 2011).

[44] Donal B. Cruise O'Brien, *The Mourides of Senegal. The Political and Economic Organization of an Islamic Brotherhood* (Oxford: Clarendon Press, 1971), and Jean Copans, *Les Marabouts de l'arachide* (Paris: Karthala, 1980).

trade, the Murīdiyya turned to production, in particular of peanuts, Senegal's main agricultural export. This, while fully under the brotherhood's control and based on the work of their younger brethren, also followed the French goal of *mise en valeur* – utilization of the colony. The Murīdiyya was thus allowed an almost free hand in building their centre at Touba, which became a city that in many ways expressed a Sufi urbanism, the city structure reflecting the religious ideals of the brotherhood.[45]

Nevertheless, the French relations with this brotherhood had a rather rocky start. Its founder, Aḥmadu Bamba (d. 1927), had joined the Qādiriyya *ṭarīqa* in Mauritania, but developed it into a branch carrying his own name, focused on work-and-learning centres that laid the foundations for its later peanut empire.[46] When the French became aware of his increasing following in the early 1890s, they became worried. As Bamba did not appear in front of them when summoned and only sent a deputy, they charged him in 1895 with being a Tijānī and thus a supporter of *jihād* (this was, after all, before the end of the ʿUmarian campaign, but ignored the rivalry between the two *ṭarīqa*s), and exiled him to Gabon. However, the following of his brotherhood grew in his absence, and in the end forced the French to allow him to return in 1902. The following year, however, he was sent into another exile, but this time only to nearby Mauritania, where he renewed contact with his Qādirī fellows. It did not hamper the expansion of his support in Senegal, and the French made no move to restrict the brotherhood's activity. They clearly had accepted its positive economic and social function, and in 1912 Bamba was finally released from French confinement. By this time, he had also made his first public statement in favour of French colonial rule, an issue he had so far been silently aloof about.

Ḥamāhu 'llāh: Distance

Aloofness is also the main characteristic of another Sufi leader who was harassed by the French in spite of never taking any offensive stance against them in words or action. Aḥmad Ḥamāhu 'llāh had at a young age received his initiation directly from the Tijāniyya centre in the Maghreb and established himself in Nioro (today's western Mali) around 1909. He soon began to acquire followers not just in the immediate neighbourhood, but eventually

[45] Eric Ross, *Sufi City. Urban Design and Archetypes in Touba* (Rochester: University of Rochester Press, 2006)

[46] Rüdiger Seesemann, *Aḥmadu Bamba und die Entstehung der Murīdīya* (Berlin: Schwartz, 1993), and Robinson, *Paths of Accommodation*, 208–28.

throughout much of French-controlled West Africa. He distinguished himself in particular from competing Tijānī branches by the recital of a Tijānī prayer ritual that was called "eleven grain" as opposed to the regular "twelve grain" Tijānīs.[47] Ḥamāhu 'llāh lived a withdrawn and almost reclusive life, but because of the rapid expansion of his brotherhood, the "Ḥamawiyya" branch of the Tijāniyya, he became very controversial in the region, within the Tijānī circles, where in particular the ʿUmarian branch and its leader Nūru Tall criticized Ḥamāhu 'llāh, but also in a local conflict with a community at neighbouring Tinwanju, either Qādirī or non-Sufi, which became violent in 1924.

The French authorities had already looked at Ḥamāhu 'llāh's growing support with some worry, although he did not make any political statements relating to colonial rule. He had, however, studiously ignored the French authorities and did not acknowledge their summons to present himself to the colonial authorities, feeding their wariness. Using the trouble with Tinwanju as a pretext, they decided to exile him for ten years in 1925, as they had done with Aḥmadu Bamba a generation earlier, this time to the Ivory Coast. As in Bamba's case, the exile only increased the support for Ḥamāhu 'llāh, bestowing the aura of an unjustly persecuted holy man. The French were thus no less worried when he returned after the assigned period and they learned that he had changed his prayer ritual – reducing the regular four *rakʿa*s of the daily prayer to two – as a sign of possible sedition. This, because the two-*rakʿa* prayer is allowed for travellers, and the French linked that to preparations for *jihād*. Many French therefore saw "Hamallisme" as a type of crypto-militant movement, while others insisted it was just what it appeared to be – a religious movement around a charismatic leader. In any case, Ḥamāhu 'llāh was sent into exile again, this time to France, where he died in 1943.

Sufism in Colonial Politics: The Khatmiyya

A much more cordial, and even inter-dependent role for a Sufi order under colonialism can be found in the Nilotic Sudan. The Mahdi was hostile to Sufi orders, even though he himself had been a member of a Sufi order, the Sammāniyya, before he appeared as *mahdī*. In particular, he suspected the

[47] Referring to how many times this particular prayer was to be recited; C. Hamès, "Cheikh Ḥamallah, ou qu'est-ce qu'une confrérie islamique (*ṭarîqa*)?", *Archives des Sciences Sociales des Religions*, 55 (1983): 67–83; Louis Brenner, *West African Sufi. The Religious Heritage and Spiritual Search of Cerno Bokar Saalif Taal* (London: Hurst, 1984), 45–59; and Benjamin F. Soares, *Islam and the Prayer Economy. History and Authority in a Malian Town* (Edinburgh: Edinburgh University Press, 2005), 69–105.

Khatmiyya order of favouring Egyptian rule. The Khatmiyya was established by Muḥammad ʿUthmān al-Mīrghanī (1793–1852), the eldest student of Aḥmad ibn Idrīs, in the 1820s.[48] They were thus in their ideas related to the Sanūsiyya of Libya, although the relations between the two were not very close. The Khatmiyya had spread extensively in the Sudan to become the largest Sufi order there, keeping completely out of the political arena. But their size and importance, and the fact that they did not acknowledge his authority, clearly made the Mahdi see them as a potential challenger, and he banned them.

When the Mahdist state fell in 1898 and the British established what was formally a "condominium" under British control, the enmity from the defeated Mahdists came to the benefit of the Khatmiyya. They were favoured by the new authorities and their leader, ʿAlī al-Mīrghanī (1873–1968), forged close links with the British. Between the world wars, however, the remnants of the defeated Mahdists re-invented themselves as a religious-political organization, the Anṣār, under the Mahdi's youngest son, ʿAbd al-Raḥmān (1885–1959), borrowing largely from a Sufi pattern of organization rather than a Mahdist one.[49] Overcoming British suspicions, ʿAbd al-Raḥmān made his Anṣār an important political force. The Khatmiyya leaders saw this as a challenge to their own position, and began organizing their own political activity, in parallel with and not in place of their religious Sufi structure. The two thus became the two major rivalling political forces in the country before independence in 1956; the Khatmiyya formalized it in 1950 by establishing the "National Unionist Party" (today the Democratic Unionist Party). Since independence the two parties – the Khatmiyya-based DUP and the Anṣār-based Umma party – have dominated civilian politics in the Sudan to this day. Both are fairly conservative, notable-dominated parties, and both are dominated by the heads of the two respective religious families, the Mīrghanīs and the Mahdī family.

ORGANIZATION, OPPORTUNITY AND IDENTITY

While the imposition of the colonial system may, like most other political events, have affected Sufi adherents as members of the wider Muslim community more than as Sufis in particular, we can thus see that there are interactions between colonialism and Sufism in many cases. They varied

48 Karrar, *Sufi Brotherhoods*, 73–102.

49 Gabriel Warburg, *Islam, Sectarianism and Politics in Sudan since the Mahdiya* (London: Hurst, 2003).

from militant anti-colonial *jihād* to close interaction with and support for the colonialists. These differences did not follow *ṭarīqa* lines or doctrinal variations, but rather context and personal choice. Sufi brotherhoods and leaders could provide popular support, organization and a charismatic authority that had a revolutionary potential that could be released when traditional Muslim political powers were absent.

There is, however, also a clear chronological development. Once the colonial power was established and stable, Sufi-led resistance disappeared and was replaced with either cooperation with or avoidance of the temporal powers. While the resistance certainly enhanced the charisma and renown of these defenders of Islam, it was seldom of great benefit for the Sufi organizations that took part. Their conversion to militancy most often wore down the religious structures, and none of the Sufi brotherhoods that were most active in resistance grew from the efforts; most declined or faded away. The Tijāniyya, spearheaded in West Africa by *al-ḥājj* ʿUmar, certainly grew to become the dominant *ṭarīqa* in sub-Saharan Africa, spreading all over the continent with millions of adherents, but it was not the ʿUmarian branch of his descendants that came to dominate it – and that branch itself grew primarily by moving even closer to the colonial power than its rivals. The larger Tijānī branches all emphasized that they had their initiation from different sources than that of *al-ḥājj* ʿUmar, in spite of the reverence all held for his charisma and religious authority within the order.

It is undeniable that the great expansion of Sufism in colonial Africa took place *under* colonialism, not before. Some orders were present in the precolonial period, but most often in small circles, restricted locally or socially. After the French and British had taken control, however, we see a Sufi explosion that only continued after the colonies became independent states. There are probably many reasons for this, and some clearly had to do with "modernity". Practical improvements like better communication and easier movement over larger regions helped spread the message of the various *ṭarīqa*s. The increased following led to an increase in economic resources for the brotherhoods, resources that could in turn be used for further expansion. The Murīdiyya's successful economic ventures into peanut farming, which made them very rich and gave them political clout in post-colonial Senegal, is only one example of how the brotherhoods made use of the new opportunities that the colonial system afforded.

But it is probably also true that Sufi affiliations had important religious and ideological functions in the period of colonial rule. The brotherhoods were ways to focus an Islamic identity and community, and they became centres for the faith of many ordinary Muslims to a greater degree than the mosques, which were more atomized sites for religious ritual than community structures. These new functions of Sufi affiliation were not an intended or even direct result of the colonial experience, and have become even more prevalent in the period after independence in most post-colonial states. But they show how Sufism was affected by the changing contexts and how they provided a continuity beyond the vagaries of political developments.

FURTHER READING

Julia A. Clancy-Smith, *Rebel and Saint. Muslim Notables, Populist Protest, Colonial Encounters* (Algeria and Tunisia 1800–1904) (Berkeley: University of California Press, 1994).

Raphael Danziger, *Abd al-Qadir and the Algerians. Resistance to the French and Internal Consolidation* (New York: Holmes & Meier, 1977).

B. O. Oloruntimehin, *The Segu Tukolor Empire* (London: Longman, 1972).

Jean-Louis Triaud, *La Légende Noire de la Sanûsiyya. Une Confrérie Musulmane Saharienne sous le Regard Français* (1840–1930) (Paris: Éditions le la Maison des sciences de l'homme, 1995).

Said S. Samatar (ed.), *In the Shadow of Conquest. Islam in Colonial Northeast Africa* (Trenton, NJ: Red Sea Press, 1992), 33–47.

David Robinson and Jean-Louis Triaud (eds), *Le Temps des Marabouts* (Paris: Karthala, 1997).

Donal B. Cruise O'Brien, *The Mourides of Senegal. The Political and Economic Organization of an Islamic Brotherhood* (Oxford: Clarendon Press, 1971).

Benjamin F. Soares, *Islam and the Prayer Economy. History and Authority in a Malian Town* (Edinburgh: Edinburgh University Press, 2005).

David Robinson, *Paths of Accommodation: Muslim Societies and French Colonial Authorities in Senegal and Mauritania 1880–1920*, (Athens, OH: Ohio University Press, 2000).

10

Sufism in the West

Ron Geaves

This chapter raises the question of what constitutes the "West". For the purposes of this article the "West" will be understood as a geographic entity consisting of Europe and North America, but with an awareness that the term implies some kind of cultural terrain containing commonality, and in its construction standing distinct from the "East". Sufism's origins in Islam place its study firmly in the terrain of Western constructions of the "East", but this chapter will show that Sufism exists in the in-between spaces and always in transition. In parts of Europe, especially Britain and Germany, Sufism should be understood in the context of Romantic orientalist reconstructions of Islam and an appropriation of Sufism as a form of universal mysticism which removed the tradition from its Islamic roots. In the USA this reconstruction has led Marcia Hermansen to categorize various Sufi movements as "theirs" and "ours".[1] However, in addition to nineteenth and early twentieth-century Romantic interest in mysticism, Sufism also needs to be understood in the context of post-colonial Muslim migrations into Western Europe, the presence of indigenous Muslim communities in Eastern Europe left behind by the collapse of the Ottoman Empire, and finally Western conversion to Islam.[2]

Contact between Sufism and European orientalism can be dated back as far as the translations of Saʿdi's *Gulistān* into German in the early decades of the seventeenth century, reaching its pinnacle in Germany in the nineteenth century.[3] Gritt Klinkhammer informs us that Johann-Wolfgang von Goethe

[1] See Marcia Hermansen, "Global Sufism: Theirs and Ours", in *Sufis in Western Society*, eds Geaves, Ron, Dressler, Markus, Klinkhammer, Gritt (London: Routledge, 2009), 26–45.

[2] Sufism is considered by some authors to be the main route to conversion to Islam. See Ali Köse, *Conversion to Islam* (London: Kegan Paul, 1996) and Kate Zebiri, *British Muslim Converts: Choosing Alternative Lives* (London: Oneworld Publications, 2007).

[3] Saʿdi was first introduced to the West in a French translation by André du Ryer (1634) on which Friedrich Ochsenbach based his German translation (1636). Georgius Gentius

praised the writings of the Muslim mystics Rumi and Hafiz, and the writings of the Sufis were known to Friedrich Rűckert, who translated the first poetic version of the Qu'ran into German.[4] In the eighteenth century, Sir William Jones, the British orientalist, initiated his project to translate classical Persian texts at the Asiatic Society founded in Calcutta in 1784.[5] German scholarship arose out of an interest in the Orient that led to travellers, orientalists, and artists visiting various parts of the East and creating a body of literature consisting of travelogues, oriental fiction, and translations of mystical poetry. In the main the German reception of the Orient differed from that of Britain and France, in that Germany had no colonial encounter.[6] Consequently, the orientalism involved in the European study of Sufism was of a different kind to that of the classical discourse of colonization framed by Edward Said. Hourani criticizes Said for ignoring the German tradition of orientialism and the philosophy of history that was central to their work. He is more specific when he states that Said carries his criticism of the orientalists too far, when he claimed that they all "delivered the Orient bound to the imperial powers".[7] Sadiq al-Azm argues that Said had rendered a disservice to those who desired to study other cultures from a "libertarian perspective".[8] All these critiques of Said are pertinent to the Western study of Sufism.

produced a Latin version accompanied by the Persian text in 1651. Adam Olearius also made the first direct and complete German translation in 1651 (Franklin Lewis, "Golestān-e Sa'di" in *Encyclopaedia Iranica* Vol. XI, Fasc. 1, 2001, 79–86). The *Gulistan* has been translated into English many times: Stephen Sullivan (London, 1774, selections), James Dumoulin (Calcutta: 1807), Francis Gladwin (Calcutta, 1808, preface by Ralph Waldo Emerson), James Ross (London, 1823), S. Lee (London: 1827), Edward Backhouse Eastwick (Hartford: 1852; republished by Octagon Press, 1979), Johnson (London, 1863), John T. Platts (London, 1867), Edward Henry Whinfield (London: 1880), Edward Rehatsek (Banaras, 1888, in some later editions incorrectly attributed to Sir Richard Burton), Sir Edwin Arnold (London: 1899), Launcelot Alfred Cranmer-Byng (London, 1905), Celwyn E. Hampton (New York: 1913), and Arthur John Arberry (London: 1945, the first two chapters). More recent English translations have been published by Omar Ali-Shah (1997) and by Wheeler M. Thackston (2008).

4 Gritt Klinkhammer (2009) "The Emergence of Transethnic Sufism in Germany: From Mysticism to Authenticity", in *Sufis in Western Society*, eds Geaves et al., 130–147.

5 Ḥafeẓ's first ode and now familiar quatrains of 'Omar Ḵayyam appeared in Latin as early as Sir Thomas Hyde's *Syntagma Dissertationum* (1700). Both William Jones and Edward FitzGerald translated from Persian into Latin. William Jones' most famous English translation was the ghazal of Ḥafeẓ, which he entitled "A Persian Song" and published twice, first in his *Grammar of the Persian Language* (1771), in conjunction with a prose translation, and a year later in his *Poems Consisting Chiefly of Translations from the Asiatick Languages* (Michael Beard "Translations Of Classical Persian Literature" in *Encyclopaedia Iranica* Vol. VIII, Fasc. 4, 1998, 443–447.

6 Klinkhammer, "The Emergence of Transethnic Sufism in Germany", 130.

7 *Interview with Albert Hourani in Approaches to the History of the Middle East*, ed. Nancy Elizabeth Gallagher (London: Ithaca *Press*, 1994), 30, quoted in Ibn Warraq, *Defending the West: A Critique of Edward Said's Orientalism* (New York: Prometheus Books, 2007), 52.

8 Sadiq al-Azm, "Orientalism and Orientalism in Reverse" in *Forbidden Agendas: Intolerance and Defiance in the Middle East*, ed. Jon Rothschild (London: Al-Saqi Books, 1988), 350 ff.

The British history of scholarship is more complex in that many of the first translators of Sufi works were associated with the colonial enterprise, arriving in parts of the expanding Eastern territories as administrators or missionaries. In general, the perception of Islam was negative, arguably framed in an older discourse in which Islam was Christendom's hostile "other". However, the reception of Sufism was far more ambivalent. The early history of comparative religion is marked by a quest for origins. The translations of classical Sufi texts, especially those written by exponents of mysticism and poetically describing experiences of intimacy with God, appeared to the orientalists as something markedly different from the practices and teachings of Muhammad. This would lead to immense speculation on the origins of Sufism. Throughout the eighteenth and nineteenth centuries, European orientalists would develop the thesis that Sufism and Islam were separate religious phenomena, formed from diverse origins but coming together historically to create a new syncretism in the Muslim world. According to such theories, Sufism's origins are variously found in Syrian Christian monasticism, Greek neo-Platonism, Zoroastrianism, and Indian religious traditions. Sufism is assumed to have emerged as the Arab conquerors made contact with these older religious worldviews. There is never any mention of the Sufi understandings of their origins in the exemplary ethical and religious life of the Prophet and his companions or even of developments in the Muslim world after the death of Muhammad.

who are orientalists

A number of prominent orientalists, including Adalbert Merx (1838–1909), Ignaz Goldziher (1850–1921), Theodore Noeldeke (1836–1930), Miguel Asin Palacios (1871–1944), Tor Andrae (1885–1947), and Reynold Nicholson (1868–1945), have all suggested that Sufism emerged out of Islamic contact with Eastern Christianity's traditions of asceticism.[9] Some prominent Muslim religious scholars were even unsure about Sufism's origins. Ibn Taymiyya (d. 1127), the Hanbali critic of Sufism, argued that Sufis were attracted to poverty and dependence on a spiritual guide as a result of contact with Christian monasticism.[10] If some were to see Sufi practices demonstrating links with Christian monasticism, others such as E.H. Whinfield (1835–1922), E.G. Browne (1862–1926), and Louis Massignon (1883–1962) sought the origins of Sufi theosophy in the neo-Platonic writings of Plotinus, Gnostic and Dionysian cults encountered in Egypt and through translation of Greek

[9] Rida Suliyman Hishmat, "Sufism and Orientalism" in *Sufism: An Entry from Encyclopaedia of the World of Islam*, eds Gholamali Haddad Adel, Mohammad Jafar Elmi, Hassan Taromi-Rad (London: EWI Press, 2012), 205–206.

[10] Hishmat, "Sufism and Orientalism", 206.

philosophy into Arabic in the eighth and ninth centuries.[11] One of the earliest European writers on Sufism, Friedrich Thöluck (1799–1877), claimed that Sufism had emerged from the Magian or Zoroastrian religion in ancient Persia.[12] Although Thöluck would later change his view,[13] others such as Reinhard Dozy (1820–1883),[14] Edgard Blochet (1870–1937),[15] and Browne continued to endorse this viewpoint, with Blochet also speculating that Sufism had parallels with Manichaen and Mazdakite religious practices.[16] The German orientalists Max Horten (1874–1945), Richard Hartmann (1881–1965), and Alfred Von Kremer (1828–1889) would go further east for the origins of Sufism and argue that there were marked parallels between the Sufi view of the relations between God, humanity and creation with Vedantic teachings found in the Upanishads.[17] They would point towards various sayings of the famed mystics of Sufism – Husayn ibn Mansur al-Hallaj (c858–922), Abu Yazid al-Bastami, (804–874), and Abu'l Qasim al-Junayd of Baghdad (830–910) – linking them to discourses on Brahman/Atman unity and the illusionary nature of the world found in Vedantic philosophy. Others were to argue that Sufism contained diverse elements from all of the above. Significantly, Nicholson, previously an exponent of the view that Sufism had originated from an intermingling of neo-Platonic, Christian, and Gnostic

[11] Hishmat, "Sufism and Orientalism", 207.

[12] Klinkhammer, "The Emergence of Transethnic Sufism in Germany", 133, and Hishmat, "Sufism and Orientalism", 209. Friedrich August Grottreu Thöluck was a Protestant theologian and linguist with an interest in the Orient who published one of the earliest books on Sufism in Europe. Born at Breslau, 30 March 1799, he studied at the universities of Breslau and Berlin. He became a university lecturer (Privatdocent) at Berlin in December 1820, and extraordinary professor of Theology there in April 1823 (D.D. from Berlin in 1826). In November 1825, he was appointed ordinary professor of Theology at Halle (http://www.hymnary.org/person/Thöluck_A1, visited on 13 September 2012).

[13] See Klinkhammer, "The Emergence of Transethnic Sufism in Germany", 133.

[14] Reinhard Dozy (b. Leiden, 21 February 1820; d. Leiden, 29 April 1883) was a Dutch orientalist renowned especially as a lexicographer of Arabic and a historian of Muslim Andalusia. He began his studies at Leiden University in 1834 with H.E. Weijers (1804–1840), who introduced him to Arabic philology through the Warner collection of manuscripts in the university library (http://www.iranicaonline.org/articles/dozy, visited 12 September 2012).

[15] Edgard Blochet was a French orientalist, born at Bourges on 12 December 1870. He attended L'Ecole des Langues Orientales in Paris, where he received a diploma in Arabic; he also received a diploma from L'Ecole Pratique des Hautes Etudes and later lectured there (from 1895 to 1901). In 1895 he joined the manuscript department of the Bibliothèque Nationale as an assistant, subsequently becoming deputy librarian and finally, in 1929, adjunct curator (http://www.iranicaonline.org/articles/blochet-gabriel-french-orientalist, visited 12 September 2012).

[16] Hishmat, "Sufism and Orientalism", 209.

[17] Alwi Shihab, *Examining Islam in the West: Addressing Accusations and Correcting Misconceptions*. Jakarta: Gramedia Pustaka Utama, 2011, p. 178; Hishmat, "Sufism and Orientalism", 209.

teachings, further influenced by Hindu and Persian thought, did eventually argue that it was "categorically improper" to perceive Sufism as extraneous to Islam and defended the profound mystical truths of the Qur'ān and the *ḥadith*.[18] Paul Noya and Helmut Ritter (1892–1971) also wrote that the allegorical language of the Sufi mystics was rooted in the Qur'ān[19], but the damage had been done and it would be many decades into the latter half of the twentieth century before Sufism in the West was reclaimed by Muslims into the fold of traditional Islam.

Gritt Klinkhammer argues that the German orientalists sought the roots of Sufism outside of Islam until the beginning of the twentieth century, with Richard Hartmann, for example, describing Sufism as a new syncretistic mystical phenomenon that only later turned towards Islam.[20] Klinkhammer notes that in Weber's analysis, Islam lacked an individual search for salvation and mysticism, and Sufism was perceived as an "orgiastic and contemplative mass movement" that prevented the "development of inner-worldly acculturation of Shari'a Islam".[21] The effect on Sufism in the West was twofold. The first impacted on the academic study of Sufism and the second on the development of Sufism as a religious form in Europe and North America. The separation of Sufism from its Islamic roots led to an over-emphasis on the translation of classical Sufi mystical literature at the expense of the lived religion practised throughout the Muslim world and perceived as part and parcel of a normative Islamic worldview, even if deeply contested in the Muslim majority world. The everyday vernacular religion of saint veneration, healing practices, *shaykh/murid* transnational networks, religious disciplines and beliefs disappeared from the academic gaze, drowned out by the voices that embraced metaphysical truths associated with mystical union. Following from Weber, sociologists of religion would regard the above lived reality of Sufism in everyday Muslim life as primitive religion fit only for rural village life. Ernest Gellner would advocate a dichotomy between an intellectual urban Islam associated with compliance to the *shari'a* and a "superstitious" religion found only in rural areas of the Islamic world.[22] The focus on the

[18] Hishmat, "Sufism and Orientalism", 210.

[19] Paul Noya, *Tafsir Qur'ani wa Zaban-i 'Irfani (Exegese Coranique et Langage Mystique)*, Isma'il Sa'adat, tr., (Tehran: 1994), 9–14; and Hellmut Ritter, *The Ocean of the Soul: Men, the World and God in the Stories of Farid al-Din Atta*r (Leiden: Brill Academic Publishers, 2003).

[20] Klinkhammer, "The Emergence of Transethnic Sufism in Germany", 132.

[21] Max Weber, "Religionssoziologie" in Wirtschaft und Gesellschaft. Tubingen: J.C.B. Mohr, 1972, 375–376 (original 1922) quoted in Klinkhammer, "The Emergence of Transethnic Sufism in Germany", 132.

[22] E. Gellner, *Muslim Society* (Cambridge: University Press, 1981).

translation of classical Sufi prose by A.J. Arberry and R.A. Nicholson would lead Arberry to assert that the "lived religion" of Sufis throughout the Muslim world was a debased version of the Sufism that had existed in the eighth to eleventh centuries. Arberry claimed that "Sufi orders continue to attract the ignorant masses but no man of education would care to speak in their favour".[23] With hindsight Arberry was premature, but even so, he ignores the continuous chain of Sufi adherents who have revived the *tariqas* through the centuries to the modern period and who have reformed Sufism from within, a process which the anthropologist Pnina Werbner describes as "waxing and waning".[24] The overall impact of this history of oriental scholarship was that when Sufism was found to exist in everyday Muslim life, it was decried as "orgiastic collectivistic fanaticism" (Max Weber) or "primitive aimless spirituality" (F.A.G. Thöluck)[25] or "folk religion" (E. Gellner), but when it appeared as moral and ethical metaphysical discourse expressed in inspired poetic forms, its origins in Islam were refuted.

The orientalist understanding of Sufism as a pantheistic or monistic mystical communion with a universal Being, with origins or influences in most of the world's major religious traditions would have another unforeseen consequence. Gritt Klinkhammer notes that the German understanding of Sufism as a "universal and positive mysticism" would feed into a rising religious narrative in Western Europe amongst some intellectuals, artists and writers, in which the idea of a universal mystical experience was perceived as the common essence of religions – a "non-institutional, individual religious feeling" that would be used in opposition to the institutionalized and cultural forms of religion already demonized in the Enlightenment and further critiqued by the Romantic movement's sense of superiority of feeling over thought.[26] Thöluck had already written that the "Orient" was primarily "image and feeling" in juxtaposition to Western European Christianity and civilization, where "thought" dominated.[27] The idea of an "essential mysticism" that lay behind all the cultural or civilizational forms of religion would influence a number of scholars in both Germany and Britain and give birth to the stubborn notion of religion as a "*sui generis*" entity requiring its own separate arena of study – a notion that remained dominant, although not

[23] A. J. Arberry, *Sufism: An Account of the Mystics of Islam* (New York: Harper & Row, 1950), 122.

[24] Pnina Werbner "Stamping the Earth with the Name of Allah: Zikr and the Sacralizing of Space among British Muslims", *Cultural Anthropology* 11 (1996): 319–321.

[25] See Markus Dressler, Ron Geaves, Gritt Klinkhammer, "Introduction" *in Sufis in Western Society*, eds Geaves et al., 1.

[26] Klinkhammer, "The Emergence of Transethnic Sufism in Germany", 134.

[27] Ibid., 133–134.

unchallenged, until the second half of the twentieth century. The German orientialist Paul Klappstein wrote in 1919 in the preface to his translation of Sufi texts that Sufism was a form of universal mysticism and should be understood as a "psychic predisposition" in all human beings.[28] This understanding of Sufism was to fascinate orientalists such as Massignon, Nicholson, and scholars of comparative religion in Britain. For example, Walter Stace (1960), Geoffrey Parrinder (1976), and Ninian Smart (1978) all argue that the mystical experience has enough common features, in spite of the obvious differences arising from a multiplicity of religious traditions in which they occur, to be defined as universal.[29]

Stace provides a seven point categorization to assert the universalism of the mystical experience: 1) a unifying vision in which the One is perceived by the senses in and through many objects; 2) the One is apprehended as the inner life, or presence in all things, so that "nothing is really dead"; 3) the experience brings a sense of reality; 4) a feeling of joy and peace resulting in fulfilment; 5) a feeling of the presence of the sacred; 6) a feeling of paradoxicality; and 7) the experience is ineffable or beyond description.[30] Reynold Nicholson and A.J. Arberry appear to endorse this syncretic approach to Sufism as a Muslim form of an essential religious experience at the heart of the major religions, or, at least, the theistic ones. Ian Netton notes that Nicholson, although aware of the deep doctrinal divisions between Christianity, Judaism, and Islam, asserts that "the spiritual element of that common element can best be appreciated in Jewish, Christian, and Islamic mysticism", and quotes Arberry as stating, "the Way on man's approach or return to God is in essence the same, in Christian and non-Christian teaching. It has three stages: an ethical stage, then one of knowledge and love, leading to the mystical union of the soul with God."[31]

Perhaps the most famous scholar of Sufism to emerge from this intellectual movement was Annemarie Schimmel who argued persuasively that Sufism was a cultural form of universal mysticism, stating that "mysticism can be

[28] Paul Klappstein, *Vier Turkestanische Heilege: ein Beitrag zum Verstandnis der Islamischen Mystik* (Berlin: Mayer & Muller, 1919), cited in Klinkhammer, "The Emergence of Transethnic Sufism in Germany", 134.

[29] See Walter Stace, *Mysticism and Philosophy* (London: MacMillan, 1960); Ninian Smart, "Understanding Religious Experience", in *Mysticism and Philosophical Analysis*, ed. Steven Katz (London: Sheldon Press, 1978); Geoffrey Parrinder, *Mysticism in the World's Religions* (London: Sheldon Press, 1976).

[30] Stace, *Mysticism and Philosophy*, 131–132.

[31] Reynard Nicholson, *The Mystics of Islam* (London: Routledge and Kegan Paul, p. v. (1975 reprint of 1914 edn)), and A.J. Arberry, *Sufism: An Account of the Mystics of Islam* (London: George Allen & Unwin, 1968), 7, quoted in Ian Netton, *Islam, Christianity and the Mystic Journey* (Edinburgh: Edinburgh University Press, 2011), 3–4.

defined as love of the Absolute" and that in its widest sense it may be defined as the consciousness of the One Reality.[32] In Britain, this was echoed by the works of Evelyn Underhill (1875–1941).[33] Aldous Huxley had popularized the term "perennial philosophy" in his book of the same name published in 1945, and it came to encapsulate the notion that all religions share a common origin in a single, perennial, primeval, or primordial religion that had subsequently taken a number of forms. In common with each other, perennialists also shared in a cultural and intellectual critique of Western society in which it was posited that the problems of the Occident could be resolved by a return to the ancient truths discovered in the sacred texts of Hinduism, Buddhism, Taoism and Islam. Some of the perennialists began to travel to the sources of the traditions that they admired in search of ancient wisdom and contemporary exponents in the Orient. Their interaction with such figures would also result in a missionary thrust from the Orient to the Occident that reversed the much more dominant infiltration of Christian missionaries following behind the European powers' colonial ventures into the Orient. Out of this interaction Sufism as a Western religion took birth in Western Europe and North America.

SUFISM AS A WESTERN RELIGION

In his study on the popularity of Sufi literature in the West, Mark Sedgwick notes that Rumi and Hafiz can be located among the top ten best-selling poets in North America. Rumi also figures in the top ten in Britain.[34] Sedgwick explores the development of Sufi literature in the West, seeking the key authors and attempting to explain Sufism's popularity. He makes the important point that Westerners read the classical texts differently from Muslims, but also read different texts on Sufism written by Western authors. He considers this difference to be so great, that he prefers to use the label

[32] Annemarie Schimmel, *The Mystical Dimensions of Islam* (Chapel Hill: University of North Carolina Press, 1975), 4 and 23, also quoted in Ian Netton, *Islam, Christianity and the Mystic Journey*, 2.

[33] Evelyn Underhill, *Mysticism: A Study of the Nature and Development of Man's Spiritual Consciousness* (1911), 12th edition reprinted by Dutton 1961; reprint 1999.

[34] Sedgwick calculated from Amazon.com and Amazon.co.uk in September and October 2007. The poetry rankings were also checked in June 2007. He notes that Rumi is often referred to as America's best-selling poet, a view expressed by Marcia Nelson: "Despite the fact that Rumi has been dead for 700 years, he is commonly thought to be America's current bestselling poet" ("Islamic Publishing"). Sedgwick notes that the Amazon data suggests that this is an exaggeration (Mark Sedgwick, "The Reception of Sufi and Neo-Sufi Literature" in *Sufis in Western Society*, eds Geaves, et al., 194.

"Neo-Sufism".[35] Writing in 2000, Geaves eschews this label as it has been used to describe Sufi reform movements in the Muslim world and prefers to use "universal Sufism".[36] It is arguable that universal Sufism has nothing to do with Islam and can be traced to the need for some Western "truth-seekers" to reject Christianity and look for answers to their quest in the East. Sedgwick argues that nineteenth-century Deism and the Romantic Movement were influential in this quest. Deism is posited as one reason why Sufism came to be perceived as an ancient and universal mystical tradition.[37] The Romantic Movement, according to Sedgwick, provided an emphasis on subjectivity, manifested as experience and self-discovery, and remains free of religion. Sedgwick considers that the readers of the poetry of Rumi and Hafiz regard them as "spirituality" rather than Islamic and are also likely to read the works of Khalil Gibran, Paulo Coelho, Hermann Hesse, and Mary Oliver.[38] Klinkhammer also makes an association with a post-Second World War generation searching for new patterns of life. She argues that, along with the "students' revolt" and the "sexual revolution", German reception of Sufism entered a new phase as the influence of the established church weakened. Sufism, alongside other Eastern religions, was understood to be more compatible with a search for freedom of individualist expression. She notes that by the late 1960s and early 1970s, a more experience-based form of Sufism was introduced in Germany "by people who did not seek a new religion, but were searching for a spiritual self". However, the roots of this quest for authenticity did not originate in the diffused and uprooted Sufism described by Klinkhammer as "New Age spirituality as therapy",[39] but rather in the first half of the twentieth century when it was associated with the *angst* and *anomie* felt by the interwar generation,[40] along with a critique of Western materialism and a perceived decline of civilization, followed by an existential terror of mass destruction during the Cold War.

It is argued above that the nineteenth-century orientalists had been instrumental in creating Sufism in the West as an ancient and universal mystical tradition older than Islam and grafted on to the Arab revelation when the Arabs expanded through trade and conquest to the territories of older civilizations. Sedgwick agrees, arguing that the intellectual and artistic

[35] Sedgwick, "The Reception of Sufi and Neo-Sufi Literature", 181.
[36] Ron Geaves, *Sufis of Britain* (Cardiff: Cardiff Academic Press, 2000).
[37] Mark Sedgwick, "Quelques sources du xviii siècle du pluralisme religieux inclusif", in *Etudes d'histoire de l'ésotérisme*, (Paris: Editions du Cerf, 2007), 49–65.
[38] Sedgwick, "The Reception of Sufi and Neo-Sufi Literature", 182–183, and 192.
[39] Klinkhammer, "The Emergence of Transethnic Sufism in Germany", 135 ff.
[40] Sedgwick, "The Reception of Sufi and Neo-Sufi Literature", 184.

European elites were in a state of obfuscation regarding Sufism and that this created a environment in which some religious innovators of the early twentieth century could locate their teachings with reference to Sufism, as in the case of Georges Gurdjieff (1866–1949).[41]

Gurdjieff claimed that most human beings lived in a state of hypnotic "waking sleep", from which it was possible to reach a higher state of consciousness and achieve one's full potential. He appeared to be aware that his teachings had parallels with the esoteric dimensions of the major world religions, but referred to them as "the Fourth Way" in that they were different to the methods of raising or transforming consciousness developed by Christian monks, Hindu Yogis or "fakirs" (Sufis). Little is known of Gurdjieff's early life until he appeared in Moscow in 1912 where he began to collect a small group of followers around himself including the philosopher P.D. Ouspensky and the composer Thomas de Hartmann. Any earlier biography is shrouded in mystery and obtainable from Gurdjieff's biographical work *Meetings with Remarkable Men* first written in Russian in 1927.[42] The book describes Gurdjieff's travels in Central Asia and his meetings with a number of esoteric "masters" and various ancient brotherhoods, including the mysterious Sarmoung Brotherhood. Gurdjieff records that he made contact with a representative of the Sarmoung through his friend, the Dervish Bogga Eddin, in Bukhara. He claims that the chief monastery of the society was located somewhere in the heart of Asia, about twelve days' journey from Bukhara on horseback. Several prominent followers of Gurdjieff, notably J.G. Bennett, have claimed that the Sarmoung were connected to Naqshbandi Sufis and that Gurdjieff's teachings were derived from their esoteric knowledge.[43] According to Ernest Scott, Ouspensky also believed that Gurdjieff's teachings originated in the Mevlevi Sufi order.[44] Although the claims that Gurdjieff was taught by Sufis are highly contested and likely to remain disputed even amongst his many followers today, there is no doubt about the influence of his teachings on the development of Sufism in the West. Western followers of the various offshoots of the Gurdjeffian way have throughout the twentieth century arrived at the door of Muslim Sufis expecting to find parallels in the Islamic traditions and hoping to discover universal esoteric knowledge. There are also Universal Sufi teachers in the West who encourage a synthesis of Sufism

[41] Mark Sedgwick, "European Neo-Sufi Movements in the Interwar Period", in *Islam in Europe in the Interwar Period: Networks, Status, Challenges*, Nathalie Clayer and Eric Germain, eds (London: Hurst, 2008).

[42] First translated into English in 1963 by A.R. Oranje.

[43] John G. Bennett, *Gurdjieff: Making of A New World* (Bennett Pub. Co. 1992), 56–57 ff.

[44] Ernest Scott, *The People of the Secret* (London: Octogon Press, 1983), 165.

derived from Islam and Gurdjieff's teachings. Some Gurdjieff-influenced teachers will also incorporate variations of the Mevlevi "turning".

One such example of this fluidity can be found in the Study Society based in Barons Court, London, where the successors to Ouspensky, under the guidance of their teacher Wilhelm Koren, carry out a particularly faithful version of the Mevlevi "whirling" as their primary spiritual practice. The original group do not lay claim to being Muslims or even Sufis, but they are now attracting students from London's Turkish Muslim communities who are impressed with the authentic maintenance of the spiritual discipline of the Mevlevi *samāʿ*. However, it should be noted that there is no adherence to any other Islamic religious practice or belief.[45]

Idries Shah (1924–1996) is more problematic than Gurdjieff. A prolific writer of over thirty five books, of which more than twenty are on the subject of Sufism, with sales estimated in excess of fifteen million,[46] and with claimed direct lineage back to Muḥammad and family connections to the Afghan branch of the Naqshbandi *tariqa*, it is not surprising that Shah became the representative of Sufism in Western intellectual and artistic circles in the second half of the twentieth century. Yet in spite of his Muslim background, a closer examination of Shah's teachings reveals little allegiance to any Islamic tenets. Shah, along with the perennialists, maintained that esoteric wisdom is independent of institutional religion but can sometimes be discovered within an exoteric religious form. Not surprisingly, he taught that Sufism is independent of Islam, although it may be possible to discover it within Islam. Shah's highly successful tales of Mullah Nasiruddin became almost obligatory reading for British and North American "truth-seekers" of the 1960s and 1970s counter-culture.[47] However, the Mullah is not presented as a devout Muslim, but rather as an innocent of God who highlights the hypocrisy of organized or institutionalized religion.[48] Shah was to teach that the truth of the Sufis was the inner essence of all religions. Doris Lessing, who studied with Shah in the 1960s, encapsulates his view when she wrote "It took 800 years to get Sufi thought accepted by orthodox Islam, and since then Muslims have claimed it for their own."[49] Shah, like Gurdjieff, was primarily concerned

45 For a fairly detailed account of the Study Group see Ron Geaves, *The Sufis of Britain*, 168–174.

46 Among them are *The Sufis*; *Wisdom of the Idiots*; *The Golden Caravan*; *The Spirit of the East*; *Learning how to Learn*: *The Commanding Self*.

47 *The Exploits of the Incomparable Mulla Nasiruddin*; *The Subtleties of the Inimitable Mulla Nasiruddin*; *the Pleasantries of the Incredible Mulla Nasiruddin*.

48 Geaves, *The Sufis of Britain*, 167.

49 Doris Lessing. "The Sufis and Idries Shah", http://www.serendipity.li/more/lessing_shah.htm, visited 21 July 2014.

with the transformation of human consciousness based on self-development, and there is little evidence that the small groups that gathered around him were taught any kind of allegiance to Islam, but rather were presented with a vision of a universal path of self-understanding. Geaves, however, argues that Shah may have presented the *malamati* tradition in which Sufis work hidden in the world and scorn any outer identity of Islam, including the practices of the *tariqas*.[50]

Decades before the counter-culture of the second half of the twentieth century, Shaykh Hazrat Inayat Khan's travels in 1910 throughout America and Europe in order to promote his Sufi Message to the West were the first missionary thrust by a Muslim Sufi into Europe and North America. As an initiate of the Chishtiya, an Indian Sufi *tariqa*, it might be expected that Inayat Khan would promote an Islamic version of the tradition. Yet Khan would also contribute to forming Sufism's current image in the West as a universal spirituality separated from Islam. Inayat Khan would teach an eclectic Sufism in which he would declare that "true" Sufism is above all religions. In his view, all of the world religions have the essence of inner knowledge by direct experience. Sedgwick asserts that Khan took "Sufism and dressed it up as something other than Sufism in order to make it more palatable to modern Westerners."[51] Certainly, there is no indication of any attempt to suggest that Western followers should comply in any way with the *shari'a* or even become Muslims. Sedgwick points out that the *contents* of the teachings are far closer to Sufism as found in the Muslim world than the *form* (author's italics).[52] The actuality of Inayat Khan's attempts to promote Sufism in the West is probably more complex than merely an attempt to create a form of the tradition that was "more palatable to modern Westerners". Inayat Khan was an upper class Indian who lived through the British Raj and whose Sufi affiliation had always demonstrated both eclectic and syncretistic tendencies. He had been trained as a musician by his grandfather, who had believed in the universality of all religions. Inayat Khan travelled the length and breadth of India as a musician and questioned holy men from all religious backgrounds and, although maintaining the outer obligations of Islam, studied the *Upanishads* and *Bhagavad Gita*. Khan's universalism can be found in the intellectual milieu of Northern India, the meetings between Yogis and Sufis, the mediaeval *bhakti* tradition and the eclectic tendencies of Chishti *tariqa*.[53] In addition,

50 Geaves, *The Sufis of Britain*, 167.

51 Sedgwick, "The Reception of Sufi and Neo-Sufi Literature", 185.

52 Ibid.

53 Geaves, *The Sufis of Britain*, 174–176.

the class and background of his students in North America should be taken into account. His musical talent and eclectic spirituality with its emphasis on universalism drew the same audiences who had been attracted to the theosophy of Annie Besant, the universalist expression of ancient Hindu truths presented by Vivekananda at the World Parliament of Religions in 1893. In 1923 Hazrat Khan founded the Sufi Movement to promote his teachings in the West and the result was a blending of Indian ideas of a universal truth that transcended the outer forms of religion and the Western pursuit of self-development as promoted by Gurdjieff and Idries Shah.

A similar outlook can be found among the followers of Irina Tweedie (1907–1999). Tweedie was taught by Radha Mohan Lal, who claimed to be a master of the Naqshbandiyya-Mujadiddiyya Sufi Order. She visited India, where she met her teacher, in 1959 after a spiritual crisis evoked by the death of her husband in 1954. The diaries that she kept were published as *Daughter of Fire: A Diary of a Spiritual Training with a Sufi Master*. The book was first published in its abridged form as *The Chasm of Fire*, which has sold over 100,000 copies and has been translated into five languages.[54] Tweedie returned to Britain in 1966 and started a Sufi meditation group in North London. It is claimed that Tweedie became the first Western woman to be trained in this Naqshbandi system.[55] However, Llewellyn Vaughan-Lee, Tweedie's chosen successor, writes that an unusual occurrence took place in the nineteenth century. One line of succession was passed to the Hindu disciples on Fazl Ahmed Khan's death and it has been noted that the language of Tweedie's teacher is more akin to Hindu spirituality than Islamic. In an interview with Tweedie published in 1990, the interviewer comments on the use of "*chakras, kundalini, atman*" in his discourses. Tweedie's response is typical of universal Sufism: "You see Sufism and yoga are one and the same thing. They are just words, in wisdom there is no difference. All the teachings are absolutely the same. They are only different paths to the One." Tweedie goes on to refer to Idries Shah, affirming his position that when Sufism spread, it took on the prevalent culture of the Middle East (Islam), but in India it borrowed heavily from the language of yoga. Tweedie's knowledge of Islam is summed up in the words, "I don't know what name they have for

[54] Irene Tweedie, *Daughter of Fire: A Diary of a Spiritual Training with a Sufi Master* (Golden Sufi Centre, 1971). As described at http://goldensufi.org/book_desc_DoF.html, visited 18 September 2012.

[55] Llewellyn Vaughan-Lee, "Neither of the East nor of the West: The Journey of the Naqshbandiyya-Mujaddidiyya from India to America", http://goldensufi.org/article_eastwest.html, visited 18 September 2012.

chakras in Arabic. I don't speak Arabic and I don't understand it. You see my training was with fire, which is *kundalini*."[56]

If the examples above demonstrate the fluidity of borders between "universal Sufism" and Islam, with the former an "invented tradition" with tenuous claims to be Muslim or Sufi, Sedgwick reminds us that even in the case of Frithjof Schuon (1907–1998), where teachings and practice were closer to Sufism as found in the Muslim world, there were still significant differences.[57] However, here the traversing of borders between perennial philosophy and traditional Islam become easier to negotiate. Schuon belonged to the Traditionalist School whose teachings resurrect the idea of a common mystical core at the heart of all world religions, as expressed in the writings of René Guénon, Titus Burckhardt, Martin Lings and Seyyed Hossein Nasr. Several of these figures would have a significant impact on the arrival of Sufism as a Western religion, in the process offering an even more flexible and fluid boundary between "universal Sufism" and traditional Islamic expressions of *tassawuf*.

The Traditionalists differed from Huxley's perennialism in that they posited that the mystical essence at the heart of all religions could only be discovered through adherence to the disciplines of one religion. Their viewpoint is perfectly encapsulated in the words of René Guénon: "initiation is essentially the transmission of a spiritual influence, a transmission that can only take place through a regular, traditional organization, so that one cannot speak of initiation outside of an affiliation with an organization of this kind".[58] In the case of the above exponents, Islam (Sufism) was chosen as the way to pursue the "transmission of a spiritual influence". The various branches of the Shadhiliya *tariqa* founded by Abu 'l-Ḥasan ash-Shadhili (1196–1258) and historically influential in North Africa and Egypt are important in this phase of the development of Sufism in Europe. The Swedish impressionist painter and Sufi scholar Ivan Aguéli (or Sheikh 'Abd al-Hadi Aqili; 1869–1917) was the first official *muqaddam* (representative) of the Shadhiliya in Western Europe. In 1902 Aguéli had moved to Cairo to become one of the first Western Europeans to be enrolled at al-Azhar University, where he studied Arabic and Islamic philosophy. In the same year he was also initiated into the al-'Arabiyya Shadhiliya by the Egyptian Shaykh

56 "Daughter of Fire: An Interview with Irina Tweedie", published in Yoga and Life, Vol. 5, No. 5, Autumn 1990 and reproduced at http://www.goldensufi.org/a_yoga_and_life.html, visited on 18 September 2012.

57 Sedgwick, "The Reception of Sufi and Neo-Sufi Literature", 184.

58 René Guénon, *Perspectives on Initiation (Collected Works of Rene Guenon)* (Sophia Perennis, 2004), 48.

'Abd al-Rahman Ilaysh al-Kabir (1840–1921).In 1911 he founded a Sufi society in Paris named Al Akbariyya to promote the teachings of Ibn 'Arabi among the "scholarly, educated and freethinking classes", drawing upon the practices of the Shadhili and Malamati Sufi paths. Among its first members was René Guénon (1886–1951).[59]

The writings of René Guénon, known to Muslims as Shaykh 'Abd al-Wahid Yahya, demonstrate his perennialism. His approach to Eastern metaphysics claims a "universal character" which can be adapted to Western audiences whilst faithfully maintaining their spirit.[60] His first attempt to write on Eastern mysticism was confined to aspects of Hinduism, primarily the teachings of Advaita Vedanta.[61] In 1930, Guénon left Paris for Cairo, where he remained for many years. In this period of his life, he apparently practised a more orthodox allegiance to Islam. He remained embedded in Sufism through his further initiation by Shaykh Salama Hassan ar-Radi, founder of the Hamidiyya Shadhiliyya. Guénon lived with the Shaykh until the latter's death in 1938. In 1934 he married the daughter of Shaykh Mohammad Ibrahim.

Frithjof Schuon (1907–1998) is known as the inspiration of the Traditionalists and an exponent of the perennialist school. Schuon was critical of the relativist stance of the academic study of religion, arguing that it was necessary to maintain a confessional position with regard to the existence of God. This search for the Absolute would lead him on a journey through the world's sacred texts, including the *Upanishads* and the *Bhagavad Gita*. He discovered the works of René Guénon and was influenced by his metaphysical position. He studied Arabic in Paris at the local mosque school and travelled to Algeria in 1932, where he met the Shaykh Ahmad al-Alawi and accepted initiation, taking the name 'Isa Nur al-Din Ahmad. In 1935, he visited Algeria and Morocco and, in 1938 and 1939, Egypt, where he finally met Guénon after correspondence with him for nearly thirty years.

Schuon's meeting with Shaykh Ahmad al-Alawi in Algeria would be instrumental in shaping Sufism in Europe and North America, and was especially influential in Britain. The Darqawiyya was a Moroccan branch of the Shadhiliya founded in the last decades of the eighteenth century by Muhammad al-'Arabi al-Darqawi (1760–1823). The Alawiyya branch of the

[59] Axel Gauffin, *Ivan Aguéli – Människan, mystikern, målaren* I–II (Sveriges Allmänna Konstförenings Publikation, 1941), 188–189.

[60] René Guénon, *The Symbolism of the Cross (Collected Works of Rene Guenon)* (Sophia Perennis, 2004), foreword.

[61] René Guénon, *Introduction to the Study of the Hindu Doctrines (Collected Works of Rene Guenon)*, (Sophia Perennis, 2004).

Darqawiyya was founded by Ahmad ibn Mustafa al-'Alawi al-Mustaghanimi, popularly known as Shaykh al-Alawi, and one of the greatest renewers of Sufism in the Muslim world in the twentieth century. After his time with the Shaykh al-Alawi in Algeria, Schuon returned to the West to found the Maryamiya branch of the Shadhiliyya Order in Europe and North America where he promoted the teachings of the Shaykh. Sedgwick claims that of all the "neo-Sufi" groups, the Maryamiyya was the closest to Sufism as found in the Muslim world. However, he points out some key differences. He affirms that it was almost identical with other Shadhili branches with regard to practices, but it was far more relaxed in its approach to the *sharī'a*. He also notes that Schuon's version of the Traditionalist philosophy of René Guénon was taught alongside Sufism and included Guénon's anti-modernist philosophy of history, which was in part influenced by theosophy. Schuon's universalism continued to influence his spirituality and was demonstrated by travels in the 1960s among the Sioux and Crow American Indians where he participated in their sacred rites.

Schuon's first book, *The Transcendent Unity of Religions*, expresses fully his perennial stance, but later he wrote several texts on Islam, including *Understanding Islam*, *Dimensions of Islam*, and *Sufism: Veil and Quintessence*. However, it is the people that he attracted to his "Traditionalist" stance, often introducing them to the teachings of the Shaykh al-Alawi, that were to be most influential. Some of his most eminent students include Seyyed Hossein Nasr, Titus Burckhardt (1908–1984) and Martin Lings (1909–2005). Lings published a biography of the Shaykh al-Alawi under the title *A Sufi Saint of the Twentieth Century*, and it remains one of the most influential books on Sufism published in the Western world. He also wrote the acclaimed *Muhammad: His Life Based on the Earliest Sources*.

Sedgwick is convinced that all the "neo-Sufi" groups are rooted in Western spirituality, with an emphasis on the individual spiritual search that has no equivalent in the Muslim world. He also notes that although some Eastern Sufis may have displayed a more ecumenical spirit with regard to other forms of spirituality they came across, the Traditionalist version of perennialism that perceived Sufism as an outer manifestation of a universal and essential mysticism was not the Islamic interpretation of the tradition.[62] The relationship between the Perennials and the Muslim world is succinctly described by Klinkhammer when she states:

[62] Sedgwick, "The Reception of Sufi and Neo-Sufi Literature", 184.

> Some of the Perennials found such primeval truths in Sufism, which they experienced by living among Muslims. In the end, they went back to their homelands and found some students, but did not establish a *tariqa*. Most of them, e.g. the Swede Agueli, the French Guenon, the German Fritjof Schuon and also their well-known students such as Titus Burkhardt and Martin Lings, were considered intellectuals rather than practitioners. Their books on Sufism are more widely known than their practice as Sufis of the Alawiyya Order, which they brought with them to Europe.[63]

However, Klinkhammer and Sedgwick may have overemphasized the distinction between the Traditionalist's brand of Western Sufism and Islam. The borders between these two had always been fluid and the degree to which the *shari'a* was followed, although problematic, is not a definitive test of allegiance to Islam. *Shari'a* compliance is used to critique Sufis in the arena of contestation between Islamic forms of religiosity amongst Muslims. The trajectory of individual transformation achieved by contact with Sufis in North Africa or the Middle East would appear in a number of cases to be drifting towards a gradual Islamicization. In the German case, Klinkhammer claims that the spread of "mainstream" Sufism was only marginally connected to Muslim immigration. Like Sedgwick, she argues that trans-ethnic Sufism in Germany must be "identified and investigated as a phenomenon within the scope of the 're-sacralization' of Western society beginning in the 1970s".[64] But some evidence exists in Britain that the two phenomena were not disassociated from each other. The first migrants from India and Pakistan were arriving in Britain at around the same time as counter-culture individuals were following in the footsteps of the Traditionalists. Little is known of contact between them, but anecdotal evidence seems to suggest that the two groups were interconnected or, at least, fleetingly aware of the presence of each other.

A few individuals from counter-culture were influenced by the writings of Schuon and Lings and made their way to Algeria and Morocco. The orientalist scholar and novelist Robert Irwin has recently recorded his visits to the Al-Alawiya in Algeria whilst an Oxford undergraduate in the 1960s in his recently published *Memoirs of a Dervish*.[65] He attributes his conversion to Islam to meeting a fellow undergraduate Harvey Mellor (Sidi Ahmed), who had travelled to Algeria earlier and before returning to study Arabic at

63 Klinkhammer, "The Emergence of Transethnic Sufism in Germany", 135.

64 Daniel Bell, "The Return of the Sacred" in *The Winding Passage: Essays and Sociological Journeys 1960–1980*, ed. Daniel Bell (Cambridge University Press, 1980).

65 Robert Irwin, *Memoirs of a Dervish* (London: Profile Books, 2011).

Merton College. Mellor had also been influenced by Schuon and had decided to convert to Islam as a young teenager, seeking out Pakistani factory workers in the steelworks of Sheffield in the late 1950s. He also recounts praying whilst an undergraduate in Merton College, Oxford, in the basement of an Indian curry house alongside the Muslim waiters sometime in the mid-1960s. Although also active in counter-culture life of the mid to late 1960s, these early converts did consider themselves to be Muslim and converted to Islam, either before or when accepting *bay'at*.

The proximity of North Africa, compared with India, would attract a continuous flow of counter-culture seekers of the oriental experience from Western Europe. Contact with the Shadhili or Darqawi *tariqas* was therefore inevitable. Both of these orders had been rejuvenated from time to time by charismatic shaykhs, most notably, as we have seen, the Shaykh al-Alawi. Most significant amongst European contacts with the *tariqa* is the Mirabitun movement, founded in Britain by Ian Dallas around 1976. Dallas, a writer and actor, had travelled to Morocco in 1967 where he was initiated into the Darqawiyya and took the name Abd al-Qadir. Somewhere around 1976, a group of British and North American followers gathered around Shaykh Abd al-Qadir in a row of derelict houses in London. Little study has been carried out on the group and its activities, but Köse notes that they numbered between twenty and thirty, were all former members of 1960s counter-culture, and had taken drugs prior to contact with Sufism.[66] Although the group dressed in green turbans and traditional Moroccan dress, conversion to Islam was seen as secondary to acquiring Sufism. Yet, like the earlier Traditionalists and the Oxford undergraduates, many would embrace Islam as a feature of Sufi lifestyle. Shaykh al-Qadir would become more overtly Muslim throughout 1976. He insisted that followers withdraw from a Western lifestyle, even to the extent of removing children from mainstream schools. He initiated public prayer meetings in Hyde Park and his writings began to be translated into Arabic. After visiting Libya, he announced himself as a unifying shaykh of the Shadhili and Darqawiyya. At the end of 1976 he moved his community to near Norwich in Norfolk, with the intention of establishing a fully self-sufficient village of believers. The community purchased Wood Daling Hall, a mansion with extensive grounds. At its peak, the community numbered around two hundred families, forming the Darqawi Institute. Shaykh al-Qadir would travel extensively throughout the Muslim world achieving international fame as a scholar. For a variety of reasons, the community fragmented. Shaykh al-Qadir moved to Andalucia and, in 1994, a new offshoot of the

[66] Ali Köse, *Conversion to Islam* (London: Kegan Paul, 1966) 176.

movement was founded in Scotland. The original community remains in Norwich and is still active in promoting Islam.[67]

I have dwelt at length on the Darqawi Institute for a number of reasons. Köse notes that the movement had two distinct phases. In the first, Abd al-Qadir attracted new followers through promoting himself as a Sufi who emphasized the esoteric teachings of the tradition. In the second, he shifted to an emphasis on the outer practices of Islam and *sharīʿa* compliance. Although Sufism was perceived as the authentic version of Islamic practice, and embedded in Sunni traditionalism, the promotion of Islam in the West became the primary objective of the movement. This is significant as it confirms the fluid borders between Sufism encountered as an esoteric but universal mysticism and Islamic allegiance. Perhaps more significantly for the development of Sufism in the West, the movement would produce a number of individuals who would have an impact today, bridging the borders between convert Sufis and the British children of South Asian migrants with Sufi allegiance. Shaykh Yasin Dutton remembers that such contacts were already taking place in the 1970s, when the Sufis of the Norwich community would travel around England in order to meet with South Asian shaykhs who were beginning to teach in the inner cities where Muslims migrants had recently settled. It is also likely that the Shadhili and Darqawi British converts would have been aware that before the influx of South Asian Muslims, the Yemeni dominated seaport communities in Cardiff, Liverpool, Hull and Tyneside that had their origins in the expansion of the British merchant fleet, and the consequent mass employment of Asian sailors owed their religious and social organization to the spiritual descendents of the Shaykh al-Alawi. These British seaport Muslim communities were organized around the efforts of Shaykh Abdullah Ali al-Hakimi, a Yemeni who had discovered the Shadhili Alawi in Morocco and who arrived in Britain in 1936. These communities were the first migrant Muslim communities to organize themselves socially and politically in Britain around the *zawiya* of a prominent Sufi figure.[68]

[67] Geaves, *The Sufis of Britain*, 142–144.

[68] See Geaves, *The Sufis of Britain*, 65. The story of these Arab port communities has been told in detail by Fred Halliday, *Arabs in Exile* (London: I.B. Tauris, 1992) and more recently in Humayun Ansari, *The Infidel Within* (London: Hurst, 2004). Mohammad Sedden is also researching al-Hakimi, delivering an unpublished paper entitled "Shaykh Abdullah Ali al-Hakimi, The Alawi Tariqah and British Yemenis" at the Conference *Sufis and Scholars: The Development of Sufism in Britain*, 25 and 26 May 2012, Liverpool Hope University.

SUFIS IN THE WEST

Klinkhammer has pointed out that any assessment of the Sufi presence in European nations must take into account patterns of immigration and the different situations in the countries of origin of Muslim migrants in the twentieth and twentieth-first centuries – for example, 80 percent of Muslim migrants in Germany originate from Turkey where Sufism is not widely represented or, at least, is not publicly visible. The ban on Sufi Orders in Turkey in 1925 strongly limited the public practice of Sufism and would have significance for the public representation of Sufism amongst Muslim migrants in Germany and elsewhere.[69] In Britain, where the great majority of Muslims originate from rural Pakistan, India and Bangladesh, Sufism is practised as a popular religion in the villages and towns. This is duplicated in the strongholds of South Asian migrant presence in British cities. In France, where the majority of migrants are from North Africa, Sufism, although once dominant, is now less so due to the changing formations of Algerian Islam after the struggle for independence. Other factors influencing the development of Sufism are critical mass of migration, class and ethnicity of the migrants, and the presence of individual Sufi leaders among the migrants.

Initially the appropriation of Sufism by Western orientalists and successive generations of seekers of a "mystical truth" hid the vibrant reality of millions of traditional Muslims in the Muslim world who practised the core disciplines of Sufism as an integral part of Islam based firmly on the teachings of the Qur'ān and *ḥadith*. Until the arrival of migrant populations in post World War II Western Europe, the articulate Sufi intellectuals hid the everyday life of traditional Muslims and the role of the *tariqas* and the shrines of deceased Sufis in Muslim religious life. Sufism in the West was an elitist presence with tenuous and fluid links to Islamic religiosity. The everyday religious life of traditional Muslims would not have a significant impact on Sufism in the West until the 1960s, when some nations in Western Europe began to be transformed by the arrival of various Muslim populations, in the case of Britain predominantly from Pakistan and Bangladesh, but also from Malaysia, Turkish Cyprus, Iran, Yemen, and North, West and East Africa. These are all places where, either historically or as a living faith tradition, Sufism is significant.

Although slow to organize themselves in the British Muslim diaspora, the last twenty years have seen the transplantation of several prominent Sufi

[69] Klinkhammer, "The Emergence of Transethnic Sufism in Germany", 144.

tariqas, including various offshoots of the Naqshbandis, Chishtis, Qadiris, Mevlevis, Alawis, Shadhilis, and Tijanis. This pattern repeats itself in other nations of Western Europe, Scandinavia and North America. This significant presence of Sufis or Sufi-influenced Muslims, has done much to offset the appropriation of Sufism by Western orientalists and has to a significant degree restored the awareness of the Sufi path at the heart of traditional Islam. However, it could be argued that even with the establishment of the *tariqas*, wherever Muslim populations have settled in Western Europe and North America, Sufism remains relatively invisible both to academics and the general public as other aspects of Muslim religious life have dominated the agenda for political and security reasons.

The dominance of Muslims of South Asian origin in the British context has perpetuated custom-laden Sufism with its roots in the subcontinent and continued historic rivalries between *ṭariqas* and with other Islamic movements that have been historical competitors in the highly contested religious environment of colonial India. The subcontinent Sufis, with their custom-laden version of Islam focused on the intercession of saints and the Prophet, shrines, *baraka* (the power to bless), powers, miracles, and the performance of *dhikr* maintained within the *shaykh/murid* relationship, had never successfully organized themselves nationally in Britain in spite of their apparent numerical superiority. Even so, the arrival of a number of charismatic Sufi *pirs* and *shaykhs* from the subcontinent provided the impetus for greater cohesion as they formed powerful groups of Sufis able to construct mosques and produce promotional literature to counter the reformist movements. The traditional loyalty of each group of *murids* to their own *shaykh* undermined this push towards a stronger and more assertive national identity.

Moreover, the establishment of these *tariqas* has provided a series of organizational structures to Sufi adherents and capitalized on the strong empathy with the teachings of traditional Islam amongst British Muslim populations. The term "traditional Islam" is used in this context to distinguish a brand of Islam that acknowledges 1400 years of tradition as authoritative alongside the teachings of the Qu'ran and Sunna and recognizes the contribution of Sufi spirituality, the legal interpretations of the '*ulama*, and the four schools of law. This label of traditional Islam has been harnessed by Sufis and Sufi sympathizers in opposition to neo-orthodoxies which have vociferously criticized Sufism, accusing it of introducing *bida*' (or innovation) into the Muslim religious arena.

Thus, in recent years the representatives of the *tariqas* have provided a unifying Islamic discourse based on practice and belief and drawing upon the traditional loyalty of the above populations to the leadership of *pirs* and *shaykhs* rather than the *ʿulama*. They have also discovered a successful discourse that is able to recruit from the younger generations of British Muslims. However, unlike the USA, Sufism has made little impact on the original non-migrant non-Muslim population, and with the exception of the Haqqani Naqshbandis, led by the charismatic Shaykh Nazim, very few outside of the Muslim migrant communities have been attracted. The main contributory reason for this difference, at least, up to the end of the twentieth century, was that Sufism in Britain in particular remained associated with ethnic identity and communication in Urdu, a means of maintaining traditions and customs tightly bound with localities in the place of origin. Thus Sufism has functioned not so much as a transmission of mysticism within Islam, able to cross over to a universal mysticism sought by Western seekers, but as a boundary mechanism primarily concerned with the transmission of cultural and religious traditions. However, this is only part of the story.

In recent years, there have been signs of significant change. The British Sufi scene now demonstrates marked attempts to carve out a new cultural and religious space that creatively interacts with the new environment of Britain.[70] The *tariqas* have become more aware of the need to draw upon the transnational and trans-cultural nature of globalized memberships and to articulate the narratives of *tasawwuf* and traditional Islamic sciences in an intellectual environment, addressing both Muslims and non-Muslims in the lingua franca. The World Wide Web is an essential aspect of this globalization. The online presence of traditional Muslim *tasawwuf* does not advertise itself as Sufism or even rally behind the epithet of *ahl as-Sunna wa Jamaʿat*, but rather prefers to speak of itself as representing traditional Islam and the teachings of the four *madhhabs*. The Web sites originate in Spain, Britain, and North America and address themselves specifically to Muslims in the West.

Influential converts, notably Shaikh Nur Ha Nim Keller and Shaikh Abdul-Hakim Murad, are able to communicate fluently in English and are often members of academia. They are not exponents of an Islam imbedded in local tradition and are often fluent in their understanding and use of *fiqh*. These

[70] For detailed study of these developments, see a series of articles written by the author: R.A. Geaves, "Tradition, Innovation, and Authentication: Replicating the Ahl-as Sunna Wa Jamaat in Britain", *Journal of Comparative Islamic Studies*, Vol. 1:1, June, 1–20, 2005; "Learning the lessons from the neo-revivalist and Wahhabi movements: the Counterattack of new Sufi movements in the UK", *Sufism in the West*, Jamal Malik and John Hinnells (eds) (London: Routledge, 2006); "A Case of Cultural Binary Fission or Transglobal Sufism? The Transmigration of Sufism to Britain" in R.A. Geaves, Markus Dressler, Gritt Klinkhammer (eds), *Global Networking and Locality: Sufis in Western Society*.

Western Sufis are as scriptural as their Salafi adversaries, able to utilize the Qur'ān and *ḥadīth* to great effect to put across their message on the issues that matter to them. Ethnicity is transcended to discover common cause in either a universal consciousness of *ummah* or the ideological belonging to traditional Islam. For young British Muslims of South Asian origin, inspiration is more likely to come from such figures as it is from the South Asian elders in the *tariqas*, who are still perceived to pull up drawbridges of isolation in their respective spiritual fiefdoms of Coventry, Birmingham, Bradford or Manchester. *Tasawwuf* in Britain, North America, and Western Europe is beginning to go trans-global and escape the confines of ethnicity and locality. Marcia Hermansen comments on this drawing together of "theirs" and "ours" and argues that mobility, rapid dissemination of information, and encounters of Eastern (Muslim) and Western individuals has brought about the creation of trans-global networks that to some extent override the old orientalist discrepancies of power described by Said. She asserts that " 'theirs' and 'ours' ultimately converge in an age of globalism".[71] The re-emergence of the North-African-influenced Western converts operating on a global scale, but, above all, able to position themselves prominently in the struggle for Islamic authenticity and attract the British and North American children of the migrants whose forefathers belonged to traditional *tariqas* in their places of origin, begs a reassessment of Sedgwick's differentiation of Sufism and neo-Sufism. Sedgwick's argument that Western Sufism always emphasizes the individual spiritual search as distinguished from the Eastern approach of a guided journey may need to be reassessed as the allegiance of young European and North American children of migrants reassess their parents' and grandparents' Sufism in the light of their in-between status in Western society.

FURTHER READING

Clinton Bennett, *South Asian Sufis: Devotion, Deviation, and Destiny* (London: Bloomsbury, 2010).

Nicolaas H. Biegman *Living Sufism: Sufi Rituals in the Middle East and the Balkans* (Cairo: American University in Cairo, 2009).

Nathalie Clayer and Eric Germain, (eds) *Islam in Europe in the Interwar Period: Networks, Status, Challenges* (London: Hurst, 2008).

Markus Dressler, Ron Geaves and Gritt Klinkhammer (eds) *Sufis in Western Society: Global Networking and Locality* (London: Routledge, 2009).

Ron Geaves *Sufis of Britain* (Cardiff: Cardiff Academic Press, 2000).

[71] Hermansen, "Global Sufism: Theirs and Ours", 26.

Ron Geaves and Theodore Gabriel *Sufism in Britain* (London: Bloomsbury, 2014).
Nile Green, *Sufism: A Global History* (Oxford: Wiley-Blackwell, 2012).
Aziz El Kobaiti Idrissi, *Islamic Sufism in the West* (Norwich: Diwan Press, 2013).
Jamil Malik and John Hinnells (eds), *Sufism in the West* (London: Routledge, 2006).
Catharina Raudvere and Leif Stenberg (eds), *Sufism Today: Heritage and Tradition in the Global Community* (London: I.B. Tauris, 2008).
Mark Sedgwick, *Against the Modern World: Traditionalism and the Secret Intellectual History of the Twentieth Century* (Oxford: Oxford University Press, 2009).
Martin van Bruinessen and Julia Day Howell (eds), *Sufism and the "Modern" in Islam* (London: I.B. Tauris, 2012).
David Westerlund (ed.) *Sufism in Europe and North America* (London: RoutledgeCurzon, 2004).

11

Sufism in the Age of Globalization

Itzchak Weismann

In the closing decades of the twentieth century humanity embarked on a new phase in its history, namely the age of globalization. At its root lies the technological revolution in communications, which eliminates traditional limitations of time and space. Information, capital, and people flow with increasing ease and speed across the globe, while facing diminishing geographical or territorial restrictions. This compression of the world – in Roland Robertson's metaphor – is articulated through extending supra-local and supra-national social and cultural networks and through the growing awareness that we all inhabit one world.[1]

The ongoing scholarly and public debate about the place of Islam in the emerging global reality is overshadowed by its fundamentalist brand, and by the international terror campaign carried out in its name. Still, contrary to the impression often given by the mass media, there are also other, more moderate, faces to Islam. One of these, on which the present article focuses, is Sufism, which denotes Islam's mystical aspect. It is as old as Islam itself, and throughout history it has satisfied the ethical and emotional needs of the spiritual elites and the masses alike. More recently, Sufis – and mystics in general – have had to cope with the complex realities of the modern state, rational-scientific modes of thought, secularism, and militant fundamentalism. Globalization intensifies the attack of these formidable forces on Sufism, but also provides it with new means to overcome their multiple challenges.

The article opens with a theoretical discussion of the concept of globalization and its temporal and spatial dialectics. Next I examine the historical

[1] For an updated readable discussion of globalization see: Kate Nash, *Contemporary Political Sociology: Globalization, Politics, and Power* (Oxford: Blackwell Publishers, 2000), esp. 48–56; Chris Barker, *Cultural Studies: Theory and Practice*. 2nd edition (London: Sage Publications, 2003), 167–77.

background to the contemporary evolution of Sufism, with a view to both its diversity and its status in the period immediately preceding globalization, namely the modern era. In the main part of the article I analyze the present manifestations of Sufism around the globe: in the Muslim world, where it originated, and in the West, where it increasingly sends its tentacles. My analysis leads to two major conclusions. First, the common wisdom about the "decline of Sufism" in the face of modernity is unwarranted; "the transformation of Sufism" is a more accurate term as it allows room for Sufi agency in adjusting to the new circumstances. Secondly, Sufism continues to draw adherents in the Muslim world and among Muslim communities elsewhere, but it is also gaining new influence among Western mystics. Occurring in the postmodern era, these developments may be defined as post-Sufism.

DIALECTICS OF GLOBALIZATION

Globalization has a dialectical relation to modernity. On one hand, like late modernity it accelerates socioeconomic and political processes rooted in the modern era. On the other hand, it undermines the philosophical and cultural foundations of modernity and challenges its claim to universality. The fashionable prefixing of "post" to various "isms" coined by the moderns reflects this dialectic. Post-industrialism refers to the intensification of capitalist production (late capitalism), but also to the shift of economic weight to consumption and the mechanisms of temptation that feed it.[2] Likewise, post-nationalism points to the principal role that the nation-state continues to fill in securing law and order, but also to the erosion of its ability to bring more equality and social justice in the face of the powerful multinational corporations.[3] Postmodernism perpetuates modernity's self-critical approach, but also undermines it by applying this same critique to the basic concepts of reason and progress on which the enlightenment project is built, exposing the imaginations constituting nation and society, and dismantling language and the subject.[4] And post-colonialism indicates that the colonial regimes are

[2] Scott Lash and John Urry, *The End of Organized Capitalism* (Wisconsin: The University of Wisconsin Press, 1987).

[3] See, e.g., Jürgen Habermas, *Die Postnationale Konstellation Politische Essays* (Frankfurt: Suhrkamp, 1998); Ronald Axtman, "The State of the State: The Model of the Modern State and Its Contemporary Transformation", *International Political Science Review* 25 (2004): 259–79.

[4] One of the founding texts in the field is Max Horkheimer and Theodor W. Adorno, *Dialectics of Enlightenment* (New York: Continuum, 1990). Also see: J. F. Lyotard, *The Post Modern Condition* (Minneapolis: University of Minnesota Press, 1984); Frederic Jameson, *Postmodernism or the Cultural Logic of Late Capitalism* (Durham: Duke University Press, 1991).

gone, but colonialism continues in the "soft" forms of cultural hegemony and economic exploitation.[5]

Globalization has a dialectical relation to its modern past, but also to its local present. Post-Marxist sociologists like Zigmunt Bauman maintain that globalization inexorably generated its local antithesis; however, more clear-sighted than Marx, they are under no illusion as to a forthcoming liberating revolution that will lead us to a higher synthesis:

> Rather than homogenizing the human condition, the technological annulment of temporal/spatial distances tends to polarize it. It emancipates certain humans from territorial constrains and renders certain community-generating meanings exterritorial – while denuding the territory, to which other people go on being confined, of its meaning and its identity-endowing capacity. For some people it augurs an unprecedented freedom from physical obstacles and unheard of ability to move and act from a distance. For others, it portends the impossibility of appropriating and domesticating the locality from which they have little chance of cutting themselves free in order to move elsewhere. . . . Some can now move out of the locality – any locality – at will. Others watch helplessly the sole locality they inhabit moving away from under their feet.[6]

Postmodernist thinkers turn their attention to the subjective aspect of the global–local dialectics. In their view, the intensification of the worldwide motion itself produces a popular desire to preserve local bases, and in extreme cases to destroy the global superpower which threatens to eliminate them. For Jean Baudrillard such resistance is inherent in each of us; he explains our reaction to the terrorist attack of September 11 thus:

> All the speeches and commentaries about September 11 betray the gigantic abreaction to the event itself and people's fascination with it. The moral condemnations, the national antiterrorism sacred union, are on par with the prodigious jubilation created by the desire to see the destruction of this global superpower, or more precisely, to watch it somehow destroy itself, commit a beautiful suicide. For it is this superpower that, through its unbearable power, is the secret cause of all the violence percolating all over the world, and consequently of the terrorist imagination, which unbeknownst to us, inhabits our psyche.[7]

5 Bart Moore-Gilbert, *Postcolonial Theory: Contexts, Practices, Politics* (London: Verso, 1997).

6 Zygmunt Bauman, *Globalization: The Human Consequence* (Cambridge: Polity Press, 1999), 18.

7 Jean Baudrillard, "L'Esprit du Terrorisme", *The South Atlantic Quarterly* 101 (2002): 404.

Finally, postcolonialist thinkers, who examine globalization from non-Western viewpoints, dwell on its diverse manifestations, not unlike the multiplicity of modernities. Arjun Appaduray maintains that "The central problem of today's global interactions is the tension between cultural homogenization and cultural heterogenization", and "The new global cultural economy has to be understood as a complex, overlapping, disjunctive order", which is shaped in the framework of the relationship between the "scapes" of ethnicity, media, technology, finance, and ideology.[8] These different global points of view led one scholar to coin the term "clash of globalizations".[9]

Several witty phrases have been thought up to articulate the double dialectical dynamics of global time and space. Manuel Castells, who largely focuses on the informational revolution, posits identity, from which people draw meaning and experience, against networking, which creates space for supra-temporal and anti-social flow space.[10] Benjamin Barber, who is much concerned about the fate of democracy, uses the more acute, though less accurate, metaphors of jihad and McWorld. From his perspective, jihad denotes militant Islamic fundamentalism, but also every anti-modern and anti-universalistic struggle, while McWorld, modelled on the McDonald's fast-food restaurant chain, epitomizes the economic and cultural Americanization at the heart of globalization.[11] The new dialectic is most aptly described as "glocalization", a composite of global and local, which combine to weaken the power and the frontiers of the nation-state.[12]

THE MODERN CHALLENGE

Sufism is the major sacrifice offered by Islam on the altar of its modernization in the past century and a half. The magnitude of this offering may be appreciated only when we realize the central role that Sufism filled in pre-modern Islam, up to the mid-nineteenth century. Contemporary Muslim historiography, and in its wake much Orientalist scholarship, constructed

[8] Arjun Appadurai, "Disjuncture and Difference in the Global Cultural Economy", in *Global Culture: Nationalism, Globalization and Modernity*. ed. Mike Featherstone (London: Sage, 1990), 295–6.

[9] Stanley Hoffman, "The Clash of Globalizations", *Foreign Affairs* 81, 4 (2002): 104–15.

[10] The concepts feature in the titles of the two first books in his trilogy: Manuel Castells, *The Information Age: Economy, Society and Culture*. vol. I: *The Rise of the Network Society* (Oxford: Blackwell, 1996), and vol. II: *The Power of Identity*. (Oxford: Blackwell, 1997).

[11] Benjamin R. Barber, *Jihad vs. McWorld* (New York: Ballantine Books, 1996).

[12] Roland Robertson, "Glocalization: Time–Space and Homogeneity–Heterogeneity", in *Global Modernities*. eds. Mike Featherstone, Scott Lash and Roland Robertson (London: Sage Publications, 1995), 25–44.

the ultra-orthodox Wahhabi movement as the standard-bearer of religious reform in the declining political landscape of the time. But as John Voll and others have convincingly demonstrated, the Wahhabiyya was rather the exception in a worldwide network of movements of renewal and revival under the inspiration and guidance of Sufi shaykhs.[13] These Sufi movements shifted their focus from converting non-Muslims to a stricter application of the *sharīʿa* as the key to political and social regeneration. Moreover, during this period Sufism in both its orthodox and its popular form was reorganized and greatly expanded to become the leading religious factor in the "civil society" of the time.

The term Sufism, like the more general term Islam, is a non-generic signifier pointing to a wide array of time- and space-dependent mystical phenomena, which can be neither reduced to one essence nor fixed as against other phenomena. In the classical literature, *taṣawwuf* and its synonyms encompassed complex spiritual teachings, and inspired poetry and influential socioreligious associations, along with superstitions, spells and amulets, and outright charlatanism.[14] The translation of the term *taṣawwuf* to Sufism by Western scholars should not be seen merely as an attempt to reflect the classical concept; it is actually a reconstruction of its content in the light of modern perceptions. Sufism thus joined other "isms" (Hinduism, Buddhism, etc.) through which Orientalism, an "ism" in its own right, sought to fix and classify the flow of "oriental religions". The shifting uses of the signifier *taṣawwuf* reflect hidden scholarly presumptions, as well as power relations, and interactions, between Europe and the Muslim peoples.[15] In the early colonial period "Sufism" referred to religious manifestations that Europeans found attractive and therefore separated them from "Islam", the religion of the enemy. In the heyday of the colonial scramble, by contrast, Sufi brotherhoods often came to symbolize "Islamic fanaticism", which fights the self-designated Western "civilizational mission".[16] Such re-signification of Sufism continues in the present age of globalization.

Obviously, not all or even most of the Sufi masters of the "long eighteenth century" took part in the religious renewal project of their time, which itself

13 Nehemia Levtzion and John O. Voll, eds. *Eighteenth-Century Renewal and Reform Movements in Islam* (Syracuse: Syracuse University Press, 1987).

14 Annemarie Schimmel, *Mystical Dimensions of Islam* (Chapel Hill: The University of North Carolina Press, 1975). ch. 1: "What is Sufism?"

15 This analysis relies on the theses of Edward Said, *Orientalism* (New York: Pantheon Books, 1978), as well as on the various reservations that were raised against it within postcolonial theory.

16 Carl W. Ernst, *Sufism: An Essential Introduction to the Philosophy and Practice of the Mystical Tradition of Islam* (Boston: Shambhala, 1997), 1–18.

was far from uniform.[17] Neither did their definition as Sufi masters exhaust their religious identity. Distinguished masters were always careful to combine their mystical piety with profound learning in the fields of law, *ḥadīth*, and theology. However important, Sufism was only one component of their religious constitution.[18] The strategies available to Sufi masters who preached reform in the pre-modern period were determined at the meeting point of three specific factors: their charisma, the mystical tradition to which they belonged, and the sociopolitical situation they had to deal with. Religious reform movements were led by a master who knew how to exert personal, spiritual, and practical influence over the elite and/or common people; who were moved into action by crises, such as the one that afflicted the Muslim world during the eighteenth century as Muslim states failed while Western pressure steadily mounted; and who belonged to orthodox and activist Sufi brotherhoods. Their traditions provided both a conceptual framework to analyze the situation and a practical course of action to amend it.

The pre-modern Sufi topography consisted of dozens of major brotherhoods and innumerable branches. However, as with "Sufism" and "Sufi shaykh", we must deconstruct the signifier "Sufi brotherhood" (*ṭarīqa*). On the one hand, the identity of each brotherhood was determined by its genealogy – that is to say, by the relation of the followers to a mythical founder who usually gave it its name, rather than by any actual attachment among themselves. On the other hand, in their archaeology, all brotherhoods rely to some extent on the mystical teachings of Ibn ʿArabī (d. 1240), while many Sufis belong to more than one brotherhood. Therefore, it might be more apt to translate the term *ṭarīqa* (literally, "the way") as mystical tradition – a living tradition that constantly adapts itself to new circumstances – than as order, which conveys a Christian bias,[19] or even as brotherhood, the term I use here as a metaphor. Several brotherhoods distinguished themselves in the Sufi landscape of pre-modern Islam by combining strict orthodoxy with active involvement in the affairs of society and state. Foremost among them were the worldwide Qādiriyya, the Egyptian-based Khalwatiyya, the North African Shādhiliyya, and, above all, the Asian-wide Naqshbandiyya with its centres in the Mughal and Ottoman Empires.

The threat to Sufism began to be felt in the second half of the nineteenth century, as Western ideas and institutions were incorporated into the efforts of

[17] Ahmad Dallal, "The Origins and Objectives of Islamic Revivalist Thought, 1750–1850", *Journal of the American Oriental Society* 113 (1993): 341–59.

[18] R.S. O'Fahey and Bernd Radtke, "Neo-Sufism Reconsidered", *Der Islam* 70 (1993): 52–87.

[19] See the seminal J. Spencer Trimingham, *The Sufi Orders in Islam* (Oxford: University Press, 1971).

Muslim polities to modernize. Westernization – the imitation of Western forms of modernity – proved antagonistic to Islamic mysticism in some major respects. One was the fundamental contradiction between Western secularism, which drew on new ideas of science and human progress, and Muslim religious faith, postulating submission to the word of God and historical regression from the Prophet's time to the Day of Judgment. More specific to Sufism was the danger of rationalist thinking, which posed reason above the a-rational experience of the Truth and the love of God. It also ridiculed the uncritical acceptance of Shaykhly authority in the brotherhoods and "exotic" popular practices. Concomitantly, commercialized capitalism challenged Sufi spirituality and its struggle against the soul's worldly desires.[20] Spreading Western ideas was facilitated by the introduction of print capitalism and modern education. Reading books and newspapers undermined the conventional oral transmission of knowledge in general, and the discreet guidance cherished by the Sufis in particular,[21] while public schools disciplined and reshaped the personality, thought, and tastes of the broadening enlightened public.[22] These processes resulted in the transformation of the Muslim public sphere, in Habermas' modernist terminology, or in the creation of a new discursive formation, according to the poststructural conceptions of Foucault.[23]

The Westernization project was led in the Muslim world by several local agents, foremost among them the state, the middle class, and Islamic Modernism. The modern, centralized bureaucratic, Muslim state was born out of the struggle against the political and military hegemony of the European powers.[24] Since modernization was imposed from above, the Muslim state has often turned authoritarian, subjecting civil society and the Sufi brotherhoods within it to its authority. "The new middle class", a category reinvented every generation, denotes those sectors of the Muslim society that strive to place it on the path of progress: intellectuals, merchants, army officers, and technocrats.[25] This class imbibed the values of Western

[20] See, Elizabeth Sirriyeh, *Sufis and Anti-Sufis: The Defence, Rethinking and Rejection of Sufism in the Modern World* (Richmond, Surrey: Curzon Press, 1999), 54–9.

[21] Francis Robinson, "Technology and Religious Change: Islam and the Impact of Print", *Modern Asian Studies* 27 (1993): 229–51.

[22] Timothy Mitchell, *Colonising Egypt* (Berkeley and Los Angeles: University of California Press, 1988), 82–92.

[23] Jürgen Habermas, *The Structural Transformation of the Public Sphere* (Cambridge MA: MIT Press, 1989); Michel Foucault, *The Archeology of Knowledge* (New York: Pantheon, 1972).

[24] Sami Zubaida, *Islam, the People and the State: Political Ideas and Movements in the Middle East* (London and New York: I.B. Tauris, 1993), 121–82.

[25] Manfred Halpern, *The Politics of Social Change in the Middle East and North Africa* (Princeton: Princeton University Press, 1963), 51–78.

rationalism and secularism at the expense of religious faith in general and Sufi mysticism in particular. The Islamic modernist trend represents the religious wing of the middle class and consists of thinkers who seek to prove Islam fully compatible with Western ideas and values.[26] They thereby paved the way for the two opposite yet complementary forces of nationalism and fundamentalism, which during the twentieth century combined to exclude Sufism from the public sphere. The national movement, the leader of the struggle against colonialism, reduced Islam to merely one component in the constitution of the nation and devised new forms of mass mobilization at the expense of the popular brotherhoods.[27] The fundamentalist trend, which began as religious protest against authoritarian Muslim regimes, promoted an Islamic alternative to Western-style modernization by re-imagining the origins of the Muslim nation (*umma*) and discrediting Sufism as the principal cause of the so-called decline of Islam.[28]

Religious and social opposition to Sufism was never absent from Muslim history. The modern assault, however, was of such intensity and magnitude that the Sufis seemed to be relegated to the margins of contemporary Muslim existence. Their teachings and practices acquired a bad reputation among the enlightened public, being invariably re-imagined as foreign, superstitious, corrupt, a major impediment to progress, and outright heretical. The leading role of past Sufi masters in the reform and jihad movements was forgotten, while contemporary ones were depicted as collaborators with colonial and indigenous tyrannical regimes. The humiliation of Sufism was the other side of the magnification of the Wahhabiyya as the prototype of modern Islamic movements.[29] Lying between the hammer of Westernization and the anvil of fundamentalism and nationalism, many Sufi brotherhoods lost their appeal. Their decline was particularly acute in the big cities, the centres of Muslim modernization, whence it gradually made its way to the urban and rural peripheries. From the modernist point of view, located in the centres of the

[26] Charles Kurzman, ed. *Modernist Islam 1840–1940: A Sourcebook* (New York: Oxford University Press, 2002), Introduction.

[27] Hamid Enayat, *Modern Islamic Political Thought* (Austin: University of Texas Press, 1982), 111–25.

[28] Itzchak Weismann, *Taste of Modernity: Sufism, Salafiyya, and Arabism in Late Ottoman Damascus* (Leiden: Brill, 2001), esp. ch. 8; Roxanne L. Euben, *Enemy in the Mirror: Islamic Fundamentalism and the Limits of Modern Rationalism* (Princeton: Princeton University Press, 1999).

[29] A key figure in the dissemination of this approach was Rashid Rida, who is often mistakenly described as the founder of the Salafiyya. On his attitude toward Sufism, see his autobiography, *al-Manar wa'l-Azhar* (Cairo: al-Manar, 1353/1934). For an analysis see: Albert Hourani, "Sufism and Modern Islam: Rashid Rida", in idem, *The Emergence of Modern Islam* (London: Macmillan, 1981), 90–102; Sirriyeh, *Sufis and Anti-Sufis*, 98–111.

new politics and culture Sufism came to be seen as a residue from the past, soon to disappear.[30]

Orientalist scholarship embraced the modern Muslim historiographical view of this subject too, as can be observed, for example, in the authoritative-scientific formulation of Arthur Arberry, the pre-eminent British scholar of Sufism, from 1950:

> The age of Ibn Farid, Ibn ʿArabi and Rumi [in the thirteenth century! I.W.] represents the climax of Sufi achievement, both theoretically and artistically. Thereafter, although through the numerous and ever multiplying Religious Orders the influence of Sufi thought and practice became constantly more widespread, and though sultans and princes did not disdain to lend the movement their patronage and personal adherence . . . the signs of decay appear more and more clearly, and abuse and scandal assail and threaten to destroy its fair reputation.[31]
>
> The wheel now appears to have turned full circle. Sufism has run its course; and in the progress of human thought it is illusory to imagine that there can ever be a return to the point of departure. A new journey lies ahead for humanity to travel.[32]

Apart from the salient essentialism of the text, it also hides the underlying modernist-Orientalist presupposition that Sufi shaykhs lack agency and merely succumb to the external action of the forces of modernity. As in other cases of subaltern studies, this presupposition proved utterly false. While many shaykhs resigned themselves to the new realities, or used them for their own opportunistic ends, others explored ways to adapt in order to preserve and even modernize their heritage.[33] The latter usually came from the Sufi reformist traditions. Their basic strategy in contending with the modern challenges was to forge an alliance with one or more of its local agents: the nation-state, the middle class, and/or Islamic fundamentalism. The choice of allies, and of enemies, ultimately depended on the concrete conditions in which each shaykh operated. The Sufis made ample use of print technology to defend and spread their message, and at times were even ready to transform their brotherhoods into new forms of organization more

[30] See Itzchak Weismann, "The Politics of Popular Religion: Sufis, Salafis, and Muslim Brothers in Twentieth-Century Hamah", *International Journal of Middle East Studies* 37 (2005): 39–58.

[31] A.J. Arberry, *Sufism: An Account of the Mystics of Islam* (London: Unwin Hyman, 1990 [1950]), 119.

[32] Ibid., 134.

[33] Among the first to observe this trend during an anthropological study of a Shādhīlī branch in Egypt was Michael Gilsenan, *Saint and Sufi in Modern Egypt: An Essay in the Sociology of Religion* (Oxford: Oxford University Press, 1973).

appropriate to the realities of mass education and growing literacy. Sufi efforts to regain Sufism's place in the public sphere thus entailed disclosing its mystical secrets and recreating its organizational bases.

Moreover, in the course of the twentieth century Sufism began to acquire Western followers. Muslim mystical traditions fascinated European intellectual circles that felt revulsion at the abject materialism overtaking their civilization, and these were later joined by free-spirited youngsters in search of refuge from modern techniques of discipline. Many were influenced by the teachings of René Guénon (d. 1951 in Egypt), a French convert who depicted Sufism as the solution to the spiritual crisis of the modern world, or by the writings of Western disciples of the Algerian Shaykh Ahmad al-'Alawi (d. 1934), who fought secularism and Westernization. This strand of Western mysticism is known as traditionalism.[34] Other Sufi masters turned their attention to Western audiences, either as an extension of their work among the fast-growing Muslim immigrant communities in Europe and North America, or by preaching directly to Europeans. One of the earliest was the Indian musician Inayat Khan (d. 1927), who at the turn of the twentieth century settled in the West and propagated a universal form of Sufism cut off from Muslim law and rituals.[35] Some Western Sufis converted to an orthodox form of Islam, while others maintained interest only in its esoteric aspect, thereby reproducing the early Orientalist divide between Sufism and Islam. Transplanting Sufism to the Western environment led to its integration into the larger phenomenon of mysticism – another modern "ism" – and consequently to its objectification – that is to say, its redefinition in relation to other mystical and religious traditions and to Western culture at large.[36]

BETWEEN ISLAM . . .

What changes can we observe in the position of Sufism with the onset of the age of globalization? Which global and local strategies do Sufi masters employ to manage postmodern realities? And how do such strategies influence contemporary Sufi teachings, brotherhoods, and related religious and spiritual organizations? Any attempt to assess Sufism's standing in such an era of accelerating change must begin with the temporal–spatial dialectics between

[34] Mark Sedgwick, *Against the Modern World: Traditionalism and the Secret Intellectual History of the Twentieth Century* (Oxford: University Press, 2004).

[35] Carl W. Ernst and Bruce B. Lawrence, *Sufi Martyrs of Love: The Chishti Order in South Asia and Beyond* (New York: Palgrave Macmillan, 2002), 140–3.

[36] On objectification as a defining feature of modern religious thought, see Dale F. Eickelman and James Piscatori, *Muslim Politics* (Princeton: Princeton University Press, 1996), 37–45.

globalization and modernity on one hand and the global and the local on the other hand. As late modernity, globalization amplifies secularization and rationalization, which caused the transformation of Islam and its mystical aspect in the past 150 years. But, as postmodernism it also undermines the enlightenment and progress paradigms, thereby creating new space for alternative modes of existence, including religious-spiritual phenomena like Sufism. In the same manner, the increasing flow of capital, information, and people around the globe deepens the Americanization of Muslim states and societies, pushing Sufism ever more to the local margins. But growing networking and mobility also allow Sufi masters to reach out to new Muslim and Western publics and to set up supra-national communities in conformity with the universal ideal of Islam, but also with the double dialectics of glocality and modernitraditionality underlying globalization. In this sense Sufism too enters its post era.

In the heterogeneous and unequal process that is globalization, the Muslim world has in many respects remained behind. Some commentators maintain that incorporation of the Muslim countries into the worldwide movement has barely begun. Others, who follow Samuel Huntington's infamous "clash of civilizations", tend to present "Islam" as the ultimate Other, not only of the "West" but of the world civilization it purports to lead; after all, the anti-global struggle must take place on the global level. The truth lies in between, in what Fred Halliday has dubbed "the politics of differential integration".[37] TV channels, satellite dishes, and the Internet provide Western commercial and cultural agents with unprecedented opportunities to penetrate the homes and hearts of the Muslim masses and inculcate in them their secular rational values and consumerist ethos. Still, the local agents of modernization are quick to adjust to the fledging global realities and divert them to their own benefit. The state, which holds to its narrow nationalist imagination, has remained authoritarian and perfects its control over civil society, while democracy is nowhere to be seen.[38] Under the aegis of the nation-state, the middle class gained a free hand to exploit the liberalization of the global economy to enrich itself.[39] Additionally, a radicalized Islamic fundamentalism

[37] Fred Halliday, "The Middle East and the Politics of Differential Integration", in *Globalization and the Middle East: Islam, Economy, Society and Politics.* eds. Toby Dodge and Richard Higgott (London: Royal Institute of International Affairs, 2002), 36–56.

[38] Emmanuel Sivan, *Hitnagshut be-toch Ha-Islam* (Clash within Islam) (Tel-Aviv, Am-Oved, 2005), 66–94 (in Hebrew).

[39] On the alliance between the state and the bourgeoisie in the age of globalization, see Toby Dodge, "Bringing the Bourgeoisie back in: the Birth of the Liberal Corporatism in the Middle East", in Dodge and Higgott, *Globalization and the Middle East*, 169–87.

has appropriated the frustrations of the "victims of globalization" and, under the umbrella of Usama bin Laden and al-Qaeda, produces terrorist spectacles such as 9/11 with the help of Western technology and communications.[40]

The direct and indirect intensification of the process of modernization in the past few decades has aggravated the basic dilemma facing Sufi masters, who must choose between preserving their local heritage, which is based on the saint's charisma, and adaptation to global realities, in which interpersonal relations are mediated through the media. The way out from this dilemma involves a complex dialectic of revealing and concealing. It is certainly premature to mourn traditional forms of Sufism. Whoever travels in Muslim countries cannot miss the innumerable active Sufi shrines and saints' tombs in the cities and the countryside, while discreet circles of mystics continue to meet to study the Sufi treatises.[41] Often, however, the shaykhs' spiritual and social authority is challenged by competing local and global cultural agents,[42] while weekly *dhikr* sessions and annual *mawlīd* celebrations commemorating the saint's death draw ever fewer adherents. Sufi rituals occasionally turn into folklore or a tourist attraction, as in the case of the whirling dervishes, whose picturesque performances of *dhikr* accompanied by music and dance attract large audiences throughout the world.[43]

The Sufi shaykhs whose voices are most heard in the contemporary Muslim public sphere are those who are able to keep and further tighten their strategic alliances with the agents of modernity. Normally, though by no means exclusively, such shaykhs still originate in the leading reformist brotherhoods of the modern period – the Qādiriyya, Khalwatiyya, Shādhiliyya, and Naqshbandiyya – and continue to cherish the experiential personal relationship on which the master's authority over his disciples has traditionally relied. In tackling the competing practices and discursive formations of the nation-state, the middle class, and Islamic fundamentalism, however, they often opt to conceal the Sufi component of their identity and re-invent their brotherhoods as political organizations, socioeconomic and cultural societies, or even fundamentalist movements. Paradoxically, this

[40] Rohan Gunaratna, *Inside al-Qaeda: Global Network of Terror* (London: Hurst, 2002); Marc Sageman, *Understanding Terror Networks* (Philadelphia: University of Pennsylvania Press, 2004).

[41] Michel Chodkiewicz, "Le soufisme au XXIe siècle", in *Les Voies d'Allah: Les Ordres Mystiques dans l'Islam des Origins à Aujourd'hui*", eds. Alexandre Popovic and Gilles Veinstein (Paris: Fayard, 1996), 532–43.

[42] Several shaykhs I interviewed in Egypt, India and elsewhere have complained that nowadays people are too busy to dedicate the time needed to follow the Sufi path.

[43] See, e.g., the program of the al-Kindi ensemble at www.turath.org/Events/Dervishes.htm.

concealment does not prevent Sufi masters and leaders of Sufi-inspired organizations from exploiting the most advanced communication technologies, especially the Internet, to promote their public standing and spread their message.

The major strategy of the Sufi masters of the age of globalization is to tighten their ties with the state, still the principal agent of modernity throughout the Muslim world. This relationship is particularly important under authoritarian regimes. Collaboration with the state underlies the alliance that the Naqshbandī Shaykh Aḥmad Kuftaro (d. 2004) forged with the basically sectarian and secular Ba'th regime in Syria.[44] The Grand Mufti of the country for four decades, Kuftaro responded to the anti-Sufi diatribes of the modernist-Salafi trend by suggesting abandonment of Sufi terminology, even the word *taṣawwuf* itself, for Qur'ānic terms more acceptable to his opponents. He made extensive use of the media to convey his ideas, which in his latter years came to include topics at the top of the global agenda such as interfaith dialogue, human rights, and the environment.[45] An open alliance between the Naqshbandiyya and the regime has also existed in Uzbekistan, the homeland of the brotherhood, since independence in 1991. The post-Communist government cultivates the Naqshbandiyya as part of the national heritage and as a counterweight to local Islamic fundamentalism.[46] In Saddam Hussein's Iraq, state patronage was extended to the Kasanzānī branch of the Qādiriyya from Kirkuk, apparently to offset the influence of the dominant Sufi brotherhoods among the surrounding Kurdish population. Following Saddam's removal by the US-led coalition army, the Kasanzānīs were targeted by the Islamist resistance under the aegis of al-Qaeda.[47]

44 Annabelle Böttcher, *Syrische Religionspolitik unter Asad* (Freiburg: Arnold Bergstrasser Institut, 1998), 147–223. Also see Muhammad Habash, *al-Shaykh Ahmad Kuftaro wa-manhajuhu fi al-tajdid wa'l-islah* (Damascus, n.p., 1996).

45 Leif Stenberg, "Naqshbandiyya in Damascus: Strategies to Establish and Strengthen the Order in a Changing Society", in *Naqshbandis in Western and Central Asia*. ed. Elisabeth Özdalga (Istanbul: Swedish Research Institute, 1999), 111–15. On the Salafi discourse of Kuftaro, see Itzchak Weismann, "Sufi Fundamentalism between India and the Middle East", in *Sufism and the "Modern"*. eds. Martin van Bruinessen and Julia Howell (London and New York: I.B. Tauris, 2007), 115–28. His Internet site is www.abrahamicreligions.com%20.

46 Bakhtiyar Babajanov, "Le renouveau des connunautes soufies en Ouzbekistan", *Cahiers d'Asie Central* 5–6 (1998): 285–311; Vernon James Schubel, "Post-Soviet Hagiography and the Reconstruction of the Naqshbandi Tradition in Contemporary Uzbekistan", in Ozdalga, *Naqshbandis in Western and Central Asia*, 73–87; Igor Rotar, "Uzbekistan: Government backs Sufism to Counter Wahhabism", Keston New Service, 24 May 2002, www.religioscope.com/info/notes/2002_052_uzbek_sufi.htm.

47 Muhammad 'Abd al-Karim al-Kasanzani, *al-Anwar al-rahmaniyya fi al-tariqa al-Qadiriyya al-Kasanzaniyya* (Cairo: Matba'at Madbuli, 1990): www.nytimes.com.2005/06/03/intrnational/middleeast/03cnd-iraq.html.

Sufi links to the state are also partially concealed under less authoritarian governments. In Egypt, Sufi brotherhoods regularly participate in the Prophet's birthday celebrations, while pilgrimage to Shaykh Aḥmad al-Badawī's tomb in Tanta still attracts multitudes. The state is particularly interested in cultivating the more reformist brotherhoods – the Shādhiliyya and Khalwatiyya – as a counterweight to the wide popularity of the Muslim Brethren. Many Egyptian high religious officials, as well as rectors and teachers at the prestigious al-Azhar university, belong to these two brotherhoods, though this affiliation is hardly known to the public.[48] Among Muslim minorities, ties to the government may be even more concealed and confined to the communal level. In India, the popular Chishtī shrines are packed for most of the year, but particularly during the celebrations of the saint's birthday, known there as *'urs* (wedding). Threatened by an aggressive wave of Hindu nationalism, the heads of the Indian brotherhoods prefer to focus on community affairs and avoid national politics.[49] Discreet collaboration with the state characterizes the Raḥmānī branch of the Khalwatiyya in Israel. Following the occupation of the West Bank in 1967, its Palestinian shaykh, who resides in Jenin, was allowed freely to visit his followers on the Israeli side of the border. Under the aegis of the Jewish state, the brotherhood runs an impressive Islamic College with close to a thousand students, which includes departments of English, mathematics, and computer science.[50]

Historical circumstances play their part in shaping the relations between Sufism and the state. In the Turkish republic the Sufi brotherhoods were outlawed in 1925. Officially in force to this day, the ordinance was directed primarily against the Naqshbandiyya, the leading brotherhood both in the Western parts of the country and among the Kurdish population in the east. The Turkish Naqshbandīs continued to work underground and developed unofficial institutions and discourses that gradually restored the brotherhood to its former political and social position. In Istanbul, Zahid Kotku's branch attracted many future intellectuals and politicians, including Islamic Prime

48 Valerie J. Hoffman, *Sufism, Mystics and Saints in Modern Egypt* (Columbia: University of Southern Carolina Press, 1995); Rachida Chih, *Le Sufism au Quotidian. Confrérie d'Egypt au XXème Siècle* (Aix-en-Provence: Actes Sud, 2000).

49 This description is based on my visits to the major Chishti shrines in India: Muinuddin Chishti in Ajmer, Nizamuddin Awliya in Delhi, Gisudaraz in the Deccan, and others during 2001–4.

50 'Afif ibn Husni al-Din al-Qasimi, *Adwa' 'ala al-triqa al-Khalwatiyya al-Jami'a al-Rahmaniyya* (n.p., n.d.). Also see Itzchak Weismann, "Sufi Brotherhoods in Syria and Israel: A Contemporary Overview", *History of Religions* 43 (2004): 303–18.

Ministers Nejmettin Erbakan and Recep Tayyip Erdogan.[51] In Senegal, by contrast, the Sufi brotherhoods are omnipresent. The Tijāniyya, an offshoot of the Moroccan Khalwatiyya, and the Murīdiyya, a local branch of the Qādiriyya, were both founded in the second half of the nineteenth century. Beginning in the countryside, their leaders adjusted to the growing urbanization of the colonial and post-colonial eras and turned them into powerful city-based socioeconomic organizations. Following independence, the Sufi shaykhs filled a major role in keeping the country democratic, and in every election campaign they are courted by the political parties.[52] In Sudan the major Sufi and Sufi-related brotherhoods – the Khatmiyya and the Maḥdiyya – themselves turned into political parties. Though enjoying considerable social bases, their power has been seriously eroded in the past few decades by autocratic military regimes and the Islamist movement.[53]

As allies of the state, Sufi brotherhoods may become attractive to religiously inclined members of the middle class, who seek to secure Islam's place in the politics of national identity and see it as a meaningful anchor in the era of global uncertainty. Considering the role of the middle class in the process of globalization, associating with it may also be an independent strategy, especially when the state fails the brotherhoods or in times of political crisis. Integration into the bourgeois economic and cultural project is marked, for instance, in an Egyptian–Lebanese branch of the Shādhiliyya. It is headed by a self-styled oil magnate and a female professor of philosophy, who since the 1970s have presented their group as a "family" rather than a brotherhood, and who hold intellectual liberal *dhikr* sessions for both men and women.[54] In Istanbul, Kotku's Naqshbandī successors took advantage of the 1980s economic liberalization of Turkey to reshape their brotherhood as a capitalistic enterprise, running its own TV station and newspapers.[55] A similar businesslike reorganization took place during the 1990s in such disparate countries as

[51] Thierry Zarcone, "Les Nakşhibedi et la République turque: de la persécution au repositionnement théologique, politique et social (1925–91)", *Turcica* 24 (1992): 133–51; idem, "The Transformation of the Sufi Orders (Tarikat) in the Turkish Republic and the Question of Crypto-Sufism", in *Cultural Horizons: A Festschrift in honor of Talat S. Halman*. ed. Jayne L. Warner (New York: Syracuse University Press, 2001), 198–209.

[52] Leonardo A. Villalón, "Sufi Modernities in Contemporary Senegal: Religious Dynamics between the Local and the Global", in van Bruinessen and Howell, *Sufism and the "Modern"*, 172–91.

[53] Gabriel Warburg, "Mahdism and Islamism in the Sudan", *International Journal of Middle East Studies* 27 (1995): 219–36.

[54] Mark Sedgwick, *Saints and Sons: The Making and Remaking of the Rashidi Ahmadi Sufi Order, 1799–2000* (Leiden: Brill, 2005), 195–219.

[55] Hakan Yavuz, "The Matrix of Modern Turkish Islamic Movements: the Naqshbandī Sufi Order", in Özdalga, *Naqshbandis in Western and Central Asia*, 137. The main Internet sites of Kosan Naqshbandi branch are www.gumushkhanawidargah.8m.com and www.iskenderpasa.com.

Malaysia and Mali.[56] In Indonesia, the basically secular official ideology of the Pancasila notwithstanding, renewed interest in Sufism has been awakened among elements of the upper middle class in the wake of the economic crisis and the political upheavals of the closing years of the last century.[57]

The recent awakened interest in Sufism should be seen in the context of the larger Islamic revival that overtook the Muslim world in the last quarter of the twentieth century as a result of the general disappointment with imported nationalist, capitalist, and socialist ideologies. The radical fundamentalist edge of this revival draws most public attention due to its militant attacks on the West and its local agents, but no less important is its enmity toward latter-day Muslim tradition, especially its Sufi aspect. Among moderate fundamentalist movements, however, the Sufi background is often not far from the surface, allowing dialogue, negotiation, and compromise between the two trends. This was the case for Abū al-Hasan ʿAlī al-Nadwī (d. 1999), an outstanding religious leader of the Muslim community of India in the second half of the twentieth century. Nadwī maintained his roots in the Naqshbandī brotherhood along with the close relations he developed with the Saudi Wahhabis and with fundamentalist circles in other Arab countries. His was a viable Islamic alternative to the anti-Sufi radical Abū al-Aʿla al-Mawdūdī, founder of Jamāʿat-i Islāmī, who in the wake of partition opted for Pakistan.[58] Negotiation takes place in many African states between local Sufi brotherhoods and Middle Eastern-type fundamentalism, in what has been respectively defined as "African Islam" and "Islam in Africa".[59] Shīʿī Sufi elements are discernible in the teachings of Ayatollah Khomeini, leader of the Islamic revolution in Iran, for whom spiritual revival was a major component in the new Islamic order he set out to create.[60]

. . . AND THE WEST

Muslim communities in the West constitute an integral part of the multinational and multicultural societies in which they live. Nevertheless, in the

[56] Benjamin F. Soares, "Saint and Sufi in Contemporary Mali", in van Bruinessen and Howell, *Sufism and the "Modern"*, 76–91.

[57] Julia Day Howell, "Sufism and the Indonesian Islamic Revival", *The Journal of Asian Studies* 60 (2001): 701–29.

[58] Jan-Peter Hartung, *Viele Wege und ein Ziel, Leben und Wirken von Sayyid Abu l-Hasan ʿAli al-Hasani Nadwi (1914–1999)* (Würzburg: Ergon, 2004), 250–71.

[59] Eva Evers Rosander and David Westerlund, eds. *African Islam and Islam in Africa: Encounters between Sufis and Islamists* (Athens: Ohio University Press, 1997).

[60] Alexander Knysh, "ʿIrfan Revisited: Khomeini and the Legacy of Islamic Mysticism", *Middle East Journal* 46 (1992): 631–53.

"host" European and North American societies many hold to Orientalist and racist conceptions and view them as nothing but an outgrowth of the Islamic Other. The inner contradictions in the situation of the Muslim communities, and of the surrounding societies, in themselves and in their mutual relationship, dictate different emphases in their "politics of differential integration" from those prevalent in the Muslim world. The distance from the Muslim authoritarian state opens the door for immigrants and their Western-born descendants to integrate into their new global civilization. Such integration ranges from demanding their civil right to preserve their Muslim identity, that is, by wearing the veil in French schools, to full assimilation à la Salman Rushdie, author of the controversial *The Satanic Verses*. On the other hand, Western liberal democracy reveals growing intolerance of the Muslim immigrants' otherness among indigenous populations, but also facilitates dialogue within a common public sphere. Technological improvements in communication similarly bring the immigrants nearer to their original societies and to each other, thereby inevitably strengthening their Muslim solidarity. This, however, is imagined in new ways, from a modernist liberal-bourgeois understanding of Islam to radical anti-Western militancy. Mass communications enhance Westerners' knowledge of Islam, while nevertheless demonizing it as an aggressive religious civilization of jihad.[61]

The existential postmodern condition prevalent in the West in the age of globalization leaves plenty of room for Sufi activity among both Muslim communities and host societies. It is shared by shaykhs in the traditional sense, leaders of Islamic movements that branched off from Sufism, Western converts who found their own Sufi groups, and all sorts of spiritual guides who include Sufism in their New Age culture. The central dilemma before these agents is in many ways opposite to that before Sufi shaykhs in the Muslim lands: how to market an Islamic-rooted heritage among audiences suspicious of Islam. Attempts to solve this dilemma include, apart from the basic revelation and concealment, a complementary dialectical strategy of adjustment and separation. This directs both disseminators of Sufism whose frame of reference is Islam and those more attuned to the general spiritual awakening in the West. Any visit to a bookshop specializing in mysticism, or surfing through Internet sites devoted to spirituality, cannot miss what Carl Ernst calls "the publication of the secret".[62] This inevitably involves

[61] On Muslim communities in the West see Gilles Kepel, *Allah in the West: Islamic Movements in America and Europe* (Cambridge: Polity Press, 1997); Jørgen S. Nielsen, *Towards European Islam* (New York: St. Martin's Press, 1999).

[62] Ernst, *Sufism*, 215–20. See also, idem, "Ideological and Technological Transformations of Contemporary Sufism", in *Muslim Networks from Hajj to Hip Hop*. eds. Miriam Cooke and

superficiality and commercialization through which Sufi teachings and rituals are absorbed by New Age syncretism and its consumerist setting. As against this, Sufi shaykhs in the West seek to preserve their traditions and provide their followers with personal guidance at public meetings or at least through the telephone and the Internet.

Sufi activity in the West is closely associated with the flow of Muslim workers and refugees in the post-World War II period to the rich and free countries of Western Europe and North America. Various brotherhoods followed the immigrants, particularly those with reformist background. Thus, for example, in the 1960s a Naqshbandī branch from northwest Pakistan began sending representatives to England to teach Pakistani immigrant workers the precepts of their religion. Gradually the British community of the brotherhood was established, annually recreating itself through the *ʿurs* and other traditional rituals.[63] The Murīdiyya and Tijāniyya brotherhoods formed the web of Senegalese immigrant communities that established themselves from the 1970s in France, North America, and West Africa. The spread of the Murīdiyya was facilitated by its international commercial networks,[64] while the Tijānis target the Afro-American population.[65]

Other Sufi brotherhoods were implanted in Western Europe and North America at the request of mystically-inclined immigrants as well as locals. The founder of the Jerrahi branch of the Khalwatiyya in the United States arrived there in 1980, after a succession of visits by American students to its hospices in Istanbul. Subsequently this branch spread to other countries in America and to Australia, where its centres are led by Muslim or convert shaykhs according to local circumstances. In the USA, following the *shariʿa* is deferred to advanced stages, while the *dhikr* is performed by men and women jointly.[66] Shaykh Dr. Jawad Nurbakhsh of the Shīʿī Niʿmatullāhiyya brotherhood travelled to America in response to the keen interest in Sufism he observed among American visitors to Iran and Iranian students in America. In the wake of the Islamic revolution he moved to the USA, but finally settled

Bruce B. Lawrence (Chapel Hill and London: The University of North Carolina Press, 2005), 191–207.

63 Pnina Werbner, *Pilgrims of Love: The Anthropology of a Global Sufi Cult* (Bloomington and Indianapolis: Indiana University Press, 2003).

64 Victoria Ebin, "Making Room versus Creating Space: The Construction of Spatial Categories by Itinerant Mouride Traders", in *Making Muslim Space in North America and Europe*. ed. B. Metcalf (Berkeley: University of California Press, 1996), 92–109.

65 www.tijaniyya.com%20.

66 Marcia Hermansen, "In the Garden of American Sufi Movements: Hybrids and Perennials", in *New Trends and Developments in the World of Islam*. ed. Peter B. Clarke (London: Luzac Oriental, 1997), 157–60. The main Internet site of the brotherhood is www.jerrahi.org.

in London, where he propagates a spiritual message that combines mysticism with psychoanalysis while glossing over the Islamic character of Sufism.[67]

The most visible shaykh in the global Sufi arena today is the Naqshbandī master Nazim al-Haqqani, a Turkish Cypriot who spends most of the year travelling among communities of his followers in most Muslim and non-Muslim countries of the world. His teaching combines nostalgia for the Ottoman past with uncompromising hostility to "Wahhabism" and an apocalyptic-messianic vision with universal elements. In London, where Haqqani began his global career in 1972, his community consists of three distinct groups: a majority of Indians and Pakistanis, ethnic Turks, and Western converts; each meets separately around a message that befits its spiritual economy: the master's personal charisma, keeping the *sharīʿa* in an alien environment, and spirituality, respectively.[68] His son-in-law, Hisham Qabbani, settled in the USA in 1991, where he set up a well-organized network of Sufi centres for Muslims and converts alike; he skilfully exploits capitalistic marketing strategies and the Internet to spread Islam and the brotherhood. Qabbani has testified on a number of occasions before Congressional committees and in the press about violent fundamentalist preaching in American mosques, to the chagrin of other trends in American Islam.[69]

Muslim immigrant communities in Europe and North America are also fertile soil for Islamic movements with roots in Sufism but that distance themselves from its traditional forms of organization and/or teachings. The Indian conservative Barelwis use legal opinions (sing. *fatwa*), books, and sermons to defend saint worship and the intermediary role of living masters. In Scotland, as in Britain at large, mosques affiliated to the movement serve as bases for its founder's Qādiriyya brotherhood, and many members have a *pīr* (spiritual master) in Pakistan.[70] On the continent a number of modernist

[67] Leonard Lewisohn, "Persian Sufism in the Contemporary West: Reflections on the Niʿmatu'llahi Diaspora", in *Sufism in the West*. eds. Jamal Malik and John Hinnels (London and New York: Routledge, 2006), 49–70; See also, Javad Nurbakhsh, "The Nimatullahi", in *Islamic Spirituality II: Manifestations*. ed. Sayyid Hussein Nasr (New York: Crossroads, 1991), 144–59. Also see www.nimatullahi.org.

[68] Tayfun Atay, "Naqshbandi Sufis in a Western Setting", D. Phil. thesis, University of London (SOAS), 1995.

[69] Annabelle Böttcher, "The Naqshbandiyya in the United States." www.naqshbandi.net (article posted 20 July 2002); David W. Damrel, "Aspects of the Naqshbandi-Haqqani Order in North America", in Malik and Hinnels, *Sufism in the West*, 115–26. The Internet sites the brotherhoods activates in the United States are: www.naqshbandi.org; the as-Sunna Foundation in America – www.sunna.org; the Islamic Supreme Council of America – www.islamicsupremecouncil.org; and the Muslim Women's organization – www.kamilat.org.

[70] A.Y. Andrews, "South Asian Sunni Reform Movements in the West: The Lang Scots Miles from Delhi to Dandi", in Clarke, *New Trends*, 59–73.

Turkish movements distinguish themselves from Sufism, but in one way or another are related to the Naqshbandiyya. The oldest is the Nurju movement, founded by the influential Kurdish thinker Said Nursi (d. 1960). In this movement the Sufi brotherhood was replaced by reading circles, which through the founder's writings – *Risale-i Nur* – engage in a regular modern-liberal interpretation of Islam.[71] The Nurju movement, its Fethullah Gülen offshoot, and the Suleimanji[72] maintain wide networks of Islamic schools among Turkish immigrants in Germany and other European countries, as well as in the Turkish republics of Central Asia and in the Caucasus.[73]

Sufi brotherhoods and derivative Islamic movements active in the European and North American space tend to redraw themselves as a bridge between East and West, as an alternative to the exclusive Wahhabi–Salafi trend, and as part of overall human spirituality. Inclusiveness is strongest among Western converts who lead their own Sufi movements. Theirs, however, is often an alternative to Western Christian civilization. It may range from a fundamentalist-like desire to convert the West to Islam, through the orthodox demand by Western Sufis to follow the *shari'a*, to the integration of Sufism in the general flow of world mysticism. The Sufi mission is represented by Ian Dallas (alias Abdalqadir as-Sufi), an initiate of the Moroccan Shādhiliyya, who founded the Murabitun movement with the aim of reconstituting "European Islam". Dallas initially required his followers to wear distinctive cloths and sever all contact with modern civilization, but later on was obliged to allow them to send their children to school, use electricity, and dress like Europeans. In the 1990s Dallas was accused of expressing admiration for Hitler and advocating Nazism.[74]

The traditionalist school and its various post-World War II splinters[75] show a completely different attitude. Some are orthodox, such as the French group of Michel Valsan (d. 1974), a follower of Guénon who lived as a pious Sufi shaykh in the Muslim milieu of Paris. He passed his keen interest in Ibn 'Arabī's teachings on to his disciples, foremost among them Michel Chodkiewicz, whose acclaimed studies of the Great Master gained him a professorship at

[71] Şerif Mardin, *Religion and Social Change in Modern Turkey: The Case of Bediüzzaman Said Nursi* (Albany: State University of New York Press, 1989).

[72] See Gerdien Jonker, "The Evolution of the Naqshbandi-Mujaddidi: The Sulaymançis in Germany", in Malik and Hinnels, *Sufism in the West*, 71–85.

[73] M. Hakan Yavuz, "Toward an Islamic Liberalism? The Nurcu Movement and Fethullah Gülen", *Middle East Journal* 53 (1999): 584–605; www.en.fgulen.com; www.fethullahgulen.org.

[74] Peter B. Clarke, "The Sufi Path in Britain. The Revivalist Tendency", *Update* 3 (1983): 12–16.

[75] Sedgwick, *Against the Modern World*, 133–77.

the Sorbonne.[76] On the other hand we find the Swiss Frithjof Schuon (d. 1998), a convert to Islam who ultimately replaced it with the Perennialist postulate of the infinite universal Truth underlying all religions. His ideas combined Ibn ʿArabī's teaching with Christian esotericism and Native American religion. Schuon was able to attract well-known Western Sufis such as his compatriot Titus Burckhardt and the British Martin Lings, as well as the Iranian mystic philosopher Seyyed Hossein Nasr, who after the Islamic revolution fled to the USA. Following a dream in which he saw the Virgin, Schuon changed his brotherhood's name to Maryamiyya, accepted non-Muslim adherents, and developed an esoteric teaching that focused on his own personality.[77]

Sufi shaykhs like Nurbakhsh or spiritual guides like Schuon lead us to the threshold of the New Age. This signifier encompasses a wide range of syncretistic beliefs and practices which converge in the search for spiritual perfection in the universe and in the private self.[78] Sufi groups that are part of the New Age normally separate Sufism from Islam, mingle it with all sorts of religious and spiritual systems, and make selective use of modern sciences, especially psychology and physics. In a mysticism that focuses on self-realization, prosperity and happiness, affiliation to one Sufi brotherhood or another becomes irrelevant.

The wealth of Sufi movements in the spiritual market of the New Age is hard to classify. One major question is the extent to which they remain attached to Muslim Sufi traditions or become assimilated into the overall spirituality. Reshad Field, whose fictional autobiographic book *The Last Barrier* tells the story of his initiation into the Mevlevi brotherhood, is an example of adhering to Sufism in its conventional sense. The institute he set up engages in teaching "the essence of knowledge" of the Sufi tradition.[79] The Golden Sufi Center is associated with the Sufi heritage, but an unusual type of it. The centre was established by Irene Tweedie, who was initiated into a Hindi offshoot of the Naqshbandiyya in India.[80] Her successor, Llewellyn

[76] Michel Chodkiewicz's main books are: *An Ocean Without Shore: Ibn ʿArabi, The Book, and the Law* (Albany: State University of New York Press, 1993); *Seal of the Saints: Prophethood and Sainthood in the Doctrine of Ibn ʿArabi* (Cambridge: The Islamic Texts Society, 1993); *Emir Abd el-Kader: Ecrits spirituels* (Paris: Editions du Seuil, 1982).

[77] Jean-Baptiste Aymard and Patrick Laude, *Frithof Schuon: Life and Teachings* (Albany: State University of New York Press, 2004).

[78] Philip Wexler, *The Mystical Society: An Emerging Social Vision* (Boulder, CO: Westview, 2000).

[79] Reshad Field, *The Last Barrier* (New York: Harper & Row, 1976).

[80] Sara Sviri, "Daughter of Fire by Irina Tweedie: Documentation and Experience of a Modern Naqshbandi Sufi", in *Women as Teachers and Disciples in Traditional and New Religions*. eds. E. Puttick and P.B. Clark (Lewiston: Edwin Mellen Press, 1993), 77–89.

Vaughan-Lee, combines this more than a century-old tradition with the dream interpretation of Karl Gustav Jung.[81] No less interesting is "the Abrahamic way" in Israel, which tries to make a contribution to Jewish-Arab dialogue by renewing medieval "Jewish Sufism". It embraces academics, Conservative rabbis and Sufi shaykhs, who meet in seminars combining lectures and joint *dhikr*.[82]

Commitment to Sufism, as distinct from Islam, characterizes the writings of Idris Shah (d. 1996), the most widely read Sufi author in the West. A British citizen of Afghan descent, Shah's name was associated with the Russian mystic Gurdjieff[83] through his English disciple John Bennett, as well as with the Naqshbandiyya. In his numerous works he maintained that Sufism emerged in prehistory and that it has nothing to do with Islam; it is rather a "formless truth" that redefines itself according to circumstances of time and place. Shah believed that rather than engaging in the advanced stages of the path, which only a few might attain, the role of the spiritual guide in our individualist and materialist age must be confined to a psychological preparation for the struggle against the temptations that surround us.[84] Equally uncommitted to Islam is the Muhyiddin Ibn ʿArabi Society, which was founded in Oxford in 1977 with a branch in Berkeley, California, and which accepts members from all religions. Its stated aim is to study and spread the teachings of the great Sufi master and his school, and for that purpose it seeks manuscripts of Ibn ʿArabī, organizes annual quasi-academic conferences to discuss his teachings, and publishes books and its own periodical.[85]

In many New Age movements, Sufism is part of a mixture of spiritual teachings and techniques purporting to bring instant enlightenment. Such is the case of "the Sufi order in the West" of Vilayat Khan (d. 2004), son of Inayat Khan. Pir Vilayat followed the syncretistic tendency of his father in his "universal worship of God", which includes reading selected passages from the scriptures of different world religions and meditation techniques from various esoteric traditions and Jungian psychology. The *dhikr* is one of these spiritual methods, but not necessarily the five daily prayers of Islam.[86] In the Indonesian Subud movement the pre-Islamic mystic traditions of Java are

81 www.goldensufi.org.

82 Weismann, "Syria and Israel", 317.

83 On Jurdjeiff's teachings, see P.D. Ouspensky, *In Search of the Miraculous: Fragments of an Unknown Teaching* (New York: Harcourt, Brace, 1949).

84 James Moore, "Neo-Sufism: The Case of Idries Shah", *Journal of Contemporary Religion* 3, 3 (1986): 4–8. www.sufis.org.

85 www.ibnarabisociety.org.

86 James Jervis, "The Sufi Order in the West and Pir Vilayat Khan: Space-Age Spirituality in Contemporary Euro-America", in Clarke, *New Trends*, 211–60.

combined with local forms of Sufism. The founder was originally affiliated with the Naqshbandiyya, but claimed to sever his ties. Subud is basically free spiritual training and purification that lead to awareness of God's omnipotence and personal perfection. It may be attached to any religion.[87] In "the Sufi dance movement" of Samuel Lewis – Murshid Sam (d. 1971), a member of "the Sufi Order in the West" who also studied Zen Buddhism and claimed to have "inner" authorization from Jesus – dances are performed in a circle around the guide, who sings: *la illa ila Allah*, *Hari Krishna Hari Rama*, and *Shma' Israel*.[88] Such movements led one critic of the New Age to remark sardonically that

> The New Age, besides being an "upsurge of the human spirit" and so on is also a fairly vast industry, driven by a considerable commercial dynamic. We may not have to wait too long for the more repellent aspects of the New Age spiritual Disneyland to claim another victim, and books on Sufi crystal healing, Sufi geomancy, talks with Sufi dolphins, and Sex Secrets of the Sufi Maters may be going to the press as I write.[89]

New Age Sufi guides often cooperate and learn from each other. In the USA an annual Sufi conference has convened since 2001 "to create a space where people could experience the various forms of Sufism". Invited to speak at the 2005 conference were Ziya Inayat Khan, the new head of "the Sufi Order in the West", Shaykha Farha Jerrahi of the Khalwatiyya, Llewellyn Vaughan-Lee of the Sufi Golden Center, and Peter Kingsley, who devotes his time to reviving Western mystical traditions.[90]

New Age manifestations are by no means confined to Western Europe or North America. In the present era of rapid movement of capital, information, and people they re-emerge among the agents of globalization in the Muslim world itself. In Morocco, for instance, "imported" spiritual methods like Yoga and Zen, all sorts of therapies, and the traditionalist school of Guénon have awakened a new interest in Sufism in the upper middle class. These turn particularly to the Budshishiyya brotherhood, which combines different spiritual techniques within an anti-legalist religious vision of individual self-fulfilment.[91] In Indonesia managers and senior bureaucrats, in their leisure

87 Antoon Geels, *Subud and the Javanese Mystical Tradition* (Richmond Surrey: Curzon, 1997). The official site of the world Subud movement is www.subud.org.

88 www.towardtheone.com/sufidance/index.htm; www.ruhaniyat.org/lineage/SAMBio.php.

89 Peter Wilson, "The Strange Fate of Sufism in the New Age", in Clarke, *New Trends*, 179–209. The quote is from 204.

90 www.suficonference.org.

91 Patrick Haenni, "God by All Means ... Eclectic Faith and Sufi Resurgence among the Moroccan Bourgeoisie", in van Bruinessen and Howell, *Sufism and the "Modern"*, 241–56.

time, attend abridged courses on Sufism held in luxurious hotels and conference halls.[92] Integration into the global trend is discernible even among Sufi branches that remain local. In a leaflet published by a Naqshbandī shaykh from the town of Rampur in northern India, entitled *The Light of Gnosis*, those wishing to enjoy the blessing of Islamic spirituality and Divine truth, whatever their nation or state, are invited to come and stay at his hospice.[93] During my visit to Rampur in February 2003 this offer of Sufi guidance was extended to me in person, even though I identified myself as an Israeli and Jewish.

CONCLUSION

From remote popular saints' tombs, through brotherhoods with government and middle class ties, to New Age cults that market themselves on the Internet, Sufism manages to preserve much of its charm in the age of globalization. The time/space dialectics that constitute our era sharpen the paradoxical existence of Islamic mysticism – between man and God, the now and the eternal, matter and spirit, being and nothingness – the oppositions whose transcendence, combining the contrasts in the Sufi terminology, is the root of the spiritual experience. Nowadays new paradoxes are added to these. Though retreating in the face of the secular and fundamentalist forces, the Sufi message has become more diversified and attractive than ever. While losing local ground under the growing pressures of mobilization and networking, its spread reaches all corners of the globe.

These achievements are not merely an objective effect of globalization. They are no less a product of the strategies employed by the Sufi propagators in their effort to cope with the challenge. These move in the double dialectics of revelation and concealment, adjustment and separation. Sufi masters often face serious difficulties in preserving their heritage in Muslim countries, but gain many followers in a West yearning for spirituality. This territorial movement involves an unprecedented transformation of Sufism: from an esoteric teaching leading to self-annihilation before uniting with God to a practical way of attaining individual bliss and success here and now, and from the inner-mystical aspect of Islam to another spiritual technique which may be mingled according to changing tastes and fashions with other techniques. Drawing on traditional Sufism, but also undermining it, such manifestations, like modernity itself, herald the coming of the age of post-Sufism.

[92] Noorhaidi Hasan and Ahmad Syafi'I Mufid, "When Executives Chant Dhikr", *International Institute for Asian Studies Newsleter* 28 (August 2002): 23.

[93] Obaidullah Naqshbandi Mujaddidi Inayati, *Light of Gnosis* (Rampur, n.d.), 60.

FURTHER READING

Peter B. Clarke (ed.), *New Trends and Developments in the World of Islam* (London: Luzac Oriental, 1997).

Carl W. Ernst, *Sufism: An Essential Introduction to the Philosophy and Practice of the Mystical Tradition of Islam* (Boston: Shambhala, 1997).

Jamal Malik and John Hinnells (eds), *Sufism in the West* (London and New York: Routledge, 2006).

Alexandre Popovic and Gilles Veinstein (eds), *Les Voies d'Allah: Les Ordres Mystiques dans l'Islam des Origins à Aujourd'hui* (Paris: Fayard, 1996).

Mark Sedgwick, *Against the Modern World: Traditionalism and the Secret Intellectual History of the Twentieth Century* (Oxford: Oxford University Press, 2004).

Elizabeth Sirriyeh, *Sufis and Anti-Sufis: The Defence, Rethinking and Rejection of Sufism in the Modern World* (Richmond, Surrey: Curzon Press, 1999).

Martin van Bruinessen and Julia Day Howell (eds), *Sufism and the "Modern" in Islam* (London and New York: I.B. Tauris, 2007).

Itzchak Weismann, *Taste of Modernity: Sufism, Salafiyya, and Arabism in Late Ottoman Damascus* (Leiden: Brill, 2001).

12

Transnationalism and Regional Cults

The Dialectics of Sufism in a Plurivocal Muslim World

Pnina Werbner

INTRODUCTION: THE PROBLEM OF COMPARISON IN SUFI ORDERS

This essay aims to compare Sufi orders, conceived of as focused, central place organisations, as they exist in different parts of the Muslim world. The challenge it poses is how to formulate a set of analytical concepts to create a theoretical approach that encompasses Sufi ritual and religious movement, beyond "belief", which can be applied to Sufi practice in geographically distant locations, from North Africa in the West to Pakistan and Indonesia in the East. I stress practice as against Sufi cosmology or poetry, since my aim is to understand the sociological and economic dimensions of Sufi orders.

Of course, it cannot be taken for granted in advance that comparison is a valid project. Superficially, even in a single locality, there is an enormously wide range of types and styles of Sufi shrines and saints, from major shrines of great antiquity, managed by descendants of the original saintly founder and guardians of his tomb, to minor saints with a highly localised clientele.[1] Some shrine-focused orders – cults, in my terms – are more reformist than others, preaching orthodoxy or even Salafism. Others celebrate music and mystical ecstasy or intoxication. The distance between Sufi cults often seems far greater than between them and Salafis, at least when it comes to ideology. The question is: if even in a single locality, shrines differ markedly, how much more so if we try to compare, for example, Sufi orders in Pakistan and Indonesia? By focusing on ritual practice, I believe we can, however, construct

[1] Christian Troll, *Muslim Shrines in India: Their Character, History and Significance* (Delhi: Oxford University Press, 1989); Pnina Werbner and Helene Basu (eds), *Embodying Charisma: Modernity, Locality and the Performance of Emotion in Sufi Cults* (London: Routledge, 1998).

a comparative framework to differentiate Sufi cults or shrine-focused orders from one another, and from Salafis or Reformists like the Deobandi, who engage in spiritual practices such as *dhikr* to the exclusion of other rituals and religious movements typical of Sufi cults. In the following discussion, I highlight key analytical terms that I believe are crucial for a comparative account of Sufi orders across the globe.

One problem in the project of comparison I am proposing has to do with language. In parts of the Muslim world there appears to be a reluctance to use the analytic armoury of concepts developed elsewhere. Hence, Indonesian scholars, for example, prefer to use vernacular concepts to describe the ritual and organisational practices of Sufi orders, and this then leads to a description of these cults that seems to imply that they are quite different from Sufi orders and cult practices in Pakistan, for example, or Morocco.[2] One challenge, then, in the project of comparison, is to begin to disentangle the meanings of vernacular terms in order identify the shared building blocks of Sufi orders across cultures, and where difference between them lies. I began this project of comparison when I undertook a re-analysis of research on Sufi orders in Indonesia. This seemed to expose many more unacknowledged areas of possible comparison between Indonesian, Pakistani and North African Sufi orders and the cults they generate than had been acknowledged.[3] While it had been recognised in Indonesian studies that the *ideas* of Sufi theosophy were shared with the rest of the Muslim world, ritual practices seemed quite different. My re-analysis highlighted aspects of the cults that were described but left untheorised by south-east Asian scholars.

KEY TERMS

Broadly speaking, charting the differences and similarities between Sufi orders as embodied traditions requires attention *beyond* mystical-philosophical and ethical ideas, to *the ritual performances and religious organisational patterns* that shape Sufi orders and cults in widely separated locations. We need, in other words, to seek to comparatively understand four interrelated symbolic complexes (see Figure 12.1): first, the *sacred division of labour* – by this I mean the *ritual roles* that perpetuate and reproduce the cult; second, the *sacred exchanges* between places and persons, often across great distances; third, the *sacred*

[2] P. Werbner, "Sufi Regional Cults in South Asia and Indonesia: Towards a Comparative Analysis", *Yearbook of the Sociology of Islam No 8: Dimensions of Locality: Muslim Saints, Their Place and Space*, edited by Georg Stauth and Samuli Schielke (Lit Verlag, 2008).

[3] P. Werbner, "Sufi Regional Cults in South Asia and Indonesia".

- *Sacred division of labour* – the ritual roles that reproduce the cult
- *Sacred exchanges* between places and persons across distance
- The *sacred region*, its catchment areas and sanctified central places
- *Sacred indexical events* – the rituals that co-ordinate and revitalise cult organisation and management

FIGURE 12.1: Key Dimensions of Sufi Cult Comparison

region, its catchment area and the sanctified central places that shape it; and fourth, the *sacred indexical events – the rituals* – that co-ordinate and revitalise organisational and symbolic unities and enable *managerial and logistical planning and decision-making*. Comparison requires that we examine the way in which these four dimensions of ritual sanctification and performance are linked in Sufi orders, and are embedded in a particular symbolic logic and local environment.

I begin with an example from my own research. The Sufi cult I studied in Pakistan[4] was in many senses remarkably similar organisationally to other, non-Muslim regional cults and pilgrimage systems elsewhere.[5] It also fitted the model of Sufi orders or cults analysed by Trimingham,[6] which was mainly based on his extensive knowledge of Sufi orders in the Middle East and Africa.

During his lifetime, Zindapir, founder of the Sufi order of the saint I studied, established a lodge that extended globally: to Britain and Europe, the Middle East and even South Africa. Emerging as a saint during the 1940s, in the dying days of Empire, Zindapir began his career as an army tailor contractor for the seventh Baluch Regiment, and his cult membership expanded through the recruitment of state employees, in this case soldiers and army personnel. These in turn recruited members of their families and, when they retired to civilian life, their co-villagers or townsmen. The cult expanded further as these soldiers went to work as labour migrants in the Gulf or in Britain. Disciples were also recruited from among the stream of supplicants coming to the lodge to seek blessings and remedies for their afflictions from the saint, and from among casual visitors curious to see the saint and lodge itself, a place renowned for its beauty. Some disciples joined the cult

[4] P. Werbner, *Pilgrims of Love: the Anthropology of a Global Sufi Cult* (London: Hurst Publishers, 2003).

[5] R. Werbner, "Introduction" in *Regional Cults*, ed. Richard Werbner (London and New York: Academic Press, 1977).

[6] J. S. Trimingham, *The Sufi Orders of Islam* (Oxford: Oxford University Press at the Clarendon Press, 1971).

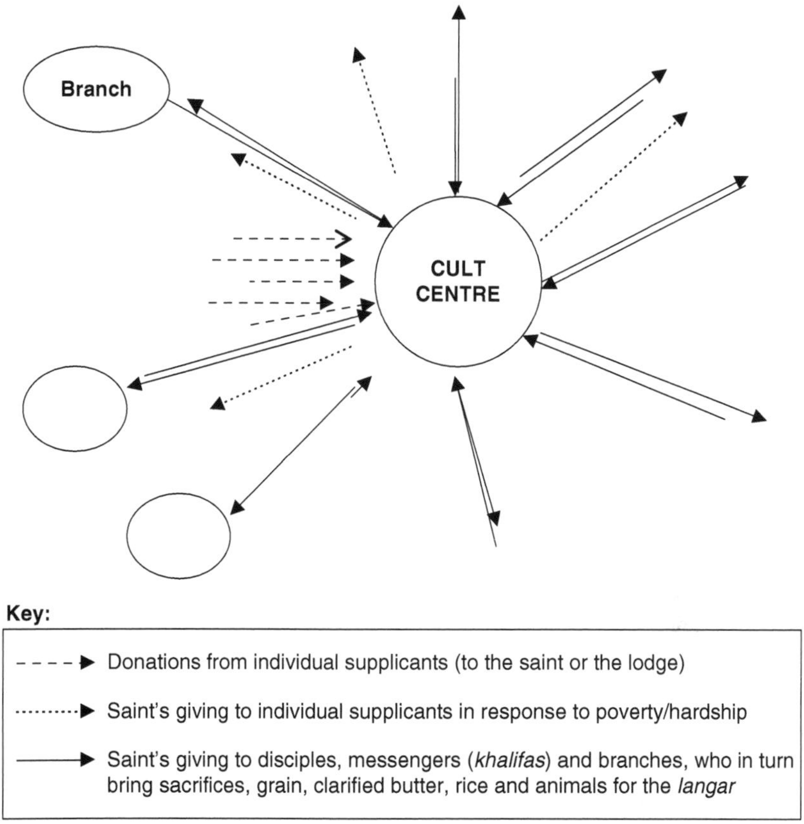

FIGURE 12.2: Redistributive Sacred Exchange at the Lodge

after meeting Zindapir or his vicegerents on the annual Hajj to Mecca. Such recruitment chains form network clusters whose members share either occupational or geographical proximity (or both).

Zindapir's disciples met regularly to perform *dhikr* at the lodge branches of the order, located throughout Pakistan. They gathered at the central lodge of Zindapir weekly, monthly, and, in most cases, annually, at the *'urs*, the three-day ritual festival commemorating the mystical "marriage" of a deceased saint with God. Some pilgrims arrived for the festival as individuals, but most came in convoys (*qafilas*) of trucks and buses from established branches, travelling in some cases for over 24 hours. The sacred exchange at the cult centre was extensive: the groups arrived bearing with them sacrificial offerings of grain, butter and animals. They returned bearing gifts from the saint – gowns or caps, and, in some instances, the sacred soil of the lodge itself (see Figure 12.2).

During their three-day stay at the *'urs*, all participants were fed and nurtured by the saint himself. The hundreds of beasts sacrificed, the hundreds of thousands of baked chappatis and nans, the enormous cauldrons of sweet and pilau rice distributed during the *'urs*, fed some 30,000 people over three days – a major logistical challenge. But the saint also feeds pilgrims to the lodge throughout the year, in what may be conceived of as a form of perpetual sacrifice. The lodge itself was built using voluntary labour in the name of God, usually in the weeks preceding the annual *'urs*. The crowds depart following the final *du'a*, the supplicatory prayer enunciated by the saint himself on behalf of the whole community.

This annual celebration at a saint's lodge or shrine is known in South Asia as the *'urs*. In North Africa it is known as *mawlīd*. It commemorates the death/rebirth of a saint, the moment of his unification or marriage with Allah. The *'urs* is the organisational hub of Sufi saints' cults. The festival gathers together individual supplicants and pilgrims alongside organised groups of devotees and disciples who visit the festival annually and cultivate a special relationship to the saint and the Sufi tarīqa or order he founded. These groups or congregations often travel great distances to attend the annual ritual. They frequently come from different linguistic, ethnic and even religious groups. Although the celebration marks the high point of the year, it cannot be understood apart from the more enduring links that constitute the organisation of the order.

REGIONAL CULTS AND SUFI INCLUSIVENESS

The mediation of cross-ethnic, inter-caste and cross-regional divisions in South Asian Sufi lodges fits *regional cult theory*, as it has been applied more widely to such cults, found in different cultures in many other parts of the world.[7] In a seminal volume on such *Regional Cults*, Richard Werbner sums up their key features. Regional cults are, distinctively, he says,

> cults of the middle range – more far-reaching than any parochial cult of the little community, yet less inclusive in belief and membership than a world religion in its most universal form. Their central places are shrines in towns and villages, by cross-roads or even in the wild, apart from human habitation, where great populations from various communities or their representatives, come to supplicate, sacrifice, or simply make pilgrimage. They are cults which have a topography of their own, conceptually defined by the people themselves and marked apart from other features of cultural landscapes by ritual activities.[8]

[7] R. Werbner, "Introduction".
[8] Ibid., XI.

Like other regional cults, Sufi cults are very often trans-regional, trans-national, and trans-ethnic. Different Sufi cults *interpenetrate* with one another rather than generating contiguous, bounded territories. They leap-frog *across major political and ethnic boundaries*, creating their own sacred topographies and flows of goods and people. These override, rather than being congruent with, the political boundaries and subdivisions of nations, ethnic groups, or provinces.[9] But, unlike the networks created by Salafi groups, connections across distance are made through collective rituals and saintly veneration.

Clearly the need is to recognise these trans-local networks. It is equally important to analyse the political and historical context in which they operate, and which changes over time. But just as one cannot study the order or cult in isolation, adopting a naïve holistic stance,[10] so too one cannot assume that different domains (ritual, political, economic) underwrite each other, so that ritual and belief become mere representations of political divisions or economic interests.[11] In Sufi regional cults in Pakistan, the symbolic order *cuts across* political divisions and remains in tension with the postcolonial and capitalist economies of modern-day Pakistan, and even more so in post-imperial Britain. Pakistani saints are often highly critical of politicians and *'ulama* (religious clerics). This is true elsewhere as well, as Villalon documents in his fine analysis of the intricate, historically evolving political-cum-economic relationships between Sufi orders (*ṭuruq*, *ṭarīqa*) such as the Mourides or Tījāniyya and political authorities in Senegal.[12]

Regional cult analysis aims to disclose hidden structural interdependencies and ruptures between different domains of action: economic, ritual, political. Like other regional cults, Sufi regional or trans-regional cults are both linked to centres of political power and in tension with them. Various historical studies have highlighted the pragmatic tendencies of Sufis in South Asia which have enabled Sufi saints to accommodate a variety of different political regimes and circumstances, over many centuries of imperial and postcolonial rule. The relationship between the political centre and the sacred centre is a

[9] R. Werbner, "Introduction", XI.

[10] Ibid., IX

[11] Ibid., XVIII. Such correspondence theories draw on simplistic Durkheimian or Marxist approaches. Werbner also cites Robertson Smith's theory of sacrifice among the Semites as an example.

[12] Leonardo A. Villalón, "Sufi Modernities in Contemporary Senegal: Religious Dynamics between the Local and the Global", in Martin van Bruinnessen and Julia Day Howell (eds), *Sufism and the "Modern" in Islam.* (London: I.B. Taurus, 2007), 172–191; see also Donal B. Cruise O'Brien, *The Mourides of Senegal: the Political and Economic Organization of an Islamic Brotherhood* (Oxford: Clarendon Press, 1971).

changing, historically contingent one, and in this sense, as in others, regional cults are historically evolving social formations. In a globalising world, this is equally the case: cults have spread transnationally, as followers have become global migrants, who must negotiate their status with the state and political authorities wherever they form branches. We may speak of such Sufi orders as trans-regional cults, since they maintain critical features of more nationally circumscribed regional cults. In particular, the branches or "circles" of disciples that form in the diaspora retain their connections, spiritual and material, to the centre and its shaykh or marabout, across great distances.

These are the bare outlines of Sufi trans-regional cult organisation. The Sufi cultural concept which best captures the idea of a *Sufi sacred region* is *wilāyat. Wilāyat*, a master concept in Sufi terminology, denotes a series of interrelated meanings: (secular) sovereignty over a region, the spiritual dominion of a saint, guardianship, a foreign land, friendship, intimacy with God, and union with the Deity. As a master concept, *wilāyat* encapsulates the range of complex ideas defining the charismatic power of a saint – not only over transcendental spaces of mystical knowledge, but as sovereign of the terrestrial spaces into which his sacred region extends. The term "regional cult", a comparative, analytic term used to describe centrally focused, non-contiguous religious organisations which *extend across boundaries*, seems particularly apt to capture this symbolic complexity.

The sacred centres and sub-centres of Sufi orders, known as *zāwiya* in North Africa, and as *darbars* or *dargāhs* (royal courts) in Pakistan and India, are places of pilgrimage and ritual celebration, with the tomb of the founder being the "focal point of the organisation, a centre of veneration to which visitations (*ziyārat*) are made".[13] The centre is regarded as sacred (*ḥaram*), a place of sanctuary for refugees from threatened violence or vengeance. Sufi regional cults (Trimingham calls them *ṭā'ifas*) are thus focused around a single living saint or his shrine after his death. The shaykh – a living saint or his descendant – heads the *ṭā'ifa* or *ṭarīqa* by virtue of his powers of blessing. Under the shaykh are a number of *khalīfas* (deputies or vicegerents) appointed by him directly to take charge of districts or town centres. Trimingham reports that in larger orders each regional *khalīfa* may have sectional leaders under him.[14]

The word *ṭā'ifa* was not used by members of Zindapir's regional cult (and appears unknown even in some parts of the Middle East). They spoke of the

[13] Trimingham, *The Sufi Orders of Islam*, 179.
[14] Ibid., 173–174, 179.

cult as a *ṭarīqa*, but to distinguish it from the wider Naqshbandī order to which it was affiliated, it was known as *ṭarīqa Naqshbandiyya Ghamkolia*. By appending the name of the cult centre, Ghamkol, to their (trans)regional cult, they marked its distinctiveness as an autonomous organisation. The saint at the head of the order, *Zindapir*, ("the living saint"), was by the time of my study the head of a vast, trans-national regional cult, stretching throughout Pakistan to the Gulf, Britain, Afghanistan and Southern Africa. He had founded the cult centre in 1948, when he first secluded himself, according to the legend, in a cave on the hill of Ghamkol. At the time the place was a wilderness.

A key feature of Zindapir's cult organisation was the way in which the exemplary centre had *replicated itself* throughout the saint's region through scores of deliberate and conscious *acts of mimesis*. In different parts of the Punjab, important *khalīfas* of the saint reproduced in their manners, dress and minute customs the image of Zindapir, along with the ethics and aesthetics of the cult he founded. In their own places they were addressed, much as Zindapir himself was, as *pīr ṣāḥib*. Such mimesis, I want to suggest, creates a sense of unity across distance: the same sounds and images, the same ambience, are experienced by a disciple who travels wherever he goes in the cult region. Along with this extraordinary mimetic resemblance, however, each *khalīfa* also fostered his own distinctiveness, his own special way of being a Sufi.

In other ways, too, Trimingham's account accords with regional cult theory. He makes the point that *ṭā'ifas* "undergo cycles of expansion, stagnation, decay, and even death",[15] but that since there are "thousands of them, new ones [are] continually being formed".[16] The point is that these key vernacular concepts have their equivalents everywhere (see Figure 12.3).

Lest it be thought that the complex regional cult structure described above has ceased to exist outside South Asia, an example of the complexity that some regional cults achieve over time can be gleaned from Edward Reeves' (1990) study, *The Hidden Government*, of the "cult of saints" in Northern Egypt, celebrated by over a million pilgrims and devotees at the annual "Big *Mulid*" at Tanta where the shrine of Sayyid Aḥmad al-Badawī is located. Most distinctively, a hierarchy of *ṭarīqas* led by a *shaykh*, and their sub-branches led by *khalīfas*, virtually all belonging to the larger Aḥmadiyya Sufi order, gather during the festival, setting up 22 huge *khidmat* (hospitality) tents for followers, with food, music and daily recitals of *dhikr* led by the *shaykh*. Each *ṭarīqa* has its

[15] Trimingham, *The Sufi Orders of Islam*, 179.
[16] Ibid., 172.

- *Wilāyat* (the *sacred* region/dominion of a saint)
- *Zāwiya, darbar, dargāh, psantren, tekke* (sacred centre)
- *Ṭā'ifa, ṭarīqa, tarixa* (central cult/focused order)
- *Ziyārat* (pilgrimage)
- *'Urs, mauled, mulid, magal* (annual popular ritual gathering)
- *Shaykh, khalīfas, marabout, walī, murshid* (saint and deputies)
- *Jamā'ats, sangats, daaira* (pilgrimage groups)
- *Qafilas* (convoys, caravans)
- *Pīr-bhai/bhen, talibe* (brother or sister disciples)
- *Langar* (free food at a saint's lodge)
- *Nazrana, shukrana* (offering)
- *Sukun/sakina* (*healing* peace, tranquility)

FIGURE 12.3: Key Vernacular Concepts in Sufi Organisation

own distinctive litanies.[17] The tents are located in the same spot, year after year.[18] The *mulid* is an occasion when "all members and officers and supposed to greet the *shaikh* and renew their fealty".[19] This is also a time when donations are collected for the *ṭarīqa*, "one of the few occasions for the common member to meet the leader of his *ṭarīqa* face to face and receive *baraka* directly from him, by shaking hands, rather than indirectly through the proxy of the *khalifas*".[20] The festival, in other words, encompasses multiple *shaykhs* who lead their own *ṭarīqas*, but are all members of Aḥmadiyya Sufi order. They come together on the last day of the festival in a big procession, the *mawkib al-khalīfa*. It is led by the cavalry, followed by the Sufi "corporations" who carry their multicoloured banners, representing different *ṭarīqas* and places.[21] They are followed by Sayyid al-Badawī's *khalīfa* riding on a fine Arabian horse.[22] Behind him are two camels in gold and red, and finally a motley crowd of wagons and people. This is the culmination of the festival. Reeves' detailed account highlights both the spatial separations and focused gatherings of regional *ṭarīqa* during the festival and the final coming together in a single procession, unifying this complex, federated organisation.

Ideologically, Sufi saints are conceived of in South Asia as tamers of the wilderness for human cultivation. In this they seem to differ from reformists, even those who practise ritual and mystical meditation such as the Deobandis. The question of the relation with the natural environment is thus a key trope

17 Trimingham, *The Sufi Orders of Islam*, 130.
18 Ibid., 122, 124–125.
19 Ibid., 128.
20 Ibid., 129.
21 Ibid.,132.
22 Ibid., 133.

in Sufi orders, which exists elsewhere as well. Ansari has shown that saints contributed to the reorganisation of canal-based agriculture in Sindh towards the end of the nineteenth century, while in Bengal, they were at the vanguard of new rice cultivation.[23]

Inclusivity is a key feature of South Asian Sufi cults. There are cases, as Mark Gaborieau documents, in which saints become patron saints of a particular occupational group,[24] but these are relatively rare. Historically, Sufis appear to have been instrumental in uniting groups across tribal or caste divisions. Rather than exclusivity, Saiyed echoes other scholars when he contends that it is through Sufi shrines that "the subcontinent saw the best part of Hindu-Muslim integration", and that it was "the personal and spiritual influence of various saints that . . . allowed for the peaceful coexistence of the two communities for several centuries on the Indian subcontinent".[25]

The catchment areas – the sacred dominions – of Sufi regional cults are importantly marked by their *instability* and by the fluctuating range of devotees drawn to them. Elizabeth Mann reports on a minor shrine which emerged in Aligarh in the 1940s and, over a short period, challenged and greatly exceeded in popularity the shrine of Shāh Jamāl, a long established Chishtī saint. The Sufi saint and world renouncer who revitalised the minor shrine lived, she argues, "within living memory, [and] stories of miraculous events are fresh in the minds of devotees who witnessed them at first hand".[26] Since his death in the 1960s, intensive building activities have greatly expanded the shrine.

Quite distinct from the fluctuating fortunes of medium-level shrines of this type are the universally venerated great shrines of the Indian subcontinent such as those of Mu'in al-Dīn Chishtī of Ajmer or Data Ganj Baksh of Lahore. These are visited by millions. Until quite recently I had assumed that such ancient shrines were not comparable to Zindapīr's regional cult, in the sense that they did not have a regional cult structure – that is, they did not have specific groups of devotees who arrive in organised pilgrimage groups for the *'urs* at these centres. Recent work on Sehwan Sharīf, an ancient thirteenth-century

[23] Sarah F. D. Ansari, *Sufi Saints and State Power: the Pirs of Sind, 1843–1947* (Cambridge: University Press, 1992); Richard W. Eaton, *The Rise of Islam and the Bengal Frontier, 1204–1760* (Berkeley: University of California Press, 1993).

[24] Marc Gaborieau, "The Cult of Saints among the Muslims of Nepal and Northern India", in Stephen Wilson (ed.) *Saints and their Cults: Studies in Religious Sociology, Folklore and History* (Cambridge: University Press, 1983), 302–303.

[25] A. R. Saiyed, "Saints and Dargahs in the Indian Subcontinent: A Review", in Troll (ed.) *Muslim Shrines in India*, 242.

[26] Elizabeth A. Mann, "Religion, Money and Status: Competition for Resources at the Shrine of Shah Jamal, Aligarh", in Troll (ed.) *Muslim Shrines in India*, 163.

Sufi shrine where Haḍrat La'l Shāhbāz Qalandar is said to be buried, by Michel Boivin and his colleagues at the EHESS, and by Juergen Wasim Frembgen, a scholar of Pakistan based in Munich, indicated that I was wrong. Groups, known as *Jhule Lal sangats*, annually travel in *qafilas* to Sehwan Sharīf shrine for the ritual festival.[27] Indeed, many of these groups seem to be newly formed, as the shrine has gained popularity. In other words, Sehwan Sharīf, founded in the thirteenth century and considered as a regional cult, has *expanded* in the late twentieth century. Similarly, in Bosnia, David Henig shows that newly formed popular dervish groups whose religious expression was repressed in socialist Yugoslav, seek continuity and authenticity by linking themselves to a sheikh of a central tekke of the Rifā'ī order in Albania, thus creating an emergent trans-regional cult by expanding centripetally.[28]

Like the shrine of Sayyid Aḥmad al-Badawī in Egypt, the ancient shrine of Bābā Fārid, a twelve century Chishtī shaykh at Pak Pattan, also has contemporary groups of devotees, known as *jamā'ats*, visiting it annually.[29] This indicates that Zindapīr's cult was not unusual and that regional cult organisation, consisting of a cult centre and branches affiliated to it, continues – sometimes for hundreds of years, with its composition fluctuating. At the other extreme are shrines of minor *pīrs* with restricted local village followings, some of whom may even be nameless, as Lukas Werth has shown.[30]

The *bonds of spirit between disciples* of a single Sufi saint often consolidate and mediate *birādarī* affinal, lineal or village ties; but they may also form the basis for new friendships forged away from home, in the absence of family or neighbourhood during labour migration, and they may introduce parochial villagers to the glories of shrines located well beyond their district and even province. In such cases, being a disciple comes to acquire many new and complex meanings. This is true for the devotees of the living saint I studied, Zindapir, and his regional cult. To explain the cult's vast catchment area, we need to look, as already mentioned, to its genesis in relations between soldiers, labour migrants and city dwellers living away from their village homes, and their continued ties to their rural communities. It is thus the intersection

[27] Juergen Frembgen, "Qalandar Networks". Unpublished paper, 2009.

[28] David Henig, "Tracing Creative Moments: Towards the Emergence of Trans-Local Dervish Cults in Bosnia-Herzegovina", *Focaal* 68, 2014, 1.

[29] A study of Nagore Sharif by Saheb also refers to visiting groups as Jama'ats. See S. A. A. Saheb, "A 'Festival of Flags': Hindu-Muslim Devotion and the Sacralising of Localism at the Shrine of Nagore-e-Sharif", in Werbner and Basu (eds), *Embodying Charisma*, 55–76.

[30] Lukas Werth, "'The Saint Who Disappeared': Saints of the Wilderness in Pakistani Village Shrines", in Werbner and Basu (eds), "Introduction: the Embodiment of Charisma", in *Embodying Charisma*.

between labour migration and village or urban roots which explains the spatial patterning of the shaykh's sacred dominion and the reach of his cult.

During his lifetime Zindapir was, above all, an army saint. His career started as a tailor contractor in the army, where his early circle of companions was forged. Sufi Sahib, who created his own regional cult centred in Birmingham, was one of these companions. Rab Nawaz, one of his trusted *khalīfas*, told me that until white hairs appeared in the shaykh's beard, he and all the *khulāfā*, the deputies or messengers, wore khaki. It was only when his beard turned white that they began to wear white gowns. Even after becoming a practising *faqīr*, Zindapir spent time in Abbotabad not far from the army base where he had worked, and he continued to recruit army followers to be his disciples. Ghamkol Sharif, the lodge he founded when he left Abbotabad, is located near his natal village and only a few miles from Kohat, a large British garrison town or cantonment which was taken over by the Pakistan army at Independence. The lodge's reputation as a place of local beauty attracts a constant stream of curious visitors. Many of his *murīds*, – that is, disciples – told me how they first visited the lodge while stationed in Kohat. On seeing the lodge, they were overwhelmed by its gloriousness and the spirituality (*rūḥaniyat*) of its *shaikh*. Later, they became his disciples.

THE REDISTRIBUTIVE ECONOMY OF SUFI CULTS

There are several other features of Sufi orders as regional cults which make comparison a fruitful exercise. These relate to the *redistributive economy of central lodges*, their reliance on *voluntary labour*, and the *myths* or miracle stories told about founder shaykhs.

The healing powers of saints are often constructed as their dominant characteristic, a key attribute of their power. Zindapir's cult was no exception. Every day truckloads of supplicants arrive at Ghamkol Sharif, the lodge and now shrine of Zindapir, to see the saint and seek redress and blessing for a wide variety of afflictions. On Fridays, holidays and *'urs* festivals the stream turned into a veritable flood as mini-buses ferried supplicants from the neighbouring town, joined by others arriving in private cars, on motorbikes or in government vehicles. Healing is undoubtedly a central activity of Ghamkol Sharif, as of most Sufi cult centres. This ritual practice too tends to differentiate Sufi orders and cults from reformist groups. While he was still alive, the saint devoted hours every day, often well into the early hours of the morning, to meeting supplicants, whom he usually took in groups of about ten men or women, supervised by a male or female gatekeeper (*darbān*). This tradition has continued since his death, sustained by his descendants who have inherited his mantle.

Zindapir prided himself on never asking anyone their name or demanding payment for his healing. During his lifetime, no donation boxes were displayed anywhere in the lodge, despite the fact that such boxes are an almost universal feature of saintly shrines elsewhere in South Asia. On the contrary, rather than asking for money, supplicants were told to eat first from the blessed food of the communal kitchen, the *langar*, as it is known in South Asia, before coming in to see the shaykh. Nevertheless, the quest for healing at Sufi shrines is associated with a cultural imperative to make a gesture of sacrificial giving or offering. There is no need to demand payment; supplicants insist on making their donations to the *langar* or in the form of *nazrana* (tribute) or *shukrana* (token of thanks) to ensure the efficacy of the cure or blessing.

The income from individual supplicants is critical to the *redistributive economy* of a saint's lodge which is ultimately sustained by *individual supplicants' donations*. These enable the saint to display his generosity to his disciples in particular, as well as the multitudes at the *'urs*. Much of the income of the place, arising from such individual supplicants' donations, is used to build up the lodge itself and support its vast regional and even trans-national organisation. In many respects the lodge is a public space, a place of God owned collectively by all the saint's disciples and open even to strangers, who are given a place to sleep and food to eat. While it is true that the shaykh's family derive material benefits from the lodge's income in the form of expensive consumer goods and superior education, much of the income from supplicants' petty donations is channelled back into the lodge itself, expanding the accommodation and facilities for pilgrims, decorating the mosque, sustaining the daily *langar* and supporting the large retinue of retainers that the saint's family has gathered over time, many of them because they were homeless or destitute. The shaykh is generous with needy disciples and supports his deputies, his *khalīfas*, in their attempts to *build up the branches* of the cult. He not only gives all disciples embroidered caps and shawls as tokens of his special connection, but he donates money for their daughters' dowries or in cases of dire need. And, as mentioned above, Sufi lodges are built with a large input of voluntary labour. In Zindapir's cult, this usually took place in the weeks preceding the annual *'urs*, with volunteers arriving to do the work of God (*khidmat*).

There is thus a symbiotic relationship between money raised through the individual traffic of supplicants coming to the lodge and the ability of a saint to build up his regional (or trans-national and global) cult organisation. One cannot exist without the other. Thus, Richard Werbner argues in relation to the organisation of the Mwali High God regional cult in South Central Africa, that

> [t]he individual supplicants' traffic, so crucial for a priest's accumulation of great wealth, is not and cannot be divorced from the congregational traffic: one sustains the other. A priest must manage both together, or risk a decline in both. This is so, in part, because the priest gets funds from the supplicants' traffic which he can use, as he sees fit, to subsidise transactions with messengers and their congregations. ... [Moreover] This traffic comes from well beyond a priest's current region, and brings to it some of its future staff. Thus members of wards about to form a congregation or would-be-messengers may first come to an oracle as individual pilgrims.[31]

As in the Mwali cult, the individual supplicant traffic is a source of *recruitment* into Zindapir's Sufi cult. Many disciples and *khalīfas* first came to visit the *pīr* in order to seek cures for their afflictions or blessings for new ventures.

Beyond the miraculous curing powers of the saint, it is important to recognise the healing qualities of the lodge itself for supplicants. The presence of the saint has transformed the site of the lodge into a sacred landscape, a haven of *sukun* or *sakīna*, peace and security, in an otherwise cruel and greedy world. The shaykh and the lodge bring to supplicants *ārām* (healing) through rest, ease, relief, quiet, comfort. Many such Sufi lodges and saints are also sanctuaries, while saints often act or have acted historically as mediators between warring tribes.[32]

The role of Sufi cults as fostering a redistributive economy is evident elsewhere as well. In Egypt, Reeves reports that pilgrims must contribute to the *ṭarīqa* while they bring home chickpeas imbued with *baraka* from the pilgrimage.[33] In the annual Magal festival at Touba in Senegal, the Mourides contribute voluntary labour and money, while the shaykhs are expected to be generous towards their followers and often give them credit.[34]

SUFI MYTHS IN COMPARATIVE PERSPECTIVE

Seen comparatively, we need to disclose what endows some men with extraordinary charismatic authority and hence the power to found new Sufi regional cults and expand their organisational ambit. To comprehend how

31 R. Werbner, "Introduction", 202.

32 As Evans Pritchard, for example, showed for the Sanusiya. E. E. Evans-Pritchard, *The Sanusi of Cyrenaica* (Oxford: Clarendon Press, 1937/1949).

33 Edward B. Reeves, *The Hidden Government: Ritual, Clientelism, and Legitimation in Northern Egypt* (Salt Lake City: University of Utah Press, 1990).

34 Stephen Golub and Jamie Hansen-Lewis, "Informal Trading Networks in West Africa: The Mourides of Senegal/Gambia and the Yoruba of Benin/Nigeria", in Nancy Benjamin and Aly Mbaye (eds), *The Informal Sector in Francophone Africa: Firm Size, Productivity and Institutions* (Washington, DC: the World Bank, 2012), 175–176.

(1) *Inner Jihad: Overcoming Inner Desires/Total Submission*
Morocco: Saint Washes with Smallpox-Infested Water
Indonesia: Saint Stands in a River for 15 Years
Result: Divine Knowledge

(2) *Outer Jihad: Overcoming External Evil/Lack of Faith*
Morocco: Triumph Over the Evil Sultan
Indonesia: Conversion of the Exemplary Centre
Result: Spiritual Power Overcomes Temporal Power

FIGURE 12.4: Sufi Myths in Morocco and Indonesia (after Geertz 1968)

the charisma of a living saint is constructed during his lifetime and underpins his authority requires a comparative analysis of the poetics of travelling theories – that is, the way that such myths tell, simultaneously, both a *local* and a *global* tale about Sufi mystical power everywhere, and the settlement of Sufis in virgin, barren or idolatrous lands, such as the lodge valley in Pakistan or industrial towns in Britain. Each Sufi cult is distinctive and embedded in a local cultural context. But, against a view of the radical plurality of Islam proposed, for example, by Geertz,[35] I propose that Sufism everywhere shares the same deep structural logic of ideas. These shape the ecological and cultural habitat and local habitus wherever Sufi saints settle. Such beliefs persist despite internal inconsistencies and evidence to the contrary, and remain powerfully compelling. At this point, then, I turn to ideology in order to return back later to ritual. As I have argued elsewhere,[36] legends about powerful Sufis from Indonesia and Morocco – which Geertz argues exemplify the contrastive localism of Islam – contain, in essence, the same fable or plot: (1) initiation through a physical and mental ordeal overcome; (2) the achievement of innate and instantaneous divine knowledge; (3) the triumphant encounter with temporal authority (see Figure 12.4). The same legends can be found in ʻAṭṭār's *Memorial of Saints*, which records the lives of the early saints of Baghdad. What differs are merely the ecological and historical details: a flowing river and exemplary centre in Indonesia, desert sands and a fortress town in Morocco, the Baluch Regiment, an anti-colonial brigand's valley, or corrupt politicians in Pakistan. A single paradigmatic underlying symbolic logic upholds this legendary corpus, while its local, familiar concrete details – regiments, rivers and desert sands – embody this logic and suffuse it with axiomatic authority. But the symbolic structure underlying this common sense is as unitary as it is inexorable.

[35] Clifford Geertz, *Islam Observed* (New Haven: Yale University Press, 1968).
[36] P. Werbner, "Sufi Regional Cults in South Asia and Indonesia".

The underlying logic of the fables constituting this religious imagination is the same logic, whether in Morocco, Iraq, Pakistan or Indonesia. It is based on a single and constant set of equations, starting from the ultimate value of self-denial or ascetiscism:

> *World renunciation (asceticism) = divine love and intimacy with God = divine "hidden" knowledge = the ability to transform the world = the hegemony of spiritual authority over temporal power and authority.*

UNIVERSALISM AND PARTICULARISM

Finally, to understand the genesis of regional cults we need to comprehend the way they mediate between a universalistic orientation to a high God and a particularistic orientation to a specific sacred site or holy person. The *tension between particularism and universalism* is the generative principle underlying the formation and expansion of such cults. And it is the *conjunction* between these apparently opposed modern and traditional religious orientations that enables the inclusive toleration evident at Sufi shrines.

In his book *Muslim Society*, Ernest Gellner famously cites the philosopher David Hume's theory of oscillation between religious pluralism and monism. Human beings, Hume suggested, tend to elevate their deities

> To the utmost bounds of perfection, [until they] at last beget the attributes of unity and infinity, simplicity and spirituality. Such refined ideas, being somewhat disproportioned to vulgar comprehension, remain not long in their original purity; but require to be supported by the notion of inferior mediators or subordinate agents, which interpose between mankind and their supreme deity. [But these mediators in turn] at last destroy themselves,

so that, as Gellner sums it up, the pendulum is bound to swing once again from the particularist towards the universalist abstract pole.[37] In regional cults, however, as I have suggested here, it is the *conjunction* rather than the oscillation between particularism and universalism which holds the key to understanding Sufi shrines. It is the simultaneous conception of a universal God for whom all men and women are equal along with the particularist conception of the saint as a unique and extraordinary individual, seen in terms of the place he has created, his person and his history – that generates the organisational features of Sufi cults. The Sufi saint is the beloved, friend, *walī*, of a distant, universal, and hence inclusive God. It is this universalism which draw followers from a wide range of different ethnic groups, regions and even religions. At the

[37] Ernest Gellner, *Muslim Society* (Cambridge: Cambridge University Press, 1981), 10.

same time, in his unique qualities of perfection, virtue and world renunciation, the Sufi saint endows God's abstract universalism with a specific uniqueness to which his followers reach out. They love the saint as they seek a distant and fearful God's grace and blessing through his mediation. The saint's specificity generates a trans-national and regional cult. The universalism inherent in the idea of an abstract, universal God draws persons beyond the local community and reaches out to people of different classes, genders, ages, languages, and regions everywhere. The saint is a universal God's vicegerent on earth. The sacred centre and sub-centres form a unique cult organisation, but the ideas and beliefs that animate them are universalist and shared across many such regional cults. Beyond ideology, to understand how such cults reproduce and perpetuate themselves in time and space as viable organisations we need to understand both the economy and the moral economy of the cult.

MOVEMENT, CIRCUITS, PILGRIMAGE ROUTES AND SUFI NETWORKS IN COMPARATIVE PERSPECTIVE

The problem of whether pilgrims achieve "communitas" at pilgrimage centres[38] has dominated debates in the literature on pilgrimage.[39] However, to my mind, this is not the key issue at stake in the comparative study of Sufi cults. The real, unstudied question has to do with circuits of pilgrims, and indeed of saints or their emissaries, who in many Sufi cults move around visiting branches and disciples, though Zindapir himself chose never to leave the lodge except to go on Hajj once a year. One gets the impression, indeed, that in some places, such as Indonesia with its multiple islands, travel circuits of the cult head and messengers may be quite extensive and distant, involving sea or plane journeys.

In many non-Sufi religious pilgrimage cults pilgrims move through a series of named stations, many of them very distant from the cult centre, before arriving there at the end of their journey. This is true, for example, of Hindus,[40] Buddhists in Japan,[41] or Christians in the Peruvian highlands[42]

[38] Victor Turner, "Pilgrimages as Social Processes", in *Dramas, Fields, and Metaphors* (Cornell: Cornell University Press, 1974).

[39] E.g. John Eade and Michael J. Sallnow, "Introduction", in *Contesting the Sacred: The Anthropology of Christian Pilgrimage* (London: Routledge, 1991).

[40] Ann G. Gold, *Fruitful Journeys: the Ways of Rajasthani Pilgrims* (Berkeley: University of California Press, 1988)

[41] Ian Reader, *Making Pilgrimages: Meaning and Practice in Shikoku* (Honolulu: University of Hawai'i Press, 2006).

[42] Michael J. Sallnow, *Pilgrims of the Andes: Regional Cults in Cusco* (Washington, DC: Smithsonian Institution Press, 1987).

and elsewhere. Pilgrims move as groups, but they can also follow the pilgrimage route as individuals. On the whole, Sufi pilgrimage routes are not so complex with few stations on the way, but most Sufi pilgrimages are cyclical and annual, not a once-in-a-lifetime project. Whatever the case, from a comparative perspective the routes, circuits and networks which pilgrimage and visitation establish are crucial for an appreciation of the organisational dimensions of Sufi cults as regional cults.

CONCLUDING REMARKS

To conclude this essay I want to defend the need to understand the way that Sufi cults are mapped in space and managed as viable organisations, as a precondition for a fuller understanding of the more experiential dimensions of Sufism. The experience of communitas at pilgrimage centres, the sense of ethical voluntarism and the bonds of friendship between disciples, forged by shared devotion to particular places, away from the centres of temporal power, as well as their shared love for the saint, are all made possible by the complex organisation of Sufi orders as regional cults. True, there are small Sufi groups that meet to perform *dhikr* and there are old shrines that are managed by the state in Pakistan and no longer have distant branches and sub-branches, but the true sense of love and camaraderie comes from membership in a specific but deterritorialised organisation. Jurgen Frembgen has recently been studying the shrine of La'l Shāhbāz Qalandar in Sehwan in Sind, a thirteenth-century shrine of a saint who preached peace between Hindus and Muslims, and which, despite its antiquity, appears nevertheless as mentioned to have sustained a regional cult organisation.[43] Its disciples are *qalandar*, dervishes who often grow their hair wild and are mendicants or *faqīrs*. They form *sangats* (devotional associations) thousands of miles away from the shrine, in Lahore and other parts of the Punjab, some focusing on a living shaykh. The fellow-disciples travel together in organised groups or *qafilas* by train to the shrine. Using posters as his primary source, Frembgen shows that devotional group membership cuts across caste and occupational divisions.[44] It is also inclusive of Sunni and Shi'a, though the buried saint was a Shi'a and so too is the shrine management. At the shrine, during the *'urs* devotees dance a devotional dance known as *dhammal*, which involves a

[43] Frembgen, *At the Shrine of the Red Sufi: Five Days and Nights on Pilgrimage in Pakistan* (Karachi: Oxford University Press, 2011).

[44] Frembgen, "From Popular Devotion to Mass Event: Placards Advertising the Pilgrimage to the Sufi Saint Lal Shahbaz Qalandar in Sehwan Sharif (Sindh/Pakistan)". Unpublished paper, 2009.

frenzied and ecstatic swirl of the head and body. This is part of a special ritual that is performed at the rhythmic beat of the *dhole* (a big barrel-shaped drum), some of which are of giant size, that are placed in the courtyard of the shrine.[45] Bells, gongs, cymbals and horns make a thunderous din, and the dervishes, clad in long robes, beads, bracelets and coloured head-bands, whirl faster and faster in a hypnotic trance, until with a final deafening scream they run wildly through the doors of the shrine to the courtyard beyond. Frembgen reports that these devotees come from all over Pakistan. They make their way, as mentioned, to the shrine in groups and convoys, to arrive in time for the annual festival. They meet regularly with one another at the places where they usually live. This aspect of shrine organisation has barely been touched upon, despite the antiquity of the shrine.

[45] See Frembgen, *Nocturnal Music in the Land of the Sufis: Unheard Pakistan* (Karachi: Oxford University Press, 2012.

Names of Individuals

Technical Terms and Names of Groups

English Terms, Place Names

OTHER TITLES IN THE SERIES (*continued from page iii*)

The Cambridge Companion to Reformation Theology
edited by David Bagchi and David Steinmetz (2004)
9780521772242 hardback; 9780521776622 paperback

The Cambridge Companion to American Judaism
edited by Dana Evan Kaplan (2005)
9780521822046 hardback; 9780521529518 paperback

The Cambridge Companion to Karl Rahner
edited by Declan Marmion and Mary E. Hines (2005)
9780521832885 hardback; 9780521540452 paperback

The Cambridge Companion to Friedrich Schleiermacher
edited by Jacqueline Mariña (2005)
9780521814485 hardback; 9780521891370 paperback

The Cambridge Companion to the Gospels
edited by Stephen C. Barton (2006)
9780521807661 hardback; 9780521002615 paperback

The Cambridge Companion to the Qur'an
edited by Jane Dammen McAuliffe (2006)
9780521831604 hardback; 9780521539340 paperback

The Cambridge Companion to Jonathan Edwards
edited by Stephen J. Stein (2007)
9780521852906 hardback; 9780521618052 paperback

The Cambridge Companion to Evangelical Theology
edited by Timothy Larsen and Daniel J. Trier (2007)
9780521846981 hardback; 9780521609746 paperback

The Cambridge Companion to Modern Jewish Philosophy
edited by Michael L. Morgan and Peter Eli Gordon (2007)
9780521813129 hardback; 9780521012553 paperback

The Cambridge Companion to the Talmud and Rabbinic Literature
edited by Charlotte E. Fonrobert and Martin S. Jaffee (2007)
9780521843904 hardback; 9780521605083 paperback

The Cambridge Companion to Liberation Theology, Second Edition
edited by Christopher Rowland (2007)
9780521868839 hardback; 9780521688932 paperback

The Cambridge Companion to the Jesuits
edited by Thomas Worcester (2008)
9780521857314 hardback; 9780521673969 paperback

The Cambridge Companion to Classical Islamic Theology
edited by Tim Winter (2008)
9780521780582 hardback; 9780521785495 paperback

The Cambridge Companion to Puritanism
edited by John Coffey and Paul Lim (2008)
9780521860888 hardback; 9780521678001 paperback

The Cambridge Companion to Orthodox Christian Theology
edited by Mary Cunningham and Elizabeth Theokritoff (2008)
9780521864848 hardback; 9780521683388 paperback

The Cambridge Companion to Paul Tillich
edited by Russell Re Manning (2009)
9780521859899 hardback; 9780521677356 paperback

The Cambridge Companion to John Henry Newman
edited by Ian Ker and Terrence Merrigan (2009)
9780521871860 hardback; 9780521692724 paperback

The Cambridge Companion to John Wesley
edited by Randy L. Maddox and Jason E. Vickers (2010)
9780521886536 hardback; 9780521714037 paperback

The Cambridge Companion to Christian Philosophical Theology
edited by Charles Taliaferro and Chad Meister (2010)
9780521514330 hardback; 9780521730372 paperback

The Cambridge Companion to Muhammad
edited by Jonathan E. Brockopp (2010)
9780521886079 hardback; 9780521713726 paperback

The Cambridge Companion to Science and Religion
edited by Peter Harrison (2010)
9780521885386 hardback; 9780521712514 paperback

The Cambridge Companion to Gandhi
edited by Judith Brown and Anthony Parel (2011)
9780521116701 hardback; 9780521133456 paperback

The Cambridge Companion to Thomas More
edited by George Logan (2011)
9780521888622 hardback; 9780521716871 paperback

The Cambridge Companion to Miracles
edited by Graham H. Twelftree (2011)
9780521899864 hardback; 9780521728515 paperback

The Cambridge Companion to Francis of Assisi
edited by Michael J.P. Robson (2011)
9780521760430 hardback; 9780521757829 paperback

The Cambridge Companion to Christian Ethics, Second Edition
edited by Robin Gill (2011)
9781107000070 hardback; 9780521164832 paperback

The Cambridge Companion to Black Theology
edited by Dwight Hopkins and Edward Antonio (2012)
9780521879866 hardback; 9780521705691 paperback

The Cambridge Companion to New Religious Movements
edited by Olav Hammer and Mikael Rothstein
9780521196505 hardback; 9780521145657 paperback

The Cambridge Companion to the Cistercian Order
edited by Mette Birkedal Bruun (2012)
9781107001312 hardback; 9780521171847 paperback

The Cambridge Companion to American Methodism
edited by Jason E. Vickers (2013)
9781107008342 hardback; 9781107401051 paperback

The Cambridge Companion to Ancient Mediterranean Religions
edited by Barbette Stanley Spaeth (2013)
9780521113960 hardback; 9780521132046 paperback

The Cambridge Companion to Pentecostalism
edited by Cecil M. Robeck, Jr., and Amos Yong (2014)
9781107007093 hardback; 9780521188388 paperback

FORTHCOMING

The Cambridge Companion to the Summa Theologiae
edited by Philip McCosker and Denys Turner

The Cambridge Companion to Reformed Theology
edited by David Fergusson and Paul T. Nimmo

Made in the USA
Columbia, SC
26 March 2021

35079689R00180